The Military Memoirs of

GENERAL JOHN POPE

CIVIL WAR AMERICA
Gary W. Gallagher, editor

EDITED BY
Peter Cozzens and Robert I. Girardi

The Military Memoirs of

GENERAL JOHN POPE

THE UNIVERSITY OF NORTH CAROLINA PRESS
Chapel Hill and London

© 1998 THE UNIVERSITY OF NORTH CAROLINA PRESS

Book Club Edition
Manufactured in the United States of America

LIBRARY OF CONGRESS CATALOGING-IN-PUBLICATION DATA
Pope, John, 1822–1892.
The military memoirs of General John Pope /
edited by Peter Cozzens and Robert I. Girardi.
p. cm. – (Civil War America)
Includes bibliographical references and index.

ISBN 0-8078-2444-5 (cloth : alk. paper)

1. Pope, John, 1822–1892. 2. United States–History–Civil War,
1861–1865–Personal narratives. 3. United States–History–
Civil War, 1861–1865–Campaigns. 4. Generals–United States–
Biography. 5. United States. Army–Biography. I. Cozzens, Peter,
1957– . II. Girardi, Robert I. III. Title. IV. Series
E467.1.P76A3 1999
973.7′82–dc21   98-13801
                                                              CIP

FRONTISPIECE: Brigadier General John Pope, early 1862
(courtesy Massachusetts Commandery Military Order of
the Loyal Legion and the U.S. Army Military History Institute).

02 01 00 99 98   5 4 3 2 1

For Eric and Ismael
With their fathers' love

Contents

Maps and Illustrations

Maps

Illustrations

Scores of Civil War roundtables meet monthly across the United States and abroad to refight America's greatest conflict. Issues of strategy, key battles, and generalship are often debated as passionately as if the outcome of the war remained in doubt. Contention about the most incompetent general in the Civil War rarely ends without reference to Major General John Pope, who was decisively defeated in the battle of Second Bull Run. Participants readily concede that Robert E. Lee and Stonewall Jackson outgeneraled Pope. Pope's contribution to the debacle remains open to discussion.

In 1990, Wallace J. Schutz and Walter J. Trenerry published the first formal biography of Pope, "the only commanding general of a major Union army in the Civil War not to have had one." After years of research on a man who kept no diary and whose surviving personal letters were scarce, Schutz and Trenerry had located only one reminiscent article by Pope. Paucity of sources proved a blessing to these ardent advocates, who found in Pope a victim of political machinations who was "abandoned by Lincoln," as the title of their book stridently asserted. Many observers concluded that their defense of Pope often effectively proved the case against him.

At long last, Peter Cozzens discovered that Pope had indeed told his own story in a lengthy series of articles that appeared in the *National Tribune*. Overlooked for more than a century, these articles shed light on many aspects of Pope's antebellum and wartime service. The rediscovery of such rich source material, now reprinted in full and with helpful annotations, provides valuable insight into the career of an important soldier.

These recollections reflect surprising generosity when discussing men and measures of the Civil War. This aspect is especially surprising because the strongest indictment against Pope, beyond his defeat at Second Bull Run, is the single-mindedness with which he pursued his subordinate, Union general Fitz John Porter, who he believed had withheld support during the battle out of loyalty to General George B. McClellan. Pope instigated the wartime court-martial of Porter, who was found guilty and cashiered. Pope invariably opposed Porter's long battle for vindication.

This struggle assumed partisan characteristics. Stalwart Republicans supported Pope, who had been a Republican general when such commanders were rarities. Democrats supported Porter, accused of alleged loyalty to McClellan, the Democratic nominee for president in 1864.

In 1879, an army review board finally found Porter innocent of military misconduct. This was merely the first step toward his rehabilitation, which required presidential and congressional action. Congressional Republicans stood firm. In 1881, Porter gained an important ally when former president Ulysses S. Grant spent three days studying testimony presented to the board, concluded that he had previously been unjust, and wrote to President Chester A. Arthur in Porter's behalf. Grant also published "An Undeserved Stigma," an article asserting forcefully that Porter had never merited condemnation. In 1882, President Arthur's pardon of Porter removed his civil disabilities. Not until 1886, however, did Congress pass legislation overruling the court-martial verdict to provide for Porter's honorable retirement.

Porter and Pope, both sixty-four years old, retired in 1886. Since entering West Point as a sixteen-year-old cadet, Pope had spent his entire life in the army, including twenty-one years as a department commander and geographical division commander in the West. When he retired, he turned quite naturally to writing memoirs.

Pope has become a staple of Civil War literature. Future discussion will owe much to the belated publication of these military memoirs and to the fortunate circumstance that their rediscovery fell to Peter Cozzens, the acclaimed author of a Western campaign trilogy: *No Better Place to Die: The Battle of Stone's River* (1990), *This Terrible Sound: The Battle of Chickamauga* (1992), and *The Shipwreck of Their Hopes: The Battles for Chattanooga* (1994). He followed this with *The Darkest Days of the War: The Battles of Iuka and Corinth* (1997). After graduating from Knox College, Cozzens entered the army for four years; he was discharged as a captain and intelligence officer. In the U.S. Foreign Service since 1983, his assignments have included Costa Rica, Peru, and Mexico, as well as Washington, D.C.

Coeditor Robert Girardi, a detective and specialist in violent crimes with the Chicago Police Department, graduated from Rosary College in River Forest, Illinois, and later acquired an M.A. in public history from Loyola University of Chicago. As a public historian, Girardi has long been active in Civil War roundtables, exhibitions, and, most recently, in editing Civil War documents.

Cozzens and Girardi already knew that Pope deserved reappraisal, an analysis that went beyond either conventional abuse or perverse praise. General Samuel D. Sturgis, otherwise obscure among Civil War commanders, immortalized himself with the ringing declaration, "I don't care for John Pope

a pinch of owl's dung." Deciding that Pope deserves better, the editors believe that the best start is to let him speak for himself through his own forgotten military memoirs.

John Y. Simon
Southern Illinois University at Carbondale

Acknowledgments

As we are presenting the work of one dead for over a century, our acknowledgments are necessarily far fewer than they would be in a work of our own.

We would like to thank Mary Abroe for her help in locating sources used in preparing the footnotes to the text.

Our sincere thanks also go to three particularly dedicated, helpful, and knowledgeable archivists for making available manuscript materials pertaining to General Pope. They are Gary Arnold of the Ohio Historical Society, Nan Card of the Rutherford B. Hayes Presidential Library, and Allen Aimone of the U.S. Military Academy Archives.

On the morning of July 29, 1862, Major General John Pope boarded a train that was to carry him seventy-five miles, from the summer swelter and noxious intrigue of wartime Washington, D.C., to the scenic foothills of the Blue Ridge Mountains, where he would assume a command he had not wanted, peopled with officers and men who did not want him. The war in the eastern theater was at a standstill, and President Abraham Lincoln and his cabinet looked to Pope to instill an aggressive, no-truck-with-traitors spirit in the Eastern soldier.

Preferring to remain in the West with his own Army of the Mississippi, Pope had marshaled a legion of arguments to convince Lincoln that he was the wrong man for the eastern job. Each of the three generals whose armies were to be consolidated under him were his senior in rank, Pope reminded the president. They undoubtedly would take offense at the slight and communicate their resentment to their troops. The appointment of a general from another theater would be especially galling and would tend to foster a divisive feeling, added Pope, rather than the close cooperation needed to mold three disparate armies quickly into an effective force. And there was an unspoken argument for his remaining in the West, perhaps more compelling to Pope than those he had made before the president: on July 19, his first-born child died in St. Louis at the age of two months. But Pope's arguments were unavailing. President Lincoln was adamant, and so Pope left for the front, feeling much like a "strange dog, without even the right to run out of the village."[1]

Pope passed the night of July 29 at a vacant girl's school in Warrenton, where "from the upper windows. . . . I caught my first view of the Blue Ridge." The scene thrilled him. "The moon was nearly full that night, the air came soft and cool from the not distant hills, and there was a deep silence and quiet upon the whole scene. A more lovely landscape or a more charming country the eye of man has not looked on, and the remembrances of that scene under the bright moonlight will always be a delight to me."

Pope continued his journey the next morning on horseback. Again, the beauty of the land caused him briefly to forget his burden. Reflecting on the occasion many years later, he was moved to delight, tempered with a soft melancholy:

A view of the country and of the Blue Ridge during that [day] served to strengthen the impressions of the night before. The intense blue of the skies melting away into more subdued coloring of the same tint along the not distant ridges of the range; the gently uneven country, with occasional abrupt trees of no great altitude, covered with forest trees, and the rapid, winding mountain streams, with solitary mansions and occasional old-fashioned villages scattered without apparent effort here and there over the country, made a landscape that I cannot think of even to this day without keen pleasure. In nothing was the manhood of Virginia (and the supremest manhood of the South shone forth in that most chivalric State) more admirably exhibited than in the resolute and uncomplaining fortitude with which they saw this beautiful region trampled into mire by hostile armies and those ancient homes and lovely villages consigned to ruin. In no part of this broad land have the courage and pluck of its people shone forth with more luster than in the Old Dominion during the late war, but God grant that never shall there arise another occasion again to test it in such a manner! Wrong no doubt they were in assenting to the attempt to break up the Union of these States, but they paid the penalty—and a penalty far heavier than was inflicted on any other State—with dignity and without complaint.[2]

That a general whom history has traduced and dismissed more thoroughly than any other army commander of the Civil War—the incompetent, bombastic, two-dimensional foil to Generals Robert E. Lee and Thomas J. "Stonewall" Jackson who would have his "headquarters in the saddle"—should pen a passage so evocative and feeling might surprise most readers, as frankly it surprised us when first we read this and the innumerable other such passages that make up the military recollections of Major General John Pope.

Much of the verdict of history is hard to reconcile with either the facts of Pope's forty-four-year military career or the benign spirit of his written recollections. There was a third dimension to Pope, as there is to all men; in his case, a manifest talent that earned for him the respect of Generals Ulysses S. Grant, William T. Sherman, and Philip H. Sheridan, all of whom held Pope in high regard long after the debacle of Second Bull Run. Though not forgetting his errors, President Lincoln and General in Chief Henry Halleck privately exculpated Pope of blame for that defeat.

Testimonials to his merit were many. Pope's fellow generals in the western theater liked and admired him, and enjoyed his keen, if sometimes biting, sense of humor. The western soldier appreciated his brusque and boisterous nature—as well as his demonstrated reluctance in early campaigns to shed blood recklessly.[3]

After Second Bull Run, Pope was sent to Minnesota to put down the bloodiest Indian uprising in American history, which happened to coincide with his defeat in Virginia. Lincoln banished Pope from the theater of war for political expediency—Pope, one of the few Republicans in the army high command, had been brought east to win a battle that would discredit George B. McClellan and the soft-war Democrats; when he failed, he became a liability, and the administration had to distance itself from him.

Contrary to popular belief today, Pope's reputation was not permanently ruined. Disgusted with the poor showing of his western departmental commanders and anxious for competent leadership in that troubled region, Lieutenant General Ulysses S. Grant in the fall of 1864 undertook a wholesale reorganization of the theater west of the Mississippi. He merged the Departments of Missouri, Kansas, and the Northwest into a single military division, with headquarters at St. Louis and Pope in command (the Department of Arkansas was added to Pope's command in early 1865). Exhorting Army Chief of Staff Henry Halleck to lay the proposal before Secretary of War Edwin V. Stanton at once, Grant wrote: "I wish you would urge that the change be immediately made. With Pope in command we secure at least two advantages we have not heretofore had, namely, subordination, and intelligence of administration." Grant followed up his recommendation with an appeal directly to the president in which he praised Pope's disinterested management of the Department of the Northwest.[4]

During the final months of the war, Pope found himself responsible for the largest geographic command in the nation. Its boundaries stretched from the Mississippi River west to the mountains of western Nevada and north from the northern frontier of Texas to the border with Canada. Command of the Military Division of the Missouri presented Pope with a wider array of problems than those faced by any other regional commander in the Union army; their magnitude gave him more responsibility than any other general in the United States, excepting Grant and Sherman.

After the Civil War, Congress thought enough of Pope to confirm him as one of seventeen generals in the peacetime army. As a district commander in the Deep South during Reconstruction, Pope championed civil rights for blacks and won the grudging admiration of his former enemies; the *Macon Telegraph* editorialized: "While looking without favor on military despotism, we can at least say of John Pope, sent to administer it, that he is disposed to exercise his office with reason and the proper regard for law and the rights of people. We are fortunate in falling into his hands." While postwar commander of the Department of the Missouri, Pope "endeared himself" to the people, the governor of Kansas told President Chester Arthur. "The general has commanded in our Indian troubles, knows completely our ways . . . so that our people have unbounded confidence in him." From Pope came pleas for forbearance in dealing with the American Indian. "Wisdom and humanity alike seem to demand some policy which shall save the Indian from complete and violent extinction," he told Grant. Benign assimilation must replace bad treaties and lies; the continuance of "such cruelty cannot be contemplated by the government." For thirteen years, as commander of a key western department, Pope would make reform of federal Indian policy a matter of almost religious zeal.[5]

This same spirit of conciliation and goodwill pervades Pope's recollections of his Civil War service. Few generals who left memoirs wielded their pen with more forbearance than did Pope, which is particularly remarkable given Pope's historical reputation as a quarrelsome liar and braggart. He dispatched his enemies with understated wit, including McClellan, whom he went to the grave believing had worked to ensure his defeat at Second Bull Run. In a passage lampooning the West Point curriculum and the failure of the cadre to prepare graduates for the realities of war, Pope had this to say of McClellan: "General McClellan was the most exquisite exponent of these West Point ideas, and he may be fairly judged, or with sufficient fairness for the present purpose, from the estimate of himself which he gives in his late autobiography. In the professional mind he was the ripest production of West Point, which of course implies that he might have been considered over-ripe for any other institution of learning in the country."[6]

To Major General Nathaniel Banks, who wrecked his corps by bringing on a general engagement with Stonewall Jackson's much larger command at Cedar Mountain contrary to Pope's orders, then tried to deflect the blame to Pope before the Joint Congressional Committee on the Conduct of the War, Pope bore no ill will. Although insisting that Banks had strayed from orders, Pope displayed genuine sympathy for his predicament at Cedar Mountain: "I have always attributed General Banks's departure from his instructions and his advance against the enemy, first, to the fact that that enemy was Stonewall Jackson, with whom he had had some unpleasant experiences in the Shenandoah Valley; and second, that he did not believe the enemy to be in much force. . . . General Banks was a most intrepid and loyal soldier."[7]

Nor did Pope bear malice toward Secretary of War Stanton, who with Lincoln had railroaded Pope into taking command of the Army of Virginia, only to accede to his banishment to Minnesota after Second Bull Run. Pope instead emphasized Stanton's invaluable contributions to the war effort. In a movingly written tribute, Pope left an unsurpassed inside view of the beleaguered secretary of war at work, lamenting that Stanton "wore out body and mind in the work, and as much and as freely gave his life to his country as any man who perished on the field of battle."[8]

That Pope forbore reopening old, private wounds, and largely abjured the kind of personal invective that enfeebled much postwar writing, is nowhere better demonstrated than in his remarks concerning Confederate general Joseph E. Johnston. Pope first made Johnston's acquaintance in 1842, when, as a twenty-year-old second lieutenant just graduated from West Point, he was assigned to duty under Johnston, then a captain, surveying public lands and laying out roads and canals in Florida. Perhaps the dull routine drove the young topographical officer to misbehave, because he and Johnston quickly developed an intense dislike of one another. Pope was reassigned after fewer than seven months. Seven years later Pope again faced the prospect of duty under Johnston, this time in Texas. But Johnston wanted nothing to do with Pope and insisted that Colonel J. J. Abert, the chief of the Corps of Topographical Engineers, assign him elsewhere. And Pope reminded Colonel Abert of his dislike for Johnston: "My relations with Colonel Johnston are and have been such for some years that it would be exceedingly unpleasant to serve with him."[9]

Rather than subject his readers to a rendition of his own, probably petty problems with Johnston, Pope related the impression the Virginian generally made on young subordinates, as this delightful anecdote demonstrates:

> Captain Johnston was the chief of my corps, at the headquarters of the Department of Florida . . . when I reported. . . . He was, and I suppose still is, a short, spare man, very erect and alert, with an engaging countenance and cordial, unaffected manners. He was in addition a man of large ability, and naturally became one of the most conspicuous figures in the Southern armies. He was genial and kindly in his manners to young officers, and was popular with them. Although he could not have been much more than thirty at the time, we youngsters looked on him as on the whole rather a venerable man. Somehow we had taken up the notion that he had been generally, and then was, in love with someone, and had had a wide experience in sentimental affairs running on many years. I don't know how such an idea originated, but it prevailed among us and invested its object with a halo of romance which constantly attracted our curiosity and interest.[10]

How might we account for the even-tempered tone of Pope's memoirs? Major General Jacob D. Cox, an astute judge of character who after the war became a close friend of Pope, thought that the trauma of Second Bull Run and the humiliation of exile to Minnesota had emptied the general of his natural combativeness.[11] Pope gradually became more reflective and more forgiving. The death in 1886 of his wife Clara, to whom he was devoted, mellowed him further. In twenty-one years of military service after the Civil War, nearly all of it spent as a departmental commander on the western frontier, he concerned himself less with his own advancement than with advocating fair treatment of the Plains Indians and pondering ways to better the Regular Army establishment. Pope became one of the most vocal proponents in the army for reform in the management of Indian affairs, on grounds both humanitarian and pragmatic.[12]

But no matter how much he might wish to, Pope could not escape the legacy of Second Bull Run. In the wake of that defeat, Pope had, through the inspector general of the Army of Virginia, Brigadier General Benjamin S. Roberts, brought charges of disobedience of orders and misbehavior before the enemy against corps commander Major General Fitz John Porter. A court-martial convicted and cashiered Porter on January 10, 1863, but the matter did not end there. Porter dedicated much of his remaining years to seeking a reversal of the verdict. He published numerous articles and pamphlets telling his side of the story of Second Bull Run and appealed to a succession of presidents and commanding generals of the army for a review of the case, based in part on new evidence garnered from former Confederates.

Pope never wavered in his belief that Porter and McClellan had wronged him, in spite of strong evidence to the contrary, and he felt compelled to contest each of Porter's appeals privately. But he largely refrained from public comment on either the Second Bull Run campaign and the Porter case in particular or on his Civil War service in general. For a number of years after the war, he had counted on his friend and former staff officer, Brigadier General Thomas C. H. Smith, an unabashed apologist for Pope, to publish a "correct history" of Second Bull Run. "All our friends are very anxious for your book to come out, knowing that it will be and always continue to be the history of that campaign," Pope told Smith in 1875. "For my children's sake and the place I am to hold in their minds in the future I am painfully anxious about the publication of your book. You will understand and appreciate what I feel and say and I beg you if it be possible to do this for me."[13]

Two years later Pope was still waiting hopefully for Smith's opus. "A very exhaustive history of our campaign in Virginia will soon be ready for the press and I trust it will settle by unassailable proof most of the controverted points," he assured an army acquaintance. But to his intimate friend, former major general and then Ohio superior court justice Manning F. Force, Pope despaired of ever seeing Smith's book in print. Smith had grown despondent after his considerable wealth literally went up in flames with the Chicago Fire, and what began as a well-documented, judicious narrative gradually deteriorated into a disjointed collection of highly opinionated, nearly illegible drafts, slashed through with deletions and heavily scratched over with cryptic additions.[14]

Smith had amassed enough evidence to refute everything Porter had published, Pope complained to Judge Force, "but he is so touchy that I don't like to say anything to him about the long delay in getting his book ready and the injury such delay is doing me by allowing false and unfair statements and books to crystallize into history." [15]

The publication of the first two volumes of a massive work on the war by Louis Philippe Albert d'Orleans, Comte de Paris, a French nobleman who had served under, and remained a partisan of, George B. McClellan, compelled Pope to speak out. Between May 1876 and April 1877, Pope engaged in a public exchange of letters with the Comte de Paris, whom he felt had taken Porter's side on the subject of Second Bull Run without examining all the evidence (see Appendix A). To the cantankerous Smith, Pope explained his purpose in writing the Frenchman:

> Everybody is writing about those battles with infinitely less information on the subject than you have and it is very certain that . . . the public sentiment will be so crystallized that it will not be changed afterwards. I cannot and do not complain that you have not written your work on that campaign since I had no claim upon you to do it more than . . . your voluntary pledge to me which of course you are at liberty to withdraw or decline to carry out at your pleasure. . . . I myself and others have rested comfortably in the belief that [your work] would be done in time to do good. . . . I have, however . . . been forced to do some work myself or see myself handed down in history in a false light.[16]

The Comte de Paris took umbrage at Pope's questioning of his version of events, and his well-reasoned rebuttal did much to expose the emptiness of Pope's arguments against Porter. Faced with the force of a logic he could not concede, Pope terminated their correspondence in disgust, saying:

> If those who are interested in this correspondence (I suppose there are not many) will take the trouble to read your letters and the narrative of the same transactions as related in your History, they will not, I think, need from any other source the admonition "not to accept without grave doubts your account of any transactions related in your history, except such as fell under your own 'observation.'" As my object in beginning the correspondence was simply to convey this caution, I rest satisfied with the result.
>
> Whilst the resolution you announce to write no more seems to me entirely wise, yet I confess that I am selfish enough to be glad that you did not adopt it sooner, as in that case I might have been deprived of your valuable assistance in accomplishing the purpose I had in view.
>
> In terminating this correspondence, however, I beg to assure you that

I entertain no ill-will whatever toward you, as I am well satisfied that your imperfect acquaintance with the facts and, what appear to me, your rather illogical deductions even from that, are faults altogether of the head; not at all of the heart.[17]

That swift verbal thrust was the last Pope had to say publicly about Second Bull Run for eight years, apart from letters to contest Porter's appeals, until circumstances again obliged him to speak out. In 1884 the monthly *Century* magazine began featuring a series of papers written by leading participants in the Civil War, North and South, and illustrated by prominent commercial artists, under the title *Battles and Leaders of the Civil War*. It was a venture that editor in chief Richard Watson Gilder trumpeted as "a flank movement on all our rivals . . . the most important thing, historically, I ever expect to live to see in this century." And it was the most successful commercially. From the first war paper, the circulation of *Century* climbed dramatically. With so much riding on their "great scheme," the editors of *Century* were unwilling to accept a polite no to their request that John Pope contribute a paper on Second Bull Run. If he would not write a history of the campaign, the editors told Pope, they would find someone "who might not possibly be friendly" to the general.[18]

Pope wrote the paper, which was published in the January 1886 issue of *Century*.[19] Former Confederate general James Longstreet, who dealt Pope the fatal blow at Second Bull Run, contributed a paper from the Southern perspective.[20]

The response to Pope's article was partisan but generally favorable. The press greeted it politely, and friends such as Judge Force, former president Rutherford B. Hayes, Brigadier General Benjamin H. Grierson, and former major general Jacob D. Cox, who four years before had penned the indictment of Porter's generalship at Second Bull Run that Pope had long hoped Smith would write,[21] applauded the paper.[22] Supporters of Porter deplored it. Brigadier General John Gibbon assured Porter that "as a contribution to history this paper of Pope's is utterly worthless, except in a negative way. . . . He reminds me of the cuttle fish which by clouding the water about him succeeds in eluding, for a time, his enemies."[23]

Pope himself was pleased with the response to the article. From his headquarters at the Presidio of San Francisco, where he was about to relinquish command of the Military Division of the Pacific, Pope wrote Judge Force merrily:

We are in the midst of packing up for our move east and I've time this morning to write you a few lines as I must go back home immediately to help Clara who is not in condition to over[see] matters though she won't

BRIGADIER GENERAL JOHN POPE, A POSTWAR IMAGE

let anyone else do it. I am glad you liked my article as it appeared in the *Century*. It seems to have been received with almost universal praise and I have seen few if any mentions otherwise of it. Even the *Nation* seems, in its reference to Longstreet's article, rather inclined to take up the cudgel for me. I am quite surprised at the reception of the article by many papers which heretofore have been very hostile.[24]

Having enjoyed his first serious effort at war history, soon after the release of his *Century* paper, Pope began devoting a great deal of time to writing. He retired from the army on March 16, 1886, and with his wife Clara settled into a house in St. Louis, at 3223 Lucas Street. Periodic bouts of lumbago kept him home much of the time, as did Clara's persistent poor health. Nor did Pope find St. Louis society particularly appealing when he did venture forth. Always deeply interested in scholarly and literary endeavors, he was disappointed to find St. Louis had become a town of philistines, concerned only with the making of money, in the years since he and Clara had lived there off and on during the Civil War. So Pope welcomed the chance to contribute his memoirs to the *National Tribune* (see Appendix B).[25]

Headquartered in Washington, D.C., the *National Tribune* was an ideal venue for Pope, as it was for thousands of other old soldiers who wished to relate their war experiences. Intended as an advocatory forum for Union army veterans, the *National Tribune* was a weekly newspaper that kept its 300,000 readers informed about congressional debates on war pensions and veterans' benefits, and on the activities of the Grand Army of the Republic. Editor John McElroy, a former Illinois volunteer cavalryman who had survived captivity at Andersonville, also reserved nearly half of the dozen odd pages of each issue for veterans' recollections. In regular columns such as "Picket Shots" and "Fighting Them Over" could be found letters and reminiscences of a few dozen lines, and the first page of each issue was given over to one or two lengthy, and often serialized, feature articles. By the time Pope began setting down his own recollections in 1886, the *National Tribune* already had run the serialized memoirs of Generals Oliver Otis Howard and William P. Carlin.[26]

Pope made his debut in the February 17, 1887, issue of the *National Tribune* with a piece on Missouri at the outbreak of the Civil War.[27] Three more installments were devoted to his service in Missouri, followed at irregular intervals over the next fifteen months by articles on the Island No. 10 campaign and the Siege of Corinth. Six installments on the Second Bull Run campaign were run on a weekly basis between August 2 and September 6, 1888.

Two years passed before Pope reappeared on the pages of the *National Tribune*. For his earlier articles, he had drawn on testimony he had given during and just after the war before the Joint Congressional Committee on the Conduct of the War, as well as reports and correspondence found in Frank Moore's twelve-volume *Rebellion Record*. With the December 11, 1890, issue of the *National Tribune*, there began a colorful, highly personal series of fifteen articles, all under the rubric "War Reminiscences: Personal Recollections of Conspicuous People, Civil and Military," in which Pope sized up for posterity the leading figures of the war, North and South, with whom he had

come in contact, while also relating his experiences with them. These he most probably penned from memory, buttressed by his own letters and the published accounts of others. In addition to the compelling portrait he painted of Secretary Stanton, Pope offered readers of the *National Tribune* an intimate glimpse at President-elect Lincoln's journey by train from Springfield, Illinois, to Washington, D.C., in February 1861, a stirring account of the Mexican War battles of Monterrey and Buena Vista, and a trenchant critique of the West Point system.

The final installment of Pope's memoirs appeared in the March 19, 1891, issue of the *National Tribune*. Eighteen months later, on September 23, 1892, Pope died in his sleep at the Ohio Soldiers' and Sailors' House in Sandusky, Ohio, where he had gone to visit Judge Force, from what the attending physician labeled "a complete breakdown of the nervous system, a letting loose of all vital force, which has been very properly called 'nervous prostration.'" He was buried at the Bellefontaine Cemetery in St. Louis beside his wife Clara, who had died four years earlier.[28]

I happened upon Pope's memoirs nearly three years ago, while scanning microfilmed reels of the *National Tribune* for articles about the 1862 Shenandoah Valley campaign. I had intended to make the Valley campaign the subject of my next book, but I was so captivated by Pope's writing that I put my extensive Valley notes on the shelf. My enthusiasm for my unexpected find grew as I read and reread his memoirs. What first struck me was the literary excellence of Pope's prose. He writes as well as Sherman or Grant and better than nearly any other general who penned postwar recollections, with dry wit, incisiveness, and a flair for epigrams.

Delving deeper, I was pleased to find that Pope's work compared favorably to those of Grant, Sherman, Sheridan, and others in terms of honesty and accuracy. The wide subject matter struck me as of unusual value. Pope provides a superb firsthand account of President-elect Lincoln's troubled journey from Springfield, Illinois, to Washington in early 1861. He paints a remarkable word picture of the anguished Secretary of War Stanton and his brusque but effective manner of conducting War Department business. Pope offers a valuable and balanced account of his capture of Island No. 10 and New Madrid and of his central role in the Siege of Corinth. He also gives us a fine account of the Mexican War battle of Buena Vista, in which he served on the staff of General Zachary Taylor.

My greatest disappointment was in finding that, when faced with the painful subject of Second Manassas, Pope reverted to what John Hennessy has aptly termed the "old veterans' medium of tedium," quoting at length from long and tiresome dispatches that reveal nothing of Pope's thinking on the

subject not found in his *Century* article. Pope treats the Battle of Cedar Mountain fairly and freshly, but he simply was unable to confess to his errors during the latter stages of the campaign.

Regrettably, Pope's memoirs died with him. For over a century, they have rested in obscurity, consulted by neither historians nor biographers. That the personal recollections of an army commander should remain so long unknown is remarkable, and it is with great enthusiasm that we, the editors, offer John Pope's own story to readers and scholars alike.

In so doing, we have sought to present Pope's words as he wrote them. Editing has been light. Like most of his contemporaries, Pope had a penchant for commas. We have eliminated a few, in cases where their overuse clouded the meaning or badly impeded the rhythm of a sentence. Apart from this, we have regularized capitalization and corrected misspelled names; otherwise, we have left the text as we found it.

Peter Cozzens
Tijuana, Mexico

Part One

MISSOURI IN 1861

The Rush to the Ranks

$\mathcal{T}$he attack on Fort Sumter was immediately followed by the president's call for 75,000 volunteers to serve for three months, and the whole country was at once wild with excitement and enthusiasm, and became, from east to west, a scene of such passionate and headlong activity as I could not have credited in so practical and self-contained a people as ours. The rush to be accepted in the ranks of the new regiments, and the rush of the officers of the regiments to the state capitals to assure that their regiments would form a part of the force called for by the president, were as gratifying as surprising. Certainly twice, and probably three times as many regiments were offered as were required by the proclamation, and it became at once apparent that the government would have no difficulty in raising all the troops needed to put down the rebellion, even if they included all the able-bodied men in the North. Whatever may have been a man's politics, or whatever he may have thought in the abstract upon the horrors of a war with our own countrymen,

3

every such idea was given to the winds in the face of the assault upon one of the forts of the United States, the capture of its garrison and the degradation of the flag, if not of its honor. No pen could describe the scenes of fierce excitement and of frantic activity in the North which followed this most unwise act of the Southern people. With the exception of the comparatively few sympathizers with the South, under all circumstances, the great body of those friendly to the Southern people who deprecated any hostile acts whatever, at once gave them up and became their most active and unrelenting enemies.

What would have been the effect upon the new administration in its support by the country, had the Southern authorities carefully refrained from any violent action against the United States and contented themselves with a passive resistance to the execution of the laws, by refusing to hold any of the public offices or render any public service, cannot now be known fully; but it is safe to say, looking back upon the almost passionate objection of the people to internecine war and their amazement at the idea that any part of our people would precipitate it upon us; that if the South had kept the peace, even for a few months, and thus have compelled the new administration to forcible action in executing the laws, the response to the president's call for troops would have been less enthusiastic, and would have come from a much smaller number of the people. Under any circumstances, however, the war was inevitable and the results exactly the same; but the South, by refraining from making the first hostile movement, would have maintained for some time the sympathy of its Northern friends, not in what they proposed, but in aiding to defer, if not altogether to prevent, the movement of Union troops against them. At all events, the South would have given its "thick and thin" supporters (the Copperheads) some more substantial basis for defending their resistance to the war, and the obstructions they tried to throw, and did throw, in the way of the loyal citizens who carried it on and through.

In the midst of this tremendous excitement I was ordered to Springfield, Illinois, to muster into the service of the United States the contingent (six regiments) from that state. There I met one, and by no means the least distinguished, of that remarkable body of men now known as the "War Governors." Governor Richard Yates was then the governor of Illinois,[1] and when I called to inform him who I was and what was my business, was surrounded by the military men, or so-called military men, of the state, engaged in heated discussion as to the organization of regiments and their acceptance for the service of the United States by him. He gave me a most cordial reception, and said that a prodigious load had been taken from his shoulders by the appearance of an officer of the Regular Army duly assigned to represent the War Department in the organization and mustering of the Union troops.

Governor Yates was of the middle height, neither spare nor too full of person, and with a very erect carriage and rapid gait. His countenance was ruddy, and his eye bright and sparkling. He had a handsome face, with the kindest and most engaging expression, and a manner full of genuine good feeling for all the world. He was in his ways and his power and devotion of attachment, as well as his great modesty and gentleness, more like a woman than a man, though he was a man of iron nerve and unshakable resolution.

Take him all in all, I think he was one of the most lovable men I ever met. He had not then fallen into the evil habit of drinking to excess, which afterward beset him and wrecked what would have been a brilliant career. I was greatly attached to him, and to this day I cannot think of him without a tender feeling. Whatever may be said of his unsuccessful and most unhappy life in the United States Senate,[2] there is no doubt that his service to the country as governor of Illinois during the war was of vital importance to the government and to the army, and was rendered with the zeal and energy born of intense loyalty to his country. No Illinois soldier who did his duty in the war will ever cease to remember Governor Richard Yates, and to honor his memory.

At the request of the governor I took command in person of the regiments and parts of regiments which had been assembled at Springfield to be mustered into the service. They were established in the fair grounds, near the city, and occupied actually the stalls and sheds which had been used for the cattle during fair weeks. They were utterly ignorant of everything military, but all were anxious to learn, and would cheerfully do anything or submit to anything which was necessary to make a soldier. This extreme anxiety to get themselves in condition to do service in the army, although it led to many absurd and ridiculous performances, which occasioned immense amusement even to themselves, had nevertheless a very touching and pathetic aspect. In looking back on it, with all that followed, the pathetic side is altogether foremost. I remember being extremely diverted, and at the same time touched by an incident I witnessed one day in the street. Two young fellows who had been undergoing drill in their camp for a week or two, stopped in front of a show window filled with military goods and ornaments, and were evidently much interested in examining these, at that day, attractive articles. Nevertheless, to avoid losing any time in perfecting themselves in military science, they continued, arm in arm to mark time and do the goose step with perfectly grave and solemn faces whilst they stood there. They evidently believed that every moment spent in any other manner than learning to be a soldier was so much time lost.

It is funny and at the same time sad, considering what happened afterward to these ardent young fellows, to think of them in those days.

Whilst the volunteers from all of the Eastern states were hurrying to Washington to defend the capital, and were being organized for service, the Western states were not less active. In the East, Washington was the point of concentration for all the regiments called, but in the West there was no such central place. St. Louis, Cincinnati, and Louisville were equally in danger and equally important to hold. The new troops, therefore, raised in the West were distributed along the whole of the long line from Pittsburg to Cairo. At the time of the First Battle of Bull Run, St. Louis, because of its position in a slave state and its importance as a great commercial center, and also because of rather peculiar transactions that had occurred and were threatened still, commanded general attention. General McClellan, who had been appointed a major general of militia by the governor of Ohio, was first given the general command west of the Alleghenies, but, I think, he never went to St. Louis, and had little to do with anything that occurred there.[3] General William S. Harney, an old officer of the Regular Army, was at the time in command of what had long been a military geographical department, which included Missouri and had succeeded to the command by virtue simply of being the senior officer serving in it.[4] He would not, for manifest reasons, have been selected to command in that state under the peculiar circumstances and the immediately impending dangers and of course, was not left long in a position for which he was in all respects unsuited. General Harney's whole service in the army had been on the frontier among the Indians, and he had no knowledge whatever of civil affairs, even in theory. He was not a man of liberal education, and possessed little of the patience and forbearance which his position demanded. He was a Southern man by birth and his associations, so far as they went, were mainly with Southern people. His nominal home was St. Louis, where he married his wife and where was the bulk of her large fortune. It would have been a difficult place for even the best-equipped man to occupy as commander of United States troops at that time, but aside from his want of knowledge and of aptitude for such relations with civil affairs, his social and business relations were of such a character that whatever ability he did have for such work was utterly unavailable. He had become accustomed, in his long personal associations in St. Louis, to trust some men implicitly and to have profound confidence in the opinions of others. Under ordinary conditions his faith would probably have been justified; but in dealing with the situation as it stood, his friends and advisers, being almost without exception Southern men and sympathizers, and many of them of shrewdness, fully enlisted in the success of the South, the counsel he got from them was, to say the least, not in the interest of the general government, so far as the affairs of the state were concerned. No one that I ever heard of suspected General Harney of disloyalty. It was not the patriotism of the soldier he lacked, but the wisdom of the serpent. He was soon superseded by General Nathaniel Lyon, and disappeared from further active service in the army.

General Harney was for many years a noted character in the army, and nearly as much so among the Western people. Perhaps the Indians knew him

MISSOURI IN 1861

better than even the whites. He had, when I first saw him, about 1845, the most perfect physique I ever saw in man. He was much above six feet in height, perfectly formed in every respect, muscular and athletic, with all the grace of movement of the feline animals. He was not only one of the strongest men, but he was the swiftest runner and the most accomplished athlete in the army, if not in the country. He easily beat the Indians at their own athletic games, especially foot-races, and was known and admired among them as "the swift runner." His wonderful physique was never impaired by any lust or dissipation, and although he very frequently indulged in strong language, he never indulged in strong drink. As a soldier he had a high reputation, and was often selected for important services on the frontier. He knew how to deal with the Indian, but with the politician and the schemer he was a child only. He still lives, an old man past ninety,[5] retaining much of his physical force, but very few of his mental faculties.

He was succeeded in command by General Nathaniel Lyon, a very different man in all respects.[6] Lyon was a Yankee of Yankees, with all the forbidding manners and stern look of the Covenanters of old, but with none of their piety. Under an exterior cold and self-possessed, he had a temper fiery and unrelenting. He believed in the government and the flag with the fury of the wildest fanatic and could scarce hold conference with those who were disloyal to either. To the Secessionist and the schemer in Missouri there could not have been found a more formidable and dangerous opponent than General Lyon. He marched his command from the arsenal in St. Louis and captured Camp Jackson, a camp of state troops near the city, and carried off its garrison as prisoners of war. He refused positively the overtures of Governor Jackson and General Sterling Price for some sort of compromise by which the United States Government would have surrendered some of its rights in Missouri.[7] He practically drove these two officials out of St. Louis and at once followed them up, defeated the force they had hastily collected near Booneville, and pursued the retreating army to Springfield in the southwestern part of the state, where they met heavy reinforcements from Arkansas under Ben McCulloch.[8] Not receiving reinforcements from St. Louis, where he had been replaced in general command by General Frémont, he fought the desperate Battle of Wilson's Creek, where he lost the battle and his own life.[9] Short as was his career, he impressed himself indelibly on the history of the war. Had he lived, there is no telling where his intense character and utter heedlessness or recklessness of results might have led him. It is extremely doubtful whether any authority would have been sufficient to control him when his passions were aroused or his loyal fanaticism was assailed. He seemed to me always to resemble a slumbering volcano capped with snow. I remember perfectly how he looked at West Point—small and spare, with a bloodless face, and hair so light in color as almost to pass for white, and the coldest blue-gray eye I ever looked into; reserved and haughty to a degree which left him without much companionship, if it did not make him absolutely unpopular—he was a marked man even then. But after years of active life, with several episodes of such disagreeable character as greatly to strengthen the intense passion which he with difficulty partially held in control, he was, when he appeared in St. Louis, inflamed with that lurid loyalty which then dominated him, a most formidable enemy to those who were plotting against the government. It is, perhaps, not unfortunate for his fame and his remembrance by his countrymen that he died when and as he did. Had he lived it is altogether probable that his uncontrollable passions, and the inflamed feelings called out by the war, would have kept him in constant difficulties with his superiors in rank, which would have embittered if they had not absolutely wrecked his life.

A short time before the Battle of Wilson's Creek, General John C. Frémont arrived in St. Louis, and under the orders of the government assumed personal command of the Western Department.[10] I had not seen him for many years, but I remember him very well as an officer of the corps to which I belonged in the army. When I saw him, about 1845, in Washington City, he was in the midst of his Rocky Mountain explorations, and was already a man of considerable note. I was, therefore, much interested in him and quite glad to have the opportunity to become acquainted with him. I met him first at dinner at Colonel Abert's,[11] who was then the chief of the Topographical Engineers Corps of the Army. He was then Brevet Captain Frémont. My first impressions of him were that he was a handsome and graceful man, short and slender, with black eyes and black curly hair, rather of the "ringlet style." He talked very little and appeared to be as reserved in character as he was frugal in words. I admired him as one of the most notable and successful young officers in the service, and doubly interesting to me as having made his exceptional reputation in the corps to which I myself belonged and in the pursuits and duties which I expected to follow and perform. I did not see him again until I practically pushed my way into his presence some little while after he had assumed command at St. Louis. When he arrived I was in northern Missouri, where I had been in command for a week or two.[12] By his request I came down to St. Louis to see him, being then next in rank to him in the department. I reached St. Louis at night, and early next morning repaired to his office. He occupied the large and very handsome mansion of Mr. Brant,[13] a relative of Mrs. Frémont. The main floor of the house was reached by a high flight of stone steps from the street, and at the lower steps stood two soldiers in uniform, with their swords crossed over the way. Instead of going up the steps to the main entrance of the house, I was directed to the doorway of the basement, which was very high and almost level with the street. A basement hall ran through the center, having rooms on both sides, which I supposed to be the offices of the house. The hall was filled with people—jammed in fact—from all classes and conditions of society, struggling and pushing for no visible purpose or result, unless ill-temper and bad words be a result. The governor of a state and a teamster, a senator and a colored workman, a general and a new recruit, speaking all the known languages of Western Europe, in all the tones of indignation and rage, or politeness and deference, were struggling and fighting in the hall, with an apparent belief that General Frémont was somewhere in the vicinity. There was a very real resolve to see him on the part of everyone, myself included. At last I pushed into a room off the right side of the hall, where I found two aides-de-camp of General Frémont fortified behind a sort of counter. One of these aides was the famous I. C. Woods, of California, the mildest and blandest man I ever saw or heard of, except, perhaps, the "Heathen Chinee" of the poem.[14] I, myself, never saw so smooth and imperturbable a man in my life. What he was doing in this apology for an office—indeed, what he or anyone else could do in such a crowd—is not easy to say, except that whilst all the rest of the persons in that noisy basement were striving to see General Frémont, the polite aide-de-camp was trying to prevent them single handedly from doing so. I never saw such a scene of confusion before, except at the door of a theater on the night of some famous performance or at a White House reception in the height of the season.

I informed the urbane Colonel Woods who I was and why I was there, and desired him to take me to General Frémont at once. With great deference and apparent regret he told me that the general just then was very much engaged, but asked me to be seated for a few moments until he was at liberty. I accordingly seated myself and watched with some amusement, but more impatience, the mixed and apparently half-crazy crowd that still struggled and crowded each other in the hall. As I have said, some of these people were official personages of high standing, who ought not to have been subjected to such indignity nor left in waiting a moment longer than was necessary, the more especially as most of them had business directly relating to the war and of very great importance to the public interests. Finding that I was left severely alone without the least intimation that I should be disturbed during the day, I again accosted Colonel Woods and told him I must see General Frémont, as I was there at his request and had very little time to wait. He made the same reply as before—that "the general was much engaged," etc. I then asked him if the room we were in was General Frémont's office. He said no; his office was on the floor above. I then told Colonel Woods I would go up to the general's office and ascertain whether he was too busy to see me. The colonel greatly deprecated this plan and objected to it in his suavest tones, with some importunity. I, however, pushed my way to the stairs which led up from the basement, Colonel Woods attending me. When I reached the hall above I found it quite solitary, except that one gentleman, in what was evidently an ill-fitting and uncomfortable uniform, was reclining on a sofa. The state apartments of the house opened on the hall and all of the doors were open. Not a solitary person was to be seen. In the long drawing-room, occupying the whole of the western side, I found General Frémont in uniform and quite alone, as he had apparently been for some time.

The room was handsomely furnished and the long tables which had been introduced for official use, were covered with maps and papers.

General Frémont himself was walking up and down the wing-room, evidently in deep thought, from his appearance and expression of face. He received me very pleasantly and cordially and we had half an hour's conversation about affairs in my own command and the general situation in Missouri.

Price was slowly advancing toward the Missouri River at Lexington from the southwest and General Frémont appeared to be satisfied that the measures he had taken to prevent the success of such a movement would be effectual, though what those measures were I did not quite make out.[15] I told him of the jam in the lower hall and of my difficulty in forcing my way to his presence. He seemed surprised and provoked and dismissed me by the main door of the house on that floor, begging me always to enter by the main entrance and not by the basement. I inferred directly from his manner and his words that he did not know of the scenes below stairs nor approve of the exclusion from his presence of persons of character and standing who wished to see him. Whether Colonel Woods and his confederates from California, of whom there were several on General Frémont's staff, desired for their own purposes to keep the general secluded in this manner without his knowledge or approval I do not know, but I do know that this withdrawal from the public view and from free and open intercourse with active and influential Union men from the neighboring states, as well as from Missouri, gave great offense and much impaired the strong partiality for him which most people felt when he first assumed the command.[16] It is related, with what truth I do not know, though the story will sufficiently illustrate the idea entertained at the time, that Governor Gamble, who had been elected Governor of Missouri by the Convention at Jefferson City after the flight of the old State officers into Arkansas and who had of course important interests in his hands, in which General Frémont was equally concerned, after several days' encounters with the army in the basement in the vain effort to see the general, was absolutely obliged to send to Washington for an order from the president to General Frémont to see him.[17] Whether this seclusion was General Frémont's own act or the unauthorized act of his subordinates, I do not know. That it did him much injury with the public and prevented much valuable information and advice from reaching him is certain. The number of foreigners also who were attached to his staff, with their strange appearance and not too good manners, gave a foreign tone and look to everything about his headquarters, which was offensive to Americans, who were, with extreme reluctance and regret, being forced into a war with their own countrymen, the prospect of which had produced this swarm of aliens, who had no interest in us or our affairs other than they could find in the spoils of war. They were not citizens, not even residents of the United States, but simply military adventurers from Europe, who had neither knowledge or respect for the institutions of a country which they were supposed to be defending. Nearly all of them I saw were cringing and subservient to their superiors in rank, but arrogant to a degree to their subordinates. They were un-American and offensive meddlers in a family outbreak and alienated people from the cause they sided with rather than attracted them to it.[18]

How much General Frémont knew of this condition or how far he encouraged it, if he did so at all, I cannot say, but that the effects were bad and the Union sentiment weakened in Missouri by it I think no one will deny who served in that state in those days. In most respects General Frémont appeared much as I expected to find him. Although a good many years had passed since I had last seen him he did not appear to have aged much and he looked very much as I remembered him. I never could, without an effort, regard him as an American. In his appearance and manner and his habits and his ideas he was essentially a foreigner and his surroundings in St. Louis caused this impression of him to prevail very generally. He appeared to be dazed with the confusion and excitement around him, and but imperfectly to realize the situation and its necessities. One may look in vain for any acts of a practical character for evidence that he was a practical man or that he possessed that robust common sense characteristic of his countrymen and essential in his position. His reign lasted only about three months. When the order relieving him from command reached him at Springfield, Missouri, it was asserted by many of the foreigners and some of the Americans also, that he was in the presence of a large force of the enemy and was on the eve of a great battle, but in fact, as is generally known now, there was no hostile force nearer to him than fifty miles and the force there was much inferior to his own and ready to retreat as soon as there was any indication that we would advance. Indeed we were in no condition to advance, having neither stores nor trains to carry them in and we had marched so far from the railroads with insufficient supplies that some of our troops actually suffered for food before we got back to them. General Frémont started back to St. Louis next morning,[19] taking with him the fine silver band of music which was attached to his headquarters and escorted by a considerable body of Indian scouts (Delawares and Shawnees), whose wild appearance and strange costumes made a very picturesque cavalcade of it.

General David Hunter, who relieved him in the command, was an old officer of the Regular Army, highly esteemed by everybody who knew him, whether in or out of the army and was altogether one of the most upright, earnest and honest men I ever knew.[20] He was intensely patriotic and could find no excuse for anyone who was not zealous and pronounced on the Union side. He was a Virginian by birth, dark of visage and healthy of complexion, with long black hair and piercing black eyes. He had a countenance so expressive and mobile that any feeling was visible at once in the sparkling of his eye and the quivering of his lip. He was a thoroughly genuine and thoroughly trustworthy man and soldier.

After ascertaining by a reconnaissance in force that there was no force of the enemy within fifty miles and assuring himself that we were nearly out of rations and had no sort of prospect of getting them from the railroad, because of want of wagons or organized trains, he gave the order for the troops to march for several points on the railroads with all speed. This withdrawal of the troops was made in view also of the suggestion of the president to General Hunter at the time the latter superseded General Frémont. Almost immediately after the arrival of General Hunter in St. Louis he was replaced in the command by General Henry W. Halleck, who had been appointed a major general in the army and assigned to this command through the influence of General Scott.[21] As Halleck was a prominent figure during the early period of the war and had a strange and rather anomalous position all through it, in that he was abused for all that went wrong in military affairs and got no credit for any success, it is not easy to give any account of him which shall be free from bias.[22] He was a black-browed saturnine man, heavy of figure and of feature; suspicious of everybody and incapable of friendship. He seemed to proceed on the theory that everyone around him was seeking to get some advantage of him and he was continually taking precautions against his officers, which did not attract their regard to him. He undid pretty much all that Frémont had done in the way of administrative acts and dissolved the military organizations he had put on foot. He had large ability of a closet kind and was in no sense brilliant—with theories often sustained and put forth by the best authorities he was familiar; acts to illustrate these theories he was utterly incompetent to do. He considered that any statement or report that might, even for the time, be beneficial to the public was justifiable whether true or not and this theory he practiced to the injury of some of the officers who served under him and to the damage of his own character. He was an office man altogether and in matters of administration he had both ability and industry.

One experiment in the field at Corinth just after the Battle of Shiloh satisfied him, no doubt, as it did everybody else, that he had none of the qualities required as the active commander of an army in the field. He certainly never repeated the experiment.[23]

I think that during the whole month spent in front of Corinth when he was in personal command, none of the troops knew him even by sight, except his immediate escort and the staff officers around and perhaps a few of the officers of rank in that army. So far as any influence he had over the troops he might as well have been in St. Louis. When he was appointed to such high rank and command he was a citizen of California, a lawyer and a successful man in so far as making money was concerned. He graduated high in his class at West Point, having plenty of intellectual ability and had such knowledge of war as his military education and subsequent studies gave him. He was a Union man, but at best exceedingly conservative, as was natural. At times he was happy, in a sort of grim humor, but in general he was too reserved and to an extent sullen, to be an attractive companion. How he managed to get along smoothly with Mr. Stanton, who had a strong feeling against him when he first arrived in Washington, I do not know; but with Stanton's fiery temper and Halleck's peculiar official relation to him I think that at times the situation must have been "strained."[24] His apparent distrust of his officers and the precautions he took to shield himself at their expense against the consequences of any misfortune that might befall any enterprise they were conducting were extremely discouraging and hateful. As an instance: In the operations against Island No. Ten it became absolutely necessary for us to cross the Mississippi in the face of the enemy with a large force. This was an operation of great hazard and difficulty, but it had to be done if we were to be successful. I reported to him all the facts, including my arrangements to effect the crossing.[25] The day before I was to make the attempt I received a telegram from him, giving it as his opinion that it had better not be undertaken and advising strongly against it, but ended his telegram by saying that as I was on the ground he would not interfere with me by any order.[26] He thus quietly placed the whole responsibility upon my shoulders and placed himself in the attitude of a looker-on who had objected to the project in hand, so that if it proved successful he as the general commander would have his full share of the glory; whereas, if it proved disastrous and a failure, he had only to publish his telegram to me to prove that it was not only not his fault, but that it had been undertaken by me wholly against his advice. This was certainly not an encouraging, nor in any sense a satisfactory, situation for the immediate commander of such an expedition to be placed in by his superior in command, nor was it fair or just. Neither was it to be defended that he should, afterward, in order to protect himself against adverse criticism in his operations at Corinth, telegraph the Secretary of War that I had reported the capture of a great many prisoners from the enemy on their retreat, when I had never reported anything of the kind nor the capture of even one prisoner.[27]

His action in this matter was in accord with his theory that any report which benefited the public interests was to be justified, whether true or not, but he displayed in this action not only the unscrupulousness born of such a theory and necessary to execute such a maxim, but the lack of manhood to attempt to lay the responsibility of the falsehood on someone else. It took some years and the action of the War Department, to right the wrong he did. He was an unlovely man, but he rendered valuable service in reorganizing the department and establishing its business on systematic and efficient foundations. He left both troops and affairs generally in much better shape than he found them. He died a bitter and disappointed man, with many enemies and few, if any, friends, though he served in such a position in Washington for most of the war that he ought to have had many and devoted friends.[28] He was a loyal man to the core and earnest and zealous in his efforts in behalf of the government.

Chapter Two

An Unpleasant Page of History

*I*t is my opinion that Missouri suffered more during the late war than any state in the Union except perhaps Virginia. It is also my opinion that the larger part of this suffering was unnecessary and was brought about by unwise and inconsiderate action, mainly on the part of the sympathizers with the South.

The political status of Missouri and its fixed connection with the Northern States did not depend at all upon the success or failure of the South in its attempt to set up another government. Whatever the outcome of the war might be, Missouri was, by its position and surroundings, firmly tied to the free states, whatever government or governments the war might evolve. It has always seemed to me singular that this condition was not recognized immediately by those most concerned. How was it possible for Missouri violently to disrupt its relations with the free states and for what purpose? The state, like a great peninsula, thrusts itself up between Illinois and Kansas and for several hundred miles is coterminous with Iowa on the north. How was it practicable for Missouri to contend successfully with these three great states, which already held her tight in their embrace and were ready to apply constriction at the first notice. Arkansas, the only neighbor on the south, was too weak to defend herself.

Of course, surrounded in this manner, slavery and slaves disappeared from the state with the first act of war.[1] What, then, was there of any material interest to bind her, or to make it in any sense desirable for her to be bound, to a system of government of which slavery was the corner-stone?

I think that everyone at this day will recognize the entire soundness of this position and ask himself why it was that the people of the state plunged themselves into civil war, which invaded every house and sat at every fireside in Missouri; when the outcome of a war, so far as they were concerned, was fixed before it began.

The disproportion between Union men and Secessionists in the state was not large.[2] In truth the parties appeared to be nearly equally divided in North Missouri, whilst St. Louis and the larger towns were quite securely Union. Fighting each other under such circumstances was simple passion, not justified by any hope of benefit to either side on the national question, or to the people themselves or their state. In short, Missouri belonged in no sense to the Southern system of states and even if permitted would never have remained joined to them. Her geographical position, the character of her soil and productions, the nature of her occupations and interests and the close embrace of the free states around her, left no tie between her and the Southern states except the sentimental remembrances of those who originally came from the South, but whose habits of life and methods of thought had been so changed by the very different conditions of society and of occupation, that they were nearly as foreign to Southern ways and ideas as those of the man from Massachusetts. The slaves among them were really only slaves in name, not onl profitless, but a burden to the so-called owners. Indeed, the slaves were the owners of the master rather than he of them and the slave-trader was nearly as odious as the abolitionist in Missouri.[3]

Nevertheless war was precipitated on the people of Missouri by their own leaders; not war in the open field and by armies duly marshaled for battle, but war by one neighbor against another. Very soon every household was in arms against some other household and in many cases the house was divided against itself. Necessarily outrageous wrongs and atrocious acts of cruelty were perpetrated and the result was almost universal suffering and misery in that state.

No man could stay quietly at home, no matter what party he belonged to or however desirous to keep the peace. Things grew worse and worse, until at last, before the war had lasted eighteen months, the condition of the people of Missouri, except in the large towns, became wretched and well nigh desperate. It was impossible for any man living in the country, away from considerable towns, to avoid taking up arms against somebody. A quiet, peaceable man, living on his farm with his wife and children and with no decided political proclivities one way or the other, would find his house suddenly surrounded by a party of bushwhackers, who, with fierce oaths and loud threats of burning his house, demanded that his wife and daughters at once prepare a meal for the party and furnish feed for their horses, regardless of the time of day or night, or whether the victim was impoverished or not. After thoroughly satisfying themselves and their horses they departed, with fearful threats of murder in case any of the family betrayed their presence or the road by which they left.

Scarcely was this party out of sight and the poor family had restored something like order to their household, when up rode a party of Union cavalry and charging these poor people furiously with having just harbored a party of rebels, made the same requisition for meals for themselves and horses. The only compensation offered to the poor man thus abused was an abundant supply of new and powerful profanity. Naturally, after one or two of these visitations, the peaceful farmer loaded his gun and took to the bush, whence he fired indiscriminately and levied taxes, without distinction of "race, color, or previous condition," on everybody who appeared. Thus one-half of the male population was loaded, watching for the other half, who were also engaged in the same pleasing occupation. The wives and children took refuge with friends in towns and villages, where numbers offered some security and practically their homes and farms were abandoned until the evil times were past. In this manner large districts in Missouri were temporarily abandoned or kept in constant terror and want and houses and fields went, at least partially, to ruin.[4]

Even in the towns and cities it was not much better, they being overrun with provost-marshals, who made life intolerable to large numbers of persons. A more unhappy and suffering people it would have been difficult to find anywhere and as I consider the larger part of this misery to have been unnecessary, I find it hard even at this day to excuse the personages whose misjudged and reckless course was the direct cause of it all. Of course this state of things did not exist at the beginning, but developed as time went on, without any application of common sense to repress or altogether to prevent it.

On the 17th of July, 1861, when I assumed the command in North Missouri, everything was in confusion and uncertainty. In North Missouri—by which is meant that part of the state which lies north of the Missouri River—the people were nearly equally divided in political sentiment. In some counties the Southern sympathizers predominated; in others, the Union men were in the majority. The Secessionists had struck the first blow in North Missouri seemingly as an experiment and to commit their friends to open hostilities.[5] The railroad leading from St. Louis via St. Charles through the central part of North Missouri had been torn up in places and several bridges burned. In nearly every county some acts of violence had been committed, almost wholly by small bands of Secessionists, but no actual hostilities on a considerable scale had been undertaken. All the civil machinery, however, of this part of the state had been arrested; courts and sheriffs had ceased to exercise their functions; every man was suspicious of his neighbor and the apprehension of complete anarchy was plainly apparent among the people. A single spark would have been enough to put the whole of North Missouri into a flame and sweep away all restraints of law and all security for life and property. The younger and more violent of the Secessionists (which party was, in the nature of things, the aggressive party) strove in every way to precipitate a collision and to involve the entire population in war against one another.

The position and condition of Missouri particularly were altogether different from those of the Southern states. Whilst the latter were so far unanimous in political sentiment that there was no open opposition to the Secession party and the civil machinery of the state governments, which that party controlled, acted freely and without interruption, Missouri was so divided in sentiment and so many of her civil officers enlisted on either side of the political question, that civil law was either not executed at all or was made the instrument of outrage and injustice to political opponents.

The governor and other high officials of the state had fled from the capital and had joined the armed insurgents, destroying or carrying off the state records and the public funds and leaving confusion, disorder and dismay behind them.[6] The chief of the state government and many of the civil officials having thus abandoned their duties, no laws were observed or executed and the people thus left without a government and inflamed with enmity and passion were in condition to inaugurate a bloody anarchy on small provocation.

Such was the situation in North Missouri when I entered that district with a few regiments of Illinois troops. General Frémont, recently appointed major general, had been assigned to the command of the Western Department, which included Missouri within its limits and it was by his telegraph order, though he himself had not joined his command, that I entered northern Missouri and assumed control.

Manifestly the first object to be attended to was the security of our railroad communications. North Missouri was divided into two nearly equal parts by the Hannibal and St. Joseph Railroad, which traversed it from east to west. It was again divided in part by the North Missouri Road, running north from St. Charles, on the Missouri River, to Macon on the Hannibal and St. Joseph Road, which was at that time its northern terminus.[7] Both roads had been torn up in places and some bridges burned by small parties of people living in the vicinity. Some firing from the roadside upon passenger trains, altogether savage and wanton, had been done also and women and children and harmless and unprotected passengers had been wounded. To have guarded those roads thoroughly from such outrages would have taken a large force and even then it could not have been effectively done.

As long as lawless parties of marauders were shielded by their neighbors and friends from punishment for these atrocious acts, if not, indeed, encouraged to commit them, it was useless to think of putting a stop to them or keeping the railroads in running order without the use of methods which any American would shrink from applying to his countrymen and yet which would have to be resorted to unless some other equally effective measures could be devised. It seemed to me that the only remedy for these lawless acts likely to be effectual was to make the whole population along the line of these roads directly responsible for the acts of the irresponsible parties of outlaws who were perfectly well known to the whole community, so that no damage or outrage could be done by them without the direct injury being laid upon the shoulders of their friends and relatives. I accordingly posted my command at one or two important points in North Missouri and put into operation the method sufficiently set forth in the following extracts from the order issued for the purpose.

A WARNING TO THE PEOPLE
H'dQ'rs District of North Missouri,
St. Charles, July 21, 1861.

An investigation of the circumstances attending the difficulties along the line of the North Missouri Road—the wanton destruction of bridges, culverts, etc.—makes it manifest that the inhabitants of the villages and stations along the road, if not privy to these outrages, at least offered no resistance to them and gave no information by which the perpetrators could have been prosecuted or merited punishment inflicted upon the criminals. I desire the people of this section of the State to understand that their safety and the security of their property depend upon themselves, and are inseparably connected with the security of the lines of railroad along which they live if they choose to do so. I therefore notify the inhabitants of the towns, villages and stations along the line of the North Missouri Railroad that they will be held accountable for the destruction of any bridges, culverts or portions of track within five miles on each side of them. If any outrages of this kind are committed within the distance specified without conclusive proof of active resistance on the part of the people, and without immediate information to the nearest commanding officer, giving names and details, the population will be held responsible, and a levy of money or of property sufficient to cover the whole damage done will be at once made and collected. To carry out these intentions, divisions and subdivisions of the railroad will be made as soon as practicable from these headquarters, and superintendents and assistant superintendents appointed by name, without regard to political opinions, who will be responsible for the safety of the railroad track within these specified limits. They will have authority to call on all persons living within these limits to appear in such numbers and at times and places as they may deem necessary to accomplish the object in view. All good citizens who value peace and the security of their families and their property will, I am sure, respond willingly to these arrangements.[8]

These appointments were promptly made and the proposed machinery put into operation. It was effectual. All attempts to molest the railroad were given up immediately.[9]

I recollect well one portly old gentleman, the principal citizen in one of the largest towns along the road and a rabid Southern man, whom I had appointed superintendent of the railroad in his locality. He came up to see me at the town of Mexico. He was a good-natured old gentleman, though he took his new appointment rather hard. He was anxious to resign, but I told him that his office was one of those that should not be sought, but could not be declined.[10] He admitted that the people could stop these raids on the railroads and promised to do his best to accomplish it. He told me that it had never been within the compass of his imagination that he would come to be an officeholder under Abe Lincoln, but he meant to be a faithful one and I have no doubt he was.

The security of the railroads against any considerable damage being thus assured, I addressed myself to the task of allaying as far as I could the general excitement which had been occasioned by these incipient hostilities and if possible restoring and maintaining the due execution of the laws through the usual civil officials. It would have been natural, perhaps, in such a condition of lawlessness and with a long war on a great scale absolutely on our hands, to have declared martial law in northern Missouri and to have at once applied military force to quiet disturbances and to keep order; but to a declaration of martial law and the subjection of any portion of the people to military rule I was greatly opposed. Nor did I consider martial law the best or even an efficient mode of bringing about the condition of fact and of feeling which appeared to me so desirable.[11]

Chapter Three

Quiet and Good Order Are of All Things Desirable

$\mathscr{S}$mall bands, mainly of Secessionists, consisting mostly of young men, were scattered through every county in North Missouri. Their depredations and other acts of violence were committed without fear of personal exposure, even by the people most concerned. The fear of swift vengeance kept peaceable people quiet even in the midst of wrong and injustice. Pursuit of these bands by troops developed only men quietly working in the fields or in their offices. The moment United States troops appeared near them these bands dispersed, each man going to his home and resuming his usual occupation, being sure that for very sufficient reasons he would not be exposed. Young men attached to the Union cause were not slow to follow the evil example, either for revenge or other reason and in conjunction with the bands of Secessionists were thus keeping the whole country in an uproar, alike ruinous to good government and injurious to the people.

The systematic pursuit of these small bands by detachments of soldiers would have carried disorder and dismay into every part of the country, alike to Secessionists and Union men. In view of all these considerations, a resort to martial law, as it seemed to me then and still seems, would have been about the most unwise course that could have been adopted. It was, however, of vital importance that some means be devised by which peaceable people, regardless of their politics, who stayed at home and had no purpose to take up arms, could be brought to act together for the security of life and property and the preservation of peace and law among themselves. This joint action could not be brought about nor the desired results accomplished so long as these bands of young and restless men remained in their midst.

It was, therefore, necessary to get rid of them, if might be, by making it impossible for them to commit any overt act without the most serious consequences being at once visited upon their friends and relatives. These turbulent youths needed some outlet, and my purpose was thus to force them to join the organized forces on one side or the other. Once completely taken out of the communities they disturbed, it would be possible to keep the peace without even the presence of military force. Whatever their political opinions or their sympathies may have been, it was very certain that nine-tenths of the respectable property-holders in North Missouri never had the least idea of taking an active part on either side.[1]

This great majority of the people it was most desirable to enlist in strenuous efforts to keep the peace, which I knew they could do by combined action. As the best means to accomplish this purpose I issued an order, extracts from which will sufficiently indicate what was proposed and what machinery put in motion:

AN APPEAL TO ALL GOOD CITIZENS.

HeadQ'rs, District of North Missouri,

Mexico, July 31, 1861.

It is plainly demonstrated by sufficient testimony, and by the experience of the past two weeks, that the disturbances in North Missouri have been made by small parties of lawless marauders, who at any other time could have been easily suppressed with no more than the usual exertions of the people against breaches of the peace in times past. Quiet and good order are of all things desirable in civilized communities, and their preservation should form a common bond of union among citizens of all shades of political opinion. When this desirable condition is securely established, there will be no need of military force among you. It is therefore, the purpose of the Commanding General in this region of the country, before removing the military forces under his command from their present stations, to visit with a considerable force every County seat and considerable town in North Missouri, and in each to appoint a Committee of Public Safety, of persons selected from both political parties, who have social, domestic and pecuniary interests at stake. Each committee will consist of five persons, and, whenever it can be consistently done, the County officers shall be chosen. . . . These committees will be charged with the duty of maintaining peace and order in their respective Counties, and shall have power to call out all citizens of the County, to assemble at such times and places and in such numbers as may be necessary to secure this object. . . . If the people of the Counties are not willing or not able to preserve peace among themselves and to prevent the open organization of military companies to make war, the military forces of the United States will perform the service; but, as this service is wholly in the interest and for the benefit of the people of each County concerned, the expenses of the same must be paid by such County. . . . Upon the call of a majority of the Committee of Public Safety in any County, troops will be sent to keep the peace, subject to the above conditions. If, in consequence of disturbances not reported by the committee, the General commanding finds it necessary to send a force into any of the Counties to restore order, it will in like manner be billeted on the County, unless the combinations against the peace were too powerful to be resisted by the people, or were organized in other Counties and brought on the disturbance by actual invasion; in which case the troops will be marched into the County where such combinations were organized, and in like manner be billeted when there. To preserve the peace is the duty of all good citizens, and as, in that case, all will suffer from the breach of it, men of every shade of political opinion can act cordially together to keep it.

By performing this very reasonable service as they have done in times past, the people of North Missouri will be spared the anxiety, uneasiness and apprehension which necessarily attend the presence of armed forces, and will again enjoy that security of person and property which has heretofore been their habit. All persons who have heretofore been led away to take up arms against their fellow citizens or the United States Government are notified that by returning and laying down their arms, and by performing their duty hereafter as peaceful and law-abiding citizens, they will not be molested by the military forces; nor, so far as the Commanding General in this section can influence the matter, will they be subjected to any penalty, unless they have committed murder or some other capital offense. . . .

(signed) John Pope, Brig.-Gen. Comd'g.[2]

The purpose of this order seems to me to be clearly indicated by its terms. The object was to adopt some machinery to keep the peace which would command the united effort of all citizens who did not wish to take actual, personal part in the war and to make any hostile acts of such persons as did propose to take part in the war so injurious to their friends and relatives that they go elsewhere to indulge their inclinations in this direction. By the departure of this dangerous element the people would be left at peace and their interest in the progress of the war would be a matter of sentiment rather than of actual participation. The arrangements indicated in the foregoing order were at once inaugurated and for a time the results seemed to be as satisfactory as could be hoped.

At this early period of the rebellion, however, it was not strange that people the most loyal and best disposed should contemplate with indignation and disapproval what seemed to them, ignorant of the future before them, such unnecessary curtailment of the entire liberty they had always enjoyed and should have looked upon this order as unwise and tyrannical. It was not long until such opinions began to circulate and earnest partisans speedily seized the opportunity to urge that higher authority than mine revoke the order. Union men of high position began to complain of the order, urging that it was unjust and tyrannical; that it placed Union men on the same footing with rebels; that the latter alone should be subjected to its provisions, etc. Complaints of substantially the same character were made by persons who, although sympathizing with the South, had no purpose to disturb the peace in any manner and who thought it hard that they should be held responsible for the acts of a few violent and lawless men in their midst.[3]

It is needless to say that the whole purpose of the order was to unite all the peaceable people of that part of the state in keeping the peace by common interest and under a common penalty. If the men of either party were excepted from the requirements of this order, of course the whole plan necessarily fell to the ground. Let me repeat that the object of my order was to force the restless and dissatisfied, who wished to take active part in the fighting, to leave these neighborhoods and join the organized forces on one side or the other and thus to leave those who did *not* wish to take personal part in the war, to live quietly at home, attending to their usual vocations, without troops or provost marshals to keep them in constant terror and unhappiness.[4]

The opinions and active personal influence of these persons soon began to appear. The restless and turbulent element which it was hoped would be driven out of this section and who were anxious to be warriors at home, with midnight raiding as a pursuit, were not slow to give their aid to arrest the execution of the order. At length, when it was believed that they had succeeded, they proceeded to put to the test whether I intended to really enforce it, or whether, even if I did so intend, I would be permitted by the highest military authority then in Missouri.

They made the test as complete as possible, by making the case as bad against themselves as it was possible to make it. A party concealed in the bushes alongside the track fired into the windows of a passenger train on the Hannibal & St. Joseph Railroad, carrying unarmed men, women and children and wounded several of the passengers. This occurred within the limits of Marion County.[5] I immediately called upon the Committee of Safety to take action; but as they did not act promptly, I sent a military force into the County, with orders to hunt down the criminals and levy upon the County for supplies whilst they were doing it. This measure brought the matter to an issue, but by this time unwise counsels and unfounded representations had so influenced the department commander in St. Louis that the execution of my order was suspended by his authority.[6]

It was enough. The scheme which I had hoped would save at least North Missouri from guerrilla warfare and the torments of irresponsible military domination fell to the ground. The whole country was soon infested by bands, both of Secessionists and of Union men, waging midnight war with each other and with the peaceable citizens and carrying terror and dismay to all parts of the country. As a logical sequence General Frémont soon declared martial law and instantly small detachments of troops appeared everywhere, accompanied by that necessary evil of martial law, the provost marshal.[7]

Except in the large towns and headquarters of military departments, where men of character and standing were chosen, these officials were appointed by the irresponsible commanders of the small detachments scattered all over the state and changed almost every day. The provost marshals, like the lice of Egypt, soon infested every place and tormented everybody and adding their efforts to swell the clamor and increase the disorder, the people of Missouri were soon in a condition beyond reach of help.

Some account of these matters and the so-called campaigns which were the result, I shall hope to give in another paper, but meantime it seems pertinent to inquire why it was that Missouri was subjected to this wretched disorder and suffering, whilst Kentucky, with a governor and a large majority of the people in full sympathy with the South and which supplied troops to both armies, was almost entirely free from martial law and bushwhacking warfare. Across Kentucky, of necessity, marched the great armies of the West which finally decided the fortunes of the war; across Missouri, or within its limits, there ought to have been no need of troops from either side and there was no need except such as was created by the action of the state officials.

To that action, in the beginning, the people of Missouri are indebted for the origin of the larger part of their suffering during the Civil War.

The flight of the governor and other state officers from Jefferson City and the destruction of railroad bridges behind them was either a most pusillanimous act or a most atrocious and cold-blooded plot to plunge unwilling and unprepared people into civil war, for no other purpose than to assist some other states in setting up another government in our midst, to which Missouri, whatever sacrifices she might make or whatever misery she might suffer, could never have belonged.[8] The feeling of the Confederate Government on this subject has lately been set forth by a competent hand and justifies the opinions herein expressed.[9] If the conduct of the state officers of Missouri in abandoning their duties to the people and taking to flight was due to personal fear, they ought to be and to have been held in contemptuous pity; but if found in Missouri afterward they should have been treated as skulkers from a field of battle are dealt with.

If, on the other hand, they abandoned their duties and fled from the capital in order to leave the people without civil government and thus force a declaration of martial law and commit the people of the state to active participation in the war, having first exasperated the United States authorities by breaking railroads and destroying bridges, it is hard to see how they are to be forgiven at all. They were elected to high and responsible executive and administrative office by the people of Missouri. By what right did they abandon these obligations? Especially by what right did they carry off public papers and money belonging to the state? Was it not their duty to stand firm in their places and hold fast to their duties, so as to maintain civil government to the last?

In proportion to the personal danger which confronted them, was their obligation to stand faithful to the trust conferred upon them. If these state officers had maintained their offices and performed their duties faithfully and honorably, it is much to be doubted whether martial law would ever have been declared in Missouri, or civil courts and processes materially interfered with. It is quite certain that no such conditions could have obtained, had the state officers been faithful to their duties, as afterward brought sorrow and suffering to every family in the state.

The action of the state convention afterward called together was itself revolutionary and never, in the minds of probably a majority of the people, invested the governor and state officers of its creation with the rights and authority of the fugitive officials who had been duly elected. These fugacious personages seem to have set up a state government for Missouri in Arkansas — an interesting illustration of their ideas of state rights — to maintain which they supposed themselves to have gone to war.[10]

In the presence at Jefferson City of the state government and of the state officials duly elected carrying on the state government without hostile act toward the United States, it is much to be doubted whether General Frémont would ever have declared martial law in Missouri. I am myself satisfied, from my own experience in the state at the time, that if the state officers had remained at their posts no condition of things would have arisen to make martial law necessary or even justifiable.

The condition of affairs in North Missouri, which I have tried to describe, was strictly due to the absence of any civil government in the state. The action of the state officers in fleeing from the state had furnished an evil example to all the minor officials and had almost completely destroyed confidence in the good faith and permanency of all their civil officials. Even such of these officials as were willing to do their duty, found neither support nor encouragement.

It was to prevent anarchy on the one hand and the horrors of martial law on the other, that I undertook the measures herein described. I thought and still think, that if they had been permitted to work themselves out, they might have protected the people of Missouri from many of the evils with which they were afterward visited. Passion, however, largely ruled the hour and it may well be doubted whether any cause based on common sense and unprejudiced consideration could have succeeded in those days of fierce excitement. It appeared to me to be worth the trial, and I did what I could to set it in operation.

I repeat, however, that the larger part of this excitement and apprehension was due to the indefensible acts of the state officials and that the people of Missouri are indebted for the greater part of their suffering during the war to the fact that these state officers fled from their posts and abandoned their duties to the people who had placed them in office.

On the 30th of August General Frémont declared martial law in Missouri and the whole state, in all the relations between its citizens, passed completely into the control of the military authorities.[11] In St. Louis, where the military headquarters were established and where many, if not most, of the civil officers were Union men, a sort of civil law was kept up; but as judges, jurors and lawyers were at any moment subject to arrest and imprisonment by provost marshals and the decisions of courts likely at any time to be overruled or cases withdrawn from their jurisdiction by the same military functionary, law was so loosely and irregularly administered as to afford small protection to persons or property.

In the interior of the state little attempt was made to carry on civil government anywhere. The numerous provost marshals with their armies of assistants and followers reigned supreme and being in authority above and beyond the reach of any civil process, they worked their will practically without opposition. No man who was wronged or even outraged dared to complain to any authority high enough to redress the injury done him, lest, if he should fail in having the offending provost marshal entirely removed, worse things should befall him.

The troops under my command in North Missouri were scattered over the country in detachments, great and small and were occupied vigorously, but in general without successful result, in trying to break up or capture bands of rebel guerrillas who infested that whole region. Whenever it was possible the troops made use of the services of such Union organizations as existed at the time, but even the very limited discipline of our troops at that early stage of the war was so distasteful to these independent organizations that they did not serve together with any degree of zeal or satisfaction. To be restrained from committing violence and wrong merely for the gratification of personal revenge or malevolence, seemed to these irregular bands purely tyrannical and they did not long continue to act with the United States forces, except when fear of superior forces on the other side compelled them to unite their irregular bands with bodies of troops for temporary security.

For weeks this irregular warfare was kept up, bringing misery to all peaceful people and doing no manner of benefit to either side. As this sort of work went on, more and more all distinctions of right and wrong and all sympathies with one side or the other in the National contest melted away and these guerrilla bands depredated alike upon everybody. No man, however harmless and innocent, was safe for a moment. All lived in anxiety and terror.

One of the most active leaders of the rebels in North Missouri was Martin Green,[12] who kept the northeastern counties of the state in constant alarm, until he was finally forced to cross to the south side of the Missouri River where he joined General Sterling Price and thereafter served in his command. His most active and formidable enemy was Colonel Moore,[13] on the Union side, who organized a force of irregulars, part of whom were from Iowa, just across the Missouri line. He followed up Green with wonderful persistency, several times on the very point of capturing him and to Colonel Moore, I think, more than to any other cause, the departure of Martin Green from North Missouri is to be attributed. Colonel Moore soon after joined the Union forces with his band and was mustered into the service of the United States. He afterward attained distinction as a most gallant and valuable officer.

It would be simply harrowing to recount the thousands of barbarous atrocities committed upon the people of North Missouri during this unhappy time. From every direction and from all parties these wrongs descended upon them and if their history could be truly written it would furnish a record at which even a savage might hang his head.

One of the most characteristic feats was the destruction of the railroad bridge over Platte River near St. Joseph. A short time before the regular passenger train was due, parties of these bushwhackers, who were well known in that vicinity and who in ordinary times had been considered respectable, civilized people, sawed the sills of the bridge from beneath nearly in two, so that they would barely hold up the structure itself. Having arranged matters, they watched the result. The passenger train, with its freight of women and children and unarmed men, innocent of any hostility or desire to do injury to anyone, came rapidly to this death-trap without warning, though in the view of a large body of American citizens calling themselves Christian people. Of course the bridge gave way at once and the whole train plunged into the river. Thirty people were killed and wounded, but not one of the perpetrators of this savage act was ever identified, though it was openly stated that most of them were well known in St. Joseph and some of them residents of the town.[14]

Such was the kind of warfare carried on in Missouri. It had nothing to do with the general war going on in the country, and no thought of benefiting either the Union or Confederate cause entered into the consideration. It was simply an illustration of what the natural, savage instincts of men will lead to when once the restraints of law are abandoned. Many of the most active of these outlaws returned to their homes when peace came and became again quiet and respectable citizens and I presume often stand amazed when they consider at this day their evil deeds of those years of sorrow and trial. Believing as I do that Missouri could have been spared the larger part of these sufferings by ordinary faithful and manly conduct on the part of the state officials at the beginning, I perhaps have been led further than was needful into the details of this most melancholy episode in the history of the people of that state.

Meantime the Battle of Wilson's Creek had been fought and lost by the Union troops and the gallant Lyon killed. Whether it was in the power of General Frémont to reinforce him in time to have insured success, or at least to have prevented defeat, is a matter of opinion and it is not necessary for me to give mine in this place. General Frémont had but recently assumed the command in Missouri. The demands on him for troops from all parts of the state were incessant and far beyond any actual need. Until he could learn the situation and understand the necessities elsewhere in his command, it was natural that he should have been reluctant to engage the larger part of his troops at so remote a point, especially as it is not likely that he anticipated such decisive action on the part of General Lyon. The result of that battle, however, confirmed the condition of lawlessness and neither injured the Union cause nor benefited the Confederate. As was usual in military operations in Missouri throughout the war, the sufferers were the people of the state; the beneficiaries none.

After that battle the Union forces fell back to Rolla unmolested by the enemy. General Sterling Price, who had been engaged in the battle, commanding an irregular and almost entirely unorganized force, which was called "state troops," not having been yet mustered into the Confederate service, began leisurely and at his ease, but with great blowing of trumpets and loud announcement of his purpose, to move north toward the Missouri River to invest and capture the town of Lexington, then occupied by about 3,000 Union troops under Colonel Mulligan.[15] Of course, as he marched slowly through the country he was considerably reinforced every day by people who joined him merely for the enterprise in which he was engaged, but probably with little purpose of long remaining with him, especially if he were unsuccessful. It is safe to say that nine-tenths of the people of Missouri knew perfectly his object and his movements and positions from day to day during the weeks occupied in marching from Wilson's Creek to the Missouri River. He marched very slowly and cautiously and seemed anxiously to expect or to fear some movement of troops from St. Louis or elsewhere against him or toward his rear.

It is not my purpose to recount the details of this march, nor the capture of Lexington and its garrison after several days fighting.[16] Price was not molested on his march to Lexington, during his operations there, nor in his march back to the south with his captives and his booty. Why this was so I never knew and do not know now. It could not have been for want of troops, or want of knowledge of the condition of things in Missouri, or of Price's movements and intentions, or want of time.

About three weeks before Price reached Lexington I had been instructed by General Frémont to proceed to northeastern Missouri and personally to look into matters in that section. From there I had returned to the line of the Hannibal & St. Joseph Railroad, had partially dispersed the guerrilla band of Martin Green, and was at the time Lexington was invested engaged in clearing the railroad of bands of outlaws who had broken it in several places. I reached the bridge over the Platte River in the vicinity of St. Joseph on the 14th of September, a considerable force of the enemy, altogether irregular bands, retiring in the direction of the Missouri River so rapidly as to keep easily ahead of my infantry. I had no cavalry. Having reopened the road to St. Joseph, I sent the whole force I had with me to follow up these retreating forces toward Lexington—one column from Platte Bridge, the other from Utica, about fifty miles east. These united columns, after beating or driving off the force they were to pursue, were ordered to go to the Missouri River at a point opposite Lexington and if it were found necessary or desirable, to cross the river and report to the commanding officer in Lexington.

As Price was known to be moving toward the Missouri River before I left St. Louis and as various rumors and reports of his progress had reached me, I presumed that the reinforcements thus sent might not prove unacceptable to the threatened garrison. I had no jurisdiction over Lexington or its garrison, had had no reports from there and had not received any intimation from General Frémont concerning the place or its necessities. It was not until I got back to the junction of the Hannibal & St. Joseph and the North Missouri Railroads, 135 miles east of St. Joseph, that I heard anything official or definite concerning the situation at Lexington and even then I heard it through a telegram sent to another officer and giving orders for him to march to Lexington.

I at once sent word to the columns I had sent from Platte Bridge and Utica to push forward by forced marches and join, if possible, the beleaguered garrison, but Lexington had been surrendered before my messenger could reach the troops; nor would it have been possible for them, even had they arrived at the river before the surrender, to have crossed to Lexington, with the enemy in possession of both banks and of all the ferryboats.[17]

The surrender of Lexington with its large garrison so soon following the loss of the Battle of Wilson's Creek, had a great and most unfortunate effect in Missouri, both as encouraging the Confederates and discouraging the Union men. The numbers and boldness of the irregular bands of Southern sympathizers increased greatly in North Missouri and this effect was even more marked in the country south of the river. It was absolutely necessary that something be done and done quickly to prevent a general panic among the people.

General Frémont accordingly began to throw forward to Jefferson City all the regiments encamped around St. Louis and all the troops also which could be brought from other parts of the state and to organize at once a campaign against Price, who was moving south from Lexington very deliberately and much at his ease, inviting all those well disposed to the South to join him. He was quite unmolested even by reconnoitering parties.

The whole force at Jefferson and west of it, as indeed the whole force in Missouri, was unorganized so far as related to brigades and divisions and at Jefferson, for the first time and on the eve of a march against Price, the regiments were assigned to constitute brigades and divisions by orders from General Frémont's headquarters; but many of the regiments so assigned were stationed at remote points in Missouri and never joined their brigade organizations.

On the 24th of September General Frémont, then in St. Louis, issued an order directing these fragmentary brigades and divisions to take post at the front as the beginning of a campaign. There were five small divisions. Their post positions were Booneville, Syracuse, Georgetown, Versailles, and the reserve at Tipton.[18]

Whilst occupying these positions, the Secretary of War, accompanied by General Thomas, the adjutant general of the army, visited our commands,[19] or some of them, to make an inspection of the troops and to investigate General Frémont's administration of the Department, especially the failure to reinforce Lexington, with which it was understood the government was much dissatisfied. I only know what occurred, either of conversation or of action, as I heard it from others. I remained at my own headquarters and called upon neither of these high officials, as I had nothing to say of value to them and preferred to say nothing. I understood, however, that it had been agreed, or rather yielded to, that nothing should be done to interfere with or restrain General Frémont until the result of his campaign against Price was known.[20]

General Frémont's unusual reticence and the extreme difficulty of seeing him, much less talking with him, was a great misfortune to him and I have no doubt led to much of his trouble and disappointment. His staff officers, who naturally were supposed to reflect his wishes and to express his orders, almost completely shut him off from the highest officers of his command by denying them admittance to his presence, or by so obstructing and delaying them, that many left without seeing him and in a most unfortunate state of feeling for future success. Whether the fault of all this was General Frémont's, or for what reason either he or his staff officers, the most active of whom were peculiar, to say the least, tried to keep him as secluded from public view as the Grand Llama, even of those who should have had the right of entrance to his presence at all times, I do not know, but I do know that such a course not only alienated him from many of the highest military officials, but also deprived him of the cordial support and sympathy of the foremost Union men of the state.

General Frémont had a multitude of aides-de-camp holding various ranks, many of whom were foreigners who could not even talk with each other. I remember very well on coming out of his office one day that I found seated on a sofa in the hall just outside one of his aides-de-camp, the lieutenant-governor of a neighboring state, a man of the highest character and standing in the country as well as in the state of which he was an honored official.[21] He rose as I passed out and asked me with some embarrassment if I could get him an interview with General Frémont. He was buttoned up in uniform, but looked much less like a soldier than a distinguished citizen. I replied to him with some surprise:

"Why, Governor, you are General Frémont's aide-de-camp and it is your province to introduce people to an interview rather than to call in help to get an interview yourself."

He said he had waited three days or more to get an opportunity to see the general. I only cite this incident to show to what strange exclusiveness General Frémont condemned himself, or was subjected by other people. Of course such utter want of confidence in or of intercourse with those under his command not only lost him their affection and sympathy, but deprived him also of information and counsel that might have been and I have no doubt would have been, of great value to him.

It was an unfortunate state of feeling and the results were soon developed. The army, commanded by General Frémont in person, marched from the railroad at the points heretofore indicated, but with no sufficient supplies of anything. There was nothing like wagons enough to haul food even, much less munitions of war and shelter for the troops. We were absolutely in no proper condition to march fifty miles away from the railroad, even with all the farmers' wagons and carts we had seized and appropriated to our use. Price was known to be retreating toward Springfield, in southwest Missouri and we were to pursue him, illy fitted as we were for any active service away from railroads. It was supposed that we might live on the country and to some extent we did, but Price had made two marches over the same country before us and had not left much that could be utilized without bringing absolute starvation on the people.

Price, having neutralized the large Union force captured at Lexington by putting them on parole and having brought off all the military stores he could use, retired very slowly, picking up every day parties of recruits, who joined him because of his success. He was therefore under no necessity to wait and give us battle, being very sure that the further we marched after him the better condition he would be in and the worse we to fight a battle and the harder it would be for us to get back to our supplies, even if successful. We were therefore possessed of the absolute knowledge that he would not halt to fight us unless very sure of success.[22]

Sigel led the advance with his division and crossing the Osage River at Warsaw, where a pontoon bridge had been thrown across, he marched directly toward Springfield.[23] McKinstry with his division halted at Warsaw, whence he was, when the time came, to follow Sigel by the direct road.[24] My division also crossed the Osage at Warsaw, but inclining to the west we took post at Humansville, on the main route from Warrensburg and Osceola to Springfield. Hunter's was the most easterly of the columns, which were all within reasonable communication with each other as to distance.

Thus I remained in camp at Humansville until I received by the hands of Mr. Julian,[25] a guide, an order from General Frémont, dated November 1, directing me to move forward by forced marches to Springfield.[26] I accordingly pushed forward without delay, guided by Mr. Julian, who soon brought us into the road from Warsaw to Springfield and immediately on the rear of McKinstry's Division, whose train delayed us for many hours. Whilst at Humansville I had spies and scouts all through the country south of us and from them I ascertained to my satisfaction that Price was far south of Springfield and that we should meet with no considerable force of the enemy at that place. I was therefore at a loss to understand what pressing necessity demanded my presence at Springfield, or such rapid marches. Nevertheless, I pushed on with all speed and on the night of the 2nd of November I encamped at dark within five miles of the place, where I received a dispatch from General Frémont informing me that he had been relieved from his command by an order transferring it to General Hunter, who had not reached Springfield, the conduct of the public service there would devolve on me.

I preceded my command into Springfield early next morning and there witnessed what seemed to me singular, not to say absurd. As I approached the town I was met by a number of officers who had been in Springfield about thirty-six hours. They were much excited by the prospect of an immediate battle and congratulated me on being in time to take part in it.

They were greatly startled when I asked them with whom they were going to fight and replied, "Price, of course." I told them that of course it might be so, but that according to my impression, drawn from reliable scouts, there was no enemy within fifty miles of Springfield to fight with.

I rode on into town with them and reported my arrival in person to General Frémont. I found that he had abandoned the idea of relinquishing the command until General Hunter's arrival and appeared to be preparing for battle in all seriousness.

After a brief interview I rode out to the front, south of the town, to see if I could ascertain upon what was based what appeared to me the strange delusion that there was an enemy in force anywhere near Springfield. I found the batteries of light artillery hitched up all ready for an immediate engagement. In front of the batteries I found the cavalry, the horses saddled and the men "booted and spurred" and ready to mount and charge the enemy.

I met General Eugene Carr,[27] who commanded them, but he appeared to be as much in a maze as I was. He told me that he was only obeying orders and had been ready for battle for more than twenty-four hours, but knew nothing of the enemy or where any was to come from. I was greatly puzzled by all this strange preparation for an enemy whom no one seemed to know anything about.

Shortly after I got back to a house near which my command was encamped I received notice to attend a council of war that evening at General Frémont's quarters.[28] I attended on time and found General Frémont standing behind a long table which was stretched across one end of the room and in front of it were a number of officers of rank, most of whom seemed to be talking in earnest tones. It was a cool night early in November, and I stood with my back to the fireplace listening to what was said as well as I could, but saying nothing. There were maps and papers of some kind on the table and the conversation seemed to relate to them.

After a short time General Frémont turned to me and asked what I thought of the plan of battle. I replied that I would be glad to know first the position of the enemy, as according to the information in my possession there was no enemy near us. He seemed surprised at my remark, and at once called on

General Sigel, who said very promptly that his scouts reported heavy forces of the enemy marching on Springfield by every road from the south, and that they would be in our front by the next morning. I said no more on that point, nor on the plan of battle, because just at that moment the outer door was opened and General Hunter, much travel-worn and disheveled, strode into the room. General Frémont said: "Good evening, General," to which General Hunter replied in the same words. General Frémont inquired whether General Hunter intended to relieve him of the command, to which General Hunter replied that he did, and upon being asked when, he said, "Now!"[29]

Of course the council of war dispersed, and the next morning General Frémont marched out of Springfield to return to St. Louis, preceded by his excellent silver band, playing, "The Red, White, and Blue," and escorted by a band of Shawnee and Delaware Indians in bright colors, yelling and dashing about in a manner more picturesque than alarming.

That same morning General Hunter sent a strong force of cavalry to reconnoiter south of Springfield. They went twenty miles below the town and on their return next day reported not only that there was no enemy in that distance, but also that none of the enemy had been within twenty miles of Springfield for six weeks, except a small force of cavalry, scouting and foraging. Price was encamped with his force at a point fifty miles south. Whether this strange delusion of his being in our immediate front and ready to give battle was really believed by those who gave it circulation, or whether it was only given out for its effect upon the authorities in Washington and the people generally, to give the impression that General Frémont was relieved of his command just as he was on the point of giving battle to the enemy, I never knew; that General Sigel believed it, I cannot credit.

The second day after he took the command General Hunter called a council of war, to which the principal officers were summoned.[30] He read to us a letter from the president of the United States suggesting that the army be drawn back to the railroad. There was no order to this effect given to General Hunter, but the suggestion was so strong, and the wish of the president so manifest, that it is difficult to see how General Hunter could have ignored them, even had the situation been favorable for a further advance against Price.[31]

The fact is, however, that we were not only in no condition to move further to the front, but in no condition to remain at Springfield. It was sufficiently manifest that Price would retreat again to the south as soon as we advanced on him. No provision whatever had been made for a campaign even as far south as Springfield, a fact made clear to me by the necessity of unloading my wagons almost entirely to supply provisions to the sick in hospital, who were reported, in a letter to me asking for the supplies, to have been thirty-six hours without food.

Although I marched back to the railroad with all speed, I only succeeded in reaching there without suffering for food because I met about halfway a small train which I had sent back from Humansville for rations ten days before, with orders to load and to follow me, which, under the charge of a most energetic and efficient officer—Major Robertson, of the 5th Iowa—was so effectively done as to meet me as described just at the right time. One-half of this train I left where I met it for the division which followed me, and retaining barely sufficient for the use of my troops I pushed on to the railroad at Otterville.

By the time General Hunter reached the railroad he was superseded in command by General Halleck.[32] About one-half of the army that retired from Springfield was distributed along the railroad from Sedalia, then its western terminus, to Jefferson City. Of this force I was placed in command, and occupied with it a section of the country officially designated the "District of Central Missouri."[33]

Soon after the withdrawal of our forces to the railroad, Price began again to advance north slowly and cautiously, so that by December 1 he had reached the Osage River and encamped in and around Osceola. His army and the forces under my command were separated by the Osage River and by about seventy miles of undulating prairie country, everywhere practicable for artillery and wagons. Price issued from his camp on the Osage another of his stirring proclamations, inviting and urging the young men of Missouri to join his army.[34] His great personal popularity and commanding influence in the state worked great mischief and kept up dangerous excitement. Thousands of men, both young and middle-aged, flocked to him from almost every county of the state, carrying with them in wagons taken from the people all the supplies they could beg, borrow or take by force. So long as Price remained on the Osage River, easily accessible, the excitement grew, and every day he was reinforced by men and supplies plundered from peaceful people. There was no hope for peace or quiet in Central Missouri until he was driven off.[35]

I accordingly, after making known to him the foregoing situation, proposed a plan to General Halleck to move with my whole force against Price, and gave him the details of a movement which seemed to promise success. It is not necessary to give these details, as General Halleck did not consent to the movement, but on the 14th of December he sent me an order to move a portion of my command from Sedalia toward Lexington—the very opposite direction to Price—and try to intercept a large body of recruits for Price's army, said to be moving from the Missouri River toward Osceola. I persuaded him, however, to permit me to move southwest toward Price, instead of northeast away from him. The results, as I shall recount, were completely satisfactory and gave us the first success we had met with in Missouri since the death of Lyon.[36]

On the 15th of December, having left a sufficient garrison at Sedalia, I marched from that place with a force of infantry, cavalry and artillery, numbering between 3,000 and 4,000 men, and divided into two brigades, commanded respectively by Colonel Jeff C. Davis and Colonel F. Steele, both officers of the Regular Army holding volunteer commissions as colonel.[37] The object of this movement was to interpose between Price's army on the Osage at Osceola and a large body of recruits, reported to be about 6,000 strong, moving south to join him from the Missouri River at Lexington and Arrow Rock, and having with them a large train of supplies for his army.

Leaving Sedalia by the road to Warsaw, merely to mislead the enemy for that night, I encamped on the main road thereto about sunset. Four companies of cavalry were thrown forward to observe any movements of the enemy from Osceola, and next morning I made a forced march of twenty-five miles, and at sunset occupied a position between the direct road from Warrensburg to Osceola and the route via Chilhowee to the west. It was this latter road that the recruits and returning soldiers of Price pursued in joining his forces.

Shortly after sunset the advance, consisting of four companies of the 1st Iowa Cavalry, under Major Torrrence,[38] captured the enemy's pickets at Chilhowee, and learned that he was encamped in considerable strength about six miles north of the town. After resting horses and men for a couple of hours, I threw forward ten companies of cavalry and a section of artillery under Lieutenant-Colonel Brown,[39] of Missouri, to assault the camp, and followed with my whole force, posting the main body between Warrensburg and Rose Hill, to support his movement.

I at the same time reinforced Major Hubbard on the direct road to Osceola with several companies of Merrill's regiment of cavalry,[40] and directed him, in order to cover our flank in the movement on Chilhowee, to push vigorously as far as he was able to the enemy's lines north of the Osage at Osceola. He executed these orders with great vigor and skill, driving back and capturing the enemy's pickets and one entire company of his cavalry, with its tents, baggage and wagons.[41]

The forces encamped at Chilhowee received hurried notice of Brown's advance and broke up in a panic, scattering in every direction, in parties great and small. Brown followed in pursuit all night of the 16th and all day of the 17th, and about midnight reached Johnstown. The enemy scattered in every direction, and as they themselves and their two-horse wagons belonged to the country, the troops could not identify those living quietly at their homes and those en route to Price's army.

When the pursuit reached Johnstown, about midnight, the enemy had completely melted away. The main body of our troops moved slowly north in the direction of Warrensburg, waiting for Brown to return. He scoured the whole country within reach of Johnstown, and brought in 150 prisoners and sixteen wagons loaded with tents and supplies. Next morning, the 18th, Colonel Brown rejoined the main body.

As I knew that the force he had dispersed was not the party he intended to intercept, which must still be north of us, I moved slowly toward Warrensburg, and when near that place the spies and scouts I had sent toward Lexington and Arrow Rock before leaving Sedalia returned and informed me that the large force we had expected was then on the march from those places, and would probably encamp that night at the mouth of Clear Creek, just south of Milford.

I at once posted the main body of my command between Warrensburg and Knob Noster to close all outlet to the south between those two points, and instructed Colonel Jeff C. Davis, with seven companies of cavalry—afterward reinforced by another company of cavalry—and a section of artillery, to march rapidly on the town of Milford, so as to be in position to intercept the enemy's retreat toward the northeast, whilst Merrill's regiment of cavalry was to march also on Milford, approaching it from the northwest. The main body of my command was four miles south of Milford, and ready to prevent escape in that direction.

At a late hour in the afternoon Colonel Davis came up with the enemy encamped on the west side of the Blackwater opposite the mouth of Clear Creek. The Blackwater was deep and miry, and could only be crossed by a long narrow bridge, which was guarded by the enemy in force. The troops under Colonel Davis, led by two companies of the 4th U.S. Cavalry, commanded by Lieutenants Gordon and Amory,[42] charged the bridge and carried it in handsome style, with the loss of one killed and eight wounded. They followed up the enemy with such force and vigor that, finding himself pressed in front and cut off from retreat in every direction, he surrendered at discretion. It was the first taste of real fighting that most of the troops had had, and too much cannot be said of their gallant conduct.[43]

The enemy's force, as reported by its commander, consisted of three companies of cavalry and parts of two regiments of infantry, numbering in all 1,300 men. There were three colonels, one lieutenant-colonel, one major and fifty-one company officers. Five hundred horses and mules, seventy-three wagons loaded with powder, lead and other military stores, fell into our hands, as also a thousand stands of arms.[44]

A number of the most influential, and therefore the most dangerous, Southern men in the state were captured with this party, and the effect of the expedition was extremely useful all over the state. Within five days the infantry marched fully 100 miles and the cavalry nearly double that distance, and they swept the whole country south of Lexington as far as the Osage clear of all parties of the enemy. They captured nearly 1,500 prisoners—a number of them the most important personages in the state from the Southern point of view; 1,200 stands of arms, and nearly 100 wagons loaded with supplies.[45]

On the seventh day after marching from Sedalia the troops reoccupied their camps at Otterville.[46] As an immediate result of this operation Price broke up his camp at Osceola and fell back to Springfield, leaving all the country north of the Osage comparatively quiet.

The prisoners captured by Colonel Davis were brought into the camp of the main body of the command near Knob Noster, arriving there about midnight.[47] It was bitterly cold and a blustering snowstorm set in at daylight and continued the whole day. We marched for Sedalia early in the day and reached there with the prisoners and captured property at sunset. Everything was shipped to St. Louis as soon as cars could be collected, and the troops once more settled down into temporary quiet in their camps.

As soon as it was known that Price had fallen back to Springfield a considerable force under General S. R. Curtis was sent from Rolla to follow him up.[48] This command was reinforced by a division under Colonel Jeff C. Davis from the force under my command, and brought Price to a battle at Pea Ridge,[49] where he was defeated by Curtis, although he had been heavily reinforced from Arkansas and Texas.

I went, shortly after my return to Sedalia, to Jefferson City, and from there was called early in February to St. Louis to organize and command the troops assigned to the operations against New Madrid and Island No. Ten.

In these papers I have confined myself to a mere detail of such events as fell under my personal observation which I thought would be interesting without provoking controversy. General Frémont's policy and his administration of civil as well as military affairs in Missouri are, of course, subjects concerning which there were then and may perhaps now be to a much lesser degree, wide differences of opinion, or perhaps it is better to say, "of feeling." It is certainly a matter on which any man has the perfect right to have and to express his opinion. It is understood that General Frémont has written a book,[50] in which he deals quite fully with all these matters, and perhaps when his statements and opinions are plainly set forth it may be someone's duty, to himself at least, to review them. Certainly I have no wish now, and shall never have, to reopen that unpleasant page of history unless necessity demands it.

Part Two

NEW MADRID AND ISLAND NO. 10

Chapter Four

The Conduct of the Troops Was Splendid

$\mathcal{A}$s the operations for the reduction of Island No. Ten and the destruction thereby as the first serious resistance made by the Confederates to the navigation of the Mississippi River were unique, as well as eminently successful, they furnish an episode in the history of our Civil War solitary in its kind and worthy, therefore, to have its own record and to be studied by military men. An attempt was subsequently made to repeat these operations at Vicksburg, but it failed, as General Grant has explained.[1]

In the early part of February 1862, the enemy's forces in the West occupied a fortified line from Bowling Green on the east to the Mississippi River at Columbus on the west. On the 16th of February General Grant broke this line by the capture of Forts Henry and Donelson. His operations and their success in the capture of these two forts compelled the evacuation of Columbus, which, though strongly fortified, was turned by the advance of General Grant up the Tennessee and Cumberland Rivers. This result had been apprehended

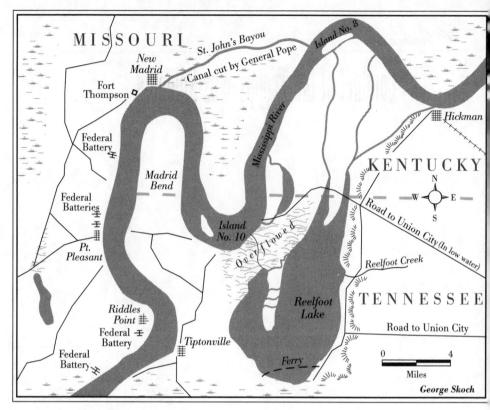

NEW MADRID AND ISLAND NO. 10

by the Confederate generals for some time, and General Beauregard,[2] who was in command in that section of country, selected Island No. Ten, sixty miles below Columbus, as the point where the navigation of the Mississippi was first to be contested. The place was strongly fortified, and further protected from open assault by its insular character. Its garrison, including the troops on the mainland, directly south, at New Madrid, consisted of about 7,000 men, and the earthworks at the island and at New Madrid were armed with 150 heavy guns.[3]

In order that this account of the operations against these places may be clearly understood, some brief description of the topography of the immediate locality is necessary.

The Mississippi River, flowing south from Columbus, makes suddenly, and at a distance of sixty miles south, a sharp bend to the west and returns almost on its course toward the northwest. At the bottom or southern point of this abrupt turn of the river lies Island No. Ten—a small island, about a mile and a half long by half a mile wide—placed in the channel about a third of the way from the south or left shore to the north shore.[4] The main channel of the river is between the island and the northern bank. Leaving the island the river runs to the northwest about six miles,[5] to New Madrid, the most northerly point of the bend. At New Madrid it makes another sharp turn to the southwest and thence south, returning at Tiptonville, nine miles below,[6] to a point within four miles by land of Island No. Ten.[7] Beginning some distance above the island, and on the left bank of the river, an immense swamp and lake puts out from the river and extends about three miles inland, thence to a point below Tiptonville, where it re-enters the main river. The swamp and lake are known as Reelfoot Lake. Tiptonville, at the lower end of the swamp, as also all the land in the great bend between that place and the island, is itself an island, the Mississippi being on three sides and Reelfoot Lake on the fourth.

From Island No. Ten and the strip of land on the mainland south of it there is no communication with the interior, except by a small flatboat, which plies across Reelfoot Lake about two miles, through an opening cut in the cypress swamps for the purpose. The only means to supply Island No. Ten and its garrison on the mainland was by steamboat, and as soon as navigation was interrupted by the capture of New Madrid, the boats landed below Tiptonville[8] and the supplies were hauled in wagons four miles across the peninsula to the island.[9] Supplies and reinforcements or escape, except in very small parties, was impossible on the land side. One mile below Tiptonville begin the great swamps, which line both sides of the river for sixty miles below, and which make access to the interior impracticable on either side of the river during high water. Almost exactly the same condition existed on the north side of the river opposite the island. A narrow strip of dry land follows all around the bend near to the river, but beyond this lie the interminable swamps, which line also the west side of the river for at least fifty miles above New Madrid. This town itself is on the narrow strip of dry land near the river bank, and northeast, north, and west of it are the great swamps.[10]

The garrison of Island No. Ten, both on the island and on the mainland, was absolutely cut off from the interior, except by the little ferryboat I have mentioned and was wholly dependent on the river for supplies and reinforcements. While it was entirely secure against attack from the interior or land side, it had the great disadvantage of being unable to escape in that direction, should the Union forces succeed in crossing the river at New Madrid or below in sufficient strength. The enemy knew, of course, that we could not cross without boats and they believed that their batteries on the island and their gunboats below it would prevent even the gunboats from descending the river.

In this condition of things they deemed themselves secure, especially during the season of high water. The whole country north of New Madrid, nearly as far up as the little town of Commerce, on the Mississippi, is an immense and dismal swamp and at the time of these operations was overflowed by the river, so that the water was from two to ten feet deep over the whole of it. An old corduroy road in wretched condition, on top of an embankment which was broken in a hundred places, extended part of the way from Commerce to New Madrid, but it had not been repaired for years and was nearly impassable. The swamp was known as the Great Mingo, or "Nigger-wool" Swamp. It was thought wholly impracticable to take wagons or artillery through it.

In considering the position and the measures necessary to reduce a system of defense so strong, it became apparent that some point on the river below the island must first be occupied and batteries planted to prevent steamboat communications from below. That done, it would be easy to push our advance down to a position opposite Tiptonville, which was the lowest point of dry land along the river for many miles. By preventing steamboats from landing at Tiptonville all communication with the island would be closed to the Confederates, except by crossing Reelfoot Lake and swamp which, as I have explained, was impracticable for military stores or for the passage of men, except in very small parties and with long delay. Having accomplished this, every effort was to be made to get boats in which to cross the river in force sufficient to capture the Confederate garrison.

The first thing to be done, therefore, was to attack and occupy a position below the island, and in this view New Madrid presented the most practicable point. It was known to be occupied by the enemy in force. It was also known that the high waters of the Mississippi had flooded to the depth of several feet the Great Mingo Swamp to the north, and made a passage across it next to impossible.

Such was the problem and such the conditions of it when I was directed, on the 14th of February, 1862, to report to General Halleck, in St. Louis, to undertake its solution. I was at Jefferson City, Missouri, when the order reached me and I at once reported in St. Louis. On the 18th General Halleck presented the subject to me and after some conversation asked me if I thought it practicable to open the river by capturing or otherwise reducing Island No. Ten and whether I would be willing to undertake it.

I accepted the duty and by General Halleck's order began to organize a force for the purpose. He promised me everything at his command that I might need and assured me that I could rely upon his cordial support. His action during the subsequent operations at Island No. Ten justified these assurances.

I went first to Cairo,[11] at the mouth of the Ohio, which at that time was the base of supplies for the force under General Grant and was besides an important strategic point in view of further military operations in that section.

At the time I left St. Louis, February 19th there was apprehension at military headquarters that the enemy at Columbus, Kentucky, was preparing, before final evacuation of the place, to make an assault on Cairo, which was feebly garrisoned. I was instructed, therefore, by General Halleck, that if I found anything to indicate such a movement I should assume the command there until all danger was over, before entering upon the movement against New Madrid.

On the 21st of February, finding that the apprehension of an attack at Cairo was groundless, I left there in a steamboat with a guard of 140 men, and landed at the little village of Commerce, on the Mississippi, thirty miles above, and on the west side of the river. Commerce was selected as the point to organize my force for the advance on New Madrid, because it was at the first point of the bluffs which impinged on the river above that place, and the only road toward New Madrid from the north—the wretched corduroy road heretofore mentioned—left the river at that place. Commerce is about fifty miles by land above New Madrid. The bluffs, however, barely touch the river at that one point and retreat from it immediately below, leaving the Great Mingo Swamp at least thirty miles wide toward the west, and extending all the way to New Madrid, and many miles below it.

It was dark on the night of February 21 when I landed at this little village with the escort mentioned. Regiments were sent to me rapidly from St. Louis, Cairo, and Cincinnati. Most of them were entirely green regiments just enlisted, and having arms placed in their hands for the first time when they embarked to join me. Very few of them had ever served at all. Even those which had served had done so separately and had never been even assigned to brigades.

I was obliged to organize this force ab initio, a difficult and troublesome task. So efficient, however, was the assistance I received from Generals Stanley, Hamilton, Palmer, and Granger,[12] that within one week after I landed nearly alone at Commerce we marched south with a well-equipped force, ready to do and capable of doing the work before it.[13]

This organization was the nucleus of the army corps afterward designated the "Army of the Mississippi," widely known and greatly distinguished in the West for its discipline, its gallantry and its effectiveness and the soldierly and cordial good feeling which prevailed among both men and officers. It is not only proper, but I consider it a duty, to record here that during my whole experience in the army, I have never seen troops, either in large or in small bodies, with which that small army would not compare on terms of advantage. To the mobility and "esprit," the courage in battle and patience under excessive exposure and fatigue; to the good will for each other and regard for their commanders, their subsequent services and their reputation, even when broken up as an organization and distributed to other corps and other armies, amply testify.

I cannot even at this day think of that little army and my relations to it as its commander, without emotions which could not be properly expressed in such a paper as this. As long as I live I shall not cease to remember it, nor fail to acknowledge the deep gratitude I owe it for its cordial support whilst I commanded it and for its earnest and avowed sympathy with and confidence in me in the darkest hours of my life afterward. I esteem it my greatest honor to have belonged to that little army, and look upon every officer and soldier of it as a personal friend, from whom nothing can ever estrange me.

On the 28th we marched from Commerce. The day was cold and wintry, a drizzling snow and rain falling upon us. Almost immediately on leaving the village we entered upon the corduroy road which led through the swamp, which, with two or three dry places of limited extent, spread out all the way before us to New Madrid. The camp measles, a familiar enemy to all soldiers of the war, broke out among us and I was, myself, one of the first victims. Fortunately the attack was not severe and well wrapped up, I was able to ride my horse part of each day.

We toiled and struggled through deep mud and water, repairing as often as was absolutely necessary the broken corduroy road and the crumbling embankment along which it was built. The drizzling rain was succeeded during the day by a driving snow, and the temperature by no means mitigated the disinclination to plunge into the water every few miles to push forward the wagons or to mend the embankments.

Patiently and steadily, without complaint and with the cheerful faces which our men always wore when there was a prospect of a fight ahead, we waded and trudged for three of the most disagreeable days I ever passed. The men and animals were cased in mud more inches in thickness than I would venture to tell and if there had been any way of melting them out of their mud envelopes without breaking the casing, we could have presented a complete and striking collection of dirt-colored statues of the Army of the Mississippi. Although there was "water, water everywhere," and plenty of it to drink, no one considered it worth while to wash in it, for the very short time the effects would last.

We bivouacked for the night on a patch of dry ground called Hunter's farm,[14] much after dark, some of the command not being able to get there before midnight. The next morning I directed General Hamilton to send the 7th Illinois Cavalry, under the command of Colonel Kellogg,[15] to scout for General M. Jeff Thompson,[16] an irregular sort of Confederate, known in that section as the "Swamp Fox," who seemed to operate on his own account, but who was reported to have with him several hundred men and two or three small—very small—guns. It was understood that he had taken up a position on a narrow plain in the causeway in front of us, and intended to oppose our advance. Colonel Kellogg found him thus posted, with his "artillery" planted on the causeway and at once rode over him without even stopping to form his command. General Thompson's command melted away and fled from the ground, each one for himself, leaving the "artillery" in our hands. It was extremely funny and not at all dangerous and furnished the command with amusement for several days.[17]

At length, on the 3rd of March and nearly four days wading and dragging wagons and artillery by hand, we debouched on the dry lands and cornfields near New Madrid. It was a small village, having generally a population of about a thousand, but at this time was practically abandoned by inhabitants. I found the defensive works at and below the place occupied by five regiments of infantry and several companies of artillery. These works consisted of one bastioned earthwork half a mile below the town, on which were mounted fourteen heavy guns and a larger irregular work at the upper end of the town, armed with seven heavy guns.[18] These two works, with the lines of intrenchments between them, constituted the land defenses of the place. In addition six gunboats, carrying from four to eight heavy guns each, were anchored close against the shore between the upper and lower redoubts.

The country for miles about the place is almost a dead level, the highest line being directly along the bank of the river, from which it descends very gradually toward the swamps. The river was very high and almost on a level with the banks, so that the guns on the gunboats looked easily over the banks and completely commanded the country within their reach.

Thus the approaches to the town were covered by the crossfire of at least sixty pieces of heavy artillery.[19] The enemy's pickets were promptly driven in and under cover of our skirmishers we made a sufficient reconnaissance of the place to confirm the information acquired before from other sources. The troops went into camp just on the edge of the swamp and hardly beyond long range of the enemy's guns.

We could, beyond doubt, have stormed these works by open assault. Our troops, though green in service, were full of courage and spirit and could have been safely relied on to do the work; but such a movement would have been attended with heavy loss, which could not and should not have been justified, in view of the certainty that by short delay the place would be taken with little loss to us. The delay was simply for the purpose of sending to Cairo for a few heavy guns, which I felt certain we could drag by hand through the swamps and along the causeway.

They were sent for and whilst waiting their arrival forced reconnaissances and several feints of an advance in force were kept up, as much to accustom our troops to act promptly and coolly under fire as for any harm to the enemy. Meantime the enemy continued to reinforce New Madrid from Island No. Ten until on the 12th of March they had on the redoubts and trenches and on the gunboats, not less than 8,000 or 9,000 according to the information received from within their lines.[20] The enemy's fleet consisted of nine gunboats, under command of Commodore Hollins.[21] The land forces were commanded by Generals McCown, Stewart, and Gantt.[22]

On the 11th of March the heavy guns were delivered at Cairo to Colonel Bissell, of the Engineer regiment whom I had sent for them.[23] They were at once brought forward, dragged part of the way by hand, and reached our camp on the night of the 12th.[24] During that same night the 10th and 16th Illinois, under Colonel Morgan,[25] were pushed forward under cover of the darkness to within 800 yards of the lowest redoubt of the enemy; and sufficient earthworks were thrown up by them on which to mount our heavy guns and short lines of trenches to shelter the immediate support of the battery. Before daylight the work was finished and the guns were mounted in it. Stanley's Division was posted within supporting distance of the battery and ready to meet any attempt of the enemy to sally out of his works to assault.

In such silence was all this work done that the enemy had not the least intimation of the construction of the battery directly in front of his principal work, nor that we had received any heavy guns.[26] In fact, they had no idea that heavy guns could be brought through the swamps at all. The roar of our heavy guns at dawn of day carried to the enemy the first knowledge he had of either guns or earthworks. Our fire was promptly replied to by all of the enemy's heavy artillery on land and water, and for a time the din was tremendous. Captain J. A. Mower, 1st U.S. Infantry,[27] was in immediate charge of the siege-guns, which were served by the two companies of the 1st U.S. Infantry under his command. Having but a small supply of ammunition for heavy guns, I directed Captain Mower to concentrate his fire first on the gunboats and when they were driven off, on the lower fort. The guns were served with admirable rapidity and skill. In a few hours, several of the gunboats hauled off and three of the heavy guns in the enemy's main work were dismounted. The cannonading was continued furiously all day by the enemy's batteries and gunboats, without any damage, except disabling one of the 24 pounder guns in our battery. Meantime our trenches were being advanced and extended and it was my purpose, under cover of night, to push forward the heavy battery much nearer to the enemy's works. During the day demonstrations were made against the works at the upper end of the town, but with no purpose to make a serious assault.

About 11 o'clock at night a furious thunderstorm broke on us, and continued without ceasing until morning. Just before daylight and in the worst of the storm, Stanley's division was relieved in the trenches by Hamilton.[28] A few minutes after daylight a flag of truce approached our lines with information that the enemy had hurriedly abandoned the works both below and above New Madrid, and been carried to the other shore of the river by the gunboats.

A brief examination showed how precipitate had been their flight. Their dead were found unburied; their suppers were standing untouched on the tables; candles were burning in the tents, and there was every indication of a panic. Neither provisions nor ammunition were carried off. Efforts had been made to take away the latter, numbers of ammunition boxes being on the bank where the troops embarked. Their artillery—field and siege guns, thirty-three pieces; magazines filled with excellent fixed ammunition; several thousand stands of small-arms, with abundant ammunition for them; tents for an army of at least 5,000 men; horses, wagons, etc., fell into our hands. Their troops carried off little except what they stood in. They were carried to the opposite side of the river and no doubt reinforced the garrison of Island No. Ten.

Thus New Madrid was occupied and the first phase of the problem was solved. This strong position on the bank of the river below Island No. Ten enabled us to close the river to vessels from below,[29] except the gunboats and even their passage was most dangerous and unpleasant.

During the time spent in these operations the flotilla, under the command of Commodore Foote,[30] anchored just around the point of land above the island and though out of sight of it, had been trying for seven consecutive days to throw shell from the mortar boats on the point of land so as to fall on the island. Of course such work was utterly without results and was rather a cause of amusement than of apprehension to the enemy. Such work might have been kept up till this time without bringing those who were doing it any nearer to capturing, or even alarming, Island No. Ten.

On the 16th of March I received a telegram from General Halleck, directing me to try and reach a point on the river bank above New Madrid and opposite Island No. Ten and to plant a heavy battery there if possible, to help the commodore cannonade the island. It did not appear to me that anything could be accomplished by such an operation. The river was at least a mile wide, and we had no guns except the old smooth 24's and 32's. All the bombardment in the world could not have reduced Island No. Ten. To do that it was necessary to either starve out its garrison by cutting off its supplies or to find some means to cross the river with sufficient force to overcome resistance. How to do this was the question.[31]

After some consultation with the division commanders on the subject, General Hamilton suggested the idea of bringing boats across the neck of land opposite the island by means of a canal.[32] I dispatched Colonel Bissell—a most active, intelligent and valuable officer—to ascertain if it was possible to accomplish such an undertaking. After rapid examination of the ground, or rather of the swamps, he reported the plan practicable, with considerable modification.[33] He proposed to dig a short ditch to connect the river with the swamps, which then had eight or ten feet of water in them; then to cut a passage through them by sawing out an avenue fifty feet wide through the dense forest in the direction of New Madrid to the point where a bayou left the swamp and cut into the river just above the town. By stopping two or three small steamers through the ditch, swamp and bayou we should be furnished with the means to carry a force across the river sufficient to deal with the garrison for the defense of the island.

Colonel Bissell was therefore instructed to begin at once the work as he proposed it. Supplies of such articles as were needed and four steamers of light draft were sent to him at Island No. 8, and with his regiment numbering then about 800 men, he began the work. It was beyond conception difficult and trying. The ditch was dug of sufficient depth to float the small steamers. When opened into the swamps the current through it was so rapid that it was necessary to let the boats and barges down into the swamps by ropes.

Then began the heavy work. An avenue fifty feet wide and six miles long was cut through the forest of immense cottonwood trees which filled the swamp. The trees were sawed off four and a half feet below the water-line, to admit of the passage of the steamers over the stumps. To do this a cross-cut saw was attached, or rather was made the lower side of a triangle, the upper angle of which was fastened to the tree just at the water-line, and the depth from this point to the lower side of the triangle (the cross-cut saw) was about five feet. In the barges on both sides of the trees to be sawed off were parties of men to pull the saw backward and forward until the tree was cut through. The trunk was immediately cut up and pushed out of the channel.

In this manner an avenue was made through heavy timber for six miles with incredible labor and by men wet to the skin in the cold month of March from morning to night. At the end of the six miles of swamp the so-called canal intersected the course of the large bayou which enters the Mississippi at New Madrid. The bayou was everywhere full of snags and dead trees imbedded in the mud. These had to be hauled out to leave a channel wide enough for the boats, and the labor in this part of the canal was not appreciably less than it was in the swamps.

Nineteen consecutive days were spent in this tremendous work by Colonel Bissell and his engineer regiment, at the end of which time he reported to me that not only was the canal finished, but his regiment was finished also. Of the 700 or 800 men with whom he began the work scarcely a score were fit for duty at the end.[34]

We had thus acquired the means to cross the river with a sufficient force the moment we could command a point of land on the other side, but to do this required that at least one of our gunboats from the flotilla be sent to us to cover the landing of the troops, which were to cross in the steamers. Meantime the boats were kept up the bayou out of sight of the enemy, who, as it afterward appeared, had heard of our digging a canal, but had treated the subject rather as a hoax than as a matter that demanded attention.[35]

Every effort was made by letter and by messenger to induce Commodore Foote to send one of his gunboats to us.[36] He was assured that in the darkness of night and with the river at so high a stage, the boat need never come within two-thirds of a mile of the island; it would be easily practicable to run the boat past the batteries without one chance in a hundred that it would ever be touched. It was represented to him that by the use of one of his gunboats the landing of the troops on the opposite shore could be made in comparative safety, whereas without it several thousand men might be vainly sacrificed; that the danger to the gunboat with its small crew and iron plating was infinitesimal compared with the risk to 2,000 or 3,000 men in frail river steamers; in short, that with the gunboats a certain and most satisfactory result would be secured, without it, the outcome was very doubtful.

It was in vain. He could be moved neither by entreaties nor by strong language. As the gunboats were at that time the property of the War Department, I asked that Department, through General Halleck, very urgently to direct Commodore Foote to turn over one or two of the gunboats to me, after removing his officers and crews from them.[37] I had men perfectly competent to man and manage them. It had become very plain that Island No. Ten could not be captured (except after the long delay involved in starving out its garrison) until our forces could be thrown across the river. The river was bankfull and running with a furious current, and so wide that our heaviest guns would barely reach the opposite shore.

During our long delay, however, the enemy, foreseeing no doubt such an attempt, had erected earth batteries along the shore all the way from the island around to Tiptonville at every point where it was practicable for troops to effect a lodgment on the bank.[38] The difficulties of making a crossing in force had therefore greatly increased and what might have been comparatively an easy matter at first, had now become an undertaking full of peril. The passage of a great river lined with batteries, and in the face of an enemy nearly equal in strength, is of all military operations the most hazardous and difficult, and can only be justified in case of absolute necessity.

Such a case was here presented. Unless this crossing were made, operations against the island must be abandoned and the forces withdrawn. The effect upon the morale of both sides would have been vastly injurious to us. It is but justice to say that the full peril of the projected movement was entirely realized by my whole command. There was not an officer or soldier who was not ready to head the advance. Whatever therefore the dangers before us, they were in our front and not in our midst.

There seemed little hope of any help from Commodore Foote, who was pounding away at space during all this time. Something in the shape of a floating battery was absolutely necessary to cover our landing on the opposite shore until the advance force could make good its lodgment and we accordingly set to work to improvise such a battery with what means we had. Several heavy coal barges were brought down through the canal. Each of the batteries was to consist of three of these heavy barges lashed together and heavily bolted with iron. The middle barge, on which the guns were mounted, was bulkheaded both along the sides and ends, so as to give four feet in thickness of heavy timber all around. Three heavy guns, protected by traverses of sandbags, were mounted on it. It carried also eighty sharpshooters.

The barges lashed on each side of it had first a layer along the bottom of empty, water-tight barrels securely lashed, then layers of cotton bales and cottonwood rails packed close; they were then tightly floored over at the top to keep everything in place, so that a shot penetrating the outer barges had to pass through twenty feet thickness of cottonwood and cotton bales before reaching the outer bulkheads of the barge carrying the guns. The arrangement of the empty water barrels and cotton bales was made, so that even if penetrated frequently by the enemy's shot and filled with water, these outer barges could not sink.

It was my purpose when all was ready to have at least two of these batteries towed out into the river by one of the small steamers, to a point immediately opposite New Madrid, where a swamp presented access to the opposite shore, and where the enemy therefore had not been able to plant guns. When these barges had been towed over toward this point to about two-thirds of the way across the river, they were to be cast loose from the steamers and allowed to drift down the river, with only such guidance as their crews of soldiers could give them, until they came opposite the point selected for landing our troops on the opposite bank. As soon as they arrived opposite this point, they were to throw out their heavy anchors and man the batteries.

I have no doubt that these batteries would have answered their purpose. My whole command volunteered to man them. They were all well supplied with small boats to get away in case the worse befell. Whilst this work was going on, our lines were extended down the river, and two important points — Point Pleasant and a point opposite Tiptonville — were occupied and batteries planted, which effectually sealed the navigation of the river.[39]

On the third of April the steamers and barges were brought near to the mouth of the bayou, but were kept carefully out of sight of the river whilst the floating batteries were being completed. After long persuasion and pretty strong pressure, Commodore Foote finally yielded to the demand for one of his gunboats. Captain Walke, who commanded the *Carondolet*, volunteered for the service and was permitted to undertake it.[40] On the night of April 4, a dark and stormy night, he ran his gunboat past the batteries of Island No. Ten and although many shots were fired not one struck his vessel. He was received with great enthusiasm and satisfaction, and to him we were largely indebted for the success of our undertaking. A more gallant, zealous and capable officer I do not know; nor have I ever been able to understand, except on a supposition much to the discredit of some of his superior officers, how it came about that he never received the reward for his service in the capture of Island No. Ten to which he was clearly entitled.[41]

On the morning of April 6, I selected several officers to make a reconnaissance of the river below to ascertain what batteries the enemy had established on the other shore and to develop their position and strength. I requested Captain Walke to convey them over the river in his gunboat to make this examination. The whole day was spent in this reconnaissance, the *Carondolet* steaming down the river under fire from the enemy's batteries along the shore. The whole shore was lined with earthworks armed with heavy guns. No two of these redoubts were more than a mile apart.

On the night of the 6th, at my urgent request, Commodore Foote sent down the gunboat *Pittsburg*, which also passed the batteries on Island No. Ten without injury. She arrived at daylight. Immediately on the arrival of the *Pittsburg* I requested Captain Walke to proceed down the river with both gunboats and if possible silence the battery at Watson's Landing, the point I had selected for landing the troops on the opposite shore. It was about a mile below New Madrid.

At the same time I had the steamers brought into the river from the bayou and embarked upon them Paine's Division, consisting of the 10th, 16th, 22d and 51st Illinois, together with Houghtaling's battery of light artillery.[42] The land battery of 32-pound guns, under Captain Williams, 5th U.S. Infantry,[43] which had been established several days before at a point directly opposite Watson's Landing, was ordered to open fire at daylight. It had rained heavily all night of the 6th and the morning of the 7th was dark and gloomy, with overhanging masses of black clouds, from which the rain poured down in torrents, accompanied by terrific thunder and lightning.

At daylight our batteries on land opened on the enemy's batteries opposite, and were promptly replied to. The two gunboats ran down the river to a point just below Watson's Landing, and then turning up the stream they began a rapid fire upon the battery at that place. I cannot speak too highly of Captain Walke during the whole of these operations. At 12 o'clock he signaled me that the enemy's battery was silenced. I immediately signaled the steamers containing Paine's Division to move out into the river and cross at once, preceded by the gunboats. Our whole force had been formed in line along the shore and saluted the passing steamers with yells of delight and encouragement.

As soon as the troops began to cross the river the enemy commenced to abandon hastily his batteries and trenches along the banks. His whole force was in motion toward Tiptonville, except a few artillerists, who had been left on the island, and who in the hurry of the retreat were forgotten. As Paine's steamers were passing the place where I stood on the river bank one of our spies, who had returned on the gunboats from the batteries they had silenced, informed me of this hurried retreat of the enemy and I at once communicated the fact to Paine and ordered him as soon as he effected a landing to leave a guard and push on himself with his command as rapidly as possible to Tiptonville, to which point all the forces of the enemy were tending, assuring him that the rest of the troops would cross rapidly and be up with him soon.[44] I sent no force up to the deserted batteries opposite Island No. Ten, on the Tennessee shore, as my first object was to capture the whole of the enemy's forces. At 8 or 9 o'clock that night—April 7—a small party of artillerists, who were thus abandoned on the Island, finding themselves deserted and fearing an attack in the rear from our troops which had crossed the river, sent a message to Commodore Foote, surrendering themselves to him.[45]

The divisions of the army pushed forward to Tiptonville as fast as they were landed, Paine leading. The enemy several times undertook to make a stand, but Paine did not once deploy his column. By midnight our troops were all across the river and were making forced marches to Tiptonville. The enemy, retreating before Paine and from Island No. Ten, met in Tiptonville during the night in great confusion, and were driven back into the Reelfoot Swamp by the advance of our forces until, about 4 o'clock on the morning of the 8th, finding themselves cut off and unable to offer effective resistance, they laid down their arms and surrendered without conditions. They were so scattered in the woods and swamps that it was several days before any accurate account of their number could be made.[46]

I had directed Colonel W. L. Elliott, 2nd Iowa Cavalry, who had crossed with his regiment after dark, to proceed as soon as the day dawned to take possession of the enemy's abandoned works on the Tennessee shore opposite Island No. Ten and to take all the steamers he could. He reached there before sunrise the next morning and took possession of the encampments, filled with an immense quantity of stores and supplies, and also of the land batteries along the shore. He captured 200 prisoners.

I reached Tiptonville about sunrise and found Hamilton's Division drawn up near the landing. The surrendered forces were marched inland and stacked their arms in front of this division. After posting his guards and taking possession of the enemy's camps, stores and steamers, he remained until the forces from the flotilla arrived, and after turning everything over to Colonel Buford,[47] who commanded them, he proceeded to scour the peninsula between Reelfoot Lake and the Mississippi. An immense amount of ammunition and military stores of all kinds fell into our hands.

Very few, if any, of the enemy escaped, and such as did waded or swam across the lake. The enemy's forces consisted of three generals, and as nearly as we could determine, about 6,000 men. One hundred and twenty-three pieces of heavy artillery, thirty of field artillery, 7,000 stands of small-arms, tents for 12,000 men, several wharf-boat loads of provisions, and hundreds of horses and mules were among the spoils.[48]

The conduct of the troops was splendid throughout. We crossed a great river in the face of an active enemy, we pursued and captured their whole force and all its supplies and works, and recrossed the river to New Madrid without an accident or any loss in men or material. Such results certainly demonstrate excellent discipline and great effectiveness. Nothing too good can be said of the troops engaged in these operations.

Stanley, Granger, Elliott, Mower, and Palmer all became major generals, and were highly distinguished during the war; and of the officers of less rank nearly all afterward became men of distinction. This small army was broken up after I left it, and its brigades and regiments were distributed to different armies and army corps. They were always distinguished in whatever organizations they were placed, and I am glad to know that they have always cherished with particular satisfaction the memory of their service in the Army of the Mississippi.

One of the things which was most noticeable among the volunteers of 1861 was their extreme eagerness to learn everything connected with war and their duties as soldiers, and they had but small regard to time, place or circumstance in pursuing their questions. Although they did many things which they themselves now look back on as exceedingly funny, there was yet about them, even in the eyes of those who saw the ridiculous aspect at the time, a certain touching and pathetic phase, which completely redeemed their absurdity.

Perhaps I cannot end this paper better than by telling an incident which occurred before New Madrid which fairly illustrates what I have said. When we first appeared before the place the enemy, both from forts and gunboats, poured many heavy shot upon us, and among them many shell, of which quite a number buried themselves in the ground without exploding. Colonel (now General) W. L. Elliott, then a captain in the Regular Army, and also colonel of the 2nd Iowa Cavalry, thinking it a good time to give his regiment some useful instruction, told them before dismissing them to their tents that whenever a shell fell among them they should throw themselves on their faces, as the pieces of shell after an explosion were much more likely to be thrown upward than in any other direction, and that the safest position was to lie flat on the ground. He had hardly reached his tent after this valuable piece of advice before he heard a tremendous explosion among the tents of the regiment. On running to the spot he found that his men had dug up one of the unexploded shells which had buried itself in the ground, and after picking it a little and laying a short train they had all lain flat on the ground around it and touched it off, merely to test the accuracy of their colonel's statement.

Part Three

THE SIEGE OF CORINTH

Chapter Five

We Sauntered Along Slowly

$\mathscr{T}$he moment Island No. Ten was in our hands, it became necessary to consider what was next to be done. Whilst the operations there were going on the enemy had fortified Fort Pillow and garrisoned it strongly. In a few days after the capture of the island, the surrendered prisoners had been sent to the rear, and boats on which to embark my command for the work at Fort Pillow had begun to arrive from above. At the end of a week we were ready to move.[1] About thirty steamboats, big and little, had been sent us and on these the troops were embarked. When all was ready Commodore Foote with his gunboats took the lead and the great convoy of steamers followed, each brigade and division being kept together and following in the order assigned them. It was a grand sight, this great fleet descending the great river and loaded with men and munitions of war. The health of the command was excellent and their spirits bordering on the boisterous. They had been supremely successful and had sustained no loss in achieving great results. They believed themselves capable of anything and longed for the opportunity to show it.

We arrived in front of Fort Pillow on the 14th of April. The gunboats took up the same relative position as at Island No. Ten—that is, out of sight—and again began to fire at long range and with as little effect. It was plain at once that some such operations as at Island No. Ten would have to be repeated by the land forces and again that same long delay and extremely hazardous crossing of the river must be expected. I do not think it can be claimed by the Confederates that they made a vigorous defense of the Mississippi. I believe it to have been their strongest line of defense and have often wondered that they did not assign more force to that work. Feeble as the resistance was, it was recognized that every point they did maintain along the river needed to be reduced by long and hazardous operations.

As I foresaw at Fort Pillow the same delays and difficulties as we had met at Island No. Ten and as also I did not know the necessity of troops elsewhere which might make it unwise to involve so large a force as I had in such protracted operations, I telegraphed to General Halleck the situation and all the circumstances and received an order from him to leave a small detachment with the gunboats to occupy any position they might capture and with my whole force to proceed as rapidly as possible up the Tennessee River to Pittsburg Landing.[2] I left two Indiana regiments, under command of Colonel Fitch,[3] with the fleet and at once started up the river with the rest of my troops. Commodore Foote objected very much to my leaving, but I thought then and still think, that it was the best disposition to make of my command.

I do not suppose there was ever a happier or more jolly and self-satisfied body of men in the world than the Army of the Mississippi as it steamed up the Mississippi with flags flying and bands playing from nearly all of the steamers in this grand procession. It was altogether the most inspiring sight I ever witnessed and I do not think that any portion of that command ever afterward experienced quite the same feelings or to the same degree as they did during the five days spent in steaming up the Mississippi, Ohio and Tennessee to Pittsburg Landing. General Payne's adventure at Paducah furnished us with amusement for the voyage up the Tennessee.[4]

Old Captain White, an old steamboat man and president of the steamboat company which supplied our transportation and the owner of most of the boats, happened to be on a boat coming down the Tennessee while the boats containing Payne and his division were lying against the bank. In trying to make a landing, Captain White's boat drifted against the boat on which Payne was with his headquarters and stove in the lower guards of that boat, without really doing any considerable damage. Payne sent a guard to bring to his presence the captain of the offending boat and the guard marched old Captain White on to Payne's boat a prisoner. Payne assailed him with a language of more power than piety and it appeared for a time that the old captain was to be drawn and quartered at the least. Payne, however, after expending much indignant invective, decided that Captain White must pay at once to the captain of his (Payne's) boat the full amount of the damage done by what he was pleased to call the old captain's d——d stupidity and carelessness. Under Payne's orders, the captain of his boat (an employee of Captain White, who also owned the boat) proceeded gravely to assess the damage at fifty dollars. Payne, in complete ignorance of Captain White's relation to these boats and their captains, and too impatient to listen to any explanation, ordered Captain White to pay over then and there fifty dollars to his captain, assuring him that if he did not pay the money down, he would be carried up the river a prisoner in irons. Captain White, with a perfectly serious face, borrowed the money from the captain to whom he was to pay it, and who received it back with a countenance equally grave, and Payne sailed off with a chuckle of satisfaction, often repeated, that he had executed condign punishment on a refractory steamboat captain. I do not think anybody ever undeceived him.

The Tennessee is a narrow and on its lower course, a sluggish stream, with low banks and rank bottomland vegetation on both sides of it. It looks like the home, or rather the breeding place, of fever and ague and indeed all forms of intermittent disease. It had fallen a good deal within a few weeks, but even when we ascended it the water was so high that from the deck of the steamer we could overlook the whole country for many miles.

At length, on the night of the 21st of April, we reached Pittsburg Landing and I reported in person to General Halleck, my troops being kept on the boats until it was known where we should disembark. I climbed the steep bank at the landing in soft, tenacious clay so deep I was in danger every moment of having my boots dragged off my feet; indeed, it was only by the greatest care that I avoided such a catastrophe. Boots in those days by no means grew on trees.

I found General Halleck in a tent planted in the mud and lying on a cot with as woebegone a countenance as I ever saw. After some conversation I returned to my steamer to wait till morning and learn out destination.[5]

As a result of the Battle of Shiloh, the enemy's force fell back to Corinth, Mississippi, about twenty-five miles and there fortified. Whatever may be said or thought of the Battle of Shiloh, one thing can be certainly asserted—it was not a decisive battle. The army which made the attack was not successful, but neither was the army that was attacked left in any condition to advance until it was largely reinforced and resupplied. One entire month the two armies, one at Shiloh Church, the other at Corinth, scarcely out of sight of each other, watched and waited, neither even threatening to advance. The question as to which army should advance first seemed to be simply a question of which should be reinforced first, and to what relative extent. With such an outcome so long continued it would hardly be justifiable to say that either side achieved decisive results.

General Halleck in person joined the army,[6] which then consisted of the Army of the Tennessee, under General Grant, and the Army of the Ohio, commanded by General Buell. The regiments engaged at Shiloh were being collected together and reorganized, but it was some days before order was restored and the men all returned to their colors. Practically the camps occupied almost the exact positions of the troops during battle, and it may certainly be said that more uncomfortable quarters have seldom been occupied by troops. The deep, tenacious mud made it difficult to walk even a few yards from the tents and the atrocious and sickening smells arising from a battlefield where the dead—both men and horses—had of necessity been thrown into shallow trenches and barely covered over, so poisoned the atmosphere that no air could be breathed not contaminated by this horrible effluvium of animal decomposition.

It is also certain that the feeling of the troops encamped on this dismal burying-ground was far from pleasant or satisfactory. Indeed, when I arrived there, two weeks after the battle (April 21), there was still a great bitterness of feeling and of expression and I myself met no one who seemed to be satisfied.[7]

The morning after I reached Pittsburg Landing I was instructed by General Halleck to proceed up the river three miles to the little village of Hamburg and there disembark my command. I accordingly landed there early in the day and posted my command in camp in front of the town. The country was still muddy everywhere, but the roads were quite practicable for the movement of troops from the time I landed at Hamburg to the end of the operations against Corinth.[8]

My small army consisted of about 25,000 men of all arms. We landed at Hamburg and a more effective and willing force never was marshalled in arms. On my immediate right and on the other side of a deep, miry creek, was Buell's Army of the Ohio, in splendid condition and spirits, as I was told by his officers. Beyond him lay the Army of the Tennessee, which had fought the Battle of Shiloh until dark of the first day. I did not for some time have the opportunity to visit either of the armies on my right. Before I did so the Army of the Tennessee had been divided into two and General Grant removed from the command of it and given merely the nominal position of "second in command."[9]

Although I saw General Grant several times, both in his own camp and in mine, he never alluded to his anomalous position nor complained to me of the action of General Halleck. That he had little or nothing to do I knew from the fact that he came more than once to my tent and spent almost the entire day there, sitting about and lying on a cot. Those were the days in which he talked of resigning and indeed, determined to do so.[10] What might have been the outcome had he carried out his intention, it is hardly worthwhile to try to forecast. No man living is essential to any administration in this country or to the people of the United States, if indeed he is to any government or any people; and it is a fact, which no man in this country will seriously dispute, that we might cut off the heads of the highest officials of the executive, legislative and judicial departments of the government with extremely little injury or embarrassment in carrying on the business of the country. Fortunately for General Grant himself, he did not resign, but lived to achieve fame and high place in the defense of his government and in the esteem of his countrymen.

I never could understand the long delay in our advance on Corinth. Certainly my troops, and I feel sure that those of both the armies on my right also, were as able and ready to march on Corinth the day after I landed at Hamburg, as at any time afterward. Two days would easily have brought us to the positions it took us five weeks to reach. Outside of Corinth the enemy practically had nothing. Our smallest scouting parties met with but trifling resistance anywhere, nor was there any obstruction to our advance offered by the enemy until after we occupied a line within three or four miles of the town.

We moved forward two or three miles at a time, but no steady or continuous movement to the front was made at all. I did not then and do not now know either why we moved when we did, nor why we halted after making two or three miles. Certainly the reason was not to be found in anything the enemy did or even threatened to do. It was understood that we had an effective army of not much, if any, less than a hundred thousand men. It was not believed that the enemy in and around Corinth had more than half that number, if so much. As we afterward learned, our army rather exceeded the strength I have mentioned, whilst that of the enemy was somewhat less than our estimate. I heard a good deal said about the demoralization of some portions of our army and the necessity of proceeding slowly, so as to give time to restore confidence, but certainly I never saw any of the demoralization spoken of, nor did I ever hear anything of the kind from anyone belonging to the troops which were reported "to lack confidence."

What amounts to intrenching, if any, was done by the troops on my right I do not know, although I heard a good deal about that also. Nothing of the kind was done by the troops under my command, nor did there appear any sort of necessity for it. There seemed, however, to be in the air, coming from somewhere, the impression that we must, above all, certainly "not bring on" a general engagement and this notion prevailed to the last. Why we were not to bring on a general engagement no one seemed to know. We had all the troops we needed for a general engagement with the enemy and we expected no more. A general engagement was, as I supposed, precisely what we wanted and had come there to seek and certainly a general engagement with the enemy brought on outside of his intrenchments at Corinth was far more desirable and likely to be more successful than an attack on his fortified position. Whatever may have been the reason, I was myself cautioned more than once against bringing on a general engagement.[11]

We continued, therefore, to saunter along slowly and irregularly until the 3rd of May, about two weeks after I landed at Hamburg, by which time the advance of my command had reached a point within five miles of Corinth—that is, about twenty-five miles from Hamburg[12]—an average rate of less than two miles a day, along an entirely unobstructed road. On the 3rd of May, however, finding myself near the village of Farmington, which stands on high ground, overlooking quite an expanse of country in our front, I advanced Payne's Division rapidly upon it, supporting his advance with my whole force.[13] The enemy occupied the village in considerable force. The roads which led from it conducted to Corinth and to the enemy's left from several directions, and it was therefore a position of considerable consequence. Payne advanced promptly and rapidly to the attack and after a sharp skirmish carried the position handsomely and the enemy fell back hastily toward Corinth, four miles distant, leaving their tents and baggage and thirty men killed on the field. Our cavalry followed the retreating enemy toward Corinth, whilst Payne, with the greater part of his division, pushed south to the Memphis & Charleston Railroad about two miles and tore up some of the track.[14]

His command drew back to the north side of a small but miry stream about two miles behind Farmington and the next day my whole force moved forward to the same ground. This movement brought my whole army within five miles of Corinth and less than half that distance of the outer earthworks of the enemy.

From the third to the eighth of May I awaited in my camps to be informed that the troops on my right were again ready to advance, but on that day (May 8) I again occupied Farmington. From there I pushed reconnaissances toward Corinth on two roads, with the purpose to develop their works, which was satisfactorily done along our front. No considerable resistance was encountered. My army was, however, again drawn back to its camps as I was informed that the troops on my right were not yet ready to move forward and I must not bring on a general engagement.[15] However, I left one brigade, under General I. N. Palmer,[16] about one mile north of Farmington. It is well to say here that the country between Corinth and the Tennessee River is drained by numerous small streams, which put into the Tennessee and that the streams are lined with swamps on both sides and that both beds and banks are boggy and miry. These swamps and streams are passed by corduroy roads.

On the morning of May 9 the enemy sallied from Corinth in heavy force with the purpose of beating or checking my corps, which they supposed to be in considerable advance of and separated from, the main body of the army. It happened that Palmer's Brigade was in the act of being relieved by Plummer's Brigade when the enemy made his attack, so that we had eight regiments on the ground.[17] As these regiments were full of spirit and anxious to meet the enemy, they accepted battle with a force at least three times larger than their own. The action was very severe and continued the greater part of the day. My whole command was drawn out and ready and anxious, from the moment the fight began, to push forward to join the battle, but I was forbidden by General Halleck positively to advance at all and instructed that if the enemy pressed Palmer's force too heavily to withdraw it. Finding about five o'clock in the afternoon that the enemy had succeeded in turning Palmer's flanks and being forbidden myself to go to his support, I withdrew the two brigades to the north side of the stream, where the enemy did not venture to follow him. Both Palmer's Brigade and my whole corps were greatly dissatisfied with this outcome.[18]

I received during the afternoon a message from General Palmer, in answer to my inquiry whether he could hold his ground until night, that he "could hold his position against the world, the flesh and the devil." [19] He did not exactly do that, but he came near enough to justify the expression. Another long delay before we again made an advance succeeded these events. About the 25th of May I again occupied Farmington with my whole command and by order of General Halleck threw up some lines of intrenchment in front of the town. The whole army under General Halleck was at this time well closed up and the three wings about equal distance from Corinth — Sherman on the extreme right, Buell in the center and I on the left.

The place was thus completely invested on three sides. Unfortunately the south side still remained open. On the 27th, in order to break up the communication with Corinth from the South, I organized and sent out the first cavalry raid ever made by our troops, or, I think, the Confederates and as it was well conducted and as successful as any such ever were, I recount it in detail.[20] It is interesting, too, as the first record of General Sheridan as a commander of troops during the war.[21] The force designated to make the raid consisted of two regiments of cavalry — the 2nd Iowa, commanded by Lieutenant-Colonel Edward Hatch[22] and the 2nd Michigan Cavalry under Colonel P. H. Sheridan, who had been appointed its colonel only a few days before; the whole force numbering about 1,000 men and commanded by Colonel William L. Elliott,[23] who was the colonel of the 2nd Iowa and also a captain in the Regular Army. His subsequent successful and honorable career in the army is well known. The orders to Colonel Elliott were that he should proceed by roundabout and unusual routes to a point whence he could descend upon the Mobile & Ohio Railroad, forty miles south of Corinth and destroy as much of the track and as many bridges as possible; indeed, to do all the damage he could to the road, so as to break up its use by the enemy either to receive reinforcements or retreat by it.[24]

At eleven o'clock[25] on the night of May 27 this raiding party left my camp and going east crossed the Memphis & Charleston Railroad about five miles east of Iuka. Small parties of the enemy's cavalry were met, but they were driven off or captured and Elliott's command was fairly on its way, unknown to the enemy at Corinth, as well as to most of the army from which it was detached. They encamped the first night just south of Jacinto, when, two miles more to the south, Elliott approached the Mobile & Ohio Road near Baldwin, on the 29th. There he found that there lay a force of the enemy for him to deal which was posted at Baldwin to protect the bridge and trestlework at that place, and he pushed on therefore to Booneville, within a mile of which he arrived just before daylight on the 30th.[26] The command halted and waited for daylight, making neither noise nor fires. Meantime small parties were sent quietly to cut the telegraph wires both north and south of Booneville.

At dawn of day the troops moved into Booneville deployed in line of battle. No enemy was found and Elliott accordingly proceeded to destroy the railroad and all the military stores he could lay his hands on. One locomotive hauling a train of twenty-five freight cars loaded with arms, ammunition, military stores, etc.;[27] platform cars carrying one iron and two brass field pieces;[28] large depot filled with military stores of all sorts, including a large amount of ammunition, were burnt up. Two culverts and more than a mile of track were also destroyed. By this raid we secured, among other things, nine or ten locomotives and 100 freight cars, which were afterward used to our great benefit north of Corinth.[29] Between 1,500 and 2,000 convalescent sick were made prisoners, but at once released on parole. After destroying everything that could be used by the enemy, the command started on its return march and passing through Iuka rejoined us on the 31st of May. This detachment of cavalry marched 200 miles and worked much injury to the enemy, with loss of one man killed and five captured. The whole affair reflected great credit on all engaged in it.

On the 28th a short advance was made from Farmington by our left and after a sharp skirmish by Stanley's Division he occupied a position in close contact with the outer works of the enemy, and at once intrenched himself.[30] Corresponding movements were made by the rest of the army and we now occupied a line so near to the enemy's works that any farther advance by either party must of necessity bring on that long-standing "bugaboo," a general engagement. No movement of our army was made on the 29th—why I do not know; but during that whole day and night the enemy was evacuating Corinth and before daylight Beauregard had disappeared toward the south with all of his army and most of his material of war. The constant running of trains into and out of Corinth all that night made it plain that important movements were going on, but whether the enemy was retreating or reinforcements coming in it was not easy to tell. Just before daylight on the morning of the 30th heavy and continuous explosions in Corinth made it very plain that the enemy was leaving or had left the place and was blowing up and otherwise destroying such material of war as he could not carry off. An advance force from each of the three armies pushed at once into the town and penetrated without opposition to the middle of it. There was some dispute at the time as to which of these parties first occupied the town, but I presume that there was so little interval, if any, between these respective entrances into the place as to leave the question of priority of no consequence, if it ever had any.[31] The line of retreat of the enemy was by his right flank and along or near to the Mobile & Ohio Railroad and my position on our extreme left placed me nearest to the retreating enemy.

The intrenchments which surrounded the town were of no formidable character. They were built of earth and heavy logs, and whilst they afforded excellent shelter for troops they were not of themselves a formidable obstacle.

The enemy was gone, however and we had nothing to compensate us for our long operations and all the labor the troops had undergone, except an empty little village, dilapidated and dirty.

Late in the day (May 30) I was directed to take up the pursuit of the retreating enemy and was reinforced by one division of Buell's army for that purpose.

I accordingly marched as soon as possible, passing through the abandoned camps of Price and Van Dorn,[32] only two miles or so from my own camp at Farmington. About seven miles from Corinth I came upon the rear-guard of the enemy posted on the opposite bank at the crossing of Tuscumbia Creek. This creek is a considerable stream and like all other watercourses in this section, it is bordered by dense and impenetrable swamps. It is passed by a narrow corduroy road cut through the swamp. On the opposite bank, commanding the line of this road with their artillery, a considerable force of the enemy was posted, simply to delay our march as long as possible and having destroyed the bridge, were able to delay us for a time. By next morning, however, we succeeded in passing the creek by penetrating the swamp below and continued the pursuit. We pushed on with little opposition to Booneville, about thirty miles south of Corinth.[33] I found when I reached there that the whole force of the enemy was posted behind what is called Twenty Mile Creek. The main body seemed to be in and in advance of Baldwin, twenty miles south of Booneville, whilst his left was thrown forward as far as Blacklands, about ten miles to our right front. As soon as I ascertained these facts

I determined to move at once against him, making a feint with a portion of my command against Baldwin by the direct road from Booneville and at the same time to throw the bulk of my forces on his left by way of Blacklands.

It was not easy to get up supplies from our depots beyond Corinth even to keep us as far to the south as Booneville, much less to go much beyond and we were delayed longer than we should have been by want of provisions. Orders were given accordingly for the movement of the several divisions of the army at daylight next morning[34] and all preparations made for battle. I communicated those facts to General Halleck, but he thought it best to make no attack on the enemy, but to let him retreat without molestation. He directed me, therefore, to discontinue the pursuit.[35] Two days after the enemy resumed his retreat toward Okolona, followed by our cavalry as far as Guntown. As soon as the continued retreat of the enemy was known, I was instructed to post a sufficient force at suitable points to cover the front of the army and to place my army in some convenient position to support them. As the water was bad everywhere south of Tuscumbia Creek, as well as in that stream itself, I drew back my army to Clear Creek, a tributary well supplied with springs, and there went into camp, within four miles of Corinth, on the 12th of June.

In our pursuit of the enemy from Corinth we took few prisoners though we might have picked up many thousands had there been any object in doing so. The woods on both sides of the road were full of stragglers, who had abandoned their army and were making their way to their homes. They seemed to be not at all unwilling to be captured and fed, but as they were deserting their army we gained all we could have gained by their capture and without any of the trouble and expense of keeping them. No effort whatever was made even to stop them. I estimated the number I saw at 8,000 or 10,000. General Buell's estimate was even higher.[36] This fact, with everything else of importance that occurred, was reported to General Halleck, and, no doubt, by some mistake or misunderstanding on his part was made the basis of a telegram from him to the War Department of an extraordinary character and which afterward — and for a long time afterward, if not to this day — has been quoted to my discredit. The telegram is as follows, viz:

Gen. Halleck's Headquarters,
June 4, 1862.

Gen. Pope, with 4,000 men, is 30 miles south of Corinth pushing the enemy hard. He already reports 10,000 prisoners and deserters from the enemy and 15,000 stands of arms captured. Thousands of the enemy are throwing away their arms. A farmer says that when Beauregard learned that Col. Elliott had cut the railroad on his line of retreat he became frantic and told his men to save themselves the best way they could. We

have captured nine locomotives and a number of cars; one of the former is already repaired and running to-day. Several more will be in running order in two or three days. The result is all I could possibly desire.
H. W. Halleck,
Major General Commanding.[37]

I copy this telegram in full, though I shall only advert to a portion of it. I need scarcely say, after what I have already intimated, that I never made such a report as General Halleck speaks of in his telegram, nor anything like it. I saw it for the first time in the papers, received when we had returned from Booneville and I immediately called the attention of my adjutant-general and of other officers of my staff to it as a most extraordinary and unfounded report. So far from being thirty miles south of Corinth on the date of General Halleck's telegram, I was sick in my tent on Clear Creek and confined to my camp from the second to the seventh of June.[38] I was only four miles from General Halleck's headquarters when he sent his telegram to Washington and as I was in hourly communication with him by letter and telegram he must have known it.[39] I sent him no reports by telegraph or otherwise, except abstracts of such as were sent me from the front by Generals Rosecrans and Granger.[40] There is but one telegram or report from me to General Halleck, dated during those days, which mentions numbers at all; and I here transcribe it:

HeadQ'rs Army of the Mississippi
Near Danville, June 3, 1862

Maj. Gen. Halleck: The two divisions on the advance under Rosecrans are slowly and cautiously advancing on Baldwin this morning, with the cavalry on both flanks. Hamilton, with two divisions, is at Rienzi and between there and Booneville, ready to move forward should they be needed. One brigade from the reserve occupied Danville. Rosecrans reports this morning that all testimony shows that the enemy has retreated from Baldwin, but he is advancing cautiously. The woods for miles are full of stragglers from the enemy, who are coming in squads. Not less than 10,000 men are thus scattered about, who will come in within a day or two.
John Pope
Major General Commanding.[41]

This dispatch contains the substance of reports from Generals Rosecrans and Granger, but it contains neither the word "deserter," "prisoner," nor "capture." Upon this dispatch, however, General Halleck probably based this telegram, if he ever sent the telegram at all. I say "if," because it will be noticed in the following correspondence between him and myself on this subject, which I trust will prove conclusive, so far as I am concerned at least:

Washington, D.C. July 3, 1865

General: The war has now ended and the events and incidents connected with it are passing into history. As I do not wish that any report or misconception which has been circulated to my prejudice, and which is susceptible of explanation, should stand recorded against me; and as the reasons which actuated me in preserving silence until this time no longer exist, I desire to invite your attention to a dispatch published in the newspapers, dated at Corinth, Miss. June 4, 1862, purporting to have been sent by you to the Secretary of War, and containing substantially the following words, viz: "Gen. Pope is 30 miles south of Corinth, pushing the enemy hard. He already reports 10,000 prisoners and deserters, and 15,000 stands of arms captured," etc. I do not know that you ever sent such a dispatch, but as I do know that I never made such a report, I infer that if you sent the dispatch in question you must have done so under a very great misapprehension. I have, therefore, to request that you furnish me a copy of any report made by me upon which such a dispatch as that in question was sent. I have full records of all my letters, dispatches and reports to you during the operations at Corinth, and no such report is among them.

I am, General, respectfully, your obedient servant,
John Pope,
Major General
Maj. Gen. H. W. Halleck,
U.S. Army, Washington, D.C.

General Halleck's Reply:

Washington, D.C. July 5, 1865

General: I have to acknowledge the receipt of your communication of the 3d inst. As my papers are all boxed up for transportation to California, I am not able to refer to the dispatches to which you allude, nor can I trust my memory in regard to communications made more than three years ago, further than to say that I never reported to the secretary of War dispatches received from you, which were not so received.

Respectfully, your obedient servant,
H. W. Halleck,
Major General.
Maj. Gen. John Pope, Present.

General Pope's reply:

Washington, D.C., July 5, 1865

General: Your note in reply to my letter of yesterday's date was received this afternoon too late to be answered before you left the city.

I regret that you did not see fit to make the very brief examination of your files necessary to make it plain to you that the correction asked for in my letter was due to me. I was at least entitled to an assurance that such examination should be made at the earliest practicable moment. Certainly the three weeks you are to pass in New York afford ample time to inspect all your papers bearing on the subject of my letter. As you do not promise an examination now or at any other time, I am constrained to say that the statement which, "trusting to your memory," and without inspection of your files, you do make it altogether unsatisfactory, and leaves me at a loss to determine whether you are to be understood as denying that you sent the dispatch to the Secretary of War which was the subject of my letter, or whether, in the face of my positive denial, you mean to insist that the dispatch was a correct transcript, or anything like it, of a report made to you by me. If it be your purpose to make such a statement as an answer to my deliberate and unqualified assertion that no such report as that attributed to me was ever made by me, it becomes more necessary than ever that you should examine your files and furnish me the papers I ask for. In short, General, I utterly deny that the dispatch purporting to be sent by you to the Secretary of War was based on any report from me such as is therein stated, and I therefore call on you either to disavow this dispatch or to furnish me with a copy of the report attributed to me.

In almost any other case this question could be easily and conclusively settled by a reference to the official files at the headquarters of the Department which you then commanded; but I have ascertained, General, that when you left the West you ordered that portion of the dispatches and reports concerning the operations around Corinth which bore upon this question, to be cut out of the official books and brought with you to Washington, leaving the official records in St. Louis mutilated and incomplete; these dispatches thus taken are believed to be in your possession. It is not necessary for me to comment on this transaction further than to say that it manifestly leaves the question I make with you to be settled by my files and those now in your possession; together with the evidence of officers, telegraph operators, and others whose duties and positions enable them to speak with knowledge on the subject. I trust, General, that you understand that this correspondence has not been begun by me without due consideration, or without abundant testimony to maintain my position on the question involved. You must, therefore, see that the matter cannot be disposed of by such a note as yours of this date.

The question between us is very simple. You are believed to have sent a dispatch to the Secretary of War asserting that I had made certain reports. I deny utterly that I did so. The onus of proof is, therefore, with you, and I might well be contented to rest the matter here, but it is proper to inform you that I have abundant evidence to establish the negative of the statement contained in the dispatch attributed to you as far as that dispatch relates to me. My main purpose in writing to you on the subject was to give you the opportunity to explain the matter in a manner that, while it would relieve me from the misconception arising from your dispatch, would leave unimpaired the personal relations which have always existed between us. It is my wish to maintain those relations if possible; but you must be aware that I cannot long do so unless you act toward me in the same spirit of frankness in which my letter of yesterday was written. It will afford me real satisfaction, on receipt of a copy of the report attributed to me in the dispatch in question, accompanied by such an explanation as a spirit of frankness and candor would dictate, to recall and destroy, this letter. Such explanation, however, is due to me, and I trust sincerely that you will not leave New York, where, I understand, you are to remain three weeks, without making the brief examination of your files necessary to a full explanation of the subject. I send the original of this to you by the hands of Maj. Scott, your staff officer, and a copy by mail to the care of John C. Hamilton, esq. I shall leave for St. Louis on Friday, the 7th inst., at which place any communication will reach me.

I am, General, respectfully, your obedient servant,

John Pope, Major General,

Maj. Gen. H. W. Halleck,

U.S.A. New York, N.Y.[42]

To this letter no answer was ever received, but it is proper to state about ten years subsequent to the date of these letters, and after General Halleck's death, the reports, dispatches, etc., which were cut out of the official records in St. Louis and carried away by General Halleck, were recovered by the War Department, and the files there are complete. The only report from me on the subject of "capturing prisoners" is that found copied in this paper immediately preceding these letters.[43]

I was called to Washington immediately after the dispatch which occasioned these letters was published and my relations to General Halleck needed to be so close and harmonious, in the face of the extraordinary difficulties that confronted us, that it would have shown neither wisdom nor patriotism to open a controversy at that time. I chose, therefore, to bear unmerited reproach rather than to make an open explanation which, at that time, might have done far more injury to the country than any temporary misconception could do to me. No opportunity presented itself during the war which was not involved in the same objection, but when the war ended it seemed to me reasonable and proper to put at rest unfounded reports which had been so long and so persistently circulated to my injury.

I could have wished that General Halleck had pursued a different course in this matter, but he had not so chosen and leaves me no recourse except to publish this correspondence.

The long delays and extremely deliberate movements of this great army of 100,000 men against a force certainly not half so large, and the wholly unsatisfactory result, are made still more incomprehensible when it is considered that, nearly without exception, every great soldier of our Civil War—that is, every one of those who commanded armies and held the highest places both in rank and fame during the war—were in that army under General Halleck and held high commands.

Grant, Sherman, Sheridan, Thomas, McPherson, Logan, Buell, Rosecrans and many others I might mention held commands in that army, and surely their subsequent history frees them from even the suspicion of responsibility for these operations at Corinth or their outcome. What influence they had in the matter is sufficiently apparent.

This great army, in splendid condition in every respect, could have marched anywhere through the South without effective opposition and an enterprising commander would not have hesitated to undertake any military movement with it. Yet in less than two months it was scattered in such a manner and to such an extent that the war was half over before it was again reunited. Stretched along from Memphis to Nashville in a long, thin line, weak everywhere, it invited attack at every point. Having occupied positions, it was as difficult, nearly, to give them up as to hold them.

For more than a year it moved forward not one foot nor accomplished anything toward suppressing the rebellion. The capture of Vicksburg and the subsequent Battle of Chickamauga once more brought this admirable army together and from that time they went "forth conquering and to conquer."

Chapter Six

Confederate Generals at Corinth

$\mathscr{I}$t is a curious fact that the Confederate government seems to have found as much fault with their commander at Corinth as we did with ours. What they expected Beauregard to accomplish is not clearly understood. With an army certainly not half so large as ours—at times, perhaps not one third so large—occupying open fieldworks in comparatively open country, he kept nearly our whole Western army at bay for six weeks and finally carried off his army and his military stores, leaving us to occupy the ruined village and deserted intrenchments. What more could have been looked for or accomplished with such inferiority of force is not easy to conceive. Certainly there was concurrence on our side in the opinion that the enemy had done more than anyone expected that they would or could do. It is probable that the Confederate president's dislike of Beauregard had much to do with his judgment of his action at Corinth.

However great a man Mr. Jefferson Davis may have been, I do not suppose that his warmest admirers would assert that he was above personal prejudices, or that they did not influence his actions toward individuals.

It was also asserted by Beauregard's friends that the Confederate president was unfriendly to him and certainly some better reason than the facts presented must be found to explain the disapproval of the results at Corinth from the Confederate standpoint, and the almost immediate removal of Beauregard from the chief command in that part of the South.

No doubt I have said as much as is necessary, certainly as much as I desire to say, concerning General Beauregard in this in a preceding article;[1] but it may not be inappropriate here to venture a few remarks upon his predecessor in command, General Albert Sidney Johnston.[2] This appears to me desirable on many accounts, but especially to invite a statement of the reasons for what appears to be a general belief (or rather impression) of his great ability as a soldier. The origin of this impression may be easily traced to Mr. Jefferson Davis, who by words and acts, both before and during the war, made it clear that he at least upheld, if he did not believe in, that theory.[3] Carefully fostered, it has grown at last to a sort of conviction in the South, accepted also in the North, that General A. S. Johnston was not only the ablest general of the war on either side, but that he was a wonderful military genius, whose death not only caused the loss of the Battle of Shiloh to the Confederates, but actually fatally impaired the vitality of the Southern Confederacy so that it languished from that hour. It is actually held by many intelligent people that, if he had lived, the fortunes of the Confederacy might and probably would, have had a very different issue. For this strange belief in the wonderful ability and power of one man, it is quite natural and altogether reasonable that we should seek some reasons not based on the sentimental utterances of any fallible man. The natural recourse of any investigator would be to the previous history of the object of so much admiration and reverence, but, strange to say, an examination of his previous life not only furnishes no confirmation of such an opinion; but would actually lead, if not to the opposite conclusion, at least to an impression of rather a common-place person in a military as well as a purely intellectual view. General A. S. Johnston was a graduate of West Point and was at least fifty years of age in 1861.[4] He resigned from the army soon after graduating and went to Texas, then a Mexican province. He passed through the war of Texas independence with a fair, but by no means great reputation. He appeared in the Mexican War, the result of the annexation of Texas and a direct consequence of her war of separation from Mexico, as an inspector on the staff of General Henderson,[5] of Texas, who led several regiments from that State to the field, but he was little known to anyone except two or three old army friends (among whom was Mr. Jefferson Davis) and the troops from Texas. He rendered no special service and was absolutely undistinguished and practically unknown during that war. Thus he emerged from two wars without distinction and almost unknown.[6]

At the conclusion of the Mexican War he returned to his home in Texas, and soon after was appointed a paymaster in the army, largely, it was understood, through the influence of Mr. Jefferson Davis.[7] In 1855, when two new regiments of cavalry and two of infantry were added to the army, Mr. Jefferson Davis being at the time Secretary of War, Major A. S. Johnston was appointed Colonel of the 2nd Cavalry. He commanded and conducted a considerable body of troops from Fort Leavenworth across the plains to Utah to suppress an anticipated rebellion of the Mormons, but there was no battle, and indeed no hostilities of any sort. In 1861, as brigadier general, he was in command on the Pacific Coast. Thus, his military appointments and the impression of his military ability are based solely on Mr. Jefferson Davis. Except in Texas he was substantially an unknown man and the belief in his ability and his fitness for high military office was confined mainly to Mr. Jefferson Davis. So far as can be ascertained this was his record when he appeared at Shiloh and this record yet remains as the only practical foundation of the strange opinion of his great capacity as a military commander.

It is to be clearly understood that in the foregoing remarks I express no opinion on the question of General Johnston's military ability. I was only giving, as I have been able to acquire them, the facts of his life upon which, in the nature of things, such opinions concerning him must be based. I shall be more than willing to share with the most ardent of his admirers the conviction that he was a great general and military genius, if I can in any way reconcile such a belief with the dictates of common sense and common experience. I knew General Johnston as well as a man so much his junior in years and rank would be likely to know him and I further knew him from the conversation of those better acquainted with him than I was and I do not hesitate to say that a more noble, generous man and altogether honorable gentleman never wore the uniform of a soldier. His engaging manners, his gracious smile, his noble countenance and fine martial figure captivated all who came near him; and I do not wonder that men were devoted to him and more than anxious to invest him with every high quality of which man is capable. In truth I feel very much the same way myself when I think of him as I last saw him before the war. He was magnanimous and I believe, truly unselfish — utterly incapable of any dishonorable action or willing injury to any man. He was a man of strong feelings and warm attachments, but, from all I could ever hear, he was either without personal prejudices or incapable of being influenced by them in his official actions.

It was said that in the Spring of 1861 he was inclined to be unfaithful to his trust and was arranging that the forts and armaments in the harbor of San Francisco might be handed over or taken over by him to the Southern side; but I happened to be on the Pacific Coast and holding the very command he held himself,[8] when this charge was made and fully discussed. There was not the smallest foundation for suspicion even. He was then as true to the obligations of his duty to the government which had invested him with so great a trust as any officer in the army; and although in the nature of things he would probably have allied himself to the Southern side, he would have done so in an open and honorable way and with no taint of deception or unfaithfulness in his action. That he was a noble gentleman, high-toned and honorable, no man who knew him would think of contesting. Whether he was equally as great as a soldier, or even approximately so, is another question. I, for one, shall be rejoiced if I can be supplied with good reasons to think so.

The next officer to Beauregard in rank and command at Corinth was General Braxton Bragg and a remarkable man he was.[9] Tall and erect, with thick, bushy eyebrows and black, fierce eyes, with harsh features and a most forbidding countenance, he possessed, or was possessed, by the most sullen and devilish temper that ever afflicted a human being. Kindly feeling or soft sentiment of any kind fled before his frown and those subject to his authority retired from his presence with almost equal celerity and relief. I do not think he could ever have had warm friends.

Indeed he seemed even to detest himself, if one might judge from the dissatisfied expression which continually sat enthroned on his face and yet the South produced no more capable general than he.[10] Though his military success was greatly lessened and at times transformed into actual defeat by the bitterness of feeling created against him among his subordinates by his harsh and uncompromising dealings with them, I yet undertake to say and I am convinced that history will, in due time, confirm the opinion, that General Bragg accomplished more with less comparative force and under more unfavorable and discouraging circumstances and relations than any Southern general. It is hard to realize how difficult the position and how hopeless the outlook of military operations of a man surrounded as he was by so many personal enemies upon whose cordial support and sympathy he was compelled to do without in the most critical moments of his campaign. It is impossible that he did not often lament the infirmities of temper which deprived him of the friendship and sympathy of those nearest to him in rank and influence, but the unhappy results born of such a condition of feeling seemed only to render his temper the more bitter and unrelenting. Under every discouragement, both of sentiment and of facts, he always presented a grim front to his enemy, before and around him. How he maintained himself so long and so well under such circumstances, has always been a wonder. Had his temper and his manners been such as make friends and not enemies, it is hard to say how great might have been his success, gifted as he was, in my opinion, with military ability of the highest order.

He never appeared to be a young man at all, even in the earliest stages of his military service, nor in any way capable of enjoying the pleasures or the anticipations of youth. Even when he was a lieutenant of artillery his military capacity was recognized as quite exceptional and this knowledge of him occasioned General Taylor to do an act of great injustice to a most competent and meritorious officer.[11] Just before the army moved from Comargo upon Monterey, in 1846, Captain T. W. Sherman (afterward General Sherman, of Hilton Head fame) reported for duty as recently-promoted captain of one of the light batteries of artillery belonging to the army and of which Bragg, as senior lieutenant, was in command.[12] The future before us was quite unknown. We neither knew the force of the enemy we were to encounter, nor what preparations he had made, nor exactly where the encounter would be. General Taylor was therefore naturally anxious that his small army should be in the best possible condition for any contingency that might arise. He knew that Bragg was eminently competent to command the light battery under any condition. He did not know Sherman at all and therefore forced him to remain in Comargo whilst Bragg marched off to the storming of Monterrey in command of his (Sherman's) battery. It was a hard measure and I am sure that General Taylor regretted the necessity, but with him the question was merely whether it was better to do temporary injustice to an individual officer or risk the inefficiency of so important an element in his small army. As it turned out afterward T. W. Sherman proved to be a most competent and gallant battery commander and at Buena Vista rendered as distinguished service as was credited to any officer in that command. His name was on the list of highly-distinguished officers recommended by General Taylor for promotion.[13]

I only mention this incident to show that even when he was only a lieutenant, Bragg's military ability was so fully recognized that so fair and just a man as General Taylor was prompted by it to do injustice to a most worthy officer of his command.

Bragg's fondness of controversy sometimes induced him to resort to queer practices to get one up. It is told of him and I presume it is true, that being stationed at Fort Moultrie, S.C., with his company, which at the time constituted the whole garrison of the post and being at the same time commander of the company and quartermaster of the post, he at once began a spirited discussion as company commander with the Post Quartermaster (himself holding both offices), upon some old and long-controverted questions between the two officials in question, which had been a bone of contention ever since the army had an organization. The controversy between Bragg as company commander and Bragg as quartermaster, became at last so acrimonious that the quartermaster preferred charges against the company commander, based on his offensive letters. The commander of the post (Colonel Eustes), being just then temporarily absent, Bragg had also succeeded for the time to the command of the post. The correspondence and charges were in due course submitted to him, and he forwarded them to Washington, with a severe excoriation of both the parties concerned, for the action and decision of the Secretary of War. In reply to this effort of his to settle questions of interest in the administration of the army he received a pretty sharp reprimand, which was, perhaps, the most absurd part of the whole transaction. So far as law and army regulations are concerned, the whole correspondence and its reference to Washington was perfectly legitimate and demanded a respectful attention. It was not a dispute between individuals, but a question between two public officials on public business and in such a case the personality of the parties was not in question, nor did it make the least difference officially whether the officials were different persons or one and the same person. The whole affair was ludicrous, but it illustrates Bragg's propensity to raise controversies and the strange methods to which he would resort to inaugurate one.[14]

It was the fatal defect of his character and joined to a naturally abominable temper, it impaired his military success and no doubt embittered his life. Had he but preserved the manner of the courtier, his history would have filled a much larger space in the records of the Southern Confederacy.

Of General Hardee,[15] who was next in rank to Bragg in that army, I do not know that I have much to say. He was not a very prominent personage during the war and made little mark in its history. He was a genial gentleman, of good address and rather of reserved manners; an officer accomplished in all the details of service and thoroughly posted in all of the smaller etiquette of army ceremonies. He was a good tactician and compiled a volume of infantry tactics for the army which was used for a few years, and was a great improvement upon the old tactics in use theretofore. He was never considered a man of large ability and his record during the war would seem to confirm this estimate of him. He possessed all those traits of urbanity, effusiveness and apparent interest in whomsoever he was with, which were so wanting in Bragg, and it is probably true that he was indebted for the military positions he held and the favor with which he was regarded, to the suavity of the courtier quite as much as to the ability of the soldier. He was always an agreeable man to meet and I have no doubt always a welcome guest.

Among the most conspicuous of the generals at and in front of Corinth in the Spring of 1862 and by no means least remarkable, was General Earl Van Dorn. He arrived in Corinth during the slow movements against the place, bringing with him from the northern part of Arkansas the remnant of the army only recently defeated in a severe battle at Pea Ridge. What was the strength of this reinforcement I do not know, but the troops composing it could not have been in good heart or efficient condition after their rough experience so short a time before.[16]

Van Dorn was a classmate of mine at West Point, but I had not seen him for many years before this time. I remember him, however, very well as a boy at the Academy. He had the soft, sweet face of a girl, with the physical strength and agility of an athlete. His gentle expression of countenance, his blue eyes and long, curly, auburn hair gave him almost a feminine look and indeed he had a kindly and affectionate disposition and temper seldom found in a man. No one could help loving him in those days, and I think he had not an enemy at West Point.

He was very sentimental, and always in love with somebody, and his sentimentality was not only the great weakness of character, but it was the direct cause, without doubt, of his violent and tragical death.

He possessed very moderate abilities, indeed so moderate that it was with difficulty he managed to graduate, either at the foot or next to the foot of his class.[17] Indeed, we all feared toward the last that he might not pass his examination at all and there was genuine sorrow over the danger that such a misfortune, or indeed any misfortune, might befall him. None of his classmates in their wildest flights in his behalf, ever predicted any more successful career than that incident to the dull routine of army service in time of peace and the slow promotion from one grade to another so exquisitely regulated by law that neither character nor conduct, neither ability nor acquirement, nor qualifications of any kind, had anything to do with an officer's promotion, except the qualification of tenacity of life. Rank came by age and not merit of any kind, in the old army before the war and naturally, life and its care and preservation became objects of supreme importance to the officers both in a personal and an official sense. It was a singular thing in this condition of affairs that Van Dorn had reached the rank of major before the war — a grade not attained nor even approached by any members of his class, the most successful of whom had barely reached the rank of captain. Van Dorn was from Mississippi and Mr. Davis was Secretary of War when the new regiments were raised in 1855 and Van Dorn was appointed the senior captain of one of them. In a year or two he was promoted major and held that rank at the outbreak of the war. Naturally, he was among the very first to desert the service and cast his lot with the South; but he held a command in the United States Army in Texas at the time and committed acts of violence and wrong to brother officers serving in that Department which cannot be justified on any ground. I have heard, from one or two of the officers on duty in San Antonio when General Twiggs surrendered or tried to surrender to the enemies of the Government the military trust which had been confided to him,[18] grievous accounts of Van Dorn's treatment of them. Everybody knows the manner in which Twiggs betrayed his trust and in that manner, odious and inexcusable, Van Dorn was said to have been his zealous assistant.[19] It has always been difficult for me to reconcile his conduct at this time, especially his rough treatment of old friends and comrades, with his gentle ways and his evident unwillingness to offend or harm anyone, when I knew him in his early youth. Indeed, I find it hard to believe that he could have done things so foreign to his nature as he is represented to have done in the violent seizure of the property of the government in Texas, and the arrest and confinement of some of the officers who only a few days before were his friends and intimate associates. The passions of 1861, however, transformed, temporarily at least, the characters of many persons actively engaged in public affairs and in Van Dorn's case especially, I much prefer to believe that he has been misrepresented or misunderstood, or that he was only for a time afflicted with the madness which seemed to have seized upon almost everybody. He received, naturally from Mr. Davis high rank in the Confederate army, served in Virginia during the early days of the war, was finally transferred to the command of the troops under McCulloch and Price in northern Arkansas, fought the battle at Pea Ridge, in which he was badly worsted and appeared at Corinth with such of his command as were left, in May, 1862.

He played no prominent part in the war thereafter and before its close he was shot to death by a gentleman in northern Alabama for what was asserted as too intimate relations with that gentleman's wife.[20]

Considering Van Dorn's limited abilities and meager intellectual endowments, he certainly succeeded in reaching and holding far higher official positions than his friends believed him capable of reaching.

Another notable character, also a member of my class at West Point, arrived in Corinth during Halleck's siege of the place, bringing with him the fragments of his command, no very formidable force. This was General Mansfield Lovell,[21] who had recently been driven out of New Orleans by the capture of the city by Farragut and Butler.[22] His military career, so far as it had any importance, ended with the catastrophe at New Orleans, for which the president of the Confederacy appears to have held him entirely responsible, although he had neither the force nor the military appliances necessary to successfully resist the advance of such an armament as was brought against the city. It is hard to make out a reason for shelving him for the remainder of the war, except the personal dislike of the man. He was full of self-conceit and self-appreciation and carried his admiration of himself almost to an imbecility only reached by the late General George B. McClellan.[23] Farther than this man could not go. Lovell, however, had one weakness which McClellan never had. Whilst the former's main object of worship was himself, he yet admired almost equally a classmate, General G. W. Smith,[24] of whom I have ventured to say something in a former paper.[25] McClellan, on the contrary, admired himself only, and could never bear a rival near that shrine. Lovell was a fine-looking man, fair in complexion and of graceful carriage. He was a generous man, too and his attachment to G. W. Smith was genuine and unselfish. He had the ability and the acquirement to have been a successful soldier, but I do not think he had the suavity of manner nor the kindly sympathy and forbearance necessary to enlist the willing service of troops, especially of volunteer troops. General G. W. Smith has written a book within a few years, in which, on behalf of Lovell as well as of himself, he presents rather a severe case against the head of the Confederacy.[26]

All the conspicuous persons thus far mentioned in the Confederate army at Corinth were West Point men whom I had either known there or afterwards in the service, but there was one personage who held a considerable command in that army, who had joined the military forces from civil life and of whom it can truly be said that he was greatly respected and highly regarded by everybody. This was General Sterling Price,[27] of Missouri.

He was a man of decided ability as a citizen and a public man, had had some military experience in the Mexican War and exercised the completest influence over the troops he led from Missouri. In fact, these Missouri troops would probably not have been raised at all except through the influence of General Price and the belief that they were to serve directly under his command.

Personally and publicly, few men, if indeed any man, stood higher in public opinion or commanded such entire confidence in his state. His integrity was unquestioned and unquestionable, his judgment deliberate and unimpassioned and his manners genial and unsympathetic. His bearing was very dignified, without being in the least haughty or forbidding.

He was tall and portly when I last saw him before the war, with a warm red complexion and fair hair. He lived a quiet life in the interior of the state, appearing to want no public place and certainly seeking none. He was regarded by everybody in the state with the greatest respect and treated with the greatest consideration. Naturally when the difficulties of 1861 began to press upon the state it became desirable for the state government to enlist the influence and the interest of General Price on the side which the state officers inclined to and to which they sought to attach the state of Missouri. Governor Jackson and his immediate following were genuine, active Secessionists, anxious to plunge the state into rebellion.

General Price was known to be a Union man, ready to do anything possible to prevent the state from joining in the rebellion. It was at the time very doubtful which way Missouri would go and its Secession governor moved heaven and earth to persuade or to trick every prominent man in the state into active support of the purpose to withdraw Missouri from the Union.

When these men could not be prevailed on by argument to be unfaithful to the Union, they were inveigled into some questionable association or position from which they could not honorably escape except by going with the state officers. Such tactics were employed on General Price. He was invited by Governor Jackson to consult and advise with him on the situation, who pretended himself to be very anxious to keep the peace and preserve the official status of the state in the Union. Price joined him in Jefferson City for this purpose and accompanied him to St. Louis to a conference with Frank Blair,[28] then vested by the government with some extraordinary powers and with General Lyon, the military commander in the state. The conference came to grief, as it was not possible to relinquish the power and authority of the general government within the state of Missouri, as Governor Jackson asked, on any condition whatever. The conference which took place in St. Louis was broken up without any result except irritation to the parties to it, and Governor Jackson retreated rapidly to Jefferson City, burning the railroad bridges between St. Louis and the state capital.[29]

Price went with him. Still holding to his Union sentiments, but placed in command of the state militia and pressed upon by General Lyon, who followed them rapidly with what military force he had to spare from St. Louis. A crisis was precipitated and a conflict brought on near Booneville between United States troops and state militia, in which, more by surprise and because of some mistaken ideas of the obligations of honor under the circumstances, than from conviction or inclination, Price found himself in command of the rebel forces. He was thus, I do not doubt, very reluctantly drawn into action he did not approve, in a cause to which he was in reality opposed.[30] Indeed, it is hard to understand how any sensible man in Missouri could have been in favor of the secession of the state from the Union. Slavery, the prime and in fact only cause of the Civil War, not only had no value in the state, but was positively an injury to its prosperity, as nearly everybody openly admitted. Besides this, the state projects to the north like a great promontory, with the powerful abolition states of Kansas, Iowa and Illinois on three sides, able at any time to crush out any force that Missouri could put into the field and inflamed with the zeal and passion necessary to do so. Worse than all, the South did not want Missouri.[31] The great slave interest which dominated them had but feeble hold on Missouri and even had it been otherwise the South could never have retained the state in Southern hands whilst it was in the embrace of such powerful and determined neighbors. It was simply wicked to attempt an impracticable scheme which could only bring ruin upon its supporters and which was neither asked nor desired by the South. The result was—I may assert and still be much within bounds—that Missouri suffered in loss of property and the unhappiness of her citizens far more than any other state of the Union. She left, for a time, a happy home where she was honored and loved, for a new abode, where she was not even a welcome guest and where her highest interests were subordinated to those of others little concerned about her welfare or her happiness. What was not stupid in the course of her state officers in 1861 was wicked and should never have been condoned so far as they were concerned.

Beaten at Booneville, Price fell back into the southern part of the state, closely followed up by Lyon with all the troops he could muster. Price met McCulloch near the Arkansas line with heavy reinforcements, with which he moved back to Wilson's Creek, near Springfield and fought the almost savage battle of that name, in which Lyon was killed and his army defeated. The Union forces fell back to the railroad connecting with St. Louis and Price advanced slowly toward Lexington, on the Missouri River, near the scene of his defeat a month or two before. He captured Lexington, held by a considerable Union force, which he paroled and fell back again toward the south before the advance of the Union troops, taking off with him considerable supplies captured there. This success stimulated the Secession spirit in Missouri wonderfully and thousands of young men left their homes to join his army. As Frémont advanced, Price continued to march south. After the comedy at Springfield, during which General Frémont was superseded by General Hunter, the United States troops, for want of supplies, again withdrew to the railroad and Price again advanced toward the Missouri River. This time, however, he did not come north of the Osage in the presence of heavy forces along the line of the Missouri Pacific Railroad, but encamped on the south side of the Osage, flooding the state with proclamations and holding his camp as a rendezvous for the recruits these proclamations were expected to bring him. Some active operations cut off and captured considerable bodies of these recruits on the way to join him and deterred many more from even attempting it, and after a time he gradually withdrew again to southern Missouri, where he was soon followed by a heavy Union force under General S. R. Curtis. In the northern part of Arkansas, Price was again reinforced by McCulloch and his Texans, all under command of Van Dorn and the decisive battle of Pea Ridge was fought and lost to the enemy. For several years thereafter the mastery in Missouri was with the United States.

It may seem singular that I should write at such length about the military career of a man who did not hold a commission in either army and who was little known to the general public east of the Mississippi, but it must be considered that few men exercised so large an influence in the prosecution of the war in the West and none who did so by mere force of character and personal influence.

For nearly a year he kept Missouri in commotion and thereby forced the government to keep heavy forces in the state which were greatly needed elsewhere and whose absence from the front impaired greatly the success of some important enterprises and prevented the undertaking of others. In fact, the retention of so many troops in Missouri, made necessary by Price's presence and movements, greatly embarrassed the government and retarded the general military operations in progress or to be undertaken and thus, in a like degree, proved advantageous to the enemy.

It is to be remembered, too, that the Secession state officers of Missouri had fled from the state; that there was in reality no constitutional state government in existence in Missouri to encourage or give official sanction to any acts whatever done by General Price or anyone else and that he absolutely carried on the war in Missouri practically on his own responsibility and according to his own judgment and neither as an official of Missouri nor of the Southern Confederacy. A man who worked such results under such conditions is certainly a man worthy of much more extended mention than I have been able to give him.

He died as he had lived, an unassuming, unambitious citizen, of simple tastes and quiet habits, pure in character, sincere in belief and perfectly honest in every act. No man who ever lived in Missouri was more respected or loved so well. Even those against whom he fought always recognized and bore testimony to his humanity and his honorable dealing and perhaps he is even yet as truly and genuinely esteemed and regretted by many Union men as by the most ardent of his partisans.

Chapter Seven

Federal Generals at Corinth

$\mathscr{A}$n interesting fact connected with the investment of Corinth by General Halleck in May, 1862, I have not seen noticed in any papers on the war and yet it is so striking as to be well worthy of mention. It is the fact that in various grades and in various commands of the army in front of Corinth, were found nearly every one of the generals who attained the highest rank and won the greatest honors of the war. Halleck, Grant, Sherman, Sheridan, Thomas, Logan, McPherson, Buell and Rosecrans and many others who subsequently greatly distinguished themselves, were present and took active part (if any such word as active can be applied to any of the operations around Corinth) in that siege. Of course there was no opportunity for distinction in such military work as we then executed, except, indeed, in the amount and massiveness of the fieldworks we built at every step of our advance upon that ill-fortified village. In the trenches and redoubts of earth we dug and piled up there we left grave room enough for the people of the entire state of Mississippi and loose soil enough to cover them up. It was a wonderful exhibition of skill with spade and pick and it was a trial afterward to leave such a monument of digging behind us without the least compensation for the work.

With the Confederate forces defending the village were also several officers of high distinction whose subsequent careers, though unfortunate in results, redounded much to the justly-earned reputation of several of them. Among them were Beauregard, Bragg, Hardee, Price, Van Dorn and others, nearly all of whom I had known personally for a good many years before they appeared at Corinth.

Concerning General Halleck I have said in a previous article all I had to say and I need not enlarge here upon any details which might go to substantiate my estimate of him.[1]

So much has been written about General Grant, by himself as well as others, that it would seem superfluous to write more on the subject and yet it may not be uninteresting what I saw and heard of him when he came to Springfield, Illinois in 1861. I had known him slightly at West Point, where he was in no sense a man of mark, either with cadets or professors.

I met him afterward in the service during the Mexican War, and subsequently I saw him frequently in St. Louis after he was out of the army and in extreme poverty. Whilst I never was intimate with him in those days, I yet knew him very well and often talked with him and from these conversations I knew that he was profoundly discontented and unhappy. For several years before the war I did not see him at all, but heard he was in some business in Galena. I was not surprised, therefore, when he came into my office in Springfield, in 1861, when I was mustering in the volunteer regiments of Illinois. We had some conversation, mainly about himself and his plans and wishes. Of course he wanted to take suitable part and proper position in the defense of the country and thought naturally that his military education and army service entitled him to consideration. After he left me I went to see Governor Yates and told him how desirable it was, in the dearth of military men and knowledge, to secure the services of such a man as Grant. He recognized it fully, but said that it was not in his power to make Grant a general or a colonel, those offices, as all others in the regiments that were to be raised, being elective, but that he would give him a position on his staff and thus have the advantage of his military acquirements at headquarters.[2] He accordingly assigned him to duty in the office of the Acting Adjutant-General of the state, who, at the end of a week, pronounced Grant to be incompetent! Poor fellow, he was killed at Pea Ridge and did not live to realize what an absurdity he had achieved. Grant came into my office soon after this report was made and rather ruefully told me that he could not do anything at Springfield and was going back to Galena to resume his business. I told him that he could not possibly do such a thing; that the idea of his resting quietly at Galena in the midst of such a war as was impending was out of the question. I offered my services to help him to get some suitable position, but he had made up his mind to go back. I told him when he left that I had no doubt I should see him again within ten days.[3] He did accordingly return to Springfield in less than the time mentioned and one of the three years regiments being without a colonel, because of a struggle among several of its officers for the position, Grant was selected as colonel and at once took the command.[4] It was said that there were many wild young fellows in the regiment, whom it was hard to discipline and that the impracticability of controlling them had been the cause of the trouble in the regiment which had prevented it from electing a colonel. The regiment was brought into the fairgrounds at Springfield and I soon had personal reason to know that there was good grounds for the reports about it.

The regiment being ordered into northern Missouri, Grant got permission to march instead of going by rail and by the time he reached the village of Mexico his regiment was in good condition in all respects. In northern Missouri he came for a time under my command and I was with him along the line of the North Missouri Railroad for several days. I remember he had a large dun colored horse, which he valued highly and took me to see, though I admit that his beauties did not strike me forcibly.

In a few days Grant received his appointment as brigadier general of volunteers. He was sent to command the troops at Cape Girardeau, below St. Louis, which was threatened by some irregular forces under the so-called general, Jeff Thompson. He often told, in a very humorous way, his controversy about rank with a brigadier general from civil life whom he found there.[5] This gentleman insisted upon it that he ranked Grant, but in a spirit of concession he proposed that to settle the matter he would choose as umpire Deacon Bross, of the "Chicago Tribune"; Grant should choose a second and together they should choose a third and this august body were to decide which of the generals should command. Grant replied that whilst he had entire confidence in Deacon Bross and no doubt should have in the other two, yet he did not understand that any one of them possessed sufficient professional knowledge to decide such a question and even if they had he did not himself believe that the War Department would feel bound by their decision, but as he had been ordered there to command, he felt obliged to do so, until otherwise instructed by higher authority. The officer concerned in this funny proposition became, subsequently, a gallant and distinguished soldier.

Grant shortly afterward went to Cairo, then fought the unsuccessful Battle of Belmont and almost immediately organized the advance against Forts Henry and Donelson.

The next time I saw him was in front of Corinth and a more unhappy man I have seldom seen. He had been relieved from the command of the army which had fought the Battle of Shiloh and was called second in command to

Halleck. He had no actual command, nor any influence in the operations of the army. Bitter and acrimonious controversies were raging in the camp about the management and the result of the late battle, in which he was largely the sufferer. He had his personal camp in a thick grove to the rear of the right of the line and lived there in perfect solitude, except for the companionship of his personal staff and a few friends who sought him out in his seclusion. His mortification was excessive, far beyond what the circumstances demanded and but for the earnest counsel of Sherman, dictated as Grant knew by strong feelings of personal attachment, he would probably have resigned his command in the army and returned home.[6] It may not be true to say that if "C. F. Smith had lived Grant would have disappeared from the history of the war,"[7] but it is well-nigh certain that but for Sherman and Sherman's friendship he might have done so from the front of Corinth.[8] He had absolutely nothing to do in the midst of a great army where he was second in rank; his advice neglected and sneered at by those in authority and it was made manifest to him in many ways that to the higher authorities his presence with the army was not welcome. He came a number of times to my camp, on the left of the line and three or four miles from his and would spend nearly the whole day lying on a cot bed, silent and unhappy. I never felt more sorry for anyone and I am sure that, to the last day of his life, he must have recalled with a shudder the memory of those bitter days, made more bitter by the ill-natured comments and criticisms of many men who afterward became his servile worshipers.

The next time I saw him was at City Point, in 1864. I had been ordered at his request, to report to him with the purpose to take an important command there and I spent an entire day with him, during which we had much conversation about men and things which would, I am sure, prove highly interesting if it were proper to publish it. Perhaps at some more fitting time and opportunity it may be wise to utter it publicly.[9]

The next in rank to Grant afterward was Sherman,[10] though at Corinth he only commanded a division and was junior in rank to most of those I have named. But what can anyone say of Sherman at this late day? He is known of all this country as perhaps no American before him has ever been; he has been seen and talked to by nearly every man between the Atlantic and the Pacific and has probably kissed the faces of half the women. Who does not know that lofty beak and bristling mustache; those keen blue eyes and sandy hair; that pleasant smile and kindly manner; those pertinent questions so personal that from any other man they would be considered impertinent? Who is not familiar with the "tout-ensemble" of the best-known and most generally-liked man of this generation?[11] He has not only seen almost everybody and everything, but before the war he had tried almost every kind of occupation, except that of the clergy, and had practically exhausted the capabilities of all without much benefit to his own financial condition. Artilleryman, commissary of subsistence, lawyer, banker, professor in a college, railroad president, he had tried them all and was tired of all. There yet remained open to him the career of a politician when the war began, a role which his plain speaking and his original opinions on most subjects, which he could not or would not change or modify to accommodate to other people's interest or ignorance, made it quite hopeless he should succeed in. It is curious that he shared with his distinguished opponent, General J. E. Johnston, the passion for trying all varieties of occupation in life and having exhausted all, they wound up by fighting each other and if one may judge by the reputation made by each of them in the campaign, they were more successful in this occupation than they had been in any other. Sherman, though in his sixty-eighth year, seems as active as ever and as much interested in everything that is going on. There is scarcely a show, a meeting, a convention or a reunion in any part of the country that his welcome face is not seen and in which he does not take as active a part as anyone.

He is perhaps the most original and interesting talker in this country and has apparently inexhaustible stores of knowledge and experience on almost every subject to draw upon. It is not so much what he recounts as what he suggests that makes his conversation so entertaining and instructive.

Let us hope that he may live many years to accept the genuine hospitalities of his countrymen. It will be a sad day to his companions-in-arms when his well-known figure shall no longer appear among them.

Sheridan joined the army at Corinth as a captain in the regular service and quartermaster at General Halleck's headquarters. He was hardly known at all, except by a few officers of the old army present. He had had some difficulty of an unpleasant nature with General S. R. Curtis in southwestern Missouri, the merits of which I know nothing of, nor do I suppose them to have been of much consequence.[12] He first appeared, as it were, in public when, on the promotion of Gordon Granger to be brigadier general of volunteers, he was appointed to succeed him as colonel of the 2nd Michigan Cavalry by Governor Blair,[13] of the state. He came over to my camp, where the regiment was serving at the time, to report for duty. It was the first time I had ever seen him. He joined his regiment at once and almost immediately accompanied the cavalry expedition under General W. S. Elliott which raided the railroad south of Corinth with much success.[14] I left almost at once for Washington and did not see him again for several years. He at once began that career of tremendous energy and activity which he pursued during the whole war with scarce an intermission. He was soon transferred to the Army of the Cumberland, where he commanded a division with great success and distinction and when General Grant assumed the general command of the armies and went to Washington to conduct in person that part of the general military operations intrusted to the Army of the Potomac, Sheridan was ordered to report to him and was assigned to the command of the cavalry of that army.

From that time to the close of the war his rapidly acquired fame became a part of the history of the country. Perhaps no man in the army made such a reputation and one so well merited in so short a time and a reputation which, unlike many others, has been confirmed and strengthened by time. I do not know a man whose traits and characteristics are more misunderstood by the public than Sheridan. The general idea of him presents a nervous, highly-excitable person, rough and overbearing, easily put out of patience and not innocent of hard words on occasions, a restless, impetuous man who acts before he thinks, but fortunately possesses the instinct of generally doing the right thing. Nothing could well be wider of the truth. No doubt, in action, he is prompt and impetuous, but I know no man possessed of more solid common sense and who bases so much of his conduct on its dictates. His judgment is excellent and he has great capacity for public business. He is a just and fair man and no man, I believe, was ever wronged by any action of his, personal or official.[15] Hasty expressions, which often times make more enemies than absolute wrongs, he was no doubt guilty of, as are most of us, but he regretted them more than their object did and was always prompt to repair them. He is a sympathetic and to some extent an enthusiastic man, but when important action is in question or grave conclusions to be arrived at, he is not in danger of being led astray by either sentiment. I think, with General Grant, that he is capable of doing creditably the duties of any position he may occupy and with an amount of good judgment and good sense rarely to be met with. I served for many years under his command with entire satisfaction and I can say truthfully, from long experience, that no man need complain of him in such relations, unless he is given to unnecessary fault finding.[16] He is a most agreeable companion, full of humor and keen to recognize and enjoy it in others.

Like most army officers of rank, he has strong convictions as to the rights and duties of the General-in-Chief of the Army and the relations of that officer to the Secretary of War—convictions not popular in the War Department nor among the bureaux of staff officers who direct its action, but which are, nevertheless, sound opinions, which it would be well for army administration and efficiency to have put into operation.[17] The only general in the army who has no staff and no voice in the administration of his command is the General-in-Chief, a most anomalous and unexplainable arrangement and one fraught necessarily with unsatisfactory administration and consequent discontent in the army. General Sheridan shares the embarrassment of such a condition with all of his predecessors, but I have not heard that it has soured his temper or much interfered with his enjoyment of life. He is exceedingly courteous and kind in his manners and is beloved by all who know him well.

The last time I had seen General George H. Thomas before I met him in front of Corinth was at the storming of Monterrey, Mexico, in September, 1846 and I only saw him then for a moment.[18] I was at the time an officer of engineers on General Taylor's staff and on duty with the advanced troops entering, or trying to enter, the place. I was occupied for the moment in tearing away with a small body of pioneers, the rough abatis which lined the face of the town, so as to admit more easy passage of troops, especially of artillery. Bragg's battery was in column, waiting and at the head of it sat Thomas on horseback. He was, as always, tall and stalwart, but in those days he had not put on the flesh which rather disfigured him in later years. Even then he wore the impassive, unmoved countenance in dangerous places which became during the Civil War so marked a characteristic. He sent, at my request, a man of the battery with a lighted port-fire to set fire to the dry branches and brush of the abatis,[19] which accomplished, I parted from him until April, 1862. It is hard to fix upon any prominent trait to describe in a man so cool and unemotional as Thomas. His subsequent career, great and honored as it was, was only the natural outcome of his unmoved and unexcitable temperament. He was great in defensive operations, and in no case was he ever driven from any position he occupied. His mind seemed to work slowly, but the results of his deliberate thought were always sound, and what is more to the purpose as illustrating his character, he always maintained them with a persistency that might sometimes be called obstinacy.

I presume he had the natural ambition of the soldier who occupies high place and command in a great war, but if he did have it, he certainly never betrayed it to his closest observers. He steadily declined and with perfect good faith, all offers of independent command and was content during the whole war to serve in subordinate place.[20] He served with the same troops and commanded the same divisions and army corps almost from first to last. He was utterly without arrogance or ostentation and easily approachable by persons of all ranks. His manner, whilst undemonstrative, was kind and considerate and when his troops began to know him they began to feel that confidence in his judgment and affection for his person which finally became an unreasonable passion which scarcely permitted criticism of anything he did or said. It was this general devotion of a mass and not the personal attachment of an individual, that he commanded.

He was not very sympathetic nor effusive, nor had he, so far as I ever heard, that sort of disposition which invited or encouraged intimacy. Being a native-born Virginian, he was more or less at the beginning under a doubt, but that feeling soon passed away. Certainly no more loyal or single-hearted man ever trod the earth. Perhaps no soldier of the war was more generally loved and esteemed and certainly not one whose great reputation will go down to posterity less questioned than his.

General Schofield has in a public letter laid claim to most of the honors of the campaign terminating in the Battle of Nashville,[21] but I have not heard that his claim has attracted much attention or commanded any assent from anybody.[22]

General Thomas died in San Francisco in 1869,[23] and it is safe to say that few men in the country have been more generally and genuinely mourned than he.

When the war broke out McPherson was a young officer of engineers and on duty in California.[24] He was ordered East almost immediately and assigned to duty on the staff of General Halleck, in St. Louis, where I first saw him. Naturally he was little known, but his handsome presence and cordial, winning manners soon attracted kindly feeling on the part of all who came into contact with him. He was as affectionate and gentle as a woman, but a man amongst men. Not only was his physique perfect, but he had intellect of the highest order and possessed the military coup d'oeil in a wonderful degree.[25]

He soon joined the headquarters of the army under General Grant, although still on the staff of General Halleck and almost at once was recognized as a man of superior ability and a soldier of excellent judgment. He was extremely active and useful in the military operations of General Grant and at Shiloh was distinguished not only for his gallantry but for his fine military foresight and sagacity. He was soon known to all the troops and was greatly admired by them. From the first he disliked staff duty and was anxious to get a command of troops. He was soon appointed brigadier general of volunteers and assigned to a command in the Army of the Tennessee. He served with the highest distinction in that army through all its military operations and as a conspicuous figure in all. He grew so rapidly in reputation and in personal popularity that he soon became the favorite general in the Northern armies.[26] As is well known, he was killed at the Battle of Atlanta, July 22, 1864, in the prime of his life and in the midst of a career which promised soon to crown him with the highest military honors. He was tall, graceful and very erect in person, with dark complexion and dark hair and eyes. He had a smile which irradiated his countenance like a sunbeam and lighted up the rather rugged features of his dark visage. Young as he was and short as was his military career, he was and still is, idolized by one of the most successful armies that ever took the field and one well fitted to judge correctly of the merits of the soldier who commanded them in campaign and battle — The Army of the

Tennessee. To say that he was mourned by that army is telling but little of that feeling of personal and individual sorrow which his bloody death brought to every soldier of the Army of the Tennessee.

He fell on the field of battle and at the head of that army in the midst of an unfinished battle and when the chances of success were against the Union army.

Except, perhaps, General Hoche, I know no general in history whose short career was rewarded by so much glory and such love and regret.

By his death, the command of the Army of the Tennessee fell into the hands of General John A. Logan and he assumed it in person amidst the smoke and roar of a battle apparently lost.[27]

The only occasion on which I ever saw General Logan before I met him in front of Corinth was in Washington, in February, 1861, during the interval between the arrival of Mr. Lincoln at the Capital and his inauguration as President of the United States. It was in the library of Senator Douglas's house that I found the senator himself and with him several of his personal and political friends, all Democrats.[28] Among them was General Logan, then a member of the House of Representatives.[29]

They were engaged in earnest conversation on the political situation, which was renewed with warmth after I had been introduced to some and had exchanged salutations with others whom I knew. They all knew that I had come to Washington with Mr. Lincoln and put several pertinent questions concerning what was to be expected, which of course I could not answer further than my own impressions went, based upon what I had heard and seen on the journey from the West. An hour was spent in earnest conversation, which at times became quite excited, as the prospective duties of the persons present were discussed in the light of what the immediate future might bring. Although none of the company approved of or in the least attempted to justify the proceedings of the Southern wing of their party, yet all seemed to disfavor the idea of joining a party they had denounced so severely and so often in carrying on any hostilities against those who so recently and for so long had been their political friends and allies. They could not, or would not, believe that there was to be war and shrank from the very thought of waging war upon their countrymen. They were as bitter as they had always been against the "black Republicans" for bringing such troubles on the country and classed that party and the Secessionists as equally the enemies of our institutions and of the peace of the country. As is always the case in such times, the so-called conservatives, having no strong opinions of their own and those persons not having determined what to do themselves, denounced in unison all parties that had convictions.

After listening for some time without contributing much to the conversation, I took my leave, with the remark that it made little difference what results their discussion of these matters might lead them to in theory, they would find the fact to be that there would be war and that they would be forced to take up arms on one side or other, or skulk in the rear with the army of sneaks whom civil war always hatches out and who are alike despised by both parties to the conflict. I added that I did not believe that one of them would be found in the rear or fighting on the side of the enemies of the government and that when war began, if it did begin, I felt certain of finding myself by their side in the armies of the Union. I rejoice to say that within three months thereafter I met two of them in the field with their regiments and was informed that the others also were in the Union armies.[30]

To look back from this distance of time upon the condition of public sentiment and the state of public feeling in Washington City in those early days of 1861, we cannot but feel astonished at the diversities of opinion and the profound ignorance of all classes of the community concerning the fearful future so close at hand. The only persons who appeared to have any sort of realization of the situation were the extreme Southern men and their sympathizers, who knew precisely what they wanted and were resolved to have, but even they expected to attain their ends without war. The Republicans and indeed, the Northern people generally, could not be made to believe that there would be war, and treated any suggestion to that effect with scorn or ridicule. The Southern men were resolved on secession and a Southern Republic and had so little belief in the patriotism and courage of Northern people that they expected to accomplish their objects by mere threats or perhaps a few acts of violence, sufficient, as they thought, to overawe the North and commit the doubtful among their own people to their disloyal purpose. The latter they easily accomplished, but the effect of their violence in the North was precisely the opposite to what they expected. The attack on Fort Sumter was the one thing needed to compel the Northern people to see and to take to heart what they neither believed nor wished to believe. It was pitiful and to so-called pessimists, exasperating, to see the loyal people who had come in large numbers to witness the inauguration of President Lincoln, walking about the city and lounging about the halls of the hotels and public places, with an expression of assured confidence of peaceful issue out of the political storm such as had been so common theretofore; whilst the Southern men, full of a stern purpose, looked with scorn and contempt on what they thought the cowardice which prompted such groundless hopes. Between Mr. Lincoln's arrival and his inauguration a grave and dignified body of solemn old gentlemen, representing every state in the Union, were assembled every day in the chapel in rear of Willard's Hotel, devising and discussing measures for the pacification of the country and with bated breath and solemn mien exulting that they had come to an agreement on some slight modification of the fugitive slave law, or some equally slight concession on the question of state rights. If it had not been pitiful it would have been ludicrous to witness such stupendous imbecility and foolishness in the midst of such impending calamities.[31] To cap the climax of these absurdities, Mr. Buchanan,[32] then President, was proclaiming from the White House that whilst the Constitution did not sanction secession of any of the states from the Union, yet it contained no authority to coerce a state to stay in the Union; which piece of wisdom, of course, made everything clear and satisfactory. I suppose it would be hard to find in the world's annals any notice of such a carnival of absurdities as Washington City offered to the spectator in the early days of 1861.[33]

The first gun of Fort Sumter cleared away these fantastic shadows in a moment. The wild schemes, the vain hopes, the groundless theories, the determined blindness disappeared from the scene, and there stepped forth into the arena the champions of national unity and state sovereignty to do battle and to settle by its issue the questions between them which had vexed this people from the very foundation of their government.

In this conflict there never for a moment was a doubt where General Logan would be found. He returned promptly to Illinois, he raised a regiment and led it to the field early in the Summer, and had distinguished himself at Belmont, at Henry and Donelson, and at Shiloh, before I met him at Corinth, where he reminded me of our conversation in Judge Douglas's library scarce a year before. I do not propose here to write a biography of General Logan, nor even to recite the record of his military service. Both are full of interest and his military career especially illustrates what the war closed too soon to demonstrate completely, that the best school of generals is war and that whatever of value is found in the teachings of military schools is greatly modified by preconceived theories of war taught there which much interfere with the rapid acquirement of the lessons learned in actual campaign by the intelligent volunteer. Whilst a knowledge of tactics and the details of discipline and supply of troops by officers in the beginning is no doubt an advantage at the time, it is more than questionable whether theories of war in the abstract taught by men who never saw a battle or took part in a campaign and yet promulgated as a science as fixed as the laws of the Medes and Persians, does not much hamper the possession in the rapid observation and quick adaptation of the lessons daily taught in actual war.[34] It is quite certain that when the war closed the volunteer generals were coming rapidly to the front, and their capacity so fully recognized that if the war had lasted a year or two longer they might have been at the head of the armies. This subject is too large to be discussed in such a paper as this and even to touch on it lays one open to misunderstanding, if not worse, but it is worth careful examination and I hope one day to make my contribution to its literature.

Although Logan was very successful in civil life and made his mark upon the history of the country as a statesman, yet he was first and pre-eminently a soldier in instinct, in capacity and in inclination and if it be justifiable ever to regret the close of war it might perhaps be so in this case, merely to see the end of what no doubt would have been a remarkable military career. It seems unnecessary to describe Logan's personal appearance. His swarthy countenance, his fierce black eyes and long black hair, his erect martial figure and impetuous mien were known to all the armies with which he served and the representative bodies which he adorned.

Everyone, however, did not know the tenderness of his heart and the nobility of his soul. Free from envy or jealousy, he entered into whatever work was before him with perfect sincerity and with all his might. His animated face and his waving sword were seen in the front of every battle in which he was engaged, and his bold bearing and cheerful words brought encouragement and courage wherever they were seen on the line of battle. Although he was grievously wounded in feeling and greatly wronged in the opinion of the whole army by being superseded by Howard in command of the Army of the Tennessee after the death of McPherson and after he had led it to victory,[35] his patriotism and high sense of duty never flagged or weakened and he went on to the end the same loyal gentleman and efficient soldier he had been from the beginning.

When the time came that he might have profited by superseding Thomas at Nashville, as he was ordered to do, he stopped at Louisville, like the magnanimous soldier that he was and refused to go forward until Thomas had had his opportunity.[36]

In civil life afterward he regulated his conduct by the same high toned and generous rules, and dead though he is his memory is still a sacred possession of his countrymen. No man ever questioned his integrity or the purity of his motives, nor doubted his earnest faith in whatever he advocated. The only wealth he ever acquired by his services to his country in war or in peace was the wealth of regard and esteem poured out upon him by his countrymen and the cherished memories with which they still recall him.

An account of the conspicuous generals before Corinth and of those who afterward became distinguished, would be sadly deficient if it did not contain the name of General Don Carlos Buell,[37] who perhaps at that time was the most promising of all of them. He commanded a magnificent army corps, entitled the "Army of the Ohio," numbering not less than 40,000 men, which had been organized by him and disciplined under his own eye.

Certainly if a man's military capability is to be judged by his ability to organize troops and present them on the field of battle in the highest condition of discipline and effectiveness, General Buell may well be reckoned among the foremost generals of the war; but unfortunately the qualities and qualifications needed to accomplish this result do not imply, necessarily, or even probably, the requisites for a great commander in the field. The subsequent career of General Buell did not add to the reputation he took with him to Corinth and it is yet an open question whether his operations afterward at Nashville and the Battle of Perryville are to be charged to his own want of ability to command in the field, or to circumstances and interference adverse to him and beyond his control. Two opinions are held on the subject within the army he then commanded, but I should not myself even venture to suggest an opinion on the matter. There was a strong and growing feeling all over the country that he had been greatly wronged, and thereby a valuable officer removed from the service of his country, but this feeling was completely checked and its attendant sympathy for the man brought to a sudden end by a letter understood to be written by General Buell himself and published over his name.[38]

The letter was written subsequent to the Emancipation Proclamation of the President and took political grounds and expressed political opinions which absolutely prevented the Government from giving him high place and command. It was unfortunate for General Buell and perhaps also for the country, that he should have avowed such sentiments at such a time and I have always thought them rather the outcome of wrath for wrongs done him, influenced by his malevolent surroundings when he uttered them, than the calm expression of his deliberate opinions. To say that he "would not lend his hand to such an act as the emancipation of the slave" reads strangely these days and yet it is what he is represented to have said in the letter referred to. Certainly his sympathies were never given to the purposes of the Administration in power farther than was involved in a strong conviction that the union of the states should be maintained by arms if necessary. I never heard General Buell talk politics and I owe to others my belief of what his political opinions were and for what I know are still, but if the letter published over his name be really his, it relieves the Government at once from any reproach for leaving him unemployed.

When the armies were reorganized, with Grant in command, in 1864, he was desirous to order into service such of the general officers as were unemployed and had the capacity to do good service and Buell was accordingly ordered, or notified that he would be ordered, to report to General Sherman for duty with that army about to begin the Atlanta campaign. He declined to do so, giving as a reason that his commission was senior to Sherman's, and he could not serve under his junior in rank. This act terminated all attempts to give him a position and command in the field.[39]

General Buell graduated at West Point the year before I did and I was therefore three years at the Academy with him and saw him almost, if not quite, every day, though I had no personal acquaintance with him. He was from the beginning a man of note at West Point, not because of his intellectual capacity or his social qualities, but rather because of something in his appearance and bearing which indicated great force of character and prompt resolution. He was in no respect social in his habits, but appeared always to be self-absorbed. He was extremely reserved in his demeanor and very silent and reticent, if not at times forbidding, in his manners. I have myself, since I have known more of him, attributed his extreme reserve, bordering at times on haughtiness, more to painful diffidence than to natural coldness of temperament and I had several times, in my acquaintance with him, a sort of impression that he suffered quite as much as his victims from the effects of his frigid deportment. He was a student always. I do not mean a student in the college sense, but a steady and close reader of history and books on military subjects and was probably as well posted on military subjects as almost any officer in the army. He was a short, square man, with an immense physique and personal strength. He was very erect, had a dark, impressive face and black eyes and from something in his bearing and general appearance always gave the impression that he was a much taller and larger man than he really was. Naturally, a man so reserved and so reticent and who trusted in consequence almost entirely for his opinions of both men and things to the evolutions of his own internal consciousness, made mistakes of judgment in such matters which alike injured himself and others. I once crossed the plains with him from Fort Leavenworth, in Kansas, to Santa Fe, New Mexico in 1851 and had, of necessity, opportunities of seeing and knowing him which a lifetime in cities would not have furnished and I came to have the greatest respect and regard for him.[40] He was a man of tremendous passion, which he with evident difficulty kept under control, but his passions were of a generous and manly character and had no quality of vice or meanness. He was and I have no doubt still is, a man of the tenderest domestic life and affections, a pure, upright and most honorable man, capable of great things and the victim rather than the author of the misfortunes which overtook him. Whatever may be the public judgment as to his military character and career, he will always be greatly respected and honored for his high character and honorable life. Like most of the Old Army officers who were in the service before the war, he has not increased in worldly goods since he entered the army.

There were several other remarkable men on the Union side in that army before Corinth who, although they never reached the high station and command of those I have mentioned, became nevertheless men of scarcely less general reputation. Among these was General William Nelson,[41] whose tragic fate is no doubt well remembered to this day. He was killed by a pistol-shot fired by General Jeff C. Davis, of his own command, in the hall of the Galt House, in Louisville, Kentucky.[42] The only surprise felt by those who knew him was that some such fate had not befallen him some time before. He was the most tyrannical, arrogant and abusive officer to those junior to him in rank that I ever saw and would use toward any of them on the smallest provocation the most outrageous and insulting language. Indeed, he did not appear to make any effort to control his violent temper, except as it was held in check in the presence of his superiors in rank. It was impossible that he could have long avoided a violent end at the hands of some of the victims of his wrath. They had only borne his violence up to the time of his death because they were new to the military service and neither knew their own rights nor the extent of his lawful authority. He was, when appointed a brigadier general of volunteers, a lieutenant in the navy and was given a position in the army mainly because he was a Kentuckian of good family and it was supposed he would exercise good influence upon the distracted counsels of the state. He was a man of fine talents, had traveled much and seen much and had withal a fine conversational ability, which enabled him to talk of his experiences in a most interesting manner. He was a great reader, too and well versed in history and general literature and had that useful faculty, said to be the birthright of all Kentuckians, of creating the impression that he did not tell the half of what he really knew; a quality known in the state as the "gift of the gab." He was naturally an enthusiast and embraced the side of the Union with a kind of furious passion. He was in all respects except his ungovernable temper, a most competent and valuable officer and in organizing and disciplining new troops he had shown wonderful capacity and rendered excellent service. How he became afflicted with such a temper and became possessed of such a vocabulary of abuse and vituperation I cannot conceive.

His two brothers, whom I knew well, were gentlemen, gentle in manners and in character and as far removed as possible from the remotest resemblance in such matters to their brother. General Nelson was tall and erect, full of habit and with a broad, red face and lofty forehead. His eyes were constantly snapping with excitement and as the boys say, he seemed to "carry a chip constantly on his shoulder." If he could only have controlled his temper and measured his language to conform to any standard of courtesy whatever, he had the ability to have achieved and certainly would have commanded, high position and a distinguished name. He was in fact the victim of his own violent temper and abusive habits. He was greatly attached to his friends and had many of them, who sincerely mourned his untimely and unnecessary death.

Another remarkable man in that army was General Gordon Granger.[43] He was at first the colonel of the 2nd Michigan Cavalry, but during the operations around Corinth he was appointed brigadier general of volunteers. He was succeeded as colonel of that regiment by General P. H. Sheridan. Fortunately for the service, Governor Blair, of Michigan, was in our camp at the time that Granger vacated the colonelcy and was prevailed on to appoint Sheridan, then a captain on duty at Halleck's headquarters, to the vacancy. Granger was a man of brains and courage, but I think a coarser-grained man, both in looks and in manners, I never saw. I do not think that any amount of experience and association could have smoothed over his roughness, or even put the slightest varnish of refinement upon him. His broad, flat face, and rugged, angular features and an expression which he always wore on his face, half insolent and half familiar, indicated pretty clearly his character and disposition and did not endear him to those brought into relations with him. His manner was not only blunt to a degree, but well nigh intolerable to strangers. He was, however, a man of great force of character and of undoubted courage, a valuable soldier in battle and a good counselor in campaign. The trouble with him was, that he could not help severely criticizing, indeed abusing, those to whom he professed friendship and to whom he really seemed to be attached. His tongue wagged at both ends and from both issued little except vitriol. He could undo by his talk at night all the good work in battle he would do in the day.

He spared nobody in his talk—not always himself even. He did not seem to have, during the war, any convictions on the politics of the government and indeed I do not know that he ever did have any, except what he derived from a friendship and association which sprang up with President Andrew Johnson and of which Granger often boasted with a wealth of detail about their intimacy and confidential talks which often amazed his hearers, but scarcely ever commanded their unqualified belief.

His conduct at Chickamauga was very fine and will always be remembered to his honor. So far as action went he played his part manfully in the war and posterity will probably not permit his manners nor his loose methods of talking to weigh much in fixing his place in history.

There were many other officers in that army who became men of fame and station, whose association and friendship I am always glad to remember. Stanley, Hamilton, Palmer, McCook and T. J. Wood[44] were among them and it seems amazing that with such an army and such wealth of commanders we did not accomplish more in that campaign.

We had 100,000 brave men, commanded, as is well known, by as brave, as enterprising and as competent officers as ever drew a sword. We spent six weeks in overcoming twenty-five miles of distance, over which we met practically no resistance whatever. We threw up miles of earthworks against an enemy too feeble to attack us in the open field and when at last we entered his very imperfect intrenchments without a fight, we found nothing; absolutely nothing. Naturally the people of the North were greatly disappointed and displeased and probably to mollify even temporarily their extreme dissatisfaction, General Halleck, in accordance with his theory on the subject, sent to the Secretary of War a dispatch couched in somewhat ambiguous language, but intended to convey the impression that he had captured thousands of Beauregard's army and great stores of small arms.

It is true that he tried to saddle the responsibility of this report upon other shoulders,[45] but it was a pure invention of his own, for which he is entitled to all the credit. The country was fully justified in feeling great dissatisfaction and disgust at the result of our operations at Corinth. They seem, at any rate, to have caused General Halleck completely to distrust his own capacity to command an army in the field and deterred him afterward from attempting it again under circumstances and conditions which would have made it impossible for any soldier except himself to refrain from doing so. Every obligation of honor and of duty required him to assume the command in front of Washington in the Summer of 1862 and the only excuse that can possibly be made for his failure to do so with any hope that it may be accepted, is that he felt himself, after his experience at Corinth, incompetent to the command.

Chapter Eight

We Frittered Away Our Strength

$\mathcal{T}$he evacuation of Corinth, preceded by the capture of Henry, Donelson and Island No. Ten and the desperate but indecisive Battle of Shiloh, appears to terminate the first period of the war in the West. By this time the troops in the field had acquired steadiness and discipline and might fairly be considered seasoned soldiers. They had been so uniformly successful that they were in the best possible spirits and ready for any enterprise and capable of carrying almost any undertaking to a successful issue. In all possible respects the outlook in the West was favorable to the government. The natural course of military operations had brought about what ought, from the beginning, to have been the main object of the Union generals – a concentration of both armies at Corinth. The superiority of the North in men and means made it certain that they would be able to appear under such conditions with largely superior forces and better equipment. To bring the war to a speedy end with the least suffering and loss to communities, it was beyond anything desirable that both parties to the conflict should concentrate their whole military strength at one or two important points and there settle by the mode selected – the resort to arms – the relative power of the two sections and their earnestness in the purpose to reap the advantage which the exercise of that power might give them in securing the results for which they respectively appealed to arms. Such concentrations and the immediate and sensible use of them by the government, furnished the only rational hope that the war might be ended in a few months, with the least harm or suffering to peaceful communities of non-combatants, especially women and children. In the West these conditions were completely effected by the assembling at Corinth of nearly the entire forces of both parties serving in the West.

Never at any subsequent period of the war were the conditions for success more favorable to the government in the West than at the siege of Corinth. Missouri, Kentucky and Tennessee were practically cleared of the armed forces of the enemy and our large army was actually within the borders of the Gulf States, with nothing to oppose their movement south, except the insufficient force with which Beauregard had just evacuated his intrenchments before our advance. We controlled the navigation of the Tennessee River, through which supplies in unlimited quantities could be conveyed to us. Corinth was a center whence railroads diverged in every direction, offering every facility for a movement south, or indeed anywhere else. The morale of our army was excellent; that of the enemy, after such severe and repeated losses, was of necessity much less satisfactory. What, then, prevented an active campaign toward the Gulf and why was not the Confederacy cut in two and the Mississippi opened in 1862, as well as the former was done by Sherman with inferior force and greatly more formidable opposition in 1864?

Before undertaking to answer this question it will be well to recount what became of Halleck's great army of more than a hundred thousand men, brought together in northern Mississippi from so many successful fields of battle.

The course of military operations in the West had led to a concentration of the armies of both sides in and around Corinth. This was precisely the condition of things most favorable to the Union cause and General Halleck received much credit from thoughtful military men, in the belief that in his military plans he had had this object principally in view and had so directed the movements of troops in the West as to bring it about in the most advantageous manner and at the most favorable point to reap its full benefits in further operations. Heretofore we had scattered our forces all over the country and were carrying on perfectly fruitless hostilities at thousands of different and widely-separated places; in fact, wherever two or three of the enemy assembled together, there we were found with a greater or less force to do what could not in the least advance the war. The troops were so scattered about that they could not even help each other. They were located at various points of the sea coast, without force enough to advance into the interior or to accomplish any decisive results, or indeed to do anything except to exasperate the surrounding inhabitants.

Great numbers of regiments had been scattered about in Missouri and Kentucky, for no apparent purpose except to protect from their neighbors a few Union men who would not try to protect themselves. In short, we were thus frittering away our superior strength, so that it was not felt by the enemy and in consequence was underrated both by them and by ourselves. It would have been as wise to try to kill a strong man by sticking pins into him, or to cure cancer by treating the farther extremities, as to expect to subdue the South by the methods which guided such military operations. It was therefore plain that our sole effort in the beginning should have been to concentrate our forces at a very important point, where the enemy also must of necessity mass their forces to meet us and thus settle the issues of the war in the shortest time and with the least loss and suffering to the Southern communities, without embittering the two sections of the country against each other further than was actually unavoidable. Indeed, the reluctance to push the war vigorously in 1861 was largely due to the sentiment in the North, that there must be some compromise of our troubles before the grim realities of war need be resorted to. By the time, however, that we besieged Corinth all such hopes had been reluctantly abandoned and we were brought face to face with the necessity to fight it out by all the means and appliances of war, or give up our Federal Government and the union of the states.

Thus when we had realized and accepted this sorrowful conclusion, we found ourselves, in the West, in the best possible condition and position to prosecute vigorous and successful war. As it was believed at the time that this most advantageous position of our Western armies was deliberately brought about by the sagacity and military foresight of General Halleck, he was looked to for further results equally satisfactory. The outcome was painfully disappointing, and made it plain to everybody that the concentration of our armies at Corinth was the accident of circumstances and not the result of design and that Halleck had no plans whatever beyond the mere occupation of Corinth, forced on him by the Battle of Shiloh and the continued presence of an inferior enemy in his front.[1] The immense possibilities—indeed, I may say certainties—of success before him with his magnificent army and with scarce a ripple of opposition to be looked for anywhere in his front, he does not appear to have had the slightest conception of, and his only idea seemed to be to hold on to the territory he had occupied. It did not appear to have occurred to him that it was not to occupy territory in the South, but to beat their armies in the field, that should be our purpose and that, unless those armies were beaten or dispersed, the occupation of every village in the South would not end the war. It is unaccountable that a man of General Halleck's military training and acquirement and acknowledged ability, should have had so little conception of the situation, of its needs and its promises of great and speedy success. Why from so successful an aggressive [*sic*] and such power to continue it, he should have subsided in a defensive and so weak a defensive, must be traced to weakness of character and want of confidence in himself and not to want of military sagacity.

🎕 In fact, it must be charged to the fact, which probably Halleck recognized more clearly than any of those around him, that he was not a man of action, nor fitted to command in person an army engaged in active campaign. His experience at Corinth must have convinced him of this fact, if he had no suspicion of it before. His subsequent conduct in August, 1862, when he was General-in-Chief of the Army and the enemy advancing on Washington in heavy force, with two armies for its defense, one of which, with inferior forces, was fighting the enemy, whilst the other was being held back and purposely kept out of the battle for the defense of the capital by its general, demonstrated this fact clearly.[2]

This fatal treachery which kept one army idle whilst its comrades in another were engaged in bloody battle within their hearing in spite of orders and of ordinary human sympathy and manhood, occurred almost in sight of Halleck's office, where he sat during all those days of anguish without making an effort to join the armies he commanded and to use the authority, in person, demanded by these shameless proceedings. Neither persuasion nor shame could drive him out of his office to his proper place at the head of the armies and not the least surprising and humiliating spectacle of the many presented during those awful days was the sight of the General-in-Chief of the Armies of the United States shut up in an office which trembled and shook day after day with the roar of a battle upon the result of which hung the safety of the Capital and when he knew that the forces for its defense were torn with dissensions and incapable of harmonious action by reason of the personal hostility of the generals in command, which could only be remedied by the prompt presence and summary exercise of command by a common superior. It was a pitiable sight and yet it was, in my opinion, the logical result of what Halleck discovered concerning himself during his experience at Corinth, viz., that he did not possess the qualities to command armies engaged in battle.

Whether because of this reason or some other of which I have no knowledge, General Halleck, as soon as Beauregard's retreat south was fully confirmed, began to disperse the great army which had been brought together with so much difficulty at Corinth and in a very short time it was distributed in detachments of greater or less strength from Nashville and Bridgeport to Memphis, passing from the offensive to the defensive without the least necessity therefore and for reasons unintelligible to the uninitiated. Scattered along this long line and to many supposed important points in rear of it, this powerful army was so placed that it was weak everywhere and barely able to defend its position anywhere. The command of it was distributed among several generals and as a great army in the field, capable of forcing its way anywhere through the South and fully equipped in every respect to do it, it became a mere system of detachments. The western half of it, heavily reinforced by new troops, succeeded in the following year in capturing Vicksburg; but, with that exception, this great army never afterward accomplished anything, except a more or less successful defense of its positions, until it was again reunited under Grant at Chattanooga. Then and from that place it began that series of operations which carried it through Georgia and the Carolinas and brought it finally to Richmond and to Washington, after a long course of victories which might as well and certainly more easily, have been achieved two years sooner.

I cannot dismiss this brief sketch of the prominent army commanders on both sides who figured in the siege of Corinth without special mention of a personage who was with us during nearly the whole time and who although not a military man, was perhaps on the whole one of the most remarkable men present with that army. I refer to Colonel Thomas A. Scott who was at the time Assistant Secretary of War.[3] He had come West to see what was going on and what was the general outlook of military operations in the West. He was a railroad man, too, in high place and with great reputation in that profession and had also the mission to rearrange and make more efficient the railroad business in that region. After making a visit of a day or two to Commodore Foote on his flagship, he came to my headquarters at New Madrid a few days before the capture of Island No. Ten. He made his home with me for the following six weeks, crossed the Mississippi with the troops which captured the enemy's forces defending the place, went with us down the river to Fort Pillow and thence to Corinth and then stayed with us until clothes actually refused to stick to him any longer. Greatly to his regret he left our camp in front of Corinth to return to Washington only a few days before Beauregard evacuated the place. I could not have wished nor have had a pleasanter or more acceptable guest. He was a man of wonderful intelligence and quickness of perception, a keen observer and a most energetic and zealous participant in all that went on. He spent a good deal of his time on the picket-line and day or night, whenever any heavy firing was heard from the front, he was on his horse and off for the scene in a "jiffy." He was everywhere and saw everything and a more genuine, cheery, good humored friend and companion I never met.

He was universally popular in the army. He possessed in a marked degree the military "coup d'oeil," and would have made a successful soldier. Indeed, I know few things he would not have succeeded at, if it had fallen in his way.

He came to us unknown and left with the strong friendship of many of us and the regard of all.

He was short, almost squat, in figure, of dark complexion and abundant black hair and bright eyes and with a face so bright, animated and cheery, that it was good to look at it. He was as active and lithe as a cat and seemed to get on equally well with or without sleep or rest. He fell a victim, while yet in the prime of life, to the inexorable demon we call business and which put an end to his life by overwork.

Part Four

THE SECOND BULL RUN CAMPAIGN

Chapter Nine

Summoned East:
I Was Most Reluctant to Leave

A few days after the evacuation of Corinth, finding that there were to be no aggressive operations from our side for some time to come, I left for St. Louis on a short leave of absence to attend to some pressing private business, leaving the command of the Army of the Mississippi temporarily in the hands of General Rosecrans. It was in the month of June and the day I left my camp was exceedingly close and hot. The boat on which I embarked at Hamburg landed at Pittsburg Landing, a few miles below and remained there for several hours. I shall not soon forget that enforced delay. The river had fallen considerably and the perpendicular clay bluff was at least twenty-nine feet higher than the water. Against this clay bank the steamboat was landed and made fast. This point was in rear of and in close proximity to the field of battle of Shiloh and many of the dead, both men and animals, had been hastily buried there in shallow trenches immediately after the battle. The whole place on the summit of the bluffs was simply a mass of animal decomposition and several small streams of water, issuing from this mass, trickled down into the river immediately adjacent to the boat. In fact, all along the bank, above and below, these small streams of filth and corruption were oozing out of the bank and flowing sluggishly over it. The stench was dreadful and nearly overcame the passengers on the boat; though there were many persons roaming about over the ground in apparent unconcern. Probably they had been there long enough to become accustomed to the dreadful filth and smell. My strongest remembrance of that part of the country is the unpleasant two hours I spent at this place and the dismal recollections called up by these disgusting surroundings.

The day after my arrival in St. Louis I received a telegram from Mr. Stanton,[1] Secretary of War, requesting me to go at once to Washington. I replied that I was only on a short leave of absence from my command, and would be unable to go to Washington and return within the limits of time at my disposal.[2]

I telegraphed this invitation to General Halleck, who at once protested against my leaving that army; but the next day I received a telegraphic order from the Secretary of War to report in person at the War Department.[3] Of course I strongly suspected that there was some intention of placing me on duty in the East. I was most reluctant to leave an Army Corps which I had myself organized and successfully commanded up to that time and to which I was greatly attached and I especially disliked the idea of service in an army of which I knew nothing beyond the personnel of its chief commanders, some of whom I neither admired nor trusted.[4] The Secretary of War, however, was imperative, and I was compelled to undertake a duty hopeless of successful performance, except under the most favorable circumstances and the most genuine and zealous cooperation, both of which were conspicuously absent, as I strongly suspected would be the case at the time.

I reported in person to Mr. Stanton, the morning after my arrival in Washington.[5] Naturally I felt much curiosity to see a man who occupied so high a position and was so closely connected with my own profession, in the midst of a great civil war, on the fortunes of which he must of necessity exact a powerful influence for good or evil. He had already begun to impress himself upon the government and the country and was then very generally well spoken of. Indeed, an immense deal was expected of him — far more than any living man could possibly accomplish. When first I saw him he was on this top wave of public hope and encouragement and was quite conscious, I think, that the country would support him in any steps he might take toward a vigorous prosecution of the war. It was generally understood that he was in favor of active, aggressive war and would use all the power and influence of his great office in that direction. When I entered his office in the War Department, the room was uncomfortably full of people, talking or listening to him, or waiting to do both. I stood to one side for a few moments, looking at him with the greatest interest. He was in no sense an imposing person, either in looks or manner. He was below the medium stature, stout and clumsy. He had a broad, rather red face, well covered with a heavy black beard, which descended on his breast and was scarcely sprinkled with gray. He had a mass of long hair, pushed off toward the back of his head from a broad, massive brow and large, dark eyes, which looked even larger behind a pair of gold-rimmed spectacles, seemingly of unusual size. His rather squat figure, sur-mounted by the Iconine bust and head above it, gave him a shaggy, belliger-ent sort of look, which, to say the least, was not encouraging to the man in search of favors. His speech was quick and apparently positive. From the abrupt and speedy departure of one after another of his visitors, I presume it was conclusive also. His face and head were full of intellectual promise, which history fully confirmed. I discovered afterwards that this curt manner and quick disposal of business was equally bestowed on all comers regardless of rank, station, or "previous or present condition" of those concerned and that, in his office, the same sort of sauce was served to both goose and gan-der. No man can compute what was the value to the government, of this terse, not to say abrupt treatment of men and business by the Secretary of War in the times when Mr. Stanton held that office. No politician nor suave man of any description could have disposed of such a mass of business and such a crowd of people as pressed on the Secretary of War from morning until night and until far into the early hours of the next day, for months together. It was no doubt unpalatable to the great men, or rather those who thought them-selves great, to meet with only such scant ceremony in the War Department as was meted out to the humblest soldier, but there was not one of them pos-sessing even ordinary common sense who did not afterwards, if he did not then, recognize the immense value, in such a position, of a man positive and prompt even if, at times, he might be actually discourteous. The room in which he generally received people on business, for an hour or more every morning, was open all the time, so that anyone could enter who chose and hear also if he chose, any other man's business, too. This publicity of itself shortened conversations and abbreviated interviews wonderfully. The only furniture in the room was a high, slightly inclined table, behind which the Secretary stood, with a piece of paper before him and a pencil in his hand. Around the room stood his visitors, who stepped up one by one to this high table, stated his business as briefly as possible and in the hearing of every-body and received a prompt and final answer as rapidly as words could con-vey it. When matters requiring secrecy were to be considered—and these were only matters of public concern—the person conveying them stood to one side until the crowd was dismissed, when he was conducted into the Secretary's own office, for such disposition of the subject as might be necessary. Of course, such methods were not entirely agreeable to self-seekers or those in search of favors for others. Neither did they suit army contractors or men in search of office or of profit. Neither did they suit officers of the army who sought details for easy or pleasant service, or who came to complain of their superiors in rank who did not estimate them as highly as they valued themselves. The necessity of taking a whole room full of strangers into their confidence much abbreviated all such communications, and whilst the Secretary's popularity among these people and their followers was not successfully established by such methods, there is no doubt that the public interests were greatly subserved. When I first saw Mr. Stanton he was in the prime and vigor of his life. His ruddy complexion, stout figure and the general impression of vigorous vitality; his nervous action and manifest energy and force gave every assurance that he was possessed of almost unlimited capacity both in intellectual and physical work. A few years, if not a few months, greatly modified this condition. To a great degree Mr. Stanton lost his health in the first years of the war and one of the officers on duty nearest to him at that time, told me that he had seen him standing for hours attending to business in his office when he was suffering the tortures of the damned. He was afflicted with a disease not immediately dangerous to life, but full of pain, which sapped health and strength day by day.[6] His constant anxiety and increasing work were a direct aggravation of the disease, for which there was no relief except in complete rest and careful diet. No doubt much of his increasing irritability of manner and roughness of speech were due to pain and suffering. Nothing but death or the successful close of the war could have forced him to pause in his fury of work to give any thought to his own troubles. There never lived the man in this country more intensely loyal to his government nor who sacrificed himself more completely to the work of protecting it against the effort to destroy it.

I saw Mr. Stanton a good many times after my first interview with him, and came to know him very well. I saw him—indeed I spent part of the day with him—on that dismal day of the execution of Mrs. Surratt and the other conspirators, when the War Department was kept closed all day, except to public officials of high grade.[7] I remember his profound conviction, which he openly expressed, of the necessity of executing these condemned prisoners, and how painfully he realized that the obligation to the public welfare and future quiet of the country should absolutely debar the government from being either persuaded or terrorized into unwise or maudlin clemency.

No one who saw and talked with him that day could have failed to be impressed with his manifest regret that such a necessity existed. To say that he took satisfaction in the execution of these criminal people or that he was in any respect cruel or revengeful in the matter, is a mistake, if indeed it not be wicked.

The tremendous panorama in which he played so conspicuous a part broke him down at last and I shall not soon forget the painful impression which my last sight of him has left with me. It was only a short time before his death that, being in Washington for a few days, I called on him at his house. He was in his dressing-gown and slippers, but still, able to be about the house during the day. Bishop Simpson and another friend were with him.[8] He rose feebly and evidently with difficulty from his armchair to speak to me, but his appearance gave me such a shock that I was hardly able to reply to his greeting. His mass of hair and the great beard, so well remembered of all who knew him in former and not so remote days, was gray and unkempt, his cheeks had fallen in and the ruddy complexion transformed into pallor almost livid. The fire of his eye was quenched and his stout figure shrunken to a mere shadow. His clothes hung loosely upon him, and when he spoke it was not in the prompt and decisive tone of the past, but in the quavering voice and stumbling pronunciation of an aged man. Thus had the war of the rebellion served this once vigorous and powerful man and thus also did it serve thousands of his countrymen who survived the battles of that bloody time. It is often said by glib orators from the forum and the pulpit, who never saw the face of an enemy or suffered a pang during those bloody four years of strife that "the results of the war were worth all the sacrifices that were made" and perhaps such cool, unsympathetic speculations contain much truth for our posterity; but no man could experience in his own person the sorrows which the war brought upon thousands of families all over this country, or look upon one such wreck, mentally and physically as the war had made of Mr. Stanton when last I saw him, and then philosophize on the subject with such cool assurance.

Mr. Stanton was not worn out with the toils and exposures of campaigns nor shot to death by hostile bullets on the field of battle, but his life was as fiercely assailed and as completely wrecked by the assaults delivered by the hands of the enemies he had made in the defense of his country.

Of course when I first saw him none of these things were dreamed of or could have been foreseen. He was then at the beginning of a great and striking career, the very success of which conducted him directly to the death from which less zeal and energy and less devotion to his duty might easily have saved him.

To recur, however, to my narrative. After he had disposed of the people who had sought him, he came to where I was standing and saluted me with great kindness and cordiality and took me into his private room where we had half an hour's conversation. He asked me many questions about the condition of affairs in the West, and expressed some rather unfriendly or rather disparaging opinions of General Halleck, with whom he had some law business of an unpleasant character in California a few years before.[9] He was so intent, however, on business (as indeed I afterwards discovered that he always was) that he did not or could not talk of anything else and as he did not wish to inform me for what purpose I had been brought East until he had seen the President, who was expected back that evening from New York, he made an appointment with me for the next morning, when the subject of my coming to Washington should be taken up. It appeared that Mr. Lincoln had gone to New York the day before to consult General Scott about the military organizations and operations which it was intended to saddle on me.[10]

My return to the hotel was signalized by the visits of a considerable number of people, representing most of the occupations of Washington life—senators, members of Congress, and public officials of "low and high degree"—all of whom knew more about the war, how it should be carried on and who should command the armies, than I did. I think I received more suggestions and advice during that afternoon and evening at Willard's than in all my life together and the advice was, perhaps, the more valuable because it was given by people who had no knowledge of me whatever, nor of the business which brought me to Washington. As I was myself quite as ignorant as the least knowing one among them of the subject of my appearance at the Capital, I neither relished nor even appreciated the banquet of good advice and wise suggestions to which I sat down. The air of mystery worn by everyone, accompanied by the knowing look, which intimated how much could be told if it were wise to do so and especially the predominance of personal over public interests, which I could not avoid noticing and which was so different from my experience in the West, that it all left an unpleasant impression of intrigue and plots extremely disagreeable in itself and unpromising for the success of the cause. In fact, there was a sort of moral odor of sewer gas in the air, which left a bad taste in the mouth, from which even a good night's sleep did not altogether relieve me.

At an early hour next morning I was with Mr. Stanton in his private room in the War Department. He had seen the President the night before, after the latter's return from New York and was prepared to unfold to me the purposes of the government in the immediate future and the part I was expected to take in carrying them out. He gave a rapid and at times humorous account of the campaign against Stonewall Jackson, in which the armies of Generals McDowell, Banks, and Frémont had been engaged and at the conclusion of which Jackson was marching off, unharmed, to Richmond, whilst the three armies, brought from three points of the compass, were huddled up together between Waterloo Bridge and Middletown, in the Shenandoah Valley.[11] Although he did not admit it or even intimate anything of the kind, this was really a campaign conducted from Washington by the President and the Secretary of War, in which the generals played no part except to obey orders. It left matters no better certainly than they were before, except that the troops under Banks, Frémont and McDowell, which had been scattered widely and beyond any possibility of supporting each other, were brought by these movements sufficiently near together to be easily united and so far as their force went, made capable of effective work. Of course these troops, never having served together and having also been subjected to every different kind of service and very diverse modes of discipline, had ideas and ways as wide apart as their training had been and could not, without time and practice, be amalgamated into that compact and harmonious body essential to such work as it was intended to do. In his account of this comic campaign against Jackson, Mr. Stanton's humor did not spare the President or himself, much less any of the generals, who, as I have said, were entirely innocent of any responsibility for those operations. Mr. Stanton proceeded then to explain to me McClellan's projects against Richmond, the force at his command and what he had done, as well as failed to do.[12] Whilst he used no harsh language and indeed, indulged in no unkind criticisms, it was evident that he shared fully the discontent of the country at the slow movements, timid vacillation and ruinous delay which had characterized all of McClellan's operations. His wonderful capacity for multiplying the number of the opposing army and increasing the strength of its positions made all his estimates on that subject quite unreliable, and no plans of any kind could be judiciously made on such data. Whether these exaggerated estimates of the enemy's force, which we now know to have been ludicrously extravagant, were the cause or the excuse for his dilatory movements and timid action was for some time a question, but his autobiography has solved all doubts concerning him or his career and has left him in a position so pitiful and humiliating that his worst enemy would now be ashamed to assail him.[13]

Mr. Stanton made it clear without unfriendly criticism that the government had been greatly discontented with the lame results accomplished by the great army under McClellan's command and also that McClellan's personal and official conduct toward the authorities had taxed the President's forbearance to the last degree. He said enough—and it was his purpose, he told me, to do so—to enable me to realize the uncertainty of vigorous and harmonious co-operation of the various forces in front of Washington and on the Peninsula, unless the whole of the forces were turned over to the unrestrained control of McClellan, whose career had not justified quite so much confidence in him as such an arrangement would have implied. Naturally the safety of Washington from any open attack by even a part of the enemy's forces, was a subject of anxious consideration. McClellan maintained that there was no danger of an attack on Washington whilst he was in front of Richmond and therefore wanted all troops sent to him; though with the wonderful magnifying power of his imagination he always (in his own mind) endowed the enemy with larger reinforcements (in buckram) than the entire

North could possibly have supplied to the Union army.[14] But as was afterward (in 1864) completely demonstrated, when Richmond was much more closely invested by a larger army and a far more formidable commander, the enemy did really detach a large force from his army there, which marched on Washington and seriously threatened its capture.[15]

Mr. Stanton, after as full a description of the situation as was considered essential to anyone who was to undertake the work intended for me, informed me that it was the purpose to unite the forces of Banks, McDowell, and Frémont into one army and to assign me to the command of it.

The general object of this army was to cover the front of Washington against any open attack of the enemy and in addition to give such aid to McClellan, by forward movement or in any other manner which might appear to me wise, as would enable him to press his advance on Richmond. I was, however, to have in mind always the safety of the Capital and not to employ my forces at such a distance or in such a direction as would endanger this main object.[16] As I remained silent when he had concluded his statement, Mr. Stanton said, with some apparent irritation:

"General, you don't seem to approve the arrangements I have outlined to you."

I replied, "Mr. Secretary, I entirely concur in the wisdom of concentrating these widely-scattered forces in front of Washington and using them generally as you propose, but I do certainly not view with any favor the proposition to place me in command of them."

He appeared surprised and disappointed and said something to the effect that he had not expected me, from what he had heard of me, to decline so great a chance and so wide a field to serve the country and that my selection for such a position was an expression of the Government's confidence, which ought to be grateful to me.

I told him that I was gratified to learn of such kind sentiments toward me and that they were as flattering as they were unexpected, but that, from my point of view, there were grave objections to my assuming such duties and such as appeared to me insurmountable. He asked me to state them. I said, in the first place, each one of the three generals whose armies it is proposed to unite into one and place under my command is my senior in rank and would in that sense consider himself deprived of his rights and wounded in his honor by being placed under the command of his junior.[17] Of course, under such conditions, harmony and zealous service could hardly be looked for and such service as was rendered by these humiliated officials must, in the nature of things, be perfunctory; that more or less of these feelings would be disseminated among the troops of the command and more or less qualify their zeal and render more difficult their amalgamation into a harmonious body; that even under the best condition of feeling much more time than could possibly be accorded to me should be devoted to perfecting the organization and discipline so necessary to the effective performance of the dangerous service before it; that necessarily the officers in that Eastern army, who had organized and served with it from the beginning, would resent the imputation that they were all unfit for such a command and that it had been found necessary to bring an officer from another part of the country and another army to do the work which they were incompetent to do. In short, that I should be much in the situation of the strange dog, without even the right to run out of the village; that the duty required of me could not be successfully done or even attempted without well nigh certain disappointment and perhaps disaster, unless there was the utmost zeal and fidelity on the part of all concerned; that the proposed assignment of a stranger to the command would have precisely the effect to create the opposite condition. With such a force so constituted and with such a feeling on the part of all, I was expected to go down to or toward Richmond and seize and hold the bear by the tail, whilst McClellan beat out its brains. If he succeeded in killing the bear, which I very much doubted, I should be invested with the tail as my share of the transaction. If, on the other hand (as was altogether likely), he should fail, the bear would turn and rend me to pieces, as he could easily do. In short, in my view, I was offered the command of a forlorn hope under the most unfavorable conditions possible for success; and to enjoy this distinction I was to give up the command of an army in the West equally large, which I had organized and commanded myself from the beginning, to which I was greatly attached and which I knew cherished the same feeling for me, which had already done great things under my command and which was capable of still more distinguished achievements, with which I could not bear to be disconnected.

All this I explained fully to Mr. Stanton and asked him whether he could reasonably expect me to enthuse over the change he proposed for me. Mr. Stanton listened to this statement with attention, but with more or less impatience and dissent and when it was made he said that in such times personal feelings and interests should not and could not be permitted to obtrude themselves; that his own office was not only personally repugnant to him, but destructive of his personal interests, but that the welfare and success of the Government was, in those unhappy days, alone to be considered by every public official. I told him that I was ready, as I hoped I had always been, to make the sacrifice he demanded, but I begged him to consider that in this case my personal feelings and interests were inextricably interwoven with those of the Government and that in my own opinion both would best be served by my declining this assignment to command. He remained unconvinced, but said he would see the President again before coming to a decision.

I told him then that I would also see the President and briefly recapitulate to him what I said. I told him, however, that I wished it distinctly understood that however the matter might be decided I might safely be counted on to do my best with cheerfulness and zeal.

I accordingly called to see the President and had half an hour's conversation with him, which, perhaps, I may recount at some other time.[18] The Secretary of War also saw him during the day, and the result was communicated to me the next morning. It was decided, for reasons no doubt satisfactory to these high officials, though not to me, that I was to remain in the East and take command of the army to be created by the union of the three corps heretofore mentioned. The order of the President announcing the creation of the Army of Virginia, and assigning me to the command of it, was made the next day and I at once entered upon the work of attempting to do what, under the circumstances and conditions which surrounded it, no living man could have accomplished.[19] It is not necessary to repeat here that almost immediately after these transactions, began the series of battles on the Peninsula which attended the retreat of McClellan to the James River and the abandonment of all operations, except such as were necessary to avoid the absolute surrender of our army.[20] I was myself present when General Marcy,[21] who had been sent by McClellan from Harrison's Landing to formulate demands upon the War Department, intimated in plain terms to Mr. Stanton that unless the large reinforcements demanded by him were sent immediately to the James River, it might become necessary for McClellan to surrender his army to the enemy.[22] I remember, too, Mr. Stanton's look of astonishment and indignation when the idea of surrender was presented to him. "What is that you say, sir? Repeat your remark," Mr. Stanton burst forth, with furious gesture and glaring eyes. General Marcy, who, perhaps, had only made the statement about "surrender" as an additional club with which to beat the War Department into compliance with McClellan's wholly unreasonable and quite impossible demands, seemed confounded by the agitated manner and violent rage of the Secretary of War and began in a stumbling and confused way to explain that he did not quite mean that the army might surrender, but only to make clear how great was the necessity for more troops on the Peninsula and that matters there were not in a satisfactory condition, and could not be until McClellan's forces were largely increased. The very manifest attempt to browbeat the War Department into yielding to any demand of McClellan, reasonable or unreasonable and whether he was victorious or defeated or to shift the blame of his failure upon the shoulders of the President and Secretary because they were not able (as he well knew they were not) to supply his extravagant and indeed impossible demands, was extremely painful to me to realize and made still clearer to me the difficult and dangerous position I occupied in being forced even to save my own small army from destruction to depend upon the vigorous and faithful co-operation of a man so constituted and so devoured by personal ambition, which he had not the moral courage

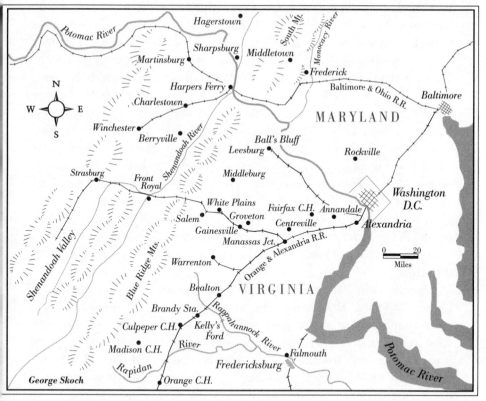

NORTHERN VIRGINIA IN 1862

to gratify and who only sought in others objects upon whom to saddle failures of which he seemed by nature to have had an instinctive anticipation before he took the field. One thing I was glad, in view of the future, to observe and that was that General Marcy left the Secretary's presence with much less appearance of confidence in his ability or McClellan's to dominate the War Department.

The three corps to constitute the Army of Virginia were at this time moving by my orders to a concentration on the east side of the Blue Ridge, at such points as would command the road to Gordonsville by the way of Madison Courthouse and Culpeper. Finding, after an honest letter and the very indefinite and unsatisfactory reply to it, that there was no hope of any effective co-operation of the Armies of the Potomac and Virginia so long as McClellan was a prominent factor in the operations to be undertaken,[23] and knowing well that without entire harmony and active and zealous efforts to the same end, there could be no hope of success, or, indeed, of escape from what might be serious disaster, I urged upon the President that in order to enforce such joint action of the two armies as absolute necessity demanded he should assign an officer as General-in-Chief of the Armies, who should have the power to enforce his orders and himself to command the two armies in the field in person as soon as a junction could be effected. General Halleck was consequently assigned to that position.[24] It had been determined to withdraw the Army of the Potomac from the Peninsula and unite it with the Army of Virginia in front of Washington, for reasons fully stated by Halleck, which it is not necessary to repeat here.[25] Mr. Stanton was greatly opposed to the assignment of Halleck to that position, and expressed himself with more force than elegance in opposition to it.[26] Yet Halleck, from his rank in the Regular Army and his high command, which embraced one-half of the country, seemed absolutely the proper person to select. After[ward] events proved the wisdom of the opposition of the Secretary of War and made manifest that Halleck's presence in Washington in such high authority[,] and his failure to take the field in front of that place in August and September of 1862, was a serious mistake and came well nigh to bring upon the Government a fatal catastrophe.

It is difficult to form a judgment upon the character of such a man, leading such a life, as Mr. Stanton. His official character and record challenge scrutiny and in greatness of deed, genuineness of purpose, unselfishness of conduct and effectiveness of action, his official career will compare favorably with that of the very best and purest patriot who ever laid down his life for his country. He was intensely loyal to the Union — in fact, passionately devoted to it — and spared neither himself nor others in the work of preserving it.

He wore out body and mind in the work and as much as freely gave his life to his country as any man who perished on the field of battle. Indeed, he died the hardest death of any, in that he was hounded to it by the malignant slanders of many men who should have been his supporters. In proportion to his success, which isolated him more and more every day from anything like intimate personal association with those who had been his companions in times past, was the bitterness of his enemies, who hated him for fancied wrongs, or it may be errors of judgment and who assailed his reputation without much regard to truth or any of the restraints which loyalty to the country and interest in the success of the war should have imposed. Those who would gladly have defended him were not sufficiently in his confidence to do so intelligently. Mr. Stanton had no time to spare from the tremendous pressure on him night and day to indulge in the personal associations and confidences necessary to the acquisition of such friends and he bore his burden alone and without even the knowledge of the sympathy felt for him by thousands of his countrymen. Except for minor errors of judgment and faults of manner, from which the fewest of mankind are free, Mr. Stanton's official character and his ability and devoted patriotism have had few parallels in the history of mankind and history more and more as time goes on will sanctify him in the hearts of our posterity.

During the war he may be said to have had no private life or friendly association outside of the business of his office, of which his mind was always full. It would puzzle anyone who did not know him before the days of the war to say anything understandingly of Mr. Stanton's personal character or social habits. He had absolutely no personal associations and attended to no social duties during all those days of the war. He appeared to have little inclination and no time for exhibitions of personal friendship and has, no doubt, justly been charged with neglect of those to whom he had once professed friendship and injustice to their rights and their interests.

Indeed, it is much to be feared that in his relations with individuals who, from their devotion to him and their supreme confidence in him, were entitled to the utmost fidelity on his part, there was a vein of duplicity in his conduct hard to reconcile with his official genuineness.

But whatever may have been the facts in such personal matters as these, Mr. Stanton will always be judged in the light of his public services and will always occupy a foremost place in the affection of and gratitude of his countrymen. When one contemplates at this day his splendid services, his unselfish patriotism, his singleness of devotion to his country, his sad and troubled life and his utter shipwreck at the last, in body and mind and contrasts his shrunken face and bowed and broken figure as he sat awaiting death, almost alone, in his darkened home, with the smug countenance and conceited air of the small specimen of humanity who was his bitterest enemy, but who never had an idea which reached beyond himself nor an emotion which concerned anything outside of his own cuticle, smiling and grimacing and followed about by a crowd of admirers, otherwise intelligent, but as blind to the weakness and bitterness of their idol as the African to his fetish, and thinks of the good natured acquiescence of thousands of good people in what he claims to have been his great services to his country, but who deny to Mr. Stanton a solitary word of commendation or even recognition; I say as one considers these things he cannot but echo the sentiment of the historian who summed up as the result of his great history that in considering the record it set forth the philosopher "according to his nature must laugh or weep at the folly of mankind."

Chapter Ten

The Battle of Cedar Mountain: Always a Source of Regret

In the January number of the *Century* magazine for 1886 will be found an account of the Second Battle of Bull Run.[1] It is prefaced by a very brief and incomplete sketch of the operations of the army under my command and transactions connected therewith which preceded that battle, but it contains no account of contemporaneous or subsequent occurrences in that army itself or at Alexandria and Washington, in the rear. Yet an acquaintance with these matters is quite essential to a fair comprehension and judgment of that campaign. It is my purpose in this paper to supply the information at least in part.

General George B. McClellan left behind him a sort of autobiography, which has been published and offered for sale by a presumedly judicious friend.[2] In that work the astounding information is given to the people of this country that President Lincoln and his Cabinet, as also some hundreds or thousands of hitherto respected people, were really traitorous conspirators against the government of the United States by secretly plotting for months the defeat of the Army of the Potomac and the destruction in battle of thousands of their fellow-citizens. There appears to have been no motive for all this attempted wickedness other than jealousy of General McClellan and envy of his superior wisdom and virtue.[3]

It would be idle at this late day to undertake to controvert statements, both direct and inferential, put forth on such authority and after twenty-five years of conscientious examination, no doubt of all the facts by the author, but as I am myself mentioned more or less honorably in this history, I venture to hope that I shall not be considered presumptuous should I devote a part of this paper to a simple recital of General McClellan's relations to the army under my command and the campaign in which it was engaged.[4]

My arrival in Washington in June 1862, under the orders of the War Department and my assignment to command the Army of Virginia by the President naturally occasioned dissatisfaction among a number of officers of high rank and no doubt a good deal of severe comment was indulged in. No one stopped to inquire whether it was by my own act or even wish that I came to Washington, or whether such a military arrangement was or was not satisfactory to me. I did not desire a transfer.

It is hardly necessary for me to repeat here that my transfer to the East was greatly against my wishes and that I tried as far as I was able to avoid duty near Washington, both before and after I arrived there. Above all things, I objected to being taken from the command of one of the finest army corps in the West, which I had organized and served with from the beginning, and to which I was bound by continuous success and by strong personal attachment.

Indeed every consideration of feeling and of hope impelled me not to separate from such a command and especially not to leave it for such service as was forced upon me in front of Washington. If there were any means which could have been properly used to avoid that service which I did not employ I know not what they were. It was all of no effect. The government commanded my service and it was rendered to the best of my ability.

The officers most directly affected by this action of the President were Generals Frémont, Banks and McDowell, who commanded respectively the three army corps which were consolidated into the "Army of Virginia." All of these generals were my seniors in date of commission and McDowell always had been my senior. Naturally they were not pleased with an arrangement which deprived them of independent commands and which subordinated them to their junior in rank. General Frémont asked to be relieved from his command because of this feeling and was so relieved.[5] Generals Banks and McDowell retained the command of their respective corps and served through the subsequent campaign with entire good faith and good feeling. It was on General McDowell's recommendation that Congress only just before passed an act authorizing the President to assign officers of the same grade to command, regardless of the date of commission and he unfortunately was one of the very first victims of the law. He accepted it in the best spirit and performed his whole duty as became a soldier and a patriot.

General Sigel was assigned by the President to command General Frémont's Corps when he left it.[6] McDowell's Corps was divided, King's Division being posted at Fredericksburg and Rickett's Division at Manassas Junction.[7] Both were in excellent condition both as to discipline and supplies. Banks and Frémont were at Middleton, in the Shenandoah Valley. Neither Corps was well supplied and Frémont's was in especially bad condition in every respect.

The following is Sigel's report of it when he took command:

> Middletown, July 5, 1862.
>
> Col. Ruggles, Chief of Staff to Gen. Pope: In reply to your inquiries I have to say that my transfer from a division which I had just succeeded in organizing, equipping and making effective, to the command of the First Army Corps (Frémont's), which I found to be in a very bad condition in regard to discipline, organization, construction of divisions and brigades, equipments, and to a great extent demoralized, has imposed severe labor upon me. In addition to this I have been greatly inconvenienced by the removal of all papers and documents by Gen. Frémont, so that I have had to learn everything by direct inquiries and inspections, etc.
>
> (Signed)
>
> F. Sigel, Major General[8]

I insert this portion of General Sigel's telegram because General Frémont, in reply to my statement of the condition of his corps at the time, published a letter in the New York *Tribune* denying the facts and asserting that General Sigel's dispatches to me did not justify my statement. My statement was literally as follows, as it will be found in my official report, viz: "Many of the brigades and divisions (Army of Virginia) were badly organized and in a demoralized condition. This was particularly the case with the army corps of Major General Frémont, a bad report of which was made to me by General Sigel when he relieved General Frémont in command of the corps." Whether the foregoing telegram from General Sigel justifies this statement the reader can determine for himself. Frémont's Corps numbered 11,500 men of all arms, Banks's Corps 8,000, and McDowell's 18,500; that is, this was the strength of these army corps on paper and on paper also, the Army of Virginia thus numbered 38,000 men.[9] This force was scattered over the country from Middletown, on the Shenandoah, to Fredericksburg, near the mouth of the Rappahannock[10] and no inconsiderable portion of it was employed in small detachments guarding private houses. These small parties were picked up and carried off as prisoners occasionally by parties of the enemy guided by some of the members of the family whose property and persons our small detachments had been posted to protect.[11] King's Division of McDowell's Corps was by the wish of the Government retained at Fredericksburg, where it was much out of position and was the occasion of constant uneasiness. It was too far separated from other parts of the army either to help or be helped. The enemy had withdrawn, at this time, all his forces from the Shenandoah and concentrated them around Richmond, so that there was no enemy in any force between Richmond and the army which I had been assigned to command.

On the twenty-seventh of June I assumed the command by an order issued in Washington and at once directed the construction within supporting distance of each other of the three corps which constituted the Army of Virginia.[12] Banks and Sigel were ordered to move forward and cross the Shenandoah at Front Royal; the former to take post at Sperryville bypassing the Blue Ridge by Thornton or Luray Gap; the latter to march direct on Little Washington. Rickett's Division of McDowell's Corps moved forward to the crossing of the Rappahannock at Waterloo Bridge, so that all the divisions of the Army of Virginia were to be well in hand, except King's Division, which was as heretofore stated, entirely out of position and kept there by the order of the Government. Whilst the movements of these three corps to the points of concentration were in progress, began the series of battles which preceded and attended the retreat of General McClellan from the Chickahominy to Harrison's Landing.[13] Before the enemy began the attack, thus promptly met by retreat, General McClellan's army had been straddled across the Chickahominy, with its left on the south side of that stream and not more than seven or eight miles from Richmond. The enemy marched out from Richmond with nearly his whole force, crossed the Chickahominy far above McClellan's bridges and assailed his extreme right, leaving nothing of any sort of effectiveness to defend their Capital, and by their movement actually placing McClellan between themselves and Richmond, so that by simply transferring his army to the south side of the Chickahominy and destroying the bridges behind him, he could have marched into Richmond in two hours without encountering serious opposition.[14] That the enemy with their much inferior force, should have made such a movement, with such extremely probable consequences in plain view, indicates a supreme confidence in General McClellan's want of enterprise, which unhappily was amply justified by results. When General McClellan first began to suggest retreat to the James River at the beginning of the attack on his right, I urged upon the President that he forbid such a movement and that he send orders to General McClellan that if he could not hold his ground, he direct his retreat toward Hanover Court-house, but under no circumstances to go farther south than the White House, on the Pamunkey River; that if he did the whole army of the enemy would be interposed between him and any reinforcements that could be sent him from the direction of the Rappahannock and would give the enemy the privilege to exchange Richmond for Washington, an exchange of the last consequence to the Government.[15] The military reasons against this retreat to the James River under such circumstances are sufficiently strong and numerous and are amply sustained by subsequent events. The enemy actually did make the choice between Richmond and Washington. General McClellan was ordered to bring back his army from Harrison's Landing by water to Fredericksburg and Alexandria, but before the first of his divisions had broken up their camps for this purpose (August 14th) Stonewall Jackson and J. E. B. Stuart had reached the Rapidan and fought with my command the Battle of Cedar Mountain and on the thirteenth of August Longstreet left the front of Rich-mond and on the fifteenth joined Jackson at Gordonsville, to which place the latter had fallen back from Cedar Mountain. General Lee assumed the com-mand at Gordonsville in person on the fifteenth of August, when General McClellan's First Division had only just completed its first day's march toward Fortress Monroe,[16] where it was to take shipping for Alexandria. The army of General Lee moved at once against the army under my command and through it against Washington.

General McClellan, however, continued his retreat to Harrison's Landing, the President being unwilling to give him orders to the contrary under the circumstances, a distinction which was shown once or twice afterward, much to the disadvantage of the army and the country. After General McClellan had intrenched himself at Harrison's Landing, against an inferior force of the enemy, I addressed him a letter giving in detail the force under my command and its position, together with the orders under which I was acting and the purposes I had had in view;[17] but at the same time offering to abandon them all for any movement or disposition of my small army which he might think best calculated to relieve his position or facilitate further operations against Richmond, bearing in mind only that I was charged with the safety of Wash-ington, which except for my command was open to the enemy's advance.

To this letter I received a reply from him very vague and general in its terms and proposing nothing whatever in the direction I had suggested.[18] It appeared useless, therefore, to look in that direction for either ideas or acts; but as the withdrawal of that army from Harrison's Landing and its junction with mine either along the Rappahannock or in front of Washington had been determined on by the government and as I felt sure a union of the two armies would never be willingly executed unless General McClellan was assured that he should have the chief command, I thought it my duty to advise that as the junction of these two armies was essential to success, if not indeed to safety and as I did not believe it was likely to be effected under present military conditions, some officer be assigned to the command-in-chief of the army over both General McClellan and myself, so that the necessary action for the purpose could be compelled.

Accordingly General Halleck was called to Washington and assigned as General in Chief of the Army. As matters turned out he was perhaps not the best choice that could have been made, but his position and years seemed to point him out as the most suitable person.

When I was first assigned to command the Army of Virginia, the Army of the Potomac occupied its positions on both sides of the Chickahominy, whence General McClellan was reporting the great hordes of the enemy who closed the road to Richmond against him and even threatened the existence of his army. One of his estimates gives the rebel army in front of Richmond at 200,000 men.[19] It was the purpose that with the small force under my command (about 38,000 men all told), I should demonstrate upon Gordonsville and Charlottesville and even upon Lynchburg, so as to draw off as much of the gigantic army under Lee (which nobody except General McClellan believed in) as I could and thus far, at least, aid the Army of the Potomac in the hoped-for capture of Richmond. The six days' battles and retreats, however, quite upset any prospects of this kind and necessitated immediate steps to cover the front of Washington now open to the enemy, except in so far as my small army could cover it.

It was determined therefore, that my army should advance to the Rappahannock on the Orange & Alexandria Railroad and farther south still, to threaten Gordonsville and Charlottesville in case the enemy did not come north of his own volition and thus relieve the Army of the Potomac, so that it could evacuate Harrison's Landing and embark for Alexandria and Acquia Creek without fear of attack. General Halleck decided, against my own judgment plainly expressed to him, that the junction of the two armies could be made along the line of the Rappahannock.

I said to him that I believed that Lee would move rapidly north with the bulk of his command and could easily reach the Rappahannock before any of the Army of the Potomac could do so and that we should be taken in detail. I therefore considered the line of the Rappahannock too far to the front. He persisted, and I said no more. It was my purpose so to post my command that if the enemy advanced with much larger force against me I could withdraw into the passes of the Blue Ridge, where, by taking up a strong position, I could maintain myself against superior forces and gain time for the Army of the Potomac to reach Alexandria or Acquia Creek; or, if the enemy should march on Washington I should be on their flank and rear and thus render such a movement extremely hazardous. General Halleck, however, insisted upon my keeping close connection with Acquia Creek, so as to cover the movement of the troops of the Army of the Potomac to join me from that place. All of these facts will be found in the report of the Committee on the Conduct of the War for 1862. I was called before the committee and set forth these facts and purposes and the forces to accomplish them, on the 8th of July, 1862, three weeks before I joined the army in the field.[20]

On the 28th of July, 1862, the day before I left Washington to join the Army of Virginia, the military situation may be thus stated: McClellan with the Army of the Potomac was intrenched at Harrison's Landing, on the James River and was loudly calling for reinforcements of over rather than under 100,000 men, to protect himself from, or further to operate against the 200,000 men in "buckram" whom he had generously bestowed on General Lee, who was in front of Richmond with less than half of that force. Stonewall Jackson, with his corps, was at Gordonsville and between there and the Rapidan, J. E. B. Stuart with his cavalry corps, was in observation of our forces at Fredericksburg.[21]

The Army of Virginia (my own command) was concentrated (except King's Division) at Sperryville, Little Washington and Waterloo Bridge. On the morning of the twenty-ninth of July I left Washington to join the command. Perhaps few men have ever been richer in treasures of advice, warnings, encouragements and assurances than I was when I crossed the Potomac to assume a command and undertake military operations distasteful to me and unpromising to the last degree. The weather had been extremely warm for several weeks, and I shall not soon forget the delightful change which the first breeze from the mountains brought with it. We passed the night at Warrenton, where from the upper windows of a female school,[22] then vacant, I caught my first view of the Blue Ridge. The moon was nearly full that night, the air came soft and cool from the not distant hills and there was a deep silence and quiet upon the whole scene. A more lovely landscape or a more charming country the eye of man has not looked on and the remembrances of that scene under the bright moonlight will always be a delight to me.

The next morning early we mounted and set off for Waterloo Bridge, where Rickett's Division, of McDowell's Corps, was encamped.

A view of the country and of the Blue Ridge during that and many successive days served to strengthen the impressions of the night before. The intense blue of the skies melting away into more subdued coloring of the same tint along the not distant ridges of the range; the gently uneven country, with occasional abrupt hills of no great altitude, covered with forest trees and the rapid, winding mountain streams, with solitary mansions and occasional old-fashioned villages scattered without apparent effort here and there over the country, made a landscape that I cannot think of even to this day without keen pleasure. In nothing was the manhood of Virginia (and the supremest manhood of the South shone forth in that most chivalric state) more admirably exhibited than in the resolute and uncomplaining fortitude with which they saw this beautiful region trampled into mire by hostile armies and those ancient homes and lovely villages consigned to ruin. In no part of this broad land have the courage and pluck of its people shone forth with more luster than in the Old Dominion during the late war, but God grant that never shall there arise another occasion again to test it in such a manner! Wrong no doubt they were in assenting to the attempt to break up the union of these states, but they paid the penalty—and a penalty far heavier than was inflicted on any other state—with dignity and without complaint.

Its geographical position made it plain to all the world that Virginia must bear the heat and burden of the war and it certainly is unfortunate that her example during the war and after the war was not that closely followed by the other states of the South.

To keep the troops of King's Division from lying in idleness at Fredericksburg and also to keep informed of any movements of the enemy on a large scale from Richmond toward the north, I instructed King to send detachments of cavalry to operate on the line of the Virginia Central Railroad and as far as was possible to interrupt or destroy communications between Richmond and the Shenandoah Valley. Several cavalry expeditions which he dispatched for that purpose were very successful and broke up the railroad at several places and on several occasions.[23] At the same time I directed General Banks to send forward a brigade of infantry and all of his cavalry, to march rapidly upon Culpeper Courthouse and after taking possession of that place to push forward some cavalry on observation toward the Rapidan.[24] On the fourteenth of July, after this movement had been successfully accomplished, I requested him to send the whole of his cavalry that night from Culpeper to Gordonsville by forced marches and to destroy the railroad for ten or fifteen miles east of that place with part of his force, whilst the remainder of the force should push on toward Charlottesville, destroying railroad bridges and breaking up communications as far as possible. At that time there was no force of the enemy of any account at Gordonsville or in the vicinity and the movement, as ordered, was quite practicable and might have worked serious inconvenience to the enemy; but to my surprise and dissatisfaction I learned by dispatch from General Banks on the seventeenth that the officer in command of the expedition had taken infantry, artillery and wagons with him and because of bad roads he had only succeeded on the seventeenth in getting as far on the way as Madison Courthouse.[25] Meantime on the sixteenth the advance of Jackson had reached Gordonsville and the movement was no longer practicable.[26]

Having completed necessary preparations I ordered Ricketts's Division to march on the sixth of August from Waterloo Bridge to Culpeper Courthouse and Banks to move forward toward Culpeper to where the Hazel River is crossed by the pike from Sperryville to Culpeper, so that the whole force under my immediate command (except some of the cavalry) was on the seventh along that pike and in close relation with each other and numbered 28,000 men on paper. King's Division remained at Fredericksburg. The cavalry forces covering the front of the army on that day were distributed as follows: General John Buford,[27] with five regiments, was posted at Madison Courthouse, with his pickets along the Rapidan from Barnett's Ford to the Blue Ridge. Sigel had been directed to post a brigade of infantry and a battery of artillery at the point where the road from Madison Courthouse to Sperryville crosses Robinson's River[28] as a support to Buford. General Bayard,[29] with four regiments of cavalry, was posted at Rapidan Station, at the point where the Orange & Alexandria Railroad crosses the river, with his pickets extending from Raccoon Ford on the east to a connection with Buford at Barnett's Ford. From Raccoon Ford to the forks of the Rappahannock above Falmouth the Rapidan was lined with cavalry pickets. On the top of Thoroughfare Mountain about half way between Bayard and Buford was established a signal station which overlooked the whole country as far south as Orange Courthouse. Thus we were prepared to know and to meet the expected movement of the enemy, which had already begun.

On the seventh of August I went to Sperryville and inspected the corps of General Sigel.[30] During the day I received reports that the enemy was crossing the Rapidan at several places between the railroad crossing and Liberty Mills and at 4 o'clock I started with my staff and escort for Culpeper Courthouse. Crawford's[31] Brigade of Banks's Corps had been there for several weeks and on the seventh of August had been joined by Ricketts's Division from Waterloo Bridge. I arrived at Culpeper on the morning of the eighth and during the whole morning I continued to receive reports from General Bayard, who was slowly falling back from the Rapidan in the direction of Culpeper before the advance of the enemy; and from General Buford, who also reported the enemy advancing in heavy force on his position at Madison Courthouse. My orders obliged me, as heretofore stated, to keep my communications with Fredericksburg perfectly secure, in order that there might be no obstacle to the free movements of the divisions of the Army of the Potomac to join me from Acquia Creek, where the troops which had left the Peninsula first debarked. These orders were a constant embarrassment and constraint to me and placed me much in the position of a man with one leg tied to a post, fighting with another free to move in every direction.

I had nothing like force sufficient to contend in the open field against any considerable portion of Lee's army and my plan, as heretofore stated, was to draw back against the Blue Ridge and occupy a strong position so as to compel the enemy to attack me in it, or by moving off toward Washington, to have me on his flank and rear. The advance on Bayard from Rapidan Railroad Station directly threatened our communications with Fredericksburg and that had to be met at once and effectively. I accordingly sent forward Crawford's Brigade of Banks's Corps toward Slaughter or Cedar Mountain early in the day, to support Bayard, who was falling back in that direction and to assist him as far as he could in determining the strength and the movements of the enemy. In view of my enforced relations with Fredericksburg and to make sure that they would not be broken up, I considered it necessary to give up my opinions and wishes and concentrate my whole army in the direction of Culpeper, so as thoroughly to cover the lower fords of the Rappahannock.

I sent orders to Banks to move forward at once from Hazel River to Culpeper Courthouse and at the same time sent the same order to Sigel at Sperryville. To my surprise I received after dark a note from Sigel, dated at Sperryville at 6:50 the same afternoon, acknowledging the receipt of this order, but asking, before he moved, to be informed by which road he should march. As there was but one road between Sperryville and Culpeper and that a broad turnpike, I was altogether at a loss to understand how there could be any such question on the subject.[32]

This unexplained and wholly absurd question, however, delayed for many hours the arrival of Sigel's Corps and proved of serious injury to the subsequent operations.[33] Early the next morning (August 9) I directed General Banks to move forward toward Cedar Mountain with his whole Corps to the position occupied by Crawford's Brigade, of his Corps, which had been sent to the front the day previous. I directed General Banks to take up a strong position at or near the point occupied by that brigade, for the purpose of checking the enemy's advance and determining his force and the character of his movements.[34] The consolidated report of General Banks's Corps received some days previously, exhibited an effective force of something over 14,000 men. It appeared subsequently, however, that he only led forward about 8,000 men; but although I several times called General Banks's attention to the discrepancy between the forces set forth in his report and those he took to the front (as he afterward stated to me), he never was able to explain, nor could I ever comprehend how he could ever have made such a mistake, if mistake it was.

When he left Culpeper Courthouse to go to the front, I instructed him that if the enemy advanced to attack him in the strong position he was ordered to take up, he should push his skirmishers well to the front and anticipate by attacking with them and notify me immediately of the situation. I was so anxious that there should be no misunderstanding in carrying out these orders that I sent General B. S. Roberts an officer of the Old Army, who was acting Inspector-General,[35] to report to General Banks and see that he thoroughly comprehended and as far as his (General Roberts's) advice went, executed them. It was not at that time quite clear whether the main forces of the enemy would move against us by way of Cedar Mountain or Madison Courthouse and Ricketts's Division of McDowell's Corps was posted three miles in rear of Banks's position and at the junction of the wagon road from Madison Courthouse and Rapidan Station to Culpeper, so as to be in the right place in either case. General Buford had reported that the enemy was advancing on his position at Madison Courthouse and early in the morning of the ninth he informed me that the enemy was in heavy force on his right, his left and partly in his rear and that he was falling back toward Sperryville.

General Sigel began to march into Culpeper late in the afternoon (August 9) having been delayed many hours by Sigel's strange uncertainty about the road he should take. I had given specific orders a number of days before that all of the troops belonging to the Army of Virginia should be ready to march at short notice and for that purpose should keep two days' cooked rations habitually in their haversacks.[36]

Notwithstanding this cautionary order, Sigel's Corps arrived in Culpeper without rations and their provision trains being considerably behind they were without food. Instead of going forward at once to reinforce Banks, as ordered, it became necessary to issue rations to them from McDowell's trains and give them time to cook and eat a meal and thereby occasion delay which worked serious injury to the troops of General Banks at the front.

Desultory firing had been kept up all day in the direction of General Banks's position, but I continued during the whole of the day to receive reports from General Banks that no considerable force of the enemy had yet come forward; that his cavalry had been ostentatiously displayed, but he did not believe him to be in any sufficient force to make an attack. As late as five o'clock in the afternoon he wrote me substantially to the same effect, but before I received this last note the artillery firing had become so rapid and continuous that I felt sure a severe engagement was going on or was being brought on.[37] I therefore instructed McDowell to lead Ricketts's Division rapidly to the front and preceded it myself. At no time during the day did General Banks express any apprehension of an attack in force by the enemy, nor did he ask for reinforcements or intimate that he needed them.

I have always regretted that General Banks thought it best to depart from my instructions and to push a battle before the troops necessary to win it could be brought to the field, but I have never failed to bear my testimony to his intrepid conduct during the Battle of Cedar Mountain, nor to his patriotic and loyal deportment throughout the campaign.[38] His corps, however, was badly cut up in that battle, as will be seen from what follows and it was always a source of regret that so much gallantry as was there displayed by that corps served directly to keep it from the front for many weeks afterward.

As has been hitherto recounted, Crawford's Brigade of Banks's Corps had been sent to take up a strong position five or six miles south of Culpeper Courthouse to support Bayard's cavalry, slowly falling back from Rapidan Station before the advance of the enemy.

On the morning of August ninth, General Banks was ordered to move forward his corps toward Cedar Mountain and take up a strong position at or near that occupied by Crawford's Brigade, of his corps.[39] My purpose was to reinforce him by Sigel's whole corps during the day, keeping Ricketts's Division, of McDowell's Corps, as a reserve at the junction of the roads from Madison Courthouse and Rapidan Station to Culpeper and about three miles south of that place, until it was certainly known on which road the strongest advance of the enemy would be made. Any advance of the enemy in sufficient force to assault a whole corps occupying a strong position would make it plain that the main force of the enemy was in his front. I directed General Banks, in case a strong attack was threatened upon him, to push his skirmishers well to the front and attack with them notifying me at once of the fact.

The object I had in view was to gain all possible time, in case of an advance of the enemy in heavy force on that road; to bring forward Sigel as well as Ricketts to the front before General Banks could be dislodged from the strong position he was ordered to take up. To render a misunderstanding of my order and intention unlikely, I sent General B. S. Roberts to report to General Banks, to repeat my orders to him and to remain with him until I arrived in person at the front. I explained fully to General Roberts my purpose in giving the order to General Banks and directed him, as far as he could by advice and suggestion, to deter General Banks from making any departure from my order.

General Roberts afterward reported to me that he had freely conferred with General Banks and had urgently represented to him my wishes and purposes, but that General Banks, contrary to his urgent entreaties and against my orders, had left the strong position which he occupied and had advanced two miles to the front to attack the enemy as soon as that enemy appeared in sight.[40]

I have never been able to believe that General Banks misunderstood my orders and wishes in this matter. They were made perfectly clear to him through every possible precaution and I think it would be hard for him or anyone else to explain what possible object there could have been in ordering him so positively to take up a "strong position" if he was to leave it and advance against the enemy as soon as he appeared.

I have always attributed General Banks's departure from his instructions and his advance against the enemy, first to the fact that the enemy was Stonewall Jackson, with whom he had had some unpleasant experiences in the Shenandoah Valley;[41] and second that he did not believe the enemy to be in much force (as indicated in his dispatches) and he would be easily able to win a success before the rest of the army should come up. General Banks was a most intrepid and loyal soldier and whilst I have ever sympathized with the sentiment that induced him to make his unwise movement against Jackson on that day, I nevertheless stated then as I do now that it was a violation of my orders to him, which had the unfortunate sequel of breaking his command so nearly to pieces that it took no foremost part in the campaign afterward. Too much, however, cannot be said in commendation of the troops under his command in the brief but bloody fight known to history as the Battle of Cedar Mountain. That command advanced against superior forces of the enemy, strongly posted and sheltered by woods and ridges, over open ground, everywhere swept by the fire of the enemy concealed in woods and ravines. Notwithstanding such disadvantages, his troops advanced with unshaken intrepidity and assaulted the enemy with great fury and determination.

The action lasted an hour and a half and during that time our forces suffered very heavy losses in killed and wounded.[42] In that fatal attack perished some of the best and bravest youth of New England. Their places it was not possible to supply and their sacrifice was not made the less sorrowful by any sufficient advantage to the cause for which they laid down their lives. As an example of courage and devotion under manifest discouragement, the action of this corps will always be admired and cherished and if there be anyone who has mourned more sincerely and grievously than I over the loss of these gallant and most loyal youth, I know not who he is.

Desultory artillery firing had been going on all day of the ninth in the direction of Crawford's position and was kept up after the rest of Banks's Corps had joined him, but I continued to receive all day reports from General Banks that no considerable force of the enemy had appeared in his front and that there were no signs of an attack on his position. As late as five o'clock in the afternoon he wrote me substantially to the same effect, but before this note was received the artillery firing had become so rapid and continuous that I feared he had been attacked and that a severe fight was going on or being brought on. Sigel not being ready to move to the front, I directed McDowell to push Ricketts's Division rapidly to the field and accompanied it myself, first giving positive orders to Sigel to come to the front with the least practicable delay. At no time did General Banks ask or suggest reinforcements, nor even intimate that they were desired. I arrived on the field with Ricketts's Division just at dusk. The firing had nearly ceased, and when I met General Banks in the open ground north of the woods where the fight had taken place, he informed me that his line of battle was just in our front, extending from an elevated point in the woods considerably to the right of us across an open field to the woods on our front and thence following the woods to the extreme left, which he indicated as being some hundreds of yards farther to the left. The main road to Rapidan Station, passing along the western base of Cedar Mountain, intersected the line of battle that General Banks pointed out as nearly exactly in the center of his line. I rode down the road at once, as it was growing dark, to a knoll about seventy-five yards north of where the road entered the woods occupied, as Banks told me, by his line of battle. I told him that I thought his line of battle, according to the right and left of it as he pointed them out, was too much extended and directed him to draw in his right and mass it on his center. I ordered Ricketts's Division to occupy the high point of woods referred to, thus vacated by Banks, which he did promptly, planting his batteries behind a low ridge in the open field in his front. These batteries commanded the whole of the north face of the woods in which Banks's Corps was supposed to be and the point where the main road entered them just south of the small knoll referred to. Having thus posted Ricketts, I rode again over to this knoll. It was then too dark to see anything in the woods. General Banks and his staff were with me. I told him I would bivouac on that knoll behind the center of his command for the night, and he proposed to remain with me.

We had hardly dismounted from our horses when a volley of musketry rattled amongst us coming from the woods directly in our front and from the point where the road entered them and where Banks's troops were understood by him to be. By this fire one man was killed and several wounded among the orderlies. As we were hastily mounting our horses, from this dangerous place behind the "center of Banks's line," there came from the same direction repeated volleys of musketry and almost immediately the sounds of galloping cavalry. We vacated the uncomfortable knoll in short order and it was rapidly occupied by the enemy, who, however, were not able to hold it in the face of the severe and rapid fire Ricketts at once opened on it. In point of fact, General Banks was wholly mistaken about the position of his corps, which had left that part of the field altogether and was much in the rear on the roads north and east, so that there was nothing whatever in the shape of troops between the bivouac selected for the night and the main forces of the enemy in the woods from whom we were only separated by a narrow open field. We were in fact on picket and like many other pickets, were very nearly being captured.

Of course, it was pell-mell riding to escape from so dangerous a place and in the confusion some one ran his horse against General Banks and so injured his leg that he was unable to mount his horse again until near the end of the campaign. But for the premature musketry firing from the woods, this absurd blunder about the position of Banks's command would probably have cost some of us dearly.[43]

By this time Sigel's Corps had begun to arrive on the field and was posted in a belt of high woods on the left (east) of the main road to the south. Ricketts was in the corresponding belt of woods terminating on a high point on the right (west) side of the road and separated from him by about half a mile of open field sloping gently to the south. A line of troops and batteries from each completed the connection between them. To their front (the south) the ground was open field and meadow for nearly a mile to the thick belt of woods in which the battle had been fought. Banks's Corps had suffered so much loss and was so broken that I directed him or his successor in command to assemble his corps on the Culpeper road, in our rear and about two miles from the front; to send back his wounded to that place and to get together his command and get them ready again for service as soon as possible. In consequence of the severe fighting and the loss he himself had sustained both from Banks's battle and Ricketts's subsequent artillery fire, Jackson drew back during the night toward Cedar Mountain and took up a strong position two miles distant from our front. Our pickets were pushed forward and occupied the field of battle. The next day was intensely hot and no movement of the forces took place on either side. My whole effective force that day, exclusive of Banks's Corps (in no condition for immediate service), was about 20,000 infantry and artillery and 2,000 cavalry.[44] It was well known that Jackson's force considerably exceeded this and it became plain that I must have King's Division from Fredericksburg, whether its departure uncovered the position there or not. Indeed, if my wishes had not been overborne in the matter and King had been with me, the result of Cedar Mountain would have been much more satisfactory.[45] As it was it accomplished our object of throwing back the enemy beyond the Rapidan and greatly delaying (ten days or more) his advance toward Washington. This ten days was gained for the Army of the Potomac to make its junction with the Army of Virginia on the line of the Rappahannock.[46] It did not avail, however, for that purpose.

Finding myself in front of Jackson with less force than his, I telegraphed King on the eighth to move forward to us with all speed by the lower fords of the Rappahannock and he accordingly joined us late on the eleventh. Although, even after King joined me, my whole effective force exceeded very little if at all the forces of the enemy. I determined that, after giving that division the night of the eleventh to rest after their forced marches, I would early on the morning of the twelfth attack Jackson by my right on his line of communications; but during the night he evacuated his positions along Cedar Mountain and retreated rapidly across the Rapidan in the direction of Gordonsville, leaving many of his dead and wounded on the field and along the road to Orange Courthouse. No material of war, no baggage trains were lost on either side, but the loss of life on both sides was severe. Generals Geary, Augur and Carroll were badly wounded and very many of our best field and company officers were killed and wounded.[47] For severe fighting at short range and for gallantry and heroism displayed, it is to be doubted if any battle of the war was more distinguished.

A strong cavalry force under Generals Buford and Bayard followed the enemy's retreating forces to the Rapidan, capturing many stragglers from Jackson's troops. The cavalry immediately resumed the positions occupied before the enemy's advance and again picketed the Rapidan from Raccoon Ford to the Blue Ridge.

On the fourteenth General Reno with nominally 8,000 (really 6,000) men of Burnside's army joined me from the direction of Fredericksburg, being the first troops that reached there from the Peninsula.[48] I immediately moved forward my whole force toward the Rapidan still farther to cover the line of the Rappahannock, occupying both flanks of Cedar Mountain and began again to operate with cavalry upon the enemy's line of communications with Richmond. From the twelfth to the eighteenth of August reports were constantly reaching me that large forces of the enemy were reinforcing Jackson from the direction of Richmond[49] and by the morning of the 18th I became satisfied that nearly or quite the whole of Lee's army had left Richmond and were concentrating in my front along the south side of the Rapidan from Raccoon Ford to Liberty Mills, with the purpose of enveloping my command by turning my right by way of Madison Courthouse and assaulting directly in front at the same time. Their greatly superior forces entirely warranted such an operation.

We now know that Lee was at Gordonsville on the fifteenth with the whole of the "200,000 men" which General McClellan assigned to him when he himself was calling for reinforcements so lustily, but a large part of which he afterward deprived Lee when he spoke of the force of the enemy when they appeared before me. The exception to this general statement is, that one small corps, under D. H. Hill,[50] of all the "vast army" McClellan pictured in his fancy, was left in Richmond to confront him and which, as events showed, was sufficient.

A cavalry expedition sent out on the sixteenth toward Louisa Courthouse captured General J. E. B. Stuart's adjutant general and among the papers taken from him was an autograph letter from General Lee to General Stuart, dated Gordonsville, August 16, which gave me quite full information of Lee's force and position and his purpose to overwhelm the small army under my command before it could be reinforced by any part of the Army of the Potomac.[51] I held on to my hazardous position so far to the front as long as it was possible to do so without utter recklessness, in order that all troops of the Army of the Potomac which could in any way do so might join me when I drew back to the Rappahannock. On the eighteenth however, it seemed manifest that it was no longer possible with such forces as I had to maintain longer this advanced position in the face of so powerful an enemy. I determined to draw back at once to the north side of the Rappahannock and defend the line of that river according to the plan of General Halleck, as heretofore explained.

I accordingly instructed Reno to send back all his trains by way of Stevensburg to Kelly's or Barnett's Ford and after the lapse of three or four hours to follow them himself and take position on the north side of the Rappahannock so as to cover these fords, leaving all his cavalry on observation toward Raccoon Ford on the Rapidan, to cover his movement to the rear. Banks's Corps, which on the twelfth had been ordered back to Culpeper Courthouse, was ordered, with its trains preceding it, to cross the Rappahannock forthwith at Rappahannock Ford, where the Orange & Alexandria Railroad crosses that river. McDowell's Corps was to follow Banks's, whilst Sigel's Corps was directed through Jefferson to Warrenton Sulphur Springs, where he was to cross the river. These movements were all duly executed with little delay and without confusion during the night of the eighteenth and day of the nineteenth, by the end of which time the entire army, with all its trains and supplies and without loss of any kind, had crossed the Rappahannock and was strongly posted behind that stream, with its left at Kelly's Ford and its right three miles above Rappahannock Station; Sigel having been instructed when he crossed at the Sulphur Springs to move down the river until he closely connected with the rest of the army.

I do not think that justice has ever been done to the celerity and complete success with which this movement was made in the presence of a superior and vigilant enemy. Considering all the impediments and want of cohesion in that army due to the hasty manner in which its various detachments, which had never served together, were united and the very short time they had served together before, it was little less than marvelous that there was neither confusion nor unreasonable delay in a movement on such a scale and through all the darkness of the night.[52]

Chapter Eleven

Leave Pope to Get Out of His Scrape

*O*ne matter only of a personal and disagreeable character had occurred up to this time in the Army of Virginia and this would not have found a record at my hands except for some rather peculiar consequences. General George H. Gordon commanded a brigade in Banks's Corps, and behaved in a most gallant and distinguished manner at the Battle of Cedar Mountain,[1] where his brigade took a foremost part and set an example of the highest courage and loyalty in duty.

A few days after that battle General Gordon, with other commanders of troops, was called on for an official report of the operations of his brigade. He rendered the report in detail and it was duly received at my office from his immediate commander. Only a few days afterward the newspapers from the North came to us with General Gordon's official report in full, containing details quite improper and dangerous to us for the enemy to know, as they did through the same papers almost, if not quite, as soon as we did.[2]

143

It appeared, after inquiry, that the report had been furnished to the newspapers by General Gordon himself. For this gross breach of military discipline, likely to be so injurious to the army with which he was serving and committed for personal advantage and not to promote any public interest, he was placed in arrest and properly so placed, either by my direct order or by suggestion to General Banks.[3] For twenty years since that battle was fought and to him that far more important event, his arrest, he has been filling the air with imprecations and epithets. In books, in papers and magazines and in the lecture rooms of historical and other societies he has been vexing the language for descriptions of me uncomplimentary enough to present to the public the figure of a "monster of such horrid mien" that Frankenstein himself would have been a moral and physical beauty in the comparison.[4] He has constituted himself the historian of events he did not witness and has created generals to direct them out of the blinding reflection of his own grievance. Fortunately, such extreme utterances carry with them, in general, their own answer.

I understand that General Gordon has recently died and I can only say that I hope he may sleep in peace, untormented by the delusion of enmities never felt and of injustice never inflicted on him.[5]

Early on the morning of August twentieth the enemy drove in our pickets at Kelly's Ford and Rappahannock Station; but ascertaining that we covered these points in strong force and that it would not be easy to force the passage of the river there, his advance halted and the main body of his army was brought forward from the Rapidan.[6]

By the night of that day Lee had brought forward his whole army to our front. All day of the twenty-first and twenty-second feints or very feeble efforts were made to cross the river at various points, but they were repulsed without trouble or much loss to either party. The artillery practice was kept up during both days and much ammunition wasted, as was generally the case in that early period of the war. Finding the fords of the river reasonably well defended and probably in the prosecution of other plans previously made, the enemy began to move slowly up the river for the purpose of turning our right.[7] For the life of me I have never been able to understand why Lee did not at once force the passage of the river in our front and fall upon our inferior force with his triumphant army. The Rappahannock above Kelly's Ford is an insignificant, narrow stream, with good fords every few hundred yards and when these events occurred was so low that there were, I think, few places where it was over a man's head. He must have known that the Army of the Potomac was leaving the Peninsula under pressing orders to join the army under my command and that every day's delay must increase the force in front of him. He must have felt confident that he could deal with the small army under my command easily, if it were not reinforced before he assailed it and yet he suffered the days from August twentieth to August twenty-eighth to pass without any serious effort in that direction.[8] If General McClellan had been in the least energetic or had had any genuine purpose to push his army to support mine,[9] Lee would have found himself confronted by superior forces and forced back behind the Bull Run Mountains and finally behind the Rapidan. His singular procrastination and his long march around by way of Thoroughfare Gap cannot be explained on any military grounds whatever and the secret of his action may perhaps be found where I do not care to look for it.

My orders still bound me to keep open the roads to Fredericksburg to receive reinforcements from the Peninsula and I therefore could not extend my line much above Rappahannock Station without weakening it so much that it might be broken through almost anywhere. I telegraphed again and again to Washington representing this dangerous movement of Lee toward my right and that I could not meet it without letting go my hold on the river below.

The following dispatches, both dated on the twenty-first, will show what ideas they held in Washington and under what assurances I held on so long to a faulty line:

Washington, Aug. 21, 1862

Gen. Pope: I have telegraphed Gen. Burnside to know at what hour he can reinforce Reno.[10] Am waiting his answer. Every effort must be made to hold the Rappahannock. Large forces will be in to-morrow. (signed)

H. W. Halleck. General-in-Chief.

And again:

Washington, Aug. 21, 1862

Gen. Pope: I have just seen Gen. Burnside's reply. Gen. Cox's forces are coming in from Parkersburg, and will be here to-morrow and next day. Dispute every inch of the ground, and fight like the devil till we can reinforce you. Forty-eight hours more, and we can make you strong enough. Don't yield an inch if you can help it. (signed)

H. W. Halleck. General-in-Chief.[11]

Finding that the continued movement of the enemy toward my right, whilst heavy masses still confronted me at Rappahannock Station, would within twenty-four hours, if allowed to continue, either render my position on the Rappahannock wholly untenable or force me to give battle to the enemy on my front and right, I determined on the afternoon of the twenty-second to mass my whole force to recross the river by the bridge and fords near Rappahannock Station and Kelly's Ford and to assail the flank and rear of the long column of the enemy slowly moving up the river. The necessary orders were accordingly made on the night of the twenty-second. It would have been a hazardous movement, no doubt, but I must have made it or utterly abandoned the plan adhered to with such pertinacity at Washington. It would have been easy for me then, as it would have been at any time afterward, to draw my force down the river to Fredericksburg and by uniting with the troops there to be strong enough to maintain myself against any forces of the enemy; but the routes to Washington would have been left open and nothing was known to me of McClellan's army or his movements. It was better that my army should be sacrificed in fighting for delay than that the Capital should be seriously endangered. I considered it my duty to hazard the movement and to fall upon the enemy's flank and rear by recrossing the Rappahannock with my whole army.

As it happened, however, a heavy rain set in that night and by morning the river had risen at least eight feet and had become a raging torrent, carrying away one bridge and destroying for some days all the fords below Sulphur Springs. It was no longer practicable to recross the river and make the attack we had prepared for, but the rise in the river which prevented the movement would also, I believed, prevent the withdrawal to the south side of the river of such of the enemy's forces as were known to have crossed to the north side at Sulphur Springs and Waterloo Bridge.

Early on the morning of the twenty-third I massed my forces in the neighborhood of Rappahannock Station, with the purpose of assaulting at once the forces of the enemy above indicated and which were supposed then to be between Sulphur Springs, Waterloo Bridge and the town of Warrenton. As the river was much too high to be forded and I felt sure that most of the bridges were gone and that this condition was likely to last at least two days, I had no fears that the enemy could interpose any of his forces between me and Fredericksburg, or make any movement against our line of supplies, the Orange & Alexandria Railroad.

I accordingly directed General Sigel, who held my right nearest to Sulphur Springs, to march promptly with his whole corps on that place; to give battle at once to whatever force of the enemy he might find there and to push forward along the river to Waterloo Bridge.[12] The corps of Reno and Banks were sent to support this movement. I directed General McDowell to move at the same time directly to Warrenton, so that from there he could march toward Sulphur Springs or Waterloo Bridge, as might be most desirable, to aid Sigel's movement. To the corps of McDowell I attached the division of Pennsylvania Reserves, under General Reynolds,[13] who had reported that day and were the first of the Army of the Potomac to join my command. General Meade,[14] who afterward commanded the Army of the Potomac with such great distinction, was next in rank to General Reynolds in that division.

On the night of the twenty-second of August a small cavalry force of the enemy, which had crossed the Rappahannock at Waterloo Bridge and had passed through Warrenton, made a raid upon our trains at Catlett's Station, on the line of the Orange & Alexandria Railroad, about ten miles distant and destroyed altogether four or five wagons out of some thousands. As it happened, quite accidentally, those wagons thus destroyed belonged to my own headquarters train and of course, a great shout and hurrah were made over this wonderful achievement, out of which the enemy possessed themselves of some private letters having no relation to the war and a few other papers equally unimportant, as also some two or three suits of clothing more or less worn.[15] It was therefore quite a brilliant affair and reflected great credit on all concerned, especially the tasteful feat of inducting a Negro into a suit of my uniform clothing and parading him through the streets of Warrenton on their retreat. This cavalry detachment was not more than 300 strong when it made this raid. Our whole army train was parked at Catlett's Station and was guarded by 1,500 men, beside being within easy reach of the whole army.

The success of this small cavalry raid, trifling as it was and attended with no loss worth mentioning, was certainly far from creditable to the force guarding the trains and through whose neglect and carelessness only such an affair was practicable.[16]

General Sigel moved up the river as he was ordered, but very slowly, in the direction of Sulphur Springs, on the twenty-third and first encountered a force of the enemy near a point where a small stream called "Great Run" puts into the river about two miles below Sulphur Springs. The enemy was driven across the stream, but destroyed the bridges. Owing to the heavy rains of the night before the stream had risen so much as to be unfordable, so the night of the twenty-third and part of the morning of the twenty-fourth were spent in replacing the bridge. McDowell's Corps occupied Warrenton on the night of the twenty-third, driving out a small cavalry force of the enemy he found there.

On the morning of the twenty-fourth Sigel crossed Great Run and occupied Sulphur Springs under some artillery fire from the opposite bank. The enemy, who had crossed at Sulphur Springs a day or two before, had recrossed to the south side before the flood carried away the bridge. Sigel at once pushed forward toward Waterloo Bridge, followed by Banks and Reno. On that same morning I sent Buford with a heavy cavalry force from Warrenton to reconnoiter the enemy at Waterloo Bridge and above. It was then believed by Sigel, who so reported to me, that a considerable force of the enemy was still on the north side of the river and retiring before his advance in the direction of Waterloo Bridge. Buford reported no enemy at Waterloo

Bridge, or between there and Sulphur Springs and Sigel's advance under Milroy occupied the place during the afternoon. On that afternoon Lee's whole army was stretched along the river from Rappahannock Station to Waterloo Bridge.

During the day of the twenty-fourth a large force of the enemy, numbering thirty-six regiments of infantry, with the usual artillery batteries and a heavy cavalry force, was detached from the main body and marched rapidly north in the direction of Rectortown. They could be distinctly seen and were several times that afternoon counted and reported from our signal stations along the east and north side of the river. This force, as we afterward ascertained, was Stonewall Jackson's Corps and the purpose of his movement was not long in doubt.

It became very apparent that it would no longer be possible for me to hold the lower Rappahannock longer if I were expected to cover the approaches to Washington. The main body of the enemy was steadily, though not rapidly, moving toward my right, keeping the Rappahannock between us and it was necessary to meet this movement in the direction of its objective. I therefore proceeded rapidly to concentrate my forces between Warrenton and Gainesville, both along the Warrenton Pike and along the railroad south of it.[17]

The day after this concentration was ordered (August 26) Jackson, passing through Thoroughfare Gap, struck the railroad at Manassas Junction. As I have recounted fully in an article for the *Century Magazine*, published in its issue for January 1886,[18] the steps taken by me to forestall and prevent such a movement and the inexcusable manner in which my wishes and advice were neglected, notwithstanding every assurance that they would be carried out, it would not be proper for me to repeat what is therein said.[19] The passage of Thoroughfare Gap by Jackson seems to mark distinctly the beginning of the Second Battle of Bull Run, and in my article for the *Century Magazine* I have begun the account of the battle at that point of time. To that article I must refer anyone interested in the subject.

In concluding the *Century* article, the following words were used: "The transactions at Alexandria and in Washington City during these eventful days and also at Centreville during part of them, are as closely connected with these battles and had nearly as much to do with the results as any part of the operations in the field."[20] For this reason I purpose now to give a careful history of them, as being essential to any thorough understanding of that campaign and especially of the Battle of Bull Run.

The Army of Virginia was made by bringing together the troops under McDowell, Frémont and Banks, which were scattered about from Fredericksburg to the Shenandoah Valley and which up to that time had had no official relation or harmony of action with each other.

The force actually disposable when I first assumed command numbered only about 28,000 men,[21] King's Division being kept at Fredericksburg by order of the government. Several of the corps and many of the divisions and brigades were badly organized and to a considerable degree demoralized and discouraged. During the concentration of this force east of the Blue Ridge, General McClellan was attacked in front of Richmond and driven back on the James River, his base of supplies on the Pamunkey River and lines of communication therewith being threatened and then occupied by the enemy.

When he had reached Harrison's Landing and his condition was known, the plans for the operations of the Army of Virginia to relieve him were determined.

It was decided to withdraw his army from the Peninsula and unite it with the army under my command along the line of the Rappahannock.

The purpose to unite these two armies, having a powerful and resolute enemy, under able commanders, interposed between them, ready to strike in either direction as might seem most judicious, involved one of the most hazardous and difficult operations of the war. It demanded from the force in front of Washington the greatest energy and activity and forced upon it such extreme danger and difficulty as an army is very infrequently exposed to. It demanded equally from the army which was to be withdrawn from the James River the same energy and activity and a zeal also which is not always found in a commander who does not willingly perform the duty imposed upon him by the orders of his government. Unless these conditions on the part of both armies are faithfully fulfilled, the chances are altogether against the success of such an operation. Whether the government was right or wrong in expecting this fidelity in its commanders, even when its orders were not satisfactory to them, I leave to the decision of the army itself and to the public sense of the country.

As the enemy pushed his force to the north with great energy and speed to crush the troops in front of Washington before they could be reinforced by General McClellan's army from the Peninsula, the Army of Virginia necessarily bore the brunt of all the fighting; whilst the army of General McClellan, exposed to no danger and not attacked at any point during its withdrawal, had nothing to do except urge forward by all possible means its movement to Alexandria and unite with the Army of Virginia with the least possible delay. That army was holding back the enemy by continued fighting and marching and with the constant risk of being overwhelmed by very superior forces.

How the Army of Virginia under my command performed its part in this operation, I have tried to recount and it now remains to tell how the army under General McClellan fulfilled the part which was assigned to and expected of it.

It does not fall properly within the province of this paper to recount in detail or to discuss General McClellan's tardy movements in the withdrawal of his army from Harrison's Landing to make its junction with the army under my command in front of Washington. It will suffice to say that he received the orders to embark his army by the fourth of August and that the first corps of that army did not move from its camps until August fourteenth.[22] On the ninth General Halleck telegraphed him that the enemy was massing his force in front of General Pope and General Burnside to crush them and move forward to the Potomac and that reinforcements must at once be sent to Acquia Creek and added, "considering the amount of transportation at your disposal your delay is not satisfactory. You must move with all possible celerity." To which General McClellan replied that "everything has been and is being pushed as rapidly as possible to carry out your orders."[23]

On the twelfth, in reply to the most pressing orders from General Halleck for immediate movement, who urged that General Burnside had moved 13,000 men to Acquia Creek in less than two days, he replied that if Washington were in danger his army could not arrive in time to save it.[24] On the fourteenth he reported that the movement had begun and on the seventeenth he said that he should not feel entirely secure until he had the whole army across the Chickahominy and that he would then begin to move forward troops by water as fast as transportation would permit.[25]

It would be hard to tell what he was afraid of, for on that date and for several days before, Lee was at Gordonsville, seventy miles away, with nearly his whole army and there was absolutely nothing in Richmond or in front of McClellan to endanger his army except the weak force of D. H. Hill.

On the tenth General Halleck telegraphed him: The enemy is crossing the Rapidan in large force. They are fighting General Pope today. There must be no further delay in your movements. That which has already occurred was entirely unexpected and must be satisfactorily explained.

Again, on the twenty-first he was informed that—"the forces of Pope and Burnside are hard pushed and require aid as rapidly as you can. By all means see that the troops sent have plenty of ammunition. We have no time here to supply them. Moreover, they may have to fight as soon as they land."[26]

Whatever may be thought of the delays thus complained of by General Halleck, it is quite certain from these telegrams that General McClellan knew perfectly well the emergency in which my army was placed and that the concentration of his army and mine was not being effected in the time expected and also as a consequence, that I was in a critical position and needed help to save my small army from certain misfortune. All this General McClellan knew when he left the Peninsula. I had asked that Franklin's Corps and other troops might be sent out to my right at Gainesville.

The movements of this corps furnish a very good illustration of the manner in which reinforcements were sent forward to, or rather withheld from, the army fighting in front of Centreville; and they are, therefore, related in some detail, according to General McClellan's own reports.

On the twenty-third Franklin's Corps started from Fort Monroe.[27] General McClellan left the next day and reached Alexandria on the evening of the twenty-sixth. Heintzelman's Corps,[28] which had arrived at Alexandria before General McClellan, had gone at once to the front and joined the army under my command near Warrenton Junction without transportation or officers' horses. Porter was understood to be on the march from Acquia Creek to the same point.[29] Of the troops which arrived at Alexandria after McClellan reached there, or which were there on his arrival, not a man reached the field of Bull Run or took any part in any of the battles which were fought there during several successive days.

In his official report, dated August 4, 1863, nearly a year after these transactions, General McClellan says as follows, viz:

> It will be seen from what has preceded that I lost no time that could be avoided in moving the Army of the Potomac from the Peninsula to the support of the Army of Virginia; that I spared no effort to hasten the embarkation of the troops at Fort Monroe myself until the mass of the army had sailed, and that after my arrival at Alexandria I left nothing in my power undone to forward supplies and reinforcements to General Pope.[30]

Is this statement true? Did General McClellan try in good faith do the things he says he did? He shall himself answer that question and I can simply premise his own account of his doings by the statement that during the four days in question, August twenty-seventh, twenty-eighth, twenty-ninth and thirtieth, severe and bloody battles were being fought at and near Bull Run and the heavy boom of the artillery was plainly heard all those days in Alexandria and in the streets of Washington.

On the twenty-seventh of August General McClellan, who had arrived at Alexandria on the twenty-sixth, was charged by General Halleck with the entire discretion of sending troops and supplies as rapidly as possible to the army under my command. The subjoined dispatches will show how he did that duty and will sustain or disprove his statement heretofore quoted. On the twenty-sixth McClellan was informed that Franklin was to go to the front and on the twenty-seventh, at ten A.M. General Halleck telegraphed General McClellan to have Franklin's Corps march in the direction of Manassas as soon as possible. It is proper here to state that the march referred to in this and the following dispatches was over a paved turnpike, which was well known both to General McClellan and to General Franklin.

In this dispatch of ten A.M. General McClellan replied:

Alexandria, August 27, 1862, 10 A.M.

Telegram this moment received. I have sent orders to Franklin to prepare to march with his corps at once, and to repair here in person to inform me as to his means of transportation. Kearny was yesterday at Rappahannock Station; Porter at Bealeton, Kelly's, Barnett's etc. Sumner will commence reaching Falmouth to-day. Williams' Massachusetts cavalry will be mostly at Falmouth to-day. I loaned Burnside my personal escort (one squadron 4th Regulars) to scout down Rappahannock. I have sent for Couch's Division to come at once.[31] As fast as I gain any information I will forward it, although you may already have it.
(signed)
Geo. B. McClellan, Major General.
Maj. Gen. H. W. Halleck, General-in-Chief[32]

At the meridian General Halleck telegraphed General McClellan the situation of the army under my command:

(Sent 12 M.)

War Department,
Washington, D.C. August 27, 1862.

Telegrams from General Porter to General Burnside, just received, say that Banks is at Fayetteville; McDowell, Sigel, and Ricketts near Warrenton; Reno on his right. Porter is marching on Warrenton Junction to reinforce Pope. Nothing said of Heintzelman. Porter reports a general battle imminent. Franklin's Corps should move out by forced marches, carrying three or four days' provisions, and to be supplied as far as possible by railroad. Perhaps you may prefer some other road than to Centreville. Colonel Haupt has just telegraphed about sending out troops.[33] Please see him, and give him your directions. There has been some serious neglect to guard the railroad, which should be immediately remedied.
(signed)
H. W. Halleck, General-in-Chief.
Maj. Gen. McClellan, Alexandria.

At 12:40 P.M. General Halleck receives General McClellan's reply dated 12:05 P.M.:

Alexandria, August 27, 1862, 12:05 P.M.
My Aide has just returned from General Franklin's camp; reports that Generals Franklin, Smith, and Slocum are all in Washington.[34] He gave the order to the next in rank to place the corps in readiness to move at once. I learn that heavy firing has been heard this morning at Centreville, and have sent to ascertain the truth. I can find no cavalry to send out on the roads. Are the works finished and ready for defense? (signed)
Geo. B. McClellan, Major General Commanding.
Maj. Gen. Halleck, General-in-Chief.[35]

And at 1:15 P.M. General McClellan again dispatched General Halleck:

(Received 1:50 P.M.)
Alexandria, August 27, 1862. 1:15 P.M.
Franklin's artillery have no horses except for four guns without caissons. I can pick up no cavalry. In view of these facts, will it not be well to push Sumner's Corps here by water as rapidly as possible,[36] to make immediate arrangements for placing the works in front of Washington in an efficient condition of defense? I have no means of knowing the enemy's force between Pope and ourselves. Can Franklin, without his artillery or cavalry, effect any useful purpose in front? Should not Burnside at once take steps to evacuate Falmouth and Acquia, at the same time covering the retreat of any of Pope's troops who may fall back in that direction? I do not see that we have force enough in hand to form a connection with Pope, whose exact position we do not know. Are we safe in the direction of the valley?
(signed)
George B. McClellan, Major General.
Maj. Gen. Halleck, Washington.[37]

War Department
Washington, D.C., August 28, 1862.
On parting with Gen. McClellan, about 2 o'clock this morning, it was understood that you were to move with your corps to-day toward Manassas Junction, to drive the enemy from the railroad. I have just learned that the General has not yet returned to Alexandria. If you have not received his orders, act on this.
(signed)
H. W. Halleck, General-in-Chief.
Major General Franklin, Alexandria, Va.[38]

To which at 1 P.M. General McClellan (not General Franklin) replied:

(Received 1:05 P.M.)

Alexandria, Va., August 28, 1862 1:00 P.M.

Your dispatch to Franklin received. I have been doing all possible to hurry artillery and cavalry. The moment Franklin can be started with a reasonable amount of artillery he shall go. In the mean time see Whipple's dispatch;[39] something must be done in that direction. Please see Barnard and be sure that the works toward the Chain Bridge are perfectly secure.[40] I look upon these works, especially Ethan Allen and Marcy,[41] as of the first importance. I have heard, incidentally, that there is no garrison in Ethan Allen, but presume it is a mistake. I have just conferred with Colonel Holabird,[42] and think the enemy is in such force near Manassas as to make it necessary for us to move in force.

(signed)

George B. McClellan, Major General Commanding

Gen. H. W. Halleck, General-in-Chief[43]

General McClellan being thus of the opinion that "it is necessary for us to move in force," it becomes a matter of interest to observe what efforts are made to that end.

At 3:30 P.M. General Halleck, in a tone that manifests his estimate of the position, telegraphed General McClellan:

War Department

Washington, D.C., August 28, 1862. 3:30 P.M.

Not a moment must be lost in pushing as large a force as possible towards Manassas, so as to communicate with Pope before the enemy is reinforced. I directed General Barnard to report to you and do not know where he is. In Barnard's absence Whipple can tell you about the garrisons and the forts. No message from Pope has reached here.

(signed)

H. W. Halleck General-in-Chief.

Maj. Gen. McClellan, Alexandria.[44]

At 4:10 P.M. this dispatch is sent:

(Received 7:31 P.M.)

Headquarters near Alexandria

August 28, 1862. 4:10 P.M.

General Franklin is with me here. I will know in a few minutes the condition of artillery and cavalry. We are not yet in condition to move; may be by to-morrow morning. Pope must cut through to-day, or adopt the plan I suggested. I have ordered troops to garrison the works at Upton's Hill.[45] They must be held at any cost. As soon as I can see the way to spare them, I will send a good corps of troops there. It is the key to Washington, which cannot be seriously menaced as long as it is held. (signed)

George B. McClellan Major General
Major General H. W. Halleck, General-in-Chief.[46]

And at 4:45 P.M. the following reply to General Halleck's dispatch of 3:30 P.M.:

> Camp near Alexandria,
> August 28, 1862. 4:45 P.M.
>
> Your dispatch received. Neither Franklin nor Sumner's Corps is now in condition to move and fight a battle. It would be a sacrifice to send them out now. I have sent Aids to ascertain the condition of the command of Cox and Tyler,[47] but I still think that a premature movement in small force will accomplish nothing but the destruction of the troops sent out. I report that I will lose no time in preparing the troops now here for the field, and that whatever orders you may give after hearing what I have to say will be carried out.
> (signed)
>
> George B. McClellan, Major General.
> Major General H. W. Halleck, General-in-Chief.[48]

Thus appreciated and replied to by General Halleck at 7:40 P.M.:

> War Department
> Washington D.C. August 28, 1862. 7:40 P.M.
>
> There must be no further delay in moving Franklin's Corps toward Manassas. They must go tomorrow morning, ready or not ready. If we delay too long to get ready there will be no necessity to go at all, for Pope will either be defeated or victorious without our aid. If there is a want of wagons the men must carry provisions with them till the wagons can come to their relief.
> (signed)
>
> H. W. Halleck, General-in-Chief.
> Major General McClellan, Alexandria.[49]

To which General McClellan answers:

(Received August 29, 12:20 A.M.)

Alexandria, August 28, 1862. 10 P.M.

Your dispatch received. Franklin's Corps has been ordered to march at 6 o'clock to-morrow morning. Sumner has about 14,000 infantry, without cavalry or artillery, here. Cox's Brigade of four regiments is here, with two batteries of artillery. Men of two regiments, much fatigued, came to-day. Tyler's Brigade of three new regiments, but little drilled, is also here. All these troops will be ordered to hold themselves ready to march to-morrow morning, and all, except Franklin's, to await further orders. If you wish any of them to move toward Manassas, please inform me. Colonel Waagner,[50] 2nd New York Artillery has just come in from the front. He reports strong infantry and cavalry force of rebels near Fairfax Courthouse. Reports numerous, from various sources, that Lee and Stuart with large forces are at Manassas; that the enemy, with 120,000 men, intend advancing on the forts near Arlington and Chain Bridge, with a view of attacking Washington and Baltimore.

General Barnard telegraphs me to-night that the length of line of fortifications on this side of the Potomac requires 2,000 additional batterymen, and additional troops to defend intervals, according to circumstances. At all events, he says an old regiment should be added to the force at Chain Bridge, and a few regiments distributed along the line to give confidence to our new troops. I agree with him fully, and think our fortifications along the upper part of our line on this side of the river very unsafe with their present garrisons, and the movements of the enemy seem to indicate an attack upon these works.

(signed)

George B. McClellan, Major General.

Major General H. W. Halleck, General-in-Chief, U.S. Army.[51]

And thus Franklin's Corps, ordered to move on the morning of the twenty-seventh had not stirred a foot on the night of the twenty-eighth.

Friday, August 29, 1862, at 10:30 A.M., General McClellan telegraphs General Halleck:

Camp near Alexandria,

August 29, 10:30 A.M.

Franklin's Corps in motion; started about 6 A.M. I can give him but two squadrons of cavalry. I propose moving General Cox to Upton's Hill to hold that important point with its works, and to push cavalry scouts to Vienna via Freedom Hill and Hunter's Lane. Cox has two squadrons of cavalry. Please answer at once whether this meets your approval. I have directed Woodbury,[52] with the Engineer Brigade, to hold Fort Lyon. Sumner detached last night two regiments to the vicinity of Forts Ethan Allen and Marcy. Meagher's Brigade is still in Acquia.[53] If he moves in support of Franklin it leaves us without any reliable troops in and near Washington. Yet Franklin is too weak alone. What shall be done? No more cavalry arrived. Have but three squadrons. Franklin has but 40 rounds of ammunition and no wagons to move more. I do not think Franklin is in condition to accomplish much if he meets strong resistance. I should not have moved him but for your pressing order last night. What have you from Vienna and Drainesville?

(signed)

George B. McClellan, Major General.

Major General H. W. Halleck, General-in-Chief.[54]

Throughout the reiterated dispatches of the two previous days General McClellan advises General Halleck that he is pushing Franklin forward and now on the morning of the third day, tells him, "I should not have moved him (Franklin) but for your pressing order last night."

General McClellan telegraphs:

> (Received 12:50 P.M.)
> Headquarters Army of the Potomac,
> Alexandria, Va., August 29 1862, 12 M.

Your telegram received. Do you wish the movement of Franklin's Corps to continue? He is without reserve ammunition, and without transportation.

(signed)

George B. McClellan, Major General.

Major General H. W. Halleck, General-in-Chief.[55]

And again:

> (Received 12:50 P.M.)
> Headquarters Army of the Potomac,
> Alexandria, Va., August 29, 1862, 12 M.

Have ordered most of the 12th Pennsylvania Cavalry to report to General Barnard for scouting duty toward Rockville, Poolsville, etc. If you apprehend a raid of cavalry on your side of river, I had better send a brigade or two of Sumner's to near Tennallytown, where, with two or three old regiments in Forts Allen and Marcy, they can watch both Chain Bridge and Tennallytown. Would it meet your views to post the rest of

Sumner's Corps between Arlington and Fort Corcoran, where they can either support Cox, Franklin, or Chain Bridge, or even Tennallytown? Franklin has only between 10,000 and 11,000 ready for duty. How far do you wish this force to advance.
(signed)
G. B. McClellan, Major General
U.S. Army Major General Halleck, General-in-Chief.[56]

To which General Halleck replies at 3 P.M.:

> War Department,
> Washington, D.C., August 29, 1862.
>
> Your proposed disposition of Sumner's Corps seems to me judicious. Of course I have no time to examine into details. The present danger is a raid upon Washington in the night time. Dispose of all troops as you deem best. I want Franklin's Corps to go far enough to find out something about the enemy. Perhaps he may get such information at Annandale as to prevent his going further. Otherwise he will push on toward Fairfax. Try to get something from direction of Manassas either by telegram or through Franklin's scouts. Our people must move more actively and find out where the enemy is. I am tired of guesses.
> (signed)
> H. W. Halleck, General-in-Chief.
> Major General McClellan, Alexandria.[57]

At 7:50 P.M. General Halleck to General McClellan:

> War Department,
> Washington, D.C., August 29, 1862. 7:50 P.M.
>
> You will immediately send construction train and guards to repair railroad to Manassas; let there be no delay in this. I have just been told that Franklin's Corps stopped at Annandale and that he was this evening in Alexandria. This is all contrary to my orders. Investigate and report the facts of this disobedience. That corps must push forward as I directed, to protect the railroad and open our communications with Manassas.
> (signed)
> H. W. Halleck, General-in-Chief.
> Major General McClellan, Alexandria.[58]

To which General McClellan replies:

(Time received 8:00 P.M.)
Camp near Alexandria,
August 29, 1862. 8 P.M.

By referring to my telegrams of 10:30 A.M., 12 M. and 1 P.M., together with your reply of 2:48 P.M., you will see why Franklin's Corps halted at Annandale. His small cavalry force, all I had to give him, was ordered to push on as far as possible toward Manassas. It was not safe for Franklin to move beyond Annandale under the circumstances until we knew what was at Vienna. General Franklin remained here until about 1 P.M., endeavoring to arrange for supplies for his command. I am responsible for both these circumstances, and do not see that either was in disobedience to your orders. Please give distinct orders in reference to Franklin's movements of tomorrow. I have sent to Colonel Haupt to push out construction and supply trains as soon as possible, General Tyler to furnish the necessary guards. I have directed General Banks's supply train to start out tonight, at least as far as Annandale, with an escort from General Tyler. In regard to to-morrow's movements I desire definite instructions, as it is not agreeable to me to be accused of disobeying orders when I have simply exercised the discretion you committed to me. (signed)
George B. McClellan, Major General.
Major General Halleck, General-in-Chief.[59]

At ten that night General Halleck advised General McClellan that he has a dispatch from General Franklin stating that "Pope is very short of provisions and the country will not support him."

(Received 10:50 P.M.)
HeadQ'rs Army of the Potomac,
Camp near Alexandria,
August 29, 1862. 10 P.M.

The following has just been received by an orderly:

"Annandale, 7:15 P.M.
General: The news picked up here from all sources passing along the road is as follows: Jackson left Centreville yesterday afternoon to march through Thoroughfare Gap. He was confronted by Sigel, whom he attacked immediately. Sigel was reinforced by Heintzelman and Porter to-day. McDowell by noon was four miles from the field, and was merely waiting for his ammunition to come up to join him. The field of battle is near Gainesville. Sigel fought all

day yesterday, slept on the enemy's ground, and this morning at 5 o'clock was attacked, and the cannonading was very heavy when a certain sutler, one of the parties who gives the information, left there. From all the evidence the inference is that we have met with no disaster, and that Stonewall is in a tight place unless he leaves to-night by Aldie. Jackson had with him yesterday three divisions — his own, Ewell's and Hill's — amounting to 40,000 men. Birney held Centreville this morning and pursued Jackson,[60] picking up many stragglers. The enemy left Centreville last evening. Many of the rebel dead are lying near Centreville. Birney ceased the pursuit on learning the force of the enemy. All of the best witnesses and all of the citizens who have passed, consider Jackson in a dangerous position. Pope's train is parked this side of Centreville.

"Truly yours,

(signed)

"W. B. Franklin, Major General, Commanding Sixth Corps.

"P.S.—Pope is said to be very short of provisions and the country will not support him.

"W. H. F."

(signed)

George B. McClellan, Major General.

Major General H. W. Halleck, General-in-Chief.[61]

And thus, on the night of the third day after General Franklin's Corps had been peremptorily ordered to join the army under my command, it had advanced as far as Annandale, six miles from Alexandria, Franklin himself being in that city as late as one P.M.

> August 29, 1862 8 P.M.
> To Commanding Officer at Centreville:
> I have been instructed by General McClellan to inform you that he will have all the available wagons at Alexandria loaded with rations for your troops, and all of the cars also, as soon as you send in a cavalry escort to Alexandria as a guard to the train.
> Respectfully,
> (signed)
> W. B. Franklin, Major General, Commanding Sixth Corps [62]

General McClellan's dispatch of ten P.M., August twenty-ninth, states that he ordered Franklin "to cover the transit of Pope's supplies." General Franklin, who doubtless understood his orders, explains them as above by saying that the supplies would be loaded "as soon as you send a cavalry escort." It was thus General Franklin was to "cover the transit."

At eleven A.M. General McClellan telegraphs General Halleck:

(Received 11:15 A.M.)
Headquarters Army of the Potomac,
Camp near Alexandria,
August 30, 1862, 11 A.M.

Have ordered Sumner to leave one brigade in the vicinity of Chain Bridge, and to move the rest via Columbia Pike on Annandale and Fairfax Courthouse. Is this the route you wish them to take? He and Franklin are both instructed to join Pope as promptly as possible. Shall Couch move also when he arrives?
(signed)
George B. McClellan, Major General.
Major General Halleck, General-in-Chief.[63]

To this inquiry as to the proper direction of the troops at the crisis of that day General Halleck's reply is comprehensive and pointed: "Send them where the fighting is."

(Sent at 12:20 P.M.)
War Department,
Washington, D.C., August 30, 1862, 12:20 P.M.

I think Couch should land at Alexandria and be immediately pushed out to Pope. Send the troops where the fighting is. Let me know when Couch arrives, as I may have other information by that time. Use the Connecticut officers and regiment as you propose. Send transports to Acquia to bring up Burnside's command. I have telegraphed to him, and am waiting his answer.
(signed)
H. W. Halleck, General-in-Chief.
Major General McClellan, Alexandria.[64]

And adds two hours later:

(Sent 2:15 P.M.)
War Department,
Washington, D.C., August 30, 1862 2:10 P.M.

Franklin's and all of Sumner's Corps should be pushed forward with all possible dispatch. They must use their legs and make forced marches. Time now is everything. Send some sharpshooters on the trains to Bull

Run. The bridges and property are threatened by bands of Prince William cavalry. Give Colonel Haupt all the assistance you can. The sharpshooters on top of cars can assist in unloading the trains.
(signed)
H. W. Halleck, General-in-Chief.
Major General McClellan, Alexandria.[65]

(Received 3 P.M.)
Headquarters Army of the Potomac,
Alexandria, Va., August 30, 1862 2:10 P.M.
I know nothing of the calibers of Pope's artillery. All I can do is to direct my ordnance officer to load up all the wagons sent to him. I have already sent all my headquarters wagons. You will have to see that wagons are sent from Washington. I can do nothing more than give the order that every available wagon in Alexandria shall be loaded at once. The order to the brigade of Sumner that I directed to remain at Chain Bridge and Tennallytown should go from your headquarters to save time. I understand you intend it also to move. I have no sharpshooters except the guards around my camp. I have sent off every man but those and will now send them with the train, as you direct. I will also send my only remaining squadron of cavalry with General Sumner. I can do no more; you now have every man of the Army of the Potomac who is within my reach.
(signed)
George B. McClellan, Major General Commanding.
Major General Halleck, General-in-Chief.[66]

As these telegrams do not appear to furnish any sort of explanation of Franklin's slow movements and of his halt at Annandale, it seems not improper to furnish a telegram of General McClellan's, which does give in part directly and in part by inference an explanation of these transactions; but before doing so it seems in place to invite attention to the strange fact that whilst in his telegrams, the first dated August twenty-ninth, at eight-thirty A.M., and the second August twenty-ninth, at one P.M., General McClellan does not consider it safe for Franklin with 11,000 men to go beyond Annandale, yet he instructs General Franklin to inform the commanding officer at Centreville (not me) that he "will have all the available wagons at Alexandria loaded with rations for your troops and all of the cars; also, as soon as you send in a cavalry escort to Alexandria as a guard to the trains." In short, whilst it was not safe, according to General McClellan's opinion, for Franklin to go beyond Annandale with 11,000 men, he did consider it safe for a cavalry escort to come in from the field of battle through Annandale to

Alexandria and take back wagon-trains by the same road. Not fear of harm to Franklin therefore was the motive to halt him at Annandale, but some other motive quite removed from such apprehension.

This motive will probably be found partly set forth in the following telegram, dated at 2:45 P.M., August 29:

> Headquarters Army of the Potomac,
> Camp near Alexandria, Va.
> August 29, 1862 2:45 P.M.
>
> The last news I received from the direction of Manassas was from strag- glers, to the effect that the enemy were evacuating Centreville and re- tiring toward Thoroughfare Gap. This is by no means reliable. I am clear that one of two courses should be adopted; first to concentrate all our available forces to open communications with Pope; second, to leave Pope to get out of his scrape and at once use all our means to make the Capitol perfectly safe. No middle course will now answer. Tell me what you wish me to do and I will do all in my power to accomplish it. I wish to know what my orders and authority are. I ask for nothing, but will obey whatever orders you give. I only ask a prompt decision that I may at once give the necessary orders. It will not do to delay longer.
> (signed)
> Geo. B. McClellan, Major General.
> A. Lincoln, President.[67]

A strange dispatch this, in view of the fact that for three successive days McClellan had been almost hourly receiving peremptory orders to send Franklin to the front and that he had been reporting almost as often that he was doing so. It must be borne in mind also that at the time this telegram was sent, Franklin, with 11,000 men; Sumner, with 14,000 men and Cox, with 5,000 men, were all in and near Alexandria under McClellan's direct control and that he had positive orders to send them forward. The sounds of battle were in his ears all the time and should of themselves have furnished him with a reason for hurrying them to the front more imperative than any orders.

As General McClellan had positively stated again and again that Franklin could not move to the front because of want of transportation, it was of course doubly impracticable for the same reason that both Franklin and Sumner should go forward and the first part of this proposition to the President, therefore, could not have been made with any purpose of being carried out. The last of the two suggestions, viz, "to leave Pope to get out of his scrape," was therefore the real one. What was the "scrape" that Pope was to be left to get out of? He had been for nearly three weeks marching and fighting almost continuously, for no other purpose than to give time for General McClellan's army to assemble at Alexandria and come forward to the field to his support. The roar of battle at the front for three or four successive days was sounding in General McClellan's ears and in answer to it he advises that Pope be left to get out of his "scrape." And was General Pope alone involved in this "scrape" so touchingly alluded to by General McClellan? Were there not also in this "scrape" thousands of loyal and gallant soldiers who had been for weeks fighting and marching with the sole hope that their comrades of the Army of the Potomac would come to their aid, as they had gone forward to aid them? How many thousands of these gallant men lie dead on bloody fields, because they were left to get out of their "scrape?"[68]

It is pitiful to continue this subject further, but perhaps it may be as well to dispose of McClellan's equally insincere excuses concerning want of transportation. The following telegram of General Halleck's very effectually disposes of them:

> War Department,
> Washington, August 30, 1862, 9:40 A.M.
> I am by no means satisfied with General Franklin's march of yesterday. Considering the circumstances of the case, he was very wrong in stopping at Annandale. Moreover I learned last night that the Quartermaster's Department could have given him plenty of transportation if he had applied for it any time since his arrival at Alexandria. He knew the importance of opening communication with General Pope's army, and should have acted more promptly.
> (signed)
> H. W. Halleck, General-in-Chief.
> Major General McClellan, Alexandria.[69]

But in addition to this General McClellan actually knew, when he was assigning want of transportation as an excuse for not moving Franklin, that there was public transportation at his command and yet he did not use it, when the fate of a campaign, if not an army, depended upon his doing so.[70]

> Camp near Alexandria, August 30, 1862 11:30 A.M.
> Major General Halleck, General-in-Chief: Your telegram of 9 A.M. received. Ever since General Franklin received notice that he was to march from Alexandria he has been endeavoring to get transportation from the Quartermaster at Alexandria, but he has been uniformly told that there was none disposable. Every effort has been made to carry out your orders promptly. The great difficulty seems to consist in the fact that the greater part of transportation on hand at Alexandria and Washington has been needed for current supplies of the garrisons. Such is the

state of the case as represented to me by the Quartermasters, and it appears to be true. I take it for granted that this has not been properly explained to you.
(signed)
George B. McClellan, Major General.[71]

It is clear that he thought or affected to think that it was better that the army under my command should be defeated, if not destroyed, than that the garrisons around Alexandria and Washington should be subjected to the slightest inconvenience. In the midst of all the pretended apprehension about Franklin's danger in moving to the front, Banks's wagon-train actually passed Franklin as it came in from the field where Franklin was to go. Much of the "news" Franklin sent to McClellan was probably obtained from this train, which, it seems, was able to come from the front with safety over a road which McClellan was afraid that Franklin should venture on with 11,000 men.

I need not proceed further in this sorry recital. All the forces in and about Alexandria were withheld for four days from the support of my army fighting Lee's whole force in front of Centreville by such groundless and trivial excuses as these.

As to the ammunition, General McClellan says in his telegram from Fort Monroe on the 21st, 10:52 P.M.: "I have ample supplies of ammunition for infantry and artillery, and will have it up in time. I can supply any deficiency that may exist in General Pope's army." But when ordered to send it forward he replied from Alexandria: "I know nothing of the calibers of Pope's artillery. All I can do is to direct my ordnance officer to load up all the wagons sent to him." Sent by whom? It need not be said that he could easily have found out from the Ordnance Department what artillery I had.

This narration of what General McClellan did is necessarily much abridged, but it is practically his own story and if it confirms the statement in his report that "after my arrival at Alexandria I left nothing in my power undone to forward reinforcements and supplies to General Pope," there is no more to be said, except, perhaps, that if this were really all he could do, it is very unfortunate, in every view, that some one else had not been charged with this work.

During these three days, twenty-seventh, twenty-eighth and twenty-ninth of August, spent by Franklin in marching from Alexandria to Annandale (six miles), over a broad turnpike, unobstructed by any obstacle, Lee marched his whole army, except Jackson's Corps, from Waterloo Bridge, on the Rappahannock, by the circuitous route of Salem and White Plains, forced the passage of Thoroughfare Gap and came on the field of Groveton (Second Bull Run), where, on the afternoon of the twenty-ninth—the third day—he fought a severe battle with the troops under my command.

The distance thus marched by Lee's army, in the face of a watchful enemy, was nearly forty miles and on the third day of this march he fought also a severe battle at Groveton.

The movements of Lee's large army and of Franklin's Corps during the same three days of August 1862, present a contrast so violent as to require no comment whatever.

What success could be expected over an active enemy with any help likely to be given by so tardy and reluctant a friend is not easy to see.

The dispatches of General Porter from the field during the same three days are essential to a sufficient understanding of the feeling which obtained among certain of the highest officers of the Army of the Potomac and which led to consequences well-nigh fatal to the cause of the government. It is with reluctance that I introduce these telegrams from a man in the unhappy condition of General Porter, but it is hard to see how it could be avoided without injustice to those who during those dreadful days cheerfully and gladfully exposed life and limb to the success of the Union army.

They are a part of General Porter's record and are so closely related to subsequent transactions that it is impossible to avoid presenting them in this paper. It has been asserted that they were private telegrams, not intended to be published or officially used and it is easy to believe that their author, considering their contents, should have been very reluctant that they should be brought to light.[72]

As they were communicated at once to the President, by the officer to whom they were sent, their privacy, if there were privacy in such a matter, was violated almost at the moment of their issue.

They were as follows, viz:

From Warrenton Junction
August 27, 1862 4 P.M.

General Burnside, Falmouth, Va.: I send you the last order from General Pope, which indicates the future as well as the present. Wagons are rolling along rapidly to the rear as if a mighty power was propelling them. I see no cause of alarm; though I think this order may cause it. McDowell moves to Gainesville, where Sigel now is. The latter got to Buckland Bridge in time to put out the fire and kick the enemy, who is pursuing his route unmolested to the Shenandoah or Loudoun County. The forces are Longstreet's, A. P. Hill's, Jackson's, Whiting's, Ewell's, and Anderson's (late Huger's) Divisions.

Longstreet is said by a deserter to be very strong. They have much artillery and long wagon trains. The raid on the railroad was near Cedar Creek, and made by a regiment of infantry, two squadrons of cavalry, and a section of artillery. The place was guarded by nearly three regiments of infantry and some cavalry. They routed the guard, captured the train and many men, destroyed the bridge, and retired leisurely down the roads toward Manassas.[73] It can easily be repaired. No troops are coming up, except new troops, that I can hear of. Sturgis is here with two regiments. Four were cut off by the raid. The positions of the troops is given in the order. No enemy in our original front. A letter of General Lee, seized when Stuart's assistant adjutant-general was taken, directs Stuart to leave a squadron only to watch in front of Hanover Junction, etc. Everything has moved up north. I find a vast difference between these troops and ours, but I suppose they were new, as to-day they burnt their clothes, etc., when there was not the least cause. I hear that they are much demoralized, and needed some good troops to give them heart and I think head. We are working now to get behind Bull Run, and I presume will be there in a few days, if strategy don't use us up. The strategy is magnificent, and the tactics in the inverse proportion. I would like some of my ambulances. I would like also to be ordered to return to Fredericksburg, to push toward Hanover, or, with a larger force, to push toward Orange Court House. I wish Sumner was at Washington, and up near the Monocacy, with good batteries. I do not doubt the enemy have large amounts of supplies provided for them, and I believe they have a contempt for this Army of Virginia. I wish myself away from it, with all our old Army of the Potomac, and so do our companions. I was informed today by the best authority that, in opposition to General Pope's views, this army was pushed out to save the Army of the Potomac—an army that could take care of itself. Pope says he long since wanted to go behind the Occoquan.

I am in great need of ambulances, and the officers need medicines, which, for want of transportation, were left behind. I hear many of the sick of my corps are in houses on the road very sick. I think there is no fear of an enemy crossing the Rappahannock. The cavalry are all in the advance of the rebel army. At Kelly's and Barnett's Fords much property was left, in consequence of the wagons going down for grain, etc. If you can push up the grain to-night, please do so, direct to this place. There is no grain here or anywhere, and this army is wretchedly supplied in that line. Pope says he never could get enough.

Most of this is private, but if you can get me away, please do so. Make what use of this you choose, so it does good.

Don't let the alarm here disturb you. If you had a good force you could go to Richmond. A force should at once be pushed on to Manassas to open the road. Our provisions are very short.
(signed)
F. J. Porter.[74]

To General Burnside: Morell left his medicine, ammunition and baggage at Kelly's Ford.[75] Can you have it hauled to Fredericksburg and stored? His wagons were all sent to you for grain and ammunition. I have sent back to you every man of the First and Sixth New York Cavalry, except what has been sent to Gainesville. I will get them to you after a while. Everything here is at sixes and sevens, and I find that I am to take care of myself in every respect. Our line of communication has taken care of itself in compliance with orders. The army has not three days' provisions. The enemy captured all Pope's and other clothing: and from McDowell the same, including liquors. No guard accompanying the trains, and small ones guard bridges. The wagons are rolling on, and I shall be here tomorrow. Good night!
(signed)
F. J. Porter[76]

Four Miles from Manassas, 28th, 2 P.M.

Major General Burnside: All that talk about bagging Jackson, etc. was bosh. That enormous Gap (Manassas) was left open and the enemy jumped through, and the story of McDowell having cut off Longstreet had no good foundation. The enemy have destroyed all our bridges, burnt trains, etc., and made this army rush back to look after its line of communication and find our base of subsistence. We are far from Alexandria, considering this moving of transportation. Your supply train of 40 wagons is here, but I can't find them. There is a report that Jackson is at Centreville, which you can believe or not. The enemy destroyed an immense amount of property at Manassas—cars and supplies. I expect the next thing will be a raid on our rear by way of Warrenton by Longstreet, who was cut-off.
(signed)
F. J. Porter. Major General.[77]

Bristoe, August 29th, 1862—6 A.M.

General Burnside:
Shall be off in half an hour. The messenger who brought this says the enemy had been at Centreville and pickets were found there last night. Sigel had a severe fight last night; took many prisoners; Banks is at Warrenton Junction; McDowell near Gainesville; Heintzelman and Reno at Centreville, where they marched yesterday, and Pope went to Centreville, with the last two as a body-guard, at the time not knowing where was the enemy and when Sigel was fighting within eight miles of him and in sight.[78] Comment is unnecessary. The enormous trains are still rolling on, many animals not being watered for fifty hours. I shall be out

of provisions tomorrow night. Your train of 40 wagons cannot be found. I hope Mac is at work, and we shall soon be ordered out of this. It would seem from proper statements of the enemy, that he was wandering around loose; but I expect they know what they are doing, which is more than anyone here or anywhere knows.[79]

(This dispatch was presented to the original court-martial which tried General Porter, embodied in one from General Burnside to General Halleck and was without signature, as shown by the record, but was quoted as being an acknowledged dispatch of General Porter by the counsel for the petitioner in his opening before the Board of Army officers in the case of Fitz John Porter in 1875).

I shall only remark that during the days on which these dispatches were sent off, Porter was not at the front at all, either personally or with his corps and that the inamiable stories and flings which these letters and telegrams contain were either suggested by his imagination or were picked up from stragglers and skulkers from the front.[80]

On the west of Porter during all this time was Banks's Corps at Warrenton Junction. On the north of him, along the Warrenton Pike and south of it at Greenwich, were the corps of McDowell and Sigel and the divisions of Reynolds, of Reno, and of Kearny. Whilst on the east of him and between him and Manassas Junction, were the division of Hooker and the Headquarters of the Army of Virginia. He was moving slowly along the chord of a semi-circle (the road from Warrenton Junction to Manassas Junction).

The arc of this semi-circle was occupied by the rest of the army, the army of the enemy being on the outside of it altogether. Our whole army, therefore, until late on the morning of the twenty-ninth, was interposed between Porter and any force of the enemy and he was in as safe a place during all that time as if he had been in the grounds of the War Department, at Washington. His condition of mind, as evinced in these dispatches, promised very little toward the active and zealous work expected of every faithful officer under the circumstances which surrounded us and little as it promised, the performance was still less.

That his corps fought on the thirtieth is true and he has made the most of it. But why and how did it do so? On the night of the twenty-ninth, after his failure to go into action that whole day, I sent him peremptory orders to march his corps to the field of battle and report to me in person.

> Headquarters Army of Virginia, in the Field near Bull Run,
> August 29, 1862, 8:50 P.M.
> General: Immediately upon receipt of this order, the precise hour of receiving which you will acknowledge, you will march your command to

the field of battle of to-day, and report to me in person for orders. You are to understand that you are expected to comply strictly with this order, and to be present on the field within three hours after its reception, or after daybreak to-morrow morning.

(signed)

Jno. Pope, Major General Commanding.

Major General F. J. Porter.

A true copy:

(signed)

T. C. H. Smith. Lieutenant-Colonel and Aide-de-Camp.[81]

This order brought him to my presence the next morning and I, myself, ordered him into the action and watched his movements from a position on the ridge in rear of him.

It would necessarily have been fatal to him personally not to go into battle under such circumstances and his fighting on the thirtieth was a matter in which his inclination or disinclination had no part.

Whatever credit is given him for his action on the thirtieth must largely be qualified by these facts.

The gallant men of his corps who did the fighting on the thirtieth would have fought equally well the day before if they had been given the chance to do so. That they had not this opportunity the day before is in no sense their fault and it is quite certain that a large number of them were both surprised and disappointed that they were not permitted to go into the action of the twenty-ninth.

Franklin arrived at Centreville, eight miles in the rear of the battlefield of Second Bull Run, late in the afternoon of the thirtieth (having marched twenty-one miles toward the field of battle in four days), too late to be of service in that battle and he, himself, was in a condition of mind which made his presence rather an injury than a benefit to the army which he was to reinforce.[82]

It was the knowledge of this feeling and the open exultation of Franklin and other officers of rank in his corps over the fact that their comrades had been worsted in the battle of the day before which induced me to recommend that the army be drawn back to the intrenchments around Washington and there thoroughly reorganized. There did not appear to me to be any hope of success for that army while such a feeling prevailed among so many of its higher officers.[83] It was therefore drawn back to Washington and McClellan succeeded to, or, as he himself intimates in his official report, usurped the command of it. The means by which such a condition was reproduced should and probably will find in time a historian.[84]

Part Five

MISCELLANEOUS RECOLLECTIONS

Chapter Twelve

Abraham Lincoln

I mentioned in a former article that I had quite a long interview with Mr. Lincoln, in which I expressed fully and frankly my disinclination to be assigned to the command of this new army in front of Washington, or indeed to be placed on duty anywhere in the East. My reasons, as given to him, were practically the same as those given to Mr. Stanton, with the additional statement that, being a Western man by birth and infused with the Western feeling and sentiment, I should naturally be unwilling to separate myself from the Western armies and their environment. It is not necessary to repeat that I did not prevail.

It would seem in order that I should say something in this connection concerning Mr. Lincoln, but it is hard to determine where to begin or to end. The constant tendency of the public mind, which grows stronger as the years go by, is to place him upon some such pedestal as Washington (mainly through the agency of the Rev. Mr. Weems) has always occupied among us.[1] It is wise

173

and properly grateful that we should hold our great men, especially those who have rendered great services to their country, in high honor and that we should perpetuate their memory in marble and bronze, as well as in the pages of history; but we should be careful, in doing this, that we do not remove them beyond the reach of human sympathy by placing them on a plane so far above us and so wholly divesting them of all the weaknesses of humanity, that we come to look upon them as demigods or at least persons so superior to all human frailties that sympathy or affection are alike out of the question. We all know how far this feeling has always separated our people from General Washington and how little is our knowledge of him as a man. The cold and dignified character and the formal and wholly irresponsive manner and habit of the man as depicted, has left us with a mere abstraction of a National hero, for whom not a ray of human regard or affection could possibly be felt.[2] So far has this idea of Washington gone that the people of the country actually resent, as a kind of sacrilege, any attempt to reproduce his actual character by offering to the public gaze some of the human weaknesses which bring him so much nearer to us and enable us to appreciate so much better his immense triumph over the difficult situation in which he was placed. It has always been hard to comprehend how a man so haughty and impassive as General Washington has been represented to be, could have commanded such strong and in some cases, impassioned personal attachment as he is known to have inspired; nor would it have been possible had he been such a man. We begin slowly to know better, but very slowly and with manifest unwillingness to accept any facts which tend to overthrow or impair our long-cherished sentiment. The famous cherry tree is still in perennial bloom and the little hatchet is brandished yet in every household in the land. Let us hope that we may hereafter make progress in an acquaintance with the real hero of the Revolutionary War and come to love him as our great friend and benefactor, who was not above us, but of and with us, who possessed virtues greater than most, but who also was afflicted with ordinary human weaknesses, to which at times he yielded like the rest of us. His great virtues enabled him to control better than most of us the exhibition of those weaknesses and the injury that might follow their indulgence and in this immense self-control is to be found the secret of his power. When we come to learn what weaknesses and blemishes in his own character he was obliged to contend with, in addition to those of his followers, in the midst of the great conflict to establish our liberties; how at times his temper gave way and he used language too strong for the Reverend Mr. Weems to record, but which most of us under like provocation would have indulged in much more copiously; how he had his favorites among the officers and his pet antipathies also, we begin to understand that he was a man like ourselves, great mainly in his immense loyalty and self control. Whilst we are beginning the effort to restore General Washington to his countrymen, we also appear to be resolved to thrust Mr. Lincoln into his place and exalt him so high and isolate him so completely that it will after a while be a sort of sacrilege to refer to him except as a saint. Even now any unfavorable criticism of any act or statement of Mr. Lincoln is widely resented and if he is to be actually known to his countrymen as he really was, no time should be lost in painting the picture. He was no more a saint than Washington and I presume no more of a sinner, but, like General Washington, he had weaknesses and peculiarities of his own, which need to be much more fully set forth before we can know him as he was and as I have doubt he would prefer that his memory should be transmitted to his posterity. Everything now written about him, however trivial, is found to be interesting to the country and it appears to me to be a sort of duty that any man who has had any relations with Mr. Lincoln should write out and publish his experience and his view of the peculiarities and conspicuous traits of our great President. In a multitude of counselors there is said to be safety. If in a multitude of writers there is not actually truth, there is at least the data from which a reasonably close approximation to the truth may be deduced. But in order to attain even this approach, to the reality, it is essential that every man who writes shall be conscientious and tell the exact impressions made on him, regardless of what people may think of him or what he says. If a man writes at all upon such a subject, it is bare justice to his readers and bare honesty in himself to state the truth; otherwise he helps to establish and to perpetuate a cheat.

Let us hope that such papers may be generally written and that some earnest and competent scholar or philosopher may collect and digest them and after consideration and comparison of them all, paint us in fitting words a picture of Abraham Lincoln which will be satisfactory to his countrymen.

I do not wish to be understood from the foregoing remarks to have any intention to attempt a biography of Mr. Lincoln, or indeed anything like a continuous narrative concerning him. I only propose to record the impressions he made on me at different times and under a variety of circumstances to be used, if they are worth it, in helping to make up some consistent knowledge of Mr. Lincoln's character.

I first saw him to know him personally in Chicago in 1850. The United States Court was in session there at the time and there was a large representation of the bar of the state in attendance. I had gone to Chicago merely to see the city and to meet some old friends whom I had not seen for some years.[3] Being a citizen of Illinois and having won some small reputation during the Mexican War, but recently ended, Mr. Lincoln, with some of the other lawyers, was good enough to call upon me. The general impression left on my mind was of a tall, gaunt, angular man, very homely and awkward, but with a very intelligent and kindly face. He appeared to be in high spirits and was overflowing with humor. He told a number of very funny stories which kept everybody laughing and appeared to be a man altogether happy and without a care. As I saw him there, during the short time of his visit, he had not an indication of that sorrowful and pathetic look which afterward became the familiar expression of his face. Altogether, at this time I should have selected Mr. Lincoln as the happiest and most joyous man I had ever met. I afterwards saw him in Indianapolis in 1861, on his way to Washington to be inaugurated President of the United States.[4]

Naturally he was an object of far greater curiosity and interest than when I saw him in Chicago and I watched him as closely as was possible under such circumstances and in the midst of such a crowd. Whilst his outward appearance was much the same, his face had strangely lost that look of careless humor which I remembered. Already a shade of care had begun to creep over his countenance and dim its joyous expression. He invited me to accompany him to Washington, which I was glad to do and at once joined the small party of friends who were with him and among whom were several officers of the army whom I knew, notably General (then Colonel) Sumner and General (then Major) David Hunter. Perhaps two more genuine and honorable men, more intensely loyal to the government, could not have been found in the army. At Indianapolis, then, I became a member, though a very insignificant one, of the party which surrounded and in a sense, guarded Mr. Lincoln in that most wonderful journey, the like of which has never been made before or since. Those who were living in the latter part of February, 1861, cannot fail even now, to remember with a pang of awakened pain and apprehension the condition of public feeling all over the North. No one was willing to believe that disunion and civil war were really contemplated by any part of the people and yet the sights and sounds forced upon them the agony of apprehension that it might be so. They did not know where to look for information or advice.

The horrid specter of war and ruin had already invaded every household and sat by every fireside in the land. Women and children, alike with the men, were distracted with fear and sorrow over the future. All classes and conditions of people were, as it were, gathered on the housetops awaiting the beginning of a civil war, which everybody knew must bring mourning to every family in the land. Much the largest portion of the people, both North and South, would not, whatever they may have thought, admit that there would be war; the Southern people, because they had been taught to believe that the North were cowardly by nature and too much absorbed in money making, to confront the South in arms; the Northern people, because they knew there was no rational cause for war which had not existed from the beginning of the government and because they had been so often threatened with secession that it had ceased to be considered worth serious notice. Nevertheless, all the indications pointed to a disruption of the government, followed by civil war and every day strengthened their force and increased their directness. A dreadful fear that we must take up arms to defend our government against our own countrymen began to brood over the land. Whilst everything was still in doubt and uncertainty, the fear was so great that men left their business and their occupations to gather into knots on the streetcorners to discuss the terrible misfortune that was about to befall them. Such excitement and the feelings which it aroused and was every day arousing, has never been paralleled in this country. It was in the midst of this great commotion and through crowds of excited people that Mr. Lincoln began his progress to Washington with the small party he had invited. Every railroad station, every hamlet and village and the greater towns in like proportion, poured forth their crowds of anxious people, eager to have some assurance or information from the new President as to what they were to expect. At all hours of the day, from early daylight till after dark, these crowds occupied the stations and pressed around the President's car with loud appeals for him to speak to them. The first rays of the sun found them still occupying every stopping place and even many stations where the train did not stop. Through this vast multitude, whose continuity was scarce anywhere broken, Mr. Lincoln pursued that memorable journey unrelieved by any of the cheerfulness and enjoyment usually attendant upon such occasions. Oppressed with care and with the awful responsibilities imposed upon him, suffering from fatigue and loss of sleep, called for by excited and anxious people at all hours for assurances he could not give and encouragement he could not honestly offer, he underwent tortures which lined his face for months. Almost half of the people of the states through which he passed were Democrats and opposed to him and the policies of his party.

They did not anticipate war because it would be ruinous to them and they never in any of their party movements contemplated the destruction of the government. Neither could they believe that their party friends of the South, to whom they had submitted their consciences and almost their manhood, would leave them to the mercies of their political enemies in the North, then largely in the majority and likely to become much more so. In short, they did not for a moment conceive it possible that they would be abandoned by their Southern allies and they presented a sullen front and aggressive tone toward the new President. The Republicans, on the other hand, would not believe in any danger of civil war, but could not escape a lively fear that there would be and their reception of the President showed a mixture of exultation and of apprehension curious but by no means encouraging to witness.

It is singular to observe how blind men are to the greatest of human events upon the immediate eve of their occurrence and how unfailingly they neglect or wholly overlook the controlling element which dominates and makes possible every such catastrophe. In the South they persuaded themselves that secession would not be resisted by war, because the Northern people were cowards and so devoted to money making that they would rather submit to anything than endanger their trade with the South.

The North, on the other side, knew that every material interest of the South would suffer, if indeed it were not destroyed, by separation and especially that the security of their slave property would be irrevocably jeoparded, if not completely destroyed, by the overthrow of the government. Both parties supposed (excepting always a few leaders) that the whole matter would turn upon such practical arguments and reasons as these, forgetting altogether that in all great movements of people, moral or political, especially such as lead to revolution and civil war, the element of passion is in the beginning the supreme authority and compels masses of people at the crucial moment to do what they had convinced themselves by deliberate reasoning ought not to be and would not be done at all. This element of passion dominated everywhere in the South and made secession and civil war acceptable to great numbers of people who were opposed to both in the beginning. In this way such states as Virginia and Georgia, known to have majorities opposed to secession, were brought to vote for measures which they abhorred.[5] Perhaps this element of passion or sentiment operated later in the North, where people act deliberately, but when it did blaze forth after the firing on Fort Sumter, it raged with equal fury and with intenser fires.

Every day of our journey brought us more alarming news and still the great mass of people we saw clung to the hope that there would be no trouble that would lead to violence. Mr. Lincoln's brief speeches, when he was forced to speak, were very carefully worded, but were apparently intended to assure the country, the South particularly, that he would not begin or encourage any measures which might lead to war.[6] The only objection to these utterances is that they were not addressed to reasonable men, or at least to men who would listen to reason. The adroit leaders in the South who were for secession per se, as we used to say in those days, paraded such remarks as an argument for secession to the doubtful among themselves, as showing that the new President had disavowed any intention to begin hostilities and thus confirmed their assertions that "the North would not fight," and therefore there was no danger in seceding.

It was not until we reached Trenton, New Jersey, where a Democratic Legislature was in session, that he gave any intimation of the course he might pursue and I remember very well the thrill that went through the chamber at his words.[7] They were few but to the point. He said substantially that conditions might arise which would require him "to put the foot down firmly." Everyone knew exactly what he meant and the sensation in the audience was very marked and suggestive. It seems a pity that there does not appear to exist any verbatim report of his speeches on that journey.[8] Whilst they were not characterized by eloquence and did not contain anything very new or startling, he said a number of things wise and worth remembering. Among others, I remember a remark in one of his speeches at Buffalo to a German society, which solicited an interview as Germans, to the effect that a resident and voter in the United States was an American or he was nothing and that he did not recognize American citizens as German, or Irishmen, or of any other nationality. This remark excited much comment, both favorable and the reverse, but in the light of the present it is very clear that it conveyed a lesson, if not a warning, to which it would have been wisdom to our foreign-born citizens to give heed then and which it is of vastly more importance that they apply now and with vigor. The time is rapidly coming when our naturalized citizens must accept Mr. Lincoln's view of their status in this country, or worse will befall them.

It seems a pity that there was not a graphic writer to paint in words the incidents of that remarkable journey and portray the scenes enacted day after day under the eyes of the party that made it; who could reproduce the continuous crowds of people who thronged every station, wherein every face, whatever else it expressed, bore the marks of extreme anxiety and apprehension. There was nothing noisy or boisterous in these assemblages of people, but there was plainly to be seen profound though unexpressed uneasiness.

I remember quite distinctly the painful impression made on me by the long ride in open carriages through the streets of New York; the crowds of people who lined the sidewalks and occupied every window and doorway which opened on the street, crowded and jammed together so that it seemed that many of them must be trampled to death. Of course, in this vast multitude there was a large representation of both political parties; but one party cheered as if uncertain whether they ought to rejoice or to lament, whilst the other, though not threatening, was silent and sullen. The ride down the city through these crowds of excited and anxious people was not encouraging and seemed a chilly welcome of the President of the United States to the metropolis of the country. It was fitly crowned and supplemented by the visit of the mayor, Fernando Wood,[9] at the Astor House.

Everybody knew his political status and that he actually was in favor of withdrawing New York City from the Union and setting it up as a free city and the seat of commercial supremacy on the Atlantic Coast. In short, to establish a small kingdom of his own quite independent of state or United States sovereignty. The contrast, between him (Fernando Wood) and Mr. Lincoln as I watched their meeting was very suggestive. Mr. Lincoln, tall, gaunt and rugged, with angular, rough-hewn features, but a kindly expression, unpolished in manner and ungraceful in speech, but evidently sincere and genuine; Mayor Wood, erect and agile, with a perfectly smooth face, easy graceful manners and fine address, but with a countenance as devoid of any indication of his thoughts and as free from the least sign of impulse or genuineness of any kind, smooth and soft, with the undulating gait of an animal of the feline tribe, made a tableau which I shall never forget. The interview lasted only a few moments and simply added to the uncomfortable feeling which had begun to invade our party when we reached the outskirts of the city.[10] Nor was that feeling relieved by our progress thence to Washington. We began to hear first in New York the rumors of insult and violence to the president, which increased in volume and directness as we approached Philadelphia.[11] The aspect of things at Trenton was decidedly chilling and when we arrived in Philadelphia reports reached the President of contemplated violence to him so specific and direct that it was no longer wise to neglect them. During the night in Philadelphia these reports of plots to assassinate Mr. Lincoln as he passed through Baltimore took official shape and came to him by official messengers,[12] under the sign manual of Mr. Seward.[13] No steps, however, were taken in the matter by Mr. Lincoln and the party went on to Harrisburg the next day without apparent excitement or change of plan. There, however, the reports from Washington became so positive and the apprehensions of prominent officials and leading Union men so forcibly urged that after some discussion it was resolved that Mr. Lincoln should return secretly and at once to Philadelphia and take the night train to Washington, which would take him through Baltimore either before or shortly after daylight next morning. Of course there was some difference of opinion among those consulted on the subject (of whom I happened to be one) concerning this procedure, some holding that it was more becoming that the President should pursue his selected route to the Capital of the country unmoved by clamor or by threats, and that any other course would lay him liable to the suspicion of lack of courage, a most unfortunate if not fatal reputation to be fixed upon him at such a crisis in public affairs.

A good deal was said in a short time on both sides of the question, but the issue was decided by Mr. Lincoln himself. In the light of subsequent events he was probably right. He returned to Philadelphia that afternoon with the knowledge of very few persons except the members of our own party—I believe none except Governor Curtin,[14] who, by the way, in the hurry and confusion of the occasion effected a change of hats with me, greatly to his own advantage. With Mr. Lincoln and by his own choice, went Colonel Ward H. Lamon,[15] of Illinois, a man of acknowledged courage and resolution and a devoted friend.

As is well known, they reached Philadelphia after dark, drove at once to the Baltimore depot, and arrived in Washington early the next morning without being recognized by anyone.[16] The rest of the party continued their journey as first determined on, and left Harrisburg the next morning for Baltimore. We were received at the station of the Northern Pennsylvania Railroad by Mr. Gittings,[17] the president and taken to his house for breakfast, where we were treated with most courteous and abundant hospitality.

Thence we went to the depot of the Baltimore & Ohio Railroad and there took the train for Washington. We waited perhaps ten minutes before the train left the station and by that time it came to be more or less public that Mr. Lincoln and the rest of the President's party were on it. A crowd began at once to collect around the car and stare in at the windows. I myself heard a number of ugly expressions and saw many scowling faces. No violence was committed, though the crowd pressing upon our car consisted precisely of the people capable of outrage and none of us were sorry when the train moved out of the station and left behind us these accomplished gentlemen, who shortly afterward distinguished themselves so much and shed such luster on their city.[18]

To this day the Plugugly of Baltimore enjoys the well-earned reputation of being the most abandoned scoundrel and miscreant on this continent.

Thus concluded a journey perhaps the most extraordinary in some respects ever made. It seems a misfortune that no one at the time recognized how deep would be its interest to posterity sufficiently to make a careful record of it, but the tremendous events which seemed so near at hand absorbed the attention of everybody and gave no inclination for the consideration of anything not directly related to them.

Until I read the paper of Nicolay and Hay on the subject, I had hoped that some one of the President's party had written up the details, or at least kept notes which could afterwards be extended, but I fear we must abandon the hope of ever getting a detailed account of one of the strangest and most significant episodes of the great rebellion.[19]

For months afterward I was haunted by the remembrance of the vast crowds of excited people through which we may be said to have in a sense forced our way from Springfield to Washington City and it is almost with a thrill that I recall the anxious and foreboding look nearly all of them wore. As the war progressed that expression in less degree became familiar to the American people; but in those days, when anxiety of that kind, or indeed of any kind, had been unknown to the mass of our people for half a century, it produced a profound impression, not only because of its character and the reason of it, but because of the vast number of people who were its victims.

During no part of this long journey did Mr. Lincoln exhibit any sign whatever of the spirit of fun and humor which always before had been the striking feature of his character and conduct. On the contrary, he had a harassed and worried look wholly unnatural to him and which seemed to increase with every mile. It was true that his car was constantly invaded by committees from the villages and towns through which we passed and by political personages of more or less local importance, all seeking information and most of them consolation also; but before this journey, as afterward, he could always find something humorous to lighten the most solemn subjects or to divert the tendency of a conversation which was becoming disagreeable. I noticed this worried look more particularly in Harrisburg and whilst he never said so, I have always had the conviction that he resolved upon the hurried night journey to Washington with great reluctance and only because of the profound alarm and hysterical appeals of his friends in Washington. It is certain, however, that his spirits were considerably lightened after he reached the Capital and found the conditions nothing like so bad as had been anticipated and indeed represented. It is much to be doubted whether he was ever afterward so much depressed in spirits and for so long a time.

The moment he arrived in Washington he was, of course, overrun by politicians of every phase of Republicanism and besieged night and day by the honest and dishonest, the former with long-winded advice or impracticable plans to save the Union; the latter with schemes for personal or political advantage. It was hard to say which of these two classes was the most annoying and wearisome, but they both consumed much valuable time and greatly tried the President's patience, of which, fortunately, he possessed a superabundance.

There was at the time a "Peace Convention" in session at Willard's Hotel, consisting of old gentlemen sent from every state in the Union, to consult together and devise and submit to the country measures which should quiet the public feeling and restore fraternal relations. They had been wise men in their day, but that day had passed and their wisdom had become folly in such a crisis as then beset us. Whilst they were with immense gravity and importance effecting some proposed modification of the fugitive slave law, or agreeing upon some small concession to the supporters of state sovereignty, the whole country was in the throes of a revolution which swept away both slavery and state sovereignty. They were a worthy and most eminent body of gentlemen in every respect, except a comprehension of the situation with which they thought they were dealing. Whilst they were hatching out small remedies for old and incurable evils and cackling over the outcome, the whole basis of their conference had practically vanished out of existence.

The Union was already gone whilst they were deciding how to save it, so far as secession could destroy it and the fugitive slave law no longer possessed interest for the dominating actors in the drama of the great rebellion. Nevertheless they were full of good intentions and what they considered wise counsel.

I remember very well the effort made by a delegation from the Republican members of the Conference to advise Mr. Lincoln on the subject of his cabinet. At that time it may be said that anybody thought himself competent to advise Mr. Lincoln. One of the members of the delegation recounted to me immediately after it occurred the result of their mission. The only person who was certainly known to have been offered and to have accepted an appointment in the Cabinet was Mr. Seward, though the public seemed to have practically made up its mind who the other members were likely to be.

The object of this Republican delegation from the Peace Conference was to advise Mr. Lincoln, in case he had determined to appoint Mr. Seward, not to appoint Mr. Chase also,[20] as the two men were so opposed to each other in many ways that discord in the Cabinet would be introduced just when harmony was of all things essential. They told him that the critical condition of affairs did not admit of any disputes or want of concert among the members of the Executive Department of the government and much else of wise counsel, which can easily be imagined, was bestowed freely as upon one ignorant of the very rudiments of public administration.

The sole reply they received was a question from the President, "if they did not think he could manage his own Cabinet." This question completely staggered them and they withdrew with the saddest forebodings. As the member of the delegation who told me remarked, "the idea of this obscure and unlettered lawyer from Illinois talking so flippantly of managing such men as Seward and Chase was too much for us."

Yet it is a fact, at which thinking people have not yet ceased to wonder, that Mr. Lincoln put into his cabinet not only Seward and Chase, but every other one of his competitors for the nomination at the Chicago Convention, and that he bumped their heads together in such manner that at the end of three years there was not one of them left who had the slightest hope of contesting his nomination for a second term. The truth was, that in those early days of March there was probably not one of the members of Mr. Lincoln's Cabinet who did not consider himself vastly Mr. Lincoln's superior and the only question appeared to be, which one of them should appropriate the Presidential functions, or at the least, how much authority or influence the new President should be permitted to exercise in their respective Departments.

One year corrected all this misapprehension and placed Mr. Lincoln where he always afterward remained, master of himself and his administration. Under that kindly, simple expression of face and those mild and gentle manners there lay concealed an iron will and a sagacity and adroitness in public affairs never before possessed by any public man in this country. Perhaps it may be going too far to say that he was cunning in the ordinary sense, but certain it is that he was impressed at the earliest moment of schemes and plots of both political friends and enemies and found little trouble in undermining them all. With a smile that was "childlike and bland," he could listen to statements and revelations the most disagreeable and obnoxious and with the same suave countenance he could deal the authors a fatal blow. The enormous burdens and difficulties of his position were far more than ought ever to have been imposed on one man with the expectation that he could support and overcome them and oftentimes his political friends, at least the members of his own political party, were the most troublesome and hard to satisfy of all.

It is not too much to say, that at the beginning of his third year of administration a majority of Republicans, both in the Senate and the House, were violently opposed to him and if they could have done so would gladly have changed him for almost any one of his cabinet. The radical Republicans to a man were bitterly opposed to him. No doubt they resorted to questionable methods to make their hostility effective, but it must be said too, that Mr. Lincoln was not above resorting to methods equally doubtful to hold his own. Witness that remarkable episode of the attempt to put Frank Blair into the House of Representatives and make him Speaker, as the President's friend, while he still held the commission of general in the army.[21] The whole story is set forth in the proceedings of Congress, accessible to everybody. He was also (as perhaps is natural) not unwilling to let the responsibility and reproach for unpopular measures or appointments to fall on the shoulders of his subordinates instead of his own, where they properly belonged.

It is not worth while to follow up these matters into further details. They only have interest as showing how an honest upright man naturally is sometimes compelled, not of his own interests merely, but even more in the public interests, in times and under conditions such as beset him, to use the weapons of his enemies, even though they be not always such as are approved by a lofty standard of morality. Mr. Lincoln was no saint, nor did I ever hear that he assumed to be. He was an earnest, loyal man, alike so to his country and his principles; but if the necessity arose, he wielded the weapons of political warfare with as little hesitation and with far more skill than did his political foes. He had been an old Whig and was therefore saturated with the idea of settling all questions by compromise, but it was also in his nature to be kind and conciliatory and he always inclined to peaceful rather than violent measures and tried to do the impossible thing in public life — make friends of his political enemies, even if it involved neglecting his own friends. It is much to be feared that, if he had lived, this tendency would have led him to go to much greater lengths in resettling the status of the Southern people than his own dispassionate judgment or the public opinion of his countrymen would have approved. He was a very wise man, a very adroit man and a very just man, unless to be just involved too great a strain on his natural kindness of heart.

This kind nature is often illustrated by stories of the manner in which he set aside capital sentences on army deserters and others of that stripe. His admirers, who publish such things for the purpose of exhibiting what they consider an admirable trait in Mr. Lincoln's character, fail to see what dreadful injustice was committed by them upon every faithful soldier on the field of battle. The absence of these deserters occasioned the loss of battles and the death of thousands of better men than they and the wounding nearly to death of thousands of others. Their presence might have assured victory and would certainly have saved many lives and much suffering. To save these deserters of their flag and their comrades from well-merited punishment for the awful fate to which their act had condemned their fellow soldiers and which penalty was provided to deter others from committing the same crime, was an act of questionable kindness, but of undeniable injustice to the country and to the soldiers of our armies. Such actions are an indication not of Mr. Lincoln's strength, but of his weakness and leave him open to the suspicion that an appeal to his feelings would in all cases have overcome his sense of justice. That some few extreme cases of this kind did occur is probably true, but that the numerous extravagant incidents of this sort every day published in books, magazines and newspapers have even a foundation of truth is beyond the reach of human credulity.

In all men who possess a keen sense of humor there is always found the element of pathos in an equal degree. When neither of them is in excess, they easily combine into a harmonious whole and make up an engaging and rounded character, but in Mr. Lincoln's case were morbidly developed and both active to a wonderful degree. They never harmonized or became fused into each other. There were always the two men in Mr. Lincoln, the pathetic and the humorous, as separate and distinct from each other as two separate personages could have been. Having seen the pathetic Mr. Lincoln, the saddest and most sorrowful of human beings, the very aspect of whom almost brought tears to one's eyes and afterward to meet the humorous part of him, full of life and fun, making jokes, sometimes not over delicate and laughing over them as loudly and as long as any of his hearers, a man seemingly without care or anxiety, was as strange and startling almost as to witness the transformations of Dr. Jekyll and Mr. Hyde. A stranger or a foreigner's opinion of him depended altogether upon whether they saw him in one or the other of these moods; and as he changed from one to the other easily and quickly, it might well happen that two strangers who had seen him at different times within an hour or two would give entirely opposite opinions of him. He apparently yielded to either impulse and was not at any pains to subdue the expression of either condition.

Certainly I have seen him at times when he was the saddest and most pathetic man my eyes had ever looked on and knowing the awful cares and responsibilities which rested on him, the falling away of political friends and the ferocious and cruel attacks of political enemies, together with the inefficiency and bad faith of some of his generals in the field, I could fully realize the look of deep dejection which overspread both face and figure. Ten minutes afterward, in the same place and under the very same conditions, I have seen him the jolliest man on earth, laughing, swinging his arms and stamping about the room, wholly overcome with mirth. It was the strangest thing I ever saw and during the week of McClellan's retreat from the Chickahominy to the James River, the most of which it was my fortune to spend with him in Mr. Stanton's office, I had the opportunity to witness this curious transformation many times. Yet I do not think it was difficult to determine that the real man was the sad and pathetic man, full of sorrows and trials, personal and public, the tremendous pressure of which he was fortunately able temporarily to throw off by his indulgence of the lower and superficial side of his nature. Toward the close of the war the humorous feature of his character in at least open and frequent exhibitions of it had nearly disappeared.

People who found fault with Mr. Lincoln for making or enjoying jokes whilst the whole country was plunged in mourning and racked by apprehension, little understood how essentially it is an effort of nature to lighten a burden of care and grief which could not otherwise be borne and that it is the same mental or emotional feeling which induces the soldier to be as gay after a bloody battle as if he had been at a feast.

But for this temperament which enabled him to throw off for the moment the tremendous cares which rested on him, Mr. Lincoln would not have lived to see the end of the first year of his administration and but for relief of exactly the same kind, no soldier could ever be persuaded to go into battle a second time.

In his personal character Mr. Lincoln was a faithful friend, true to those he loved and without malice or hatred for his enemies. Nothing could be more touching than his affection for his family and his devotion and forebearance to them. He was eminently a domestic man, more fond of his home and his own fireside than is considered politic in a public man. He was a devoted husband and father, a trusty friend and a good citizen. These traits of his personal character are well known of all men and therefore hardly worth repeating.

But he was also the greatest public man in some respects that this country has ever produced. It is strange that the general public and especially surprising that his Cabinet, did not sooner discover and adapt themselves to his immense superiority. In intellectual force, in political sagacity and in adroitness of political management he was so far beyond the members of his Cabinet that he held them absolutely in the hollow of his hand. They found this out later and it must have been a surprise as great as that of Balaam. They submitted to it ruefully no doubt, but only after their luster had been dimmed by the long shadow which his gaunt figure cast over them. There lived not the man in those days and in this country who could have done the work he did and he did it not solely nor mainly by virtue of his sagacity and intellectual force, but because of his peculiar relation to the great mass of his country-men, a relation never before held by any public man in the United States.

He was one of the people, familiar with their ideas and their ways and thoroughly acquainted with every detail of their home lives and their methods of thought and action. He was always with them; moved forward when they were ready; halted when they wished to halt and drew back when they thought it better to retire. It was not because "he felt their pulse," and learned what they wanted and would support or indeed that he asked any questions on the subject, but because he was literally one of them, moved by the same impulses and guided by the same instincts. It was himself he consulted when any great or novel thing was to be tried, knowing well enough that what he felt about the matter the great mass of his countrymen would think also and he never was deceived or misled in this matter. It was not because he was one of the people that he possessed such power, but because he was the absolute embodiment of the people in his own person and naturally in his high place their complete exponent.

Every year he grew in popularity and influence and on the day of his unhappy death he wielded a power in this country never before possessed, or probably to be possessed, by man.

He was not a saint, as I have said and I fancy he would have repudiated such a claim for him, but his virtues and his services to his country, which no other man could have rendered, will secure him a place in the hearts of his countrymen and in the eyes of the world forever.

Let us hope that the inclination to deify and set him aloft in our midst too far removed from us by the supposed perfection of his character for any human sympathy may be checked before it goes further and that we may never be condemned to contemplate Abraham Lincoln with that reverence and awe which for nearly a hundred years isolated George Washington from the sympathy and affection of his countrymen.

The Mexican War and Washington in 1861

 $\mathscr{A}$ mong the many notable persons whom I met from time to time in the office of Mr. Stanton during the three weeks I remained in Washington awaiting the concentration of the three corps which were to constitute the Army of Virginia, was Mr. Joseph Holt,[1] who from the very beginning impressed me as a remarkable man. The first time I saw him was when he was Secretary of War in Buchanan's Administration and he was then indirectly concerned in rather an absurd, certainly an abortive, episode which occurred during the very last days of Mr. Buchanan's occupation of the White House. Just before leaving Cincinnati to accompany Mr. Lincoln to Washington, I made an address on the situation of the country and especially the prospective outcome of the threatening attitude of the state authorities of South Carolina toward Fort Sumter. This address was made to the Literary Society of Cincinnati, of which I was a member and by their request.[2] It was a time when the whole country was uneasy and fearful and everything said in relation to the critical condition of affairs, especially by a military man, commanded far more attention than it would have attracted under any other conditions. After giving somewhat in detail an account of the plan and character of Sumter and its means of defense as it had been left by Mr. Buchanan and his Secretary of War, Mr. Floyd,[3] I enlarged upon the general situation and took occasion to use some not over harsh language toward those two functionaries because of their shameful neglect, to call it by no harder name, in abandoning the forts and other public property of the United States to the capture of its enemies.[4] There was not a word that was not true, nor as I remember was the name of either of these public officials made use of, but of course it was easily seen who was meant and in a strictly military view such expressions were an offense under the Articles of War.

The address was published in the papers next morning and of course was more widely read and commanded far more attention than its merits warranted or than it would have met with in ordinary times.

I left Cincinnati, however, almost immediately after to accompany Mr. Lincoln to Washington and gave no further thought to the matter. But on the second day of March, after I had been a week in Washington, I was served with an official paper placing me in arrest and ordering me to Newport, Kentucky, where a court-martial was instructed to meet on March 4 to try me on the charge of having used "contemptuous and disrespectful language" towards the President of the United States. On the morning of March 4, however, these orders were revoked, but only after the arrest and its cause had been widely published in the newspapers and had called forth all manner of unpleasant comment. There was no doubt that a technical offense had been committed, but neither the language used nor the circumstances were sufficiently serious to have called for such pointed and extreme action at any time. Whilst the whole country was under an agony of apprehension that the grim figure of war was stalking on the scene and the whole structure of our government, our institutions and our laws were about to crumble up before him, whilst there was weeping and mourning all over the land over these impending horrors, it did seem strange, not to say puerile, that the President of the United States, two days before vacating his office, in the presence of these tremendous possibilities, should turn aside from this great spectacle of apprehension and anguish, to cause the arrest of a captain in the army for an offense so trifling in the midst of such great events.

During this episode I saw Judge Holt, who had recently replaced Mr. Floyd as Secretary of War, several times and was greatly impressed by him. He is a majestic man in appearance and deportment, at least six feet in height, with a stalwart, powerful figure, swarthy complexion and black eyes and hair; he would at any time have been a striking figure, but even at that early period of our great civil strife his career had been so prominent and he had deported himself with so much courage and loyalty to the Union that it scarcely required marked physical traits to make him an object of attention. When I came afterward to know him well, I came also to realize how well worthy he was of the admiration and affection of his countrymen. Whilst I was waiting in Washington the movements of the troops to a concentration on the east side of the Blue Ridge, I saw Judge Holt several times in the office of the Secretary of War.

He appeared to be on the most intimate terms with Mr. Stanton, who was devoted to him and was so anxious to have Judge Holt closely connected with him in the War Department as friend and adviser, that he prevailed on him to accept an inferior office and one much beneath his deserts and his capabilities.[5] He was appointed Judge Advocate General of the Army for no other reason than Mr. Stanton's extreme anxiety to unite Judge Holt with himself as closely as both official and personal ties could do so. The office of Judge Advocate General of the Army at that time carried with it only the rank of major and had been held for many years by Major John F. Lee, whose Southern sympathies were too strong to justify the government in retaining him in an office of trust and confidence. Indeed, I think he felt this himself. At any rate, he resigned his commission and was immediately succeeded by Judge Holt.

The office was then given the rank of brigadier general. Judge Holt held this office, though far too obscure a position for a man of his abilities and former high official station, from 1862 to the close of General Grant's second term. During all this long period he discharged every duty of the office with the same energy, care and fidelity that he would have shown if these duties had been the highest and greatest in the land. It was always a melancholy thought to me, as it was to many others, that such a man should be wasted in such a place whilst hundreds of ephemeral creatures were grinning and capering about in great official places, by virtue merely of toadying to the great dispenser of patronage. The two principal cases in which Judge Holt was directly concerned for the government were those of Fitz-John Porter and Mrs. Surratt and the other conspirators.

The first of these cases naturally brought on him the bitter hostility of the Northern Copperheads and subsequently of the Southern men who came to Congress to legislate for those whom they had vainly sought to overthrow in the field. In the nature of things both of these classes were for Porter, not because they believed that he did not do what he was charged with doing, but because they believed he did do it. Of course they were all extremely bitter against Judge Holt because he prosecuted the case vigorously and they have pursued him to this day.

The Surratt case brought down upon him also a large body of the Catholics, many of whom affect to believe that Judge Holt was responsible that Andrew Johnson did not pardon Mrs. Surratt.[6] This was a charge from which Mr. Stanton could have fully relieved him and that he was bound to do so by every obligation of gratitude to Judge Holt; for such friendship and fidelity as is rarely met with among men no man can dispute who knows anything of their personal relations during all the years of the war.[7]

That Mr. Stanton rested quietly and without an utterance while such a friend as Judge Holt was vilified and traduced for what Mr. Stanton knew was false, only illustrates that fatal element in his make-up, from which many of his friends suffered during the war and since.

At one time, within my own knowledge, General Grant had determined to appoint Judge Holt Secretary of War and the Judge was notified of the fact and both he and his friends expected the official announcement for several days. It did not come, however and soon it began to be rumored about that opposition was being made by the same parties that had pursued him because of the Surratt business and that they were pressing their hostility through high official personages. They were successful in defeating Judge Holt's appointment. General Grant appeared to think that the appointment would be impolitic, but I know that he always had the sincerest regard and the highest esteem for Judge Holt long after he retired from the presidency. Judge Holt was the most intensely loyal man to the Union that I have ever known. It was a passion with him and no doubt intensified his feeling against the men he considered lukewarm or unfaithful. Indeed, I think that his intense patriotism greatly injured if indeed it did not entirely thwart, his public career. He was silent and reticent to a degree, even when he conversed, but perhaps that state so celebrated for its public speakers produced no finer orator or more eloquent speaker than he. He lives very quietly in Washington, having retired altogether from active life and dispenses genuine hospitality to the many friends who are devoted to him. Take him all in all, he is one of the ablest men, and one of the most loyal citizens and the most reliable friends in all this country. His diffidence and reticence were qualities which did not conduce to success in public life in this country and as a politician he never could achieve high place.

Very different in these latter respects was a veteran of the Old Army whom I saw several times during these stirring days – General John E. Wool,[8] of the army. He came into my office in Washington a few days after I had assumed the command of the Army of Virginia, or rather, a few days after McClellan's retreat (called by him a "change of base") to Harrison's Landing. I had not seen him since I parted with him at Monterrey, Mexico, in 1848 and as our parting had been far from heart-rending, I was a little surprised to see him in my office. I had been on the general's staff at his headquarters in the latter year of the Mexican War and had taken my departure from it with some unpleasantness.[9] However, whatever might be said against General Wool and no doubt much was said and justly said, no man could question his loyalty to his country nor his ability as a soldier; and everybody who knew him knew very well that he would never allow personal feeling against any man to restrain him from seeking an interview and communicating to that person any knowledge or advice which he believed to be of benefit to the country. The time had not yet come in the army when an officer would dare to subordinate the success of an army or the welfare of the country to his personal feeling toward his commanding officer, and who would bring defeat and disaster upon his comrades to gratify his personal spite or serve his personal interests.

General Wool was at that time in command of Fortress Monroe and came up to Washington to inform me of the condition of things on the Peninsula and McClellan's operations. He was extremely bitter concerning this abortive and certainly not creditable campaign and he was especially severe on McClellan for his weakness and timidity. He urged me in particular to look out for an advance of the enemy toward Washington by way of the Upper Rappahannock, remarking that the enemy had no longer the least apprehension about Richmond from any move by McClellan and that they would not hesitate to detach a large force from their army for such an operation. I told him that I was at the moment concentrating all the troops of my command on the Upper Rappahannock, so as to cover the lines of advance from the direction of Richmond and should be ready to make all the resistance possible with such a force against any such movement by the enemy as he indicated; that I had anticipated such a movement from the moment the outcome of the military operations on the Peninsula was known and felt certain that I should be obliged to bear the whole brunt of such a movement without help from the Army of the Potomac, unless McClellan were compelled to co-operate by positive command of a common superior in rank. I did not and very naturally could not, then conceive it possible that any officer could in the face of positive orders and almost in the sight of the official giving them, fail to execute peremptory commands and by evasions, mis-statements and other scandalous tricks keep a large army for three days from moving to the help of their comrades engaged in a furious battle, the sounds of which were in their ears for all those days of bloodshed and agony.

General Wool, after some general conversation, left my office apparently much relieved in mind by what I had told him. He was at this time, I think, fully sixty-five years old, beyond the age now fixed for the retirement of officers from active service, but he was still very alert and active and moved about with as much sprightliness as a man of half his age could have done. He had won distinction in the war of 1812 and fame of a higher sort in the Mexican War, where he was second to General Taylor in command at Buena Vista.[10] He selected the place where the battle was fought and himself posted the troops and commanded for some hours after the battle was engaged. General Taylor, on whose staff I was serving at the time, slept at Saltillo, five miles in the rear, the night before the battle and did not get on the field until the middle of the forenoon. By that time the whole of our left had given way and the only hold we had on the line along which we had begun the battle was on the extreme right, overlooking the main road to Saltillo, which was held by two Illinois regiments and a section of Washington's Battery.[11] I shall never forget the appearance of that field as we rode up the steep slope that conducted us to the top of the level plain on which the battle had thus far been waged. The valley in which lies the small hamlet of Buena Vista is about eight miles long from north to south and four miles wide, bounded both east and west by chains of lofty mountains. At the northern end of the valley is the large and handsome city of Saltillo.[12]

The main road to the south conducts down the middle of the valley and near and extending south of Buena Vista the road is closely bordered on the east side by abrupt ascents to the table-lands which occupy all the eastern half of the valley. The west side of the valley is so cut up by ravines and deep washes that that it is practically impassable. The great table-land on the eastern side extends from the mountains by a gentle slope to the road above referred to, but is cut up at intervals by streams, generally dry, which flow from the mountains perpendicular to them and the road so that, instead of one great table-land, the eastern half of the valley really consists of a number of parallel table-lands separated from each other by deep ravines, the washes from the mountains. Just south of the little village of Buena Vista, the steep faces of the table-lands on the eastern side of the valley approach so near to the broken and much cut up western half, that there is barely room enough left for the great public road. On the table-land immediately above this narrow place was posted Washington's Battery of artillery and extending thence along the table-land toward the east, the troops were posted in line of battle extending to the base of the mountains.[13] This table-land was about two miles in extent from east to west, and about five hundred yards wide from north to south. I was a member of General Taylor's staff at the time and of course knew what were his movements that day.[14] He was detained in Saltillo until a late hour of the morning, making some arrangements for the safety of our rear and especially the immense quantity of army supplies which were stored in the town, then threatened by a considerable body of the enemy's cavalry, which had appeared on the plain between Saltillo and Monterrey.[15]

When we started to the front the sounds of the battle were plainly heard and they increased in noise and in volume as we rode rapidly toward the field. For a mile before we reached there it became manifest from the fugitives and stragglers we met that some check if not positive disaster had occurred to our army and as we dashed up the short but steep ascent from the road to the plateau where the battle was going on, the sight which met our eyes was as far from encouraging as it well could be unless we had confronted total rout. The whole of the left and left-center of our line had given way and was in full retreat. General Wool and his staff were trying with great earnestness and much personal exposure to arrest the disorderly retreat and rally the troops to their colors, but without success. Herein was plainly demonstrated General Wool's weak point as a soldier. Most of the troops on that field had been organized by him at San Antonio, Texas and had marched thence under his command to Buena Vista. They were with him many months and under his own eye and some of them every hour of the day. Yet there was not a particle of sympathy or even of kind feeling between him and them. On the contrary, there was a feeling of dislike verging on bitterness against him on the part of the larger part if not the whole of the troops he had brought from Texas. I made a visit to the Illinois regiments in their camp a week before the battle and the animosity to General Wool was deep and outspoken.[16]

At a crisis such as occurred on this field of battle General Wool could be of no service whatever. He commanded neither the confidence nor kind feeling of the troops and lacking these things he could not, if he had possessed the military genius of Julius Caesar himself, have arrested the retreat of the regiments which were falling back, or brought them again to confront the enemy. By the time General Taylor reached the field the retreat of the left wing and part of the left center had become practically a rout. There were no reserves and apparently nothing except scattered fragments of a force to oppose the advance of the solid columns of the enemy. Where we ascended the plateau was a little to the left rear of the extreme left of our line, which still held its ground. The first view showed us our entire left just disappearing into the deep ravine in the rear of our line of battle, with General Wool and his staff officers vainly trying to halt and reform them. Immediately in our front and apparently covering the whole plateau to the base of the mountains, were the columns of the enemy, who had already advanced beyond the line occupied by our left and were pressing on in the pursuit. They did not seem to be four hundred yards distant from us and an advance of two hundred yards farther would have placed them so far in rear of our right, which still stood firm, that they could have turned the rear and completely destroyed our right wing also. The plain in front of us seemed to swarm with Mexicans, pressing forward to what, unless they were instantly checked, was certain and complete victory. The only force we had were two batteries of artillery, under Bragg and T. W. Sherman and they were much broken down by hard work the day before and that morning.[17] Nevertheless they were the only hope and a desperate hope, as all thought. General Taylor at once ordered them forward. It was with difficulty the horses could pull the guns up the steep acclivity between the road and the plateau, Bragg's battery leading, he rode up to General Taylor and reported for orders. General Taylor directed him to unlimber his battery and go into action. Bragg replied:

"General, if I go into battery here I will lose my guns."

To which the General replied, "If you do not the battle is lost."

Bragg and Sherman immediately went into action with their batteries and the effect was simply amazing. The whole plateau toward the mountains was packed by the solid columns of the Mexicans advancing on our positions at quick time and cheered on by their officers with waving swords and shouts of encouragement. Their advance had already passed the left flank of the right wing of our army, which naturally began to fall back toward its right rear. The shouts of the enemy as they came on we could plainly hear and as plainly see their swarthy, scowling faces. I was sitting on my horse immediately in rear of the right section of Bragg's battery when his guns first opened. For a moment the smoke of the guns obscured the view, but almost instantly it lifted and disclosed the scene in our front. It was appalling. Long avenues were plowed through the masses of the enemy, in which the wounded were writhing and shrieking among the dead. The whole mass had nearly come to a halt and there appeared to be wavering among them, with a decided cessation of the cheering and shouting. Scant time was given to recover the shock. Again the twelve guns of Bragg and Sherman belched forth their fiery message and the mass of the Mexicans reeled before it. First they halted, then began to break up their ranks and mix themselves together in the confusion of a mob and then to fall back faster and faster and in more disorder every moment. The danger was over from this force, the main force of the enemy, but these two batteries of artillery continued to pour volley after volley into the now terror-stricken Mexicans, piling up the dead and wounded into heaps on the plain. It was a dreadful sight, but the work was effective and settled the issue of the Battle of Buena Vista. I was of course quite near to General Taylor during all this time and he was to me far the most impressive feature of the scene. Naturally, General Taylor was a very irascible man and flew into a passion on the least provocation and for the most trifling causes. I have seen him fly into a fury with a teamster who had been careless or awkward in his driving and after using the most robust and vernacular English on the offender dismount from his horse and ply a wagon-whip over his shoulders with furious vigor. I never knew a man of his years and character so easily and completely thrown off his balance by trifles. This being his temper and habit, I watched him with peculiar interest in this crucial moment of his life, when the whole fate of a battle and of the army under his command was at stake and the chances altogether against him and when the next ten minutes would settle the question whether he was to be victorious or a dishonored general and whether his army was to be prisoners of war or victors of a glorious battle. In such a crisis it was natural that the general in command should be an object of interest and as I looked at him I was struck with surprise and admiration. He sat on his horse in an easy careless attitude, with no sign of excitement about him and with an expression of countenance as placid and pleasant and a manner as composed and quiet as if he had just risen from a very satisfactory dinner.

Meantime General Wool had been everywhere among the troops, trying to rally those who were retreating from the field and to encourage those who still held firm; but as I have said, he had failed utterly to enlist the good feeling of his command and of course they did not respond to him on the field of battle. With regular troops of long standing in the service, among whom sentiment has no place, General Wool was a capable and most efficient officer, but with volunteers he had little sympathy and less influence. Indeed, General Wool had few elements of personal popularity and was almost without friends in the army, in which he served nearly all his life. He was, however, always a marked man in the army and full credit was given him as a soldier even by his enemies. He began his military service in the war of 1812 and ended it in 1864. He was a Democrat from policy before and during the war, but an intensely loyal man both from principle and feeling. He was short and slender, very agile and vivacious, with dark hair and eyes and a perfectly beardless and mustacheless face.

When I last saw him he was still active and full of interest in all public matters, but his figure was considerably bowed and bent and he was aging fast. He lived a long life in the army and it may be said of him in the highest and truest sense that nothing became it better than its honorable and patriotic ending.

As the mention of General Wool naturally led me back to the Mexican War, so the latter recalls to me several men who, noted then, became afterward men of prominence and standing during the war of the rebellion. Among these was Ben McCulloch of Texas. I knew him very well indeed during the Mexican War. He came out with the detachment of Texas troops brought to General Taylor's army by Governor Henderson,[18] on whose staff at the time was General A. Sydney Johnston. When Governor Henderson left with his troops after the storming of Monterrey, McCulloch joined General Taylor's headquarters with a company of Texas scouts, I think about thirty strong.

He remained with us before, during and after the Battle of Buena Vista, being in the front of the army whilst it was encamped at Agua Nueva and being among the first to report the advance of Santa Anna's army against us.[19] I saw him no more after that battle, though I often saw him before. He was a most kindly and gentle man, with a low, soft voice and very quiet, pleasing manners. Like all real frontiersmen, mountainmen and trappers, as well as scouts, he was a silent, uncommunicative man, who listened much but talked little. If he came to know you well and happened to like you, he would un-bend to you and then become a very interesting companion. He had many and wild experiences in Texas before annexation, in the days when the question put to new comers was not "Who are you?" but "What have you done?" He was a scout by nature and although during the war he came to command large forces and to take part in great operations, I have no idea that he ever felt so much at home or so well satisfied as when he commanded the small company of scouts in Mexico and spent his time in hazardous escapades on the dangerous ground between two hostile armies. He was a fine specimen of the frontier scout and ranger of fifty years ago in the Southwest and belonged to a class which is produced no more.

The cowboy is a poor substitute for such men as McCulloch represented— as poor indeed as are the lean Texas steers for the great herds of buffalo, their predecessors. There have been a number of organizations since the war calling themselves "Texas Rangers," but to the Texas Ranger of McCulloch's day they bear no resemblance except in name.[20]

Another conspicuous figure in the Mexican War who acquired unenviable notoriety at the beginning of the Civil War was General David E. Twiggs,[21] of the Regular Army. He was in every respect a marked man. Tall and bulky with a highly florid face and bald head, wearing habitually a countenance half cynical, half humorous and altogether malicious and with a tongue of venom, he held all the young men and many of the old men in constant apprehension of some malicious or ill-natured remark. He seemed to delight in mishaps or mortifications to others and never failed to assist people to them whenever he could.

He was a man of keen judgment and remarkable ability and might have been one of the foremost men in the nation if he could only have rid himself of two or three distinctive traits of character which brought to grief all of his undeniable talent and capacity. His judgment was held in such high respect and his ability was so well known that his advice was often sought even by those who knew him well. It was said to be always given with a view of getting the applicant into trouble—not serious, perhaps, but mortifying—and the recipients shaped their course accordingly.

It used to be said of General Harney, who was lieutenant-colonel of Twiggs's regiment (the 2nd Dragoons) and whose head-piece was not of the highest temper, that whenever he was doubtful what to do in any special case, he consulted Twiggs and then did precisely the opposite of what Twiggs advised him; so profound was his belief in Twiggs's purpose to mislead him. With this engaging disposition and these attractive ways, it may naturally be inferred that his popularity in the army did not reach alarming proportions. He managed to keep in favor with General Taylor and in or near his proper position during the campaigns and battles between Vera Cruz and the City of

Mexico and came out of the war a brigadier general in the army without anyone being able to cite a single creditable act which he did during the war.

In 1860 he was in command of the Department of Texas, with his headquarters at San Antonio. From the first, as might naturally have been expected, he was disloyal to the government. He held on to his rank and command and used both with ability and unscrupulousness against the government in whose name he was exercising command. He encouraged every hostile act and gave aid to every movement which could cripple or destroy the troops under his command. By talk and countenance he encouraged the armed Secessionists to seize his own officers and appropriate the public money and property in their hands; in short, he acted the part of a malicious traitor to the trust reposed in him by his government. I have no doubt that these services, great as they were to the South at the time, were rendered in that cool, cynical way peculiar to him and whilst they were accepted, did by no means endear him to the recipients. I judge this to have been so as much from the nature of the man as from his subsequent history in the South, where he cast his fortunes, but fished up nothing in return.[22] He was one of the few men concerned in the rebellion whom the people of the country never would have forgiven or ought to have forgiven.

Another officer, very different in all possible respects from General Twiggs, who was famous in the Mexican War and occupied a prominent position in the early days of the Civil War, was General J. K. Mansfield,[23] who was for some months in the Fall of 1861 in command at Washington. He will, perhaps, be more generally remembered by the sign manual of his aide-de-camp Captain Drake DeKay. Everybody who was about Washington even for a short time in those last days of 1861 and especially every soldier, will remember that gigantic signature, without which no man was safe from arrest and confinement who wore the uniform of the United States, or indeed who ventured to cross the Potomac in any costume whatever.[24] The writer of that autograph was a large-hearted and valiant soldier and as loyal a man, not only to his country but to his comrades, as ever wore the uniform of the United States. I had occasion to know him well during the time I was in Washington and I not only bear my testimony thus to his character and his conduct, but I give the evidence with the deepest and warmest feeling personally for him. At the time to which I am now referring, however, the captain's signature was about the biggest thing out — bigger even than the captain and the general put together. General Mansfield himself was a peculiar man, combining in his own person two quite distinct characters, almost the precise opposite of each other. In ordinary times and circumstances he was a sort of fussy, particular man, very much given to pry into all manner of details and to meddle with other people's work, especially that of his subordinates. His manner, too, was querulous and fault-finding and altogether he was an uncomfortable person to have anything to do with and was far from popular. Place this same man on a field of battle, amidst the roar and fury of the fight and a transformation as complete as that between Dr. Jekyll and Mr. Hyde at once appeared. It was magnificent to see General Mansfield in battle. He visibly swelled before your eyes; his face flamed out with fiery ardor and his whole figure and his every movement seemed filled with a sort of terrible passion. He pervaded all places of danger and everywhere put himself in the forefront of the battle. He was like a lion and no man could look on him at such a time without a thrill of admiration and wonder. I have never yet seen a man so regardless of his personal safety or so eager to imperil it. The wonder with me has always been how he could have survived any battle with his uncontrolled inclination to thrust himself where the danger was greatest. I first saw him in action at the storming of Monterrey.[25] He was the chief engineer on General Taylor's staff and I was one of the junior officers under him. We led the advance of the column which attacked and carried some of the fortifications on the lower part of the city. Of course Mansfield was wounded, shot through the calf of the leg; but he had it bound up and the next I saw of him he was stretched out in a partly-reclining position behind a piece of artillery of Webster's battery,[26] within open sight of the enemy's intrenchments, not two hundred yards distant and from which a terrific fire from artillery and small-arms was being poured upon the spot until the dust and dirt were flying in every direction. The place was too hot even for the gunners and this one gun was served in person by Lieutenant J. L. Donaldson, the first lieutenant of the battery, who seemed as careless of his life as Mansfield. The latter was unable to walk on his wounded leg, but was lying in the midst of this tremendous fire, in which it seemed impossible to live, with his field-glass to his eye, directing Donaldson where to aim his gun. Absolutely he seemed as unconscious of danger or as indifferent to it as if he had been walking the streets of Washington. I saw him in battle under somewhat different circumstances at Buena Vista. Although still on General Taylor's staff, he did not go back with the general that night to Saltillo, but remained on the field with General Wool to help him select positions and post the troops for the next day's work. When we rode up on the plateau in the midst of a lost battle, as I have described, one of the first men I saw was General Mansfield. He rode a gray horse, which made him very conspicuous and was charging furiously back and forth across the field, trying to rally the broken columns, but without success. He was beside himself with shame and humiliation and the tears poured down his face. He was not tranquilized until the effects from Bragg's and Sherman's batteries became apparent. Mansfield had a keen military eye and most excellent military judgment, but he never afterward had the opportunity to exhibit them until the Civil War and he was killed, as it was almost certain he would be, in the first battle in which he was engaged.

General Mansfield was of middle height and robust figure. He had a broad and rather ruddy face, with a thick shock of white hair and beard. He was a man of kindly disposition and very just; but, as I have said before, he was rather fussy and fond of meddling with his subordinates, so that, although all of his officers exulted in his behavior in battle and were immensely proud of him for some time after the battle was over, he soon reduced them to their old feeling that he tormented and persecuted them unwarrantably. He was still a comparatively young man when he was killed at Antietam, but I think it may be said of him that his complete recklessness and his apparently irresistible inclination to seek the most exposed and most dangerous places on a field of battle, of necessity deprived him of the power to use his great military abilities and acquirements to the best advantage for the army or the government. He was a gallant soldier and a true and loyal man and will always be remembered with pride and respect by those who knew him in those old days.

The Adjutant-General of the Army when the war broke out was Samuel Cooper,[27] a native of New York and a graduate of West Point. He married a Virginia lady and had long before identified himself with that section of the country. It was a noticeable fact that, whilst almost every Northern man who married a Southern woman attached himself at once to his wife's country and became naturally the most violent and bitter partisan of the South, very few Northern women were able, perhaps they were not anxious, to hold their husbands loyal to the government. One of the strangest social phases that characterized the years before the war was the recognized social supremacy of the South and the deference paid to it. It does not seem important yet to inquire into the causes of this curious freak. The South did not possess the wealth, the culture, or the polish given by the experiences of foreign travel, yet in any society anywhere they dominated almost without question. Perhaps in their manner of life on isolated plantations where unquestioned authority gave a habit of command and a tone of habitual supremacy and where wide and lavish hospitality was the custom, may be found the secret of the easy assumption of the foremost place in any other company than their own. It is reported in the papers that Mr. Jefferson Davis once said in 1868, in a public speech, that the Southern people were the natural masters of their Northern brethren and that in a few years, after the passions of the war had subsided, they would again be put in control of the government. Twenty-three years only have passed since he made this utterance (if he did make it) and his forecast is already so nearly true that we can see the end plainly in view. Not only is this true in political affairs, but it is also again the fact in social life.

A glance at the social life in Washington will make this fact plain enough. The South had been ruined in fortune and their customs and habits of life altogether overthrown. Yet poor, indeed well nigh destitute, they still hold their heads high and are recognized as among the leaders of men of society by their far more prosperous fellow-citizens of the North. It has been surprising to many people to witness the resurrection of the South and its triumphant advance again to power and to place; but it is a fact worthy or not, as the case may be, of some study. If things go on as they have been for the last ten years, the South by the end of another ten years will as fully be in possession of the government and will as completely direct its policy as in 1858; and it cannot be said that this will happen because of any peculiarity in their lives nor the habits of authority and domination which were the natural outcome of their system of slavery and of the necessity for their banding together, regardless of all other questions, to protect it. Such conditions exist no longer. The South is poor and needy and her people are compelled to work as hard as any Northern laborer; but over and through it all blazes that power to rule and that fitness to command which characterized them before the war and which is rapidly being recognized and submitted to now. It is easy to dent these statements and no doubt many good people in the rural districts of the North will be prompt to do so should they see or hear of them, but the man of the cities or of public life will hardly question them in the presence of those having his own experience.

General Cooper, as I have said, was a native of New York and except through his wife could have had neither interest in the South nor sympathy with its purpose to break up the Union. He went because his wife's family were Southern, a reason which carried off in the same way hundreds of feeble-minded men who became, from the necessity of their position, the most violent of rebels. I do not now recall a single Northern officer who married a Southern woman who did not go South with her. What sort of talk concerning their friends at home and the North generally they were obliged to hear and doubtless contribute to and to what humiliations they were compelled, in the nature of things to submit, are easily imagined; but how men with the most rudimentary elements of manhood could have endured such a life is past understanding.

General Cooper left Washington suddenly. In point of fact, he deserted his post whilst still Adjutant-General of the Army. It was said at the time that he took off with him, for the use of the Confederacy, all the official papers and returns necessary to give full information as to the force of the army, its stations and its supplies of arms, ammunition, and provisions. I have not been able to believe that a man with so high a reputation for honor as he had before could have been guilty of such a breach of trust, but his going at all was even more astonishing. He went and with that departure went all the reputation, all the honor and all the happiness of his life. It has not been many years since a subscription was circulated among the officers of the Adjutant-General's Department to raise a fund for the support of a man who had betrayed and dishonored it. He died in poverty and obscurity, genuinely lamented by his personal friends, of whom he had many, who not only mourned his loss, but deplored such a sacrifice of his life as this able and distinguished officer had made to influences and associations foreign to all of his sentiments and obnoxious to his moral as well as to his common sense.

His successor in the order of rank was General Lorenzo Thomas,[28] of Delaware, also a graduate of West Point. For some reason, I know not what, but perhaps because of the state whence he came, or his Southern associations and connections, I think that there was not entire confidence felt in his loyalty, or I should rather say that he was suspected of Southern sympathies. For that reason, perhaps, but perhaps, also, because he was earnestly loyal, he became so violent in his patriotism and so malevolent toward all who were not so violent and unreasonable as himself as to induce the suspicion that he was doing it all for effect. I heard him say publicly, in May, 1861, that if he heard of any army officer using disloyal language he would strike his name from the rolls of the army; and upon being reminded by one of the officers present that army commissions were not held at his pleasure and that tenure of office in the army was in no sense dependent upon the whim of the Adjutant-General, remarked that the Secretary of War, Mr. Cameron,[29] would confirm any action of that kind he might take. Of course this was all fancy on his part, but coming from a man of his years and long service in the army, it created upon those who heard it the impression that his ardor of loyalty was not genuine.

He was soon removed from the charge of the Adjutant-General's Department and placed on detached service—I think organizing and mustering into service the Southern Negroes in those parts of the country occupied by the Union troops. The successor to his place and his duties, though unfortunately not for some time to his rank, was a man of wholly different make-up. A quiet, well-read, high-toned gentleman, to be trusted in all things, both a judicious friend and a sound advisor, General E. D. Townsend filled the position and did the duties of Adjutant-General of the Army to his own honor and the good of the service until he had reached the age when the law retired him from the active list of the army.[30]

He was a loyal man and a true man in every sense and whilst many of us oft and again differed from him in opinion and contested his action, or that taken on his advice, no man ever questioned his integrity or the purity of his motive.

He is still living and illustrates in his own person what an upright, faithful and honorable officer should be.

I will close this paper with a brief mention of one man who was conspicuous in Washington in those early days of the war and whose case furnishes and will always continue in the history of this country to furnish, one of the most unpardonable and atrocious crimes ever committed upon an upright citizen and a most honorable and faithful officer. I refer to General Charles P. Stone.[31] No man who knows the inside history of affairs in Washington during March and April 1861 has ever failed to credit to General Stone the active and efficient measures which were taken to assure the Capital of the nation from riot and bloodshed, if not indeed from violent seizure by the enemies of the government. His services during these months were of the last importance and it is hard at this day to foresee what might have happened had he been a man of less moral force and assured loyalty.

So plainly was this recognized at the time by the highest officials of the government, that when a number of regiments were added to the Regular Army for the war by the President's order, in the absence of Congress, General Stone was appointed one of the colonels and when the first great army of 300,000 men was called out he was appointed a brigadier general in that army and took the field with it in 1861. Holding an important command in front of the enemy, he was suddenly and without warning brought to Washington and thrown into a common prison, where he was kept for some time in utter ignorance of the crime imputed to him.[32] He was afterward transferred to a military prison in New York, still ignorant of what he was said to have done which could justify such treatment. No application could draw from the authorities any official statement on the subject, nor was any opportunity ever given to him to meet his accusers before a proper tribunal and answer to any charges they could make. Indeed, he did not know who his accusers were. It was the general impression that he had committed some treasonable act imperiling his command, but to those who knew him and his loyal service such a charge was simply ridiculous. He was finally released, after his life had been ruined and his reputation destroyed except among those who knew him well. He went off to Egypt, where for a number of years he was Chief of Staff to the Khedive, and retained that position until that high official was deposed. When he returned to the United States he was appointed engineer to build the pedestal and place upon it the statue of Liberty which now ornaments the harbor of New York. He died in the midst of this work. I saw him, indeed dined with him, in New York in the Spring of 1883, the last time I ever saw him. He talked to me fully but uncomplainingly of his unhappy life and told me that it had only been within a few days that he had found out certainly who had been his enemy and had caused his arrest and imprisonment. The only harsh expressions he used were in regard to this man, whom he had always regarded as his friend and to whom he had talked of this matter more than once.[33] I do not know, considering the manner in which this information came to my knowledge, that I have the right to pursue it further, but certainly it is not too much to say that, through whatever instigation, no more inexcusable, cold-blooded and atrocious wrong was ever committed by this government upon any of its citizens.

In this case the crime against right was committed against one of the most honorable and loyal men in the land, which gave it ten-fold wickedness and however misled the government was by misstatements and misrepresentations of some of its then trusted officers, the crime against General Stone will always be a dark stain on the history of that administration.

Chapter Fourteen

Prominent Confederates

*V*ery shortly after the defeat of the First Bull Run General Scott retired from the head of the army.[1] I had, of course, seen him many times during my service in the army and had such a personal acquaintance with him as a man so much younger in years and in rank would be likely to have.

Every old officer or citizen in the country knows very well the strength and the weakness of General Scott's character and it would be a thankless as well as a profitless task to discuss them here; but I shall always remember with special pleasure my last interview with him. I had come to Washington by request of the governor of Illinois, where I was mustering in the volunteers from that state, to consult with the War Department as to the advisability of concentrating the regiments for muster at important railroad points whence they could be directed with the least delay to any place where there might be a demand for them. I called at the general's office and an hour for me to see him was designated by one of the aides. I accordingly was there on time and found the general ready to see me. He bade me be seated opposite to him at his office table and after I had explained my business he began to question me about the country and the troops to be mustered in. It was queer to hear him speak of the state of Illinois as "the Illinoy," after the French pronunciation and of the Indian and emigrant trails through it as they were known fifty years before. He spoke also briefly of his own campaign against the Sacs and the Foxes, I think, in 1832, when his headquarters were in the insignificant village of Chicago; or rather at Fort Dearborn, which was the principal feature of Chicago in those days and when the cholera, which just visited this country in that year, broke out in his command. He talked for an hour in the most animated way and I was deeply interested in what he said. He was an immense man, both in height and breadth and at that time he was so unwieldy that he moved about with difficulty, but his mind was as clear and as active apparently as it ever was and I think I never before or since have looked into such a bright and piercing blue eye. I carried away with me a feeling of admiration and reverence for him which I have maintained. His weight of character, his great reputation as a soldier and a citizen, the dignity of his years, his intense loyalty to the government and the fact that he was a Virginian, made his presence in Washington at the head of the army a matter of the last consequence to the new Administration. If he had then abandoned his post and taken sides with "his section," no man can now tell how many more officers would have gone South with him. Whilst I think that the departure of the half-hearted men who would have gone because General Scott or general anybody else did, would have been a gain and not a loss to the army, I am sure that the defection of the general himself at that time would have been a serious injury to the country.

The manner in which he was forced to retire from the head of the army soon after the defeat at Bull Run is, no doubt, generally known, from the reports of the Committee on the Conduct of the War and the records in the War Department. It is a sorry story, of which any American should be ashamed.

General Joseph E. Johnston,[2] who was one of the three conspicuous figures at the First Battle of Bull Run, was the officer to whom I first reported for duty after graduating at West Point. He was then a captain of topographical engineers, of which corps I had just been appointed to the elevated position of a brevet second lieutenant, which was really (according to my estimate of it then) the highest position I have ever held in the army since. Captain Johnston was the chief of my corps, at the headquarters of the Department of Florida and was when I reported, acting as Assistant Adjutant-General of that Department. He was and I suppose still is, a short, spare man, very erect and alert, with an engaging countenance and cordial, unaffected manners. He was in addition a man of large ability, and naturally became one of the most conspicuous figures in the Southern armies. He was genial and kindly in his manners to young officers and was popular with them. Although he could not have been much more than thirty at that time, we youngsters looked on him as on the whole rather a venerable man. Somehow we had taken up the notion that he had been generally, and then was, in love with someone and had had a wide experience in sentimental affairs running on many years. I don't know how such an idea originated, but it prevailed among us and invested its object with a halo of romance which constantly attracted our curiosity and interest.[3]

He was one of the most energetic men I ever saw and did whatever he had to do with all his might; but he had apparently an uncontrollable craving to serve in all arms of service and in all positions in the army, which gave him the most diversified military career of any other officer. From the time he left West Point to the beginning of the Civil War he had been an artillery officer, a civil engineer, a topographical engineer in the army, a lieutenant-colonel of voltigeurs,[4] a captain of engineers again, a special envoy to Mexico, a lieutenant-colonel of cavalry and finally Quartermaster-General of the Army. If the war had not supervened he would probably have been Adjutant-General, Commissary-General, Surgeon-General, or any other generalship from those he had held previously and there is no doubt he would have done the duties of each with efficiency and energy. He is, I believe, still living and occupied some high public position under President Cleveland.[5]

Perhaps no officer of the Old Army sacrificed so high a position or so promising a future as he did to enter into a rebellion which, I am sure, he had too much intelligence and too much acquaintance with the Northern people to believe could be successful.

General Beauregard was the third of the principal military personages who figured at the First Battle of Bull Run. He was a Louisiana Frenchman, whose name was really "Toutant" de Beauregard, but the official in charge of the Cadet roster, being a native-born American, naturally supposed that the last name was the surname and so settled the matter, as far as his name at West Point was concerned. Why he permitted himself to be thus called at West Point and adopted and confirmed this name in his after-life, I do not know. He is a man of brilliant talents, of wonderful vivacity and is at once an able man and a delightful companion. I never knew him very well. Though he was one year at West Point whilst I was there, he was in the first class and I was a "Plebe" and in those days the relations between the oldest and newest classes might be truly said to be "strained." General Beauregard was too impulsive and quick-tempered to be a prudent or a safe counselor and too restless and enterprising to be satisfied with any condition except that of constant action. His difficulties with Mr. Davis from the very beginning hampered his military career and kept from him the chance to do more conspicuous service in the Southern army; but he will always appear in history as one of the notable personages of the war. Nominally, his controversy with Mr. Davis began on the question of an advance on Washington after the First Bull Run, but I presume that in reality the foundation of the ill-feeling existed in the heart of Mr. Davis before the war began. General Beauregard is held in high esteem by all who personally knew him. He has all the genial polished manners, all the vivacity and impulse of the French Creole, without his indolent habits of body and mind. Of all restless, energetic men whom I have known, General Beauregard is one of the foremost.

There appeared in the Confederate camp shortly after the First Battle of Bull Run a somewhat remarkable person belonging to the class of men mentioned in the first part of this article, as men whose careers had greatly disappointed all of the predictions of professors and of admirers. This was G. W. Smith, who joined the Confederate army at Manassas with the commission of major general, next in rank to Johnston and Beauregard. He was a classmate of mine and of course I knew him very well and greatly admired him as a boy at West Point. Since we left school I have seen him very rarely. Everyone called him then "G. W.," omitting altogether his surname as not necessary to identify him.

These initials did not represent George Washington, as might be naturally supposed, but they were quite distinctive of the man himself and by his classmates and friends of the old days I presume he is still called "G. W." without the Smith. From the very beginning he was very popular with his class and grew to be more and more so as the months passed on. Indeed, before he had been there half the usual term he had become known to the whole Corps of Cadets and was a prominent person at the Academy. He possessed neither grace of manner nor comeliness of figure or face, but he had a solid brain and a forceful though extremely kind and engaging countenance, which dominated almost every one brought into relations with him. By his own class he was admired beyond reason and his influence over his fellows arose from a most remarkable combination of force of character with a kind and most attractive affectionateness of disposition. He was at once loved and admired and this double feeling he was able to maintain among his associates by a powerful and commanding intellect. He graduated into the Engineer Corps of the Army, but did not long remain in the service, though he acquired some distinction in the Mexican War.[6]

When the Civil War broke out he was, I think, the Commissioner of Public Works of New York City and was recognized as a man of large brain and supreme efficiency, with a great career before him. Indeed, his classmates and friends believed that there were few things that "G. W." could not do. With these opinions concerning him, he resigned his commissionership in New York and passing through Kentucky, his native state, he reported in Richmond to the Confederate War Secretary and was at once commissioned a major general and sent to the victorious army at Manassas. He remained with that army until a short time after the Battle of Fair Oaks, during which for a short time he fell into command of the army when Johnston was wounded. He was, however, relieved almost immediately by General Robert E. Lee and thereafter seemed to fall into disfavor with the officials of the Confederate government. Mr. Jefferson Davis appears to have had a strong feeling of dislike and distrust concerning him. With him General Smith appears to have engaged in a disagreeable and at times acrimonious controversy, which terminated in Smith resigning his commission in the army and drifting down into Georgia. He was not heard of again in the North until the march from Atlanta to Savannah brought him again more or less into public notice as commanding some of the Georgia militia in their operations to prevent or retard Sherman's march to the sea. Whether ill-health and the infirmities of temper generally connected with it, occasioned his failure to make a distinguished name, or the want of some faculty required to make a harmonious whole of his certainly remarkable abilities and force of character, I do not undertake to say. He has written a book partly to explain his position and treatment in the Confederacy,[7] in which the whole controversy between that Confederate official and himself is fully set forth, and of this it may certainly be said that, although it clearly makes out a case against Mr. Davis, it fails to satisfy the extreme disappointment of his friends and admirers.

I think that there was no man in the South from whom so much was expected and so little realized. Whose fault it was and why it was, is a matter which I know too little about to express an opinion.

There died, however, at the Battle of Bull Run and in front of his command, one of the noblest and manliest of men and the most chivalric of soldiers. All who knew him loved him. He had the sweetest disposition, the kindliest and most attractive manners and was the most truly affectionate and unselfish man I ever knew. He was sincerely mourned by all who knew him in the Old Army, whether of the North or the South.

This was General Barnard E. Bee, of South Carolina, of whom it may truthfully be said that he was the very flower and pink of the typical soldier.

Chapter Fifteen

West Pointers to the Front

$\mathscr{O}$f the many surprises to which the war of the rebellion treated us, perhaps the most noticeable in a small way were the men who came to the front
both in the civil and military departments of the government. Equally surprising was the fact that of those who were expected to take the lead so few
ever did so and of that few none, or scarcely any, succeeded in maintaining
their position. Naturally the West Point officers were placed at the head of the
army in the beginning, as they were the only persons supposed from their education and experience, to have much military knowledge. It was astonishing to observe in the early part of 1861 how completely the people of the
Northern states had lost all interest in military affairs and indeed, all knowledge of war; so that when hostilities precipitated themselves upon us military operations were thought to be so scientific and mysterious that it was
considered, even by the people themselves, presumptuous for any citizen to
criticize, much less censure, any absurdity that any West Point man might

commit. Yet of all the transactions of human beings, there are none which should be (and indeed must be) under the dominion of common sense and business rules as the conduct of an army in time of war if success is to be hoped for. Whenever anything in conflict with common sense, especially business sense, is done by a commander of troops, it is quite as certain that he is doing wrong and will achieve disaster as the same violation of business rules will bring similar results to business enterprises.

Like other lessons of the war, this fact was not long in being found out by the people and the government, but until it was discovered some of the most absurd and preposterous proceedings ever witnessed in this or any other country were carried on, in the face and under the eyes of the most intelligent people and keenest observers in the world. The gravity and patience with which the people of the country witnessed the wildest and most senseless antics of military men in the summer of 1861 would have been ridiculous if it had not been invested with the pathos of a dreadful war close at hand. War was considered a mysterious specialty which none but the initiated must venture to intrude on and the first year of the war, if it accomplished little else, did make plain to all the utter groundlessness of such an idea. When we look back to-day to the absurdities, the ridiculous pretensions and to the more preposterous, not to say outrageous, conduct of some of the principal army officers in 1861, we stand astounded at the self-deception and forebearance of the people at a time when the strongest passions were aflame and the agonies of apprehension were torturing every man's soul. An entertaining and perhaps instructive paper, recounting some of these burlesque performances, both in the East and the West, might be easily made up from the official papers in the War Department, but if prepared by anyone who was in position to see behind the scenes it would be inexpressibly amusing. We are still rather too near the actors and the acts to publish such matters without giving great offense, but I presume enough will be left in manuscript to furnish our posterity with amusement we must deny ourselves.

It has always been and no doubt still is the theory of West Point professors, that after a young fellow has passed one year at the Academy, they can solve his equation and as it were, determine his x. Whatever he does or fails to do when he leaves there, in no respect shakes their estimate of him. Whatever happens to him in conflict with their opinions is charged to circumstances abnormal and unexpected and not in the least to any shortcoming in him. Naturally their method of "sizing up" of the graduates gives token of the same wisdom. The rule is full of simplicity. Every boy's capacity in life is determined by the number of scientific books they can cram into him or he can be made to absorb in a given time. It matters not in the least that the scholar does not digest or in any manner assimilate the intellectual banquet and that if you squeeze him twenty years afterward it will run out of him as undigested as it went in. The equation has been solved and there can be no dispute as to the answer. To West Point, therefore, the career of its graduates during the war was a source of constant wonder and dismay, though in justice to their wisdom it must be that these strange freaks of fortune never at all affected their previous estimates or shook their belief in the infallibility of their judgment. They always sought explanations of such impressive results in circumstances and conditions which had no relation to the capacity of the actors. To these worthy professors, with their inflexible opinions about the men whom they had taught, the career of such men as Grant and Sheridan was a fountain of wonder and perplexity and they felt themselves much in the predicament of Balaam when his ass began to talk so wisely. They began to try and remember something of these remarkable men when they were obscure cadets to account for such unexpected outcome, but without much success.

Some reminiscences of Grant at West Point were put forth before the close of the war and attributed to one of the professors,[1] but as Grant was a very quiet, reserved man, with nothing noticeable in appearance, manners or proficiency in his studies and was little, if at all, known even to schoolmates belonging to other classes than his own, much less to professors, the value of these reminiscences may be fairly questioned. General McClellan was the most exquisite exponent of these West Point ideas and he may be fairly judged, or with sufficient fairness for the present purpose, from the estimate of himself which he gives in his late autobiography. In the professional mind he was the ripest production of West Point, which of course implies that he might have been considered over-ripe for any other institution of learning in the country.

His book and letters, however, enable anyone interested in the matter to form a sufficiently accurate idea of a beloved of West Point officials. Much the same remarks may be made of the prominent civilians appointed to high military positions at the beginning of the war, except that the valuation put upon them was due to public notoriety instead of algebraic determination. The general surprise and disappointment in the last case were quite as great as in the first, but the treatment was somewhat different. The facts were recognized and the remedy was applied in the case of the high military officials appointed from civil life with promptness and dispatch, but the educated military man was suffered to go on until his incapacity became a subject of general ridicule. No doubt this difference of treatment must be ascribed to the ignorance of war everywhere the rule in the country and the very natural hesitation of those in authority to meddle with matters which they did not understand or to interfere with supposed experts.

When the first year of the war is recalled and the inefficiency of the officers, their forgetfulness of the obligations of duty, their controversies and open quarrels and the disasters, failures and disappointments which logically resulted, it is difficult to realize that we were successful in the midst of such dis-couragement. That we did succeed must be attributed to the aptitude of our people to learn and apply the lessons of experience. It is but fair to state that most of these troubles occurred among and were brought about by officers of the Old Army, mainly graduates of West Point.

The war, however, is now over and all is peace once more. Everyone has been pardoned and restored to good standing. The only enemies of peace and the gushing sentimentality which appears to be the essential element of it, appear to be the old soldiers who put down the rebellion and who scarcely dare open their mouths on any subject pertaining to the war, for fear of be-ing charged with stirring up ill-feeling. They have, perhaps, lagged superflu-ous on the stage; in fact, they have certainly done so, since they have lived long enough to see how little distinction is made between the cause for which they fought and that upheld by their opponents.

When the war began the venerable Winfield Scott was General-in-Chief of the Army. He was old and feeble, wholly unable to undergo the fatigues of camp, or even to mount a horse. But he had justly a great reputation as a sol-dier, a high position both in social and political life and beyond and above all he possessed a recommendation most valued by the administration in those early days of the Civil War. He was from the border state of Virginia and an intensely loyal man. His presence in Washington and his active zeal in behalf of the government were of immense benefit in that time of doubt and uncer-tainty, every hour aggravated by the desertion of some high official, carrying off with him valuable personal influence and information. Although General Scott was incapable of doing active duty in the field, he could do the work of administration at the head of the army in all matters pertaining to the orga-nization and supply of the new troops called into service and the general fields to which they should be sent. Had he confined himself to this work, all would probably have gone well; but the moment troops of the enemy began to take position in front of our army before Washington, the martial spirit again dominated his better judgment and he undertook to conduct from his office in Washington a campaign against an enemy in the field.

No man had condemned such an attempt, or would have done so in any other case, in stronger language than General Scott had done many a time and oft in his life and notably during the Mexican War. The result was pre-cisely what he himself had always predicted it must be—failure. McDowell,[2] who was in 1861 a comparatively young officer, a major in the Adjutant-General's Department and a former aide-de-camp on General Scott's staff, had been made brigadier general and assigned to the command of the troops arriving in Washington. As fast as regiments arrived—and they came very fast on the President's first call for troops—they were transferred to the Virginia side of the Potomac, where they soon made an army formidable in numbers, but lamentably weak in organization and discipline. Necessarily they possessed not the slightest experience of war or knowledge of military operations or obligations. In especial they were restless under the restraints and demands of military service in the field. These first levies came from all classes and conditions and the same regiment often times contained representatives of the very extremes of social life. The barkeeper and the clergyman, the coalheaver and the college graduate stood side by side in the ranks, ate the same food side by side at the mess and slept side by side in their tents. Whilst all of them had no doubt, been governed by the ordinary rules of civil life, perhaps none of them had ever had the slightest taste of army discipline, or were at all accustomed to the arbitrary orders and curt manners of the Old Army officer. As the larger part of them were men of intelligence and character and held social standing of more or less prominence at home, it was desirable, if not absolutely essential, that in the beginning of this abrupt and extreme change of life they should at first have been treated with the utmost kindness both of speech and of act. The patriotic reason which prompted them to leave everything and come forward even as private soldiers to defend their government, fully entitled them to the highest consideration and I am sure it was felt, though, perhaps, rarely shown, by Old Army officers during the first months of the war. It took these old military officials some time to shake off the habits of their lives and to comprehend clearly that the volunteers placed under their command were many, if not all of them, citizens of character and standing. They came to realize it, however, before many months had passed and to make the proper changes both in manner and method. It was discovered, too, that fear of punishment was hardly the proper incentive to the making of a good soldier and that discipline needed no military violence nor the use of bad words. They also learned in time that the trouble between the North and the South was not a political squabble, nor the volunteer a "mustang."

When McDowell was made a brigadier general and placed in command of the troops in front of Washington he was about forty-three years of age, tall and stalwart, with short hair and a full face, inclining to redness and when in uniform he had all the distinctive appearance of a marshal of the First Empire. His eyes were very bright, his tones of voice rough and metallic, his manner arbitrary and at times irritating. He was an accomplished soldier, full of the book knowledge of the science of war and full of energy and zeal. It may be said of him as it cannot be said of many in such unqualified terms, that he was an intensely loyal man, not alone to his country, but to his duty. I have never known a man in whom the obligation of duty dominated to such a degree as McDowell. The misfortune was that his arrogant manners, a habit merely and the strong metallic voice in which he not seldom uttered the harshest language when excited (and he was easily and often excited), gave him an undeserved unpopularity during the first months of the war, which he was never able entirely to overcome. In his position of commander of the troops in front of Washington, he was also handicapped by the fact that General Scott, only two or three miles in rear, was the actual command-in-chief and that he (McDowell) had been his aide-de-camp only a short time before. Naturally McDowell, who saw both troops and country with his own eyes, had come to strong convictions about attacking the enemy in his front, who, by the way, were actually blockading the Potomac below Washington with their pickets along the river, absolutely in sight of the Capital.

He also had his opinion as to the true manner in which the attack should be made. There was no question about the absolute necessity that some effort should be made as soon as possible to rid the vicinity of Washington of the presence of hostile troops.

Naturally, also, General Scott had his opinion on the subject and as usual the king and the heir-apparent disagreed on both points.

As usual, the compromise was not so good as either of the original plans. The essential feature of the plan finally adopted was that General Johnston, of the rebel army, who was in front of Winchester, should be detained there until McDowell fought the battle at Bull Run with Beauregard. For this purpose General Robert Patterson,[3] of Philadelphia, a retired merchant who knew a great deal more about a division of profits in a trade than about a division of troops in the field, was placed in command of a considerable Union force at Winchester and as guide, philosopher and friend, that impetuous soldier and desperate fighter, Fitz-John Porter, then a major in the Adjutant-General's Department, was sent to reinforce him. A perfectly logical result followed: Johnston marched away to Bull Run and determined the result of that battle; Patterson and Porter remained to adorn the village of Winchester.[4] McDowell wrote a very manly report of the battle (First Bull Run), in which, however, he took upon himself the responsibility for many misfortunes and mistakes not properly chargeable to him.[5] If he had known how much his generous act would be afterward abused to his injury, he would perhaps have shown less forebearance.

He was in all such matters a generous man and in several cases within my own knowledge this trait of character has been played upon by the unscrupulous. It is as amazing now, as it was then, to everybody who knew him, what shameful slanders were circulated about him and generally credited because of his great unpopularity. One of the most loyal men on earth, openly charged with treachery on the field of battle — treachery to the degree of communicating with the enemy during a great battle and furnishing information to defeat his comrades. The most temperate man in the army, indeed temperate to the verge of intemperance in his abhorrence of drink, he was proved by the testimony of several witnesses to have been seen in a beastly condition of intoxication on the streets of Washington. Most of this injury, to the embitterment of his life and the destruction of his military career, was due largely to the impatience of his temper and the arrogance and severity of his language and manner. One can learn from McDowell's fate how much more valuable to human success is that intangible thing called deportment than character and ability. Indeed, the successful career of several of our conspicuous officers during the early part of the war was due wholly and exclusively to "deportment."

By deportment I do not mean simply gracious manner and apparent cordiality, but also that mystery in which the possessors of it shrouded themselves, that seclusion in which they intrenched themselves, so as to be inaccessible, at times, even to the President of the United States himself. No one could look on the solemn visage, the furrowed brow and pensive face without being impressed that they indicated profound thought and that vast projects and gigantic schemes of conquest were surging in the massive brain behind. As few men in those days knew anything of war, they accepted these heroes at their own valuation and it is astonishing how long they banked on this capital alone. It is not worthwhile to mention their names. They will occur at once to anyone familiar with those times.

McDowell possessed none of these impressive ways and suffered accordingly.

Postwar Correspondence between Pope and the Comte de Paris Pertaining to the Second Bull Run Campaign

Headquarters, Department of the Missouri
Fort Leavenworth, Kansas, May 29, 1876

To M. Le Comte de Paris
Sir:

Although the general expectation in this country was, I think, that your history of our civil war would have a strong but natural bias in favor of the general on whose staff you served at the beginning of hostilities, and of the personal friends in high official station who surrounded him (an expectation confirmed by those portions of the work which have been published in the United States), yet I confess that I share the surprise of many other people that this natural sympathy, with which I believe no one finds fault, should have led you, no doubt unconsciously, into errors, contradictions and inconsistencies which cannot fail greatly to impair the value of the work, even considered as merely *"Memoires pour Servir."*

It is to be hoped, indeed I think it may be counted certain, that when the partisans on all sides of the controverted questions, raised during the war, have had their say, some dispassionate and able writer, in view of the whole subject, will give us as the result, a history of our civil war which shall recite the facts as nearly as human testimony can reach the truth.

As your work is ably written, and by a man much respected in this country, it is very likely to mislead many persons, to the prejudice of the rights and character of men who were engaged in our great conflict.

A history of the campaign of the army under my command in Virginia is now being compiled from all the data, to the minutest details, furnished by the records of both armies, and although it may possibly be thought to have a bias of an opposite character, yet I trust it will furnish data possessing at least equal value for the future historian.

I have not enjoyed the advantage of reading all those parts of your history which have been printed in this country. Indeed I have seen nothing concerning the campaign in which I was myself engaged in Virginia except a short extract concerning the Second Battle of Bull Run published in the *Army and Navy Journal* of the 27th instant.

Short as this extract is, however, it will afford me, I am sure, sufficient data to illustrate how far your sympathies seem to have carried you in the attempt to reconcile ugly facts, which you felt bound to admit, with a fair record for those in whom you show so manifest an interest, and to do this work at the expense of injustice and wrong to others.

In this extract you say, concerning the Second Bull Run battle: "The contest was prolonged after sunset, and amid the darkness of night could be heard the shouts of the combatants and could be seen the flashes of musketry. Meanwhile Porter had remained the whole of this long day in front of Longstreet's right without firing a musket." And again you say: "However this may be (the reopening of Porter's case), it is now known that the whole Confederate army was united before Porter could have executed the flank movement from which Pope anticipated such wonderful results and that he had before him Longstreet's entire right wing, part of which only had been engaged against the Federal center, at the close of the battle. His attack therefore could not have produced the results upon which the General-in-Chief had counted. But neither the impossibility of executing to the letter the order of the latter (myself), nor even the instructions McDowell may have given him during the day afford any excuse for his having remained so long inactive in the presence of the enemy, with two fine divisions, while a great battle was being fought in the vicinity. In short if the road was barred against him, if therefore he could not cut the enemy's army in two and secure its defeat, it is equally certain that a vigorous attack made by him upon Longstreet's right would have drawn out all the forces of this general, and by freeing the rest of the Union line would probably have prevented the reverse which the latter sustained at the close of the day."

Let us examine in the light of these statements the charges preferred against Porter which you seem to find fault with me for having made instead of confining myself to "blaming" him, which you admit I had a right to do. Under the principal charge against Porter upon which he was tried, there are three specifications— first, that he disobeyed a positive order to attack the enemy, and "did retreat from advancing forces of the enemy without any attempt to engage them or to aid the troops that were already fighting greatly superior numbers, and were relying on the flank attack he was thus ordered to make to secure a decisive victory," etc., etc. (To avoid making this letter too long I content myself with the substance of the specifications, and enclose them fully drawn out that you may verify my statements.) In the first specification it is also stated that if the flank attack had been made the result would have been to secure a decisive victory and capture the enemy's army.

2d Specification—That Porter "being with his army corps between Manassas Station and the field of a battle then pending between the forces of the United States and those of the rebels, and within sound of the guns and in presence of the enemy, and knowing that a severe action was being fought and that the aid of his corps was greatly needed, did fail all day to bring it on the field, and did shamefully fall back and retreat from the advance of the enemy without any attempt to give them battle and without knowing the forces from which he shamefully retreated."

Specification 3d—That Porter "being with his army corps near the field of battle at Manassas, while a severe action was being fought by the troops under Major General Pope's command, and being in the belief that the troops of the said General Pope were sustaining defeat and retiring from the field, did shamefully fail to go to the aid of the said troops and general, and did shamefully retreat away and fall back with his army [corps] to Manassas Junction and leave to the disasters of a presumed defeat the said army, and did fail, by any attempt to attack the enemy, to aid in averting the misfortunes of a disaster that would have endangered the capital of the country. All this at or near Manassas Station on the 29th of August 1862."

The only substantial difference I can discover which demand notice between your statements as heretofore quoted and the above specifications are: 1st, your assertion that Porter did not receive my order to attack until dark, and 2d, that the results of an attack made by him would not have led to consequences nearly so great as those expected by me. To the first of these differences, it may be said that no fact can be more clearly established by human testimony than the fact that Porter received this order not later than half past five o'clock in the afternoon. It is not necessary, however, to insist upon this, as you admit (and I think every soldier will agree with you), that Porter's obligations did not depend on the receipt of this order, and that it was as much his duty to go into battle without it as with it.

The second difference I will consider farther on, and content myself in this place with saying that as it is a matter of opinion what the result of an attack by Porter would have been, it may fairly be claimed that officers of high rank, known character and military ability, who were present in that action and fully acquainted with the situation by personal knowledge, are, to say the least, as competent to judge of such a question as yourself, who were not even in the State of Virginia at the time, and certainly not more likely than yourself to be influenced by prejudice.

I beg to invite your attention, however, in the first place to what appears to me a singular conclusion you arrive at. In order that it may be shown that the consequences of an attack by Porter would not have been so great as I expected, you are compelled to assume that the army under my command suffered a reverse on the afternoon of the day of that battle. Without stopping now to reply to the assumption, not only groundless but in positive contradiction to the facts, I will simply ask you to examine again your own statements. You say that if Porter had attacked Longstreet it would have drawn out the whole of that general's force and thereby relieved the rest of the Union line, so that the reverse you assert that we met with would have probably been prevented. I say that an attack by him would have given us the victory. I would wish to ask you what distinction you make between a crime which permitted a reverse and a crime which prevented a victory? You yourself charge Porter with the first, but blame me apparently for charging him with the last. Does it really make any difference in the character or degree of Porter's crime whether that crime prevented a victory or permitted a defeat? I confess that if there be a distinction which in any respect affects a judgment of Porter's conduct, it is too subtle for my comprehension.

Although it is necessary (to sustain your statement that the consequences of

Porter's attack would not have been what I expected) that you should assume that we sustained a reverse on that evening, yet it is a fact as well known to every man engaged in the battle on the 29th of August, 1862 (the first day of the Second Bull Run), as the fact that a battle was fought at all, that we sustained no reverse whatever on that day, and I shall proceed to prove it by testimony which I think even you will not dispute. So far from there having been a "reverse," at nightfall the divisions of Kearny and Reno had driven back the forces in front of them and possessed the ground occupied during the day by the left of the enemy's line. The sharp action by McDowell's corps, between sunset and dark, which you graphically describe, was fought opposite to and three-fourths of a mile in front of the line of battle occupied by our center all day. We not only encamped that night on the ground occupied during the day, but held that and much of the ground which had been occupied by the enemy, during the whole of that night and until twelve or one o'clock the next day (the 30th), when *we* and *not* the enemy advanced and renewed the engagement at a point considerably in advance of our line of battle on the 29th. These are facts known to all the army on that field. If any further proof of facts so generally known is needed it is furnished by the testimony of General McDowell before the court martial which tried Porter, and I presume that neither you nor anyone will question McDowell's opportunity or capacity to judge of such a matter, nor the evidence which he gives. His testimony is as follows:

Question—"Please state the ground on which you formed the opinion that if the accused had attacked the right wing of the rebels, as he was ordered, the battle would have been decisive in our favor?"

Answer—"Because on the evening of that day (29th of August), I thought the result was decidedly in our favor, as it was. But admitting that it was merely equally balanced, I think and thought that if the corps of General Porter, reported one of the best if not the best in the service, consisting of between twenty and thirty regiments and some eight batteries, had been added to the efforts made by the others, the result would have been in our favor very decidedly."

Question by accused—"Will you state what in your opinion would have been the result of the battle of the 29th of August if the accused had attempted to execute the order of 4:30 P.M. to attack the enemy on his right flank and in the rear, if he, the accused, had been defeated?"

Answer—"To have defeated General Porter in that attack would have required a large force of the enemy, which would have relieved the attack in front, and I think would have still resulted in a success to our side—to our army generally."

Question by accused—"Then we are to understand you as saying that a failure of the attack contemplated by the order of 4:30 P.M., had it been made, would not have materially affected the fate of the day?"

Answer—"I have stated that even if the attack had been made and had failed, it could only have failed by a very large force of the enemy attacking it, and that would have so much relieved the front as to have gained a success for the army generally."

This is General McDowell's testimony, and that he understood the situation thoroughly cannot be disputed. It settles completely the very serious error you have committed in stating that our army sustained a reverse on the evening of that day, the 29th of August, 1862, and using that error to support the theory that Porter's attack would not have led to the result I expected. Concerning this question we have in the testimony of General McDowell the opinion of an expert, of high character and station, of admitted military acquirement and skill, and it is an opinion given with knowledge of the facts. I respectfully submit to you that such an opinion, based on such statements, and by such an authority, demands much more consideration than it has received at your hands, and is, I venture to say, far weightier authority than was or is in your possession for making an assertion in absolute contradiction to it.

One more quotation from the brief extract of your history published in the *Army and Navy Journal*, and above referred to, will, I think, suffice for the purpose I have in view at present:

You say: "This indifference on the part of Porter to the cannon's appeal, the manner in which he interpreted the orders of superiors, and the tardiness with which these orders reached him, were the inevitable consequences of the confusion we have referred to in the general management of the army."

I think I have never seen a more singular statement, viewed either from a logical, a moral, or a military standpoint, and I fear it would hardly pass muster in any civilized community. Is it indeed true that "confusion in the general management of an army" has for an "inevitable consequence" the commission of a monstrous military crime, by an officer among the highest in rank and command? Surely no such idea would be maintained in any army in the world, and I am very sure it is not upheld by you. What! Because in the opinion of a subordinate officer in high command, there is confusion at the Army Headquarters, is it therefore an "inevitable consequence" that he shall commit the most monstrous of military crimes? No such "inevitable consequence" would be admitted by any soldier worthy of the name. He serves his country and is faithful to his comrades at all times, but more especially and in a far higher sense ought he so to do and be, if he has reason to think that both army and country are in danger, from "confusion in the general management of the army."

In making the plea in excuse for a great criminal, that the enormous military crime he committed was "the inevitable consequence" of presumed "confusion in the general management of the army," you cannot now fail, it appears to me, to comprehend the sorry position, both in a moral and a military sense, to which your ill-regulated sympathies have led you; a position from which I am sure your best friends would advise you to escape without delay.

"The confusion in the general management of the army" which you appear to consider, in some sort, an excuse for Porter, had no more existence than the "reverse" on the 29th August which you ascribe to us, but no doubt the "confusion" rests on the same authority as the "reverse." It is contradicted by the records as completely as McDowell's evidence establishes the misstatement about the reverse of our arms. Scarcely any order, and certainly none of importance, was issued by me in that campaign except in writing, and all the orders contained not only the most detailed instructions (very unusually detailed in campaign), but in most cases the exact hour and place of issue. These orders are on file in the War Department, and accessible to you or any other responsible person, and the most important of them have been printed and published by Congress. I ask no other proof of the utter groundlessness of your assertion of a "confusion" than these furnish, and I commend them to an attention which I am very certain you never gave them, even if you took the trouble to examine them.

If your account of other parts of the campaign of the army under my command in Virginia is based upon such groundless assumptions and such unreliable authority, as this short extract seems to have been, it is to be feared that it will scarcely take rank as one of the great histories of the world.

If it indeed be true, as you state, that the "inevitable consequence" of "confusion in the general management of an army" is the commission of the most monstrous crime known to military law, it is to be regretted that you did not also state a second "inevitable consequence" sure to have followed in your or any other civilized country in the world except this, viz: the swift execution of the criminal.

It would not be difficult, I think, to overturn several other statements you make in the short extract published in the *Army and Navy Journal*, particularly the statement that the whole Confederate Army was united before Porter could have made the attack in his front (no flank movement was needed, or ordered). I am sure you did not intend, by using the term "flank movement," to mislead the reader. A "flank movement" requires time, and in general a good deal of time and some risk. Porter's attack would have been on the enemy's flank, but directly on Porter's own front. Your use of the term "flank movement" is in error, and implies what is not true, and therefore not intended by you.

My present purpose, I hope, has been accomplished without making this letter too long. The purpose simply is to caution the reading public in this country, as far as I can do so by the publication of this letter, not to accept without great doubt your account of any transactions except such as fell under your own observation. Your manifest perplexity in trying to account for many of the occurrences which took place whilst I was in Virginia (and you were absent, it may be stated, from this country), is not surprising in the face of the extraordinary malevolence, personal bitterness, defamation of character and absolute disaster resulting therefrom during that time on the part of men, all of whom proclaimed a common purpose, and that purpose the protection of their Government. But if you will pardon me for doing so, I think I can furnish you a basis on which much of it may be explained. It is simply the bad policy of having been too much in earnest at much too early a period of the war; a time when many reputedly wise persons in this country were expecting every day to patch up a hollow peace without more fighting; when the military hero was the apotheosis you seem desirous to herald was proclaiming from the field of a lost battle, the enormity of Negro emancipation, and when the President of the United States himself hardly ventured to speak aloud the idea from what is known to have been an unfounded fear of popular disapproval. Under such circumstances zeal and earnestness in the prosecution of the war were a sin deserving condign punishment, and if I may be considered a competent judge, the punishment was duly inflicted. In short, at an inopportune time I violated an injunction of one of the shrewdest of Frenchmen, "*Surtout point de zele*," and it seems logically in order, that another eminent Frenchman should belabor me because of the results.

I am, very respectfully,

    Your obedient servant,

      John Pope,

        Brevet Major General, U.S. Army

Chateau d'Eu Inferieure, France
October 8, 1876

Major General John Pope
U.S.A., Fort Leavenworth, Kansas
Sir:

As I had already the honor to inform you, your letter of May 29 reached me only at the end of August, just at a time when the fulfillment of a military duty kept me away from my books, and left me no leisure for a conscientious revision of all the documents concerning the battle of the 29th of August, 1862. I felt, indeed, that the elaborate pamphlet which you have addressed to me, coming from such high authority as the late Commander of the Army of Virginia, imposed upon me the duty of examining anew the information upon which I had founded my account, and of completing that inquiry by the study of the new elements which recent publications could afford, to confirm or correct my original opinions. I may have failed in that task, for if I knew most of the country and of the men, I was not a witness of the campaign which brought the Federal armies back upon the bloody fields of Bull Run, as you very justly remark, but such a fact cannot disqualify me for writing on that subject. Military history would become an impossibility if each writer could speak only of what he might have seen himself. At all events, I am conscious of having brought to the difficult task I had undertaken of writing a work of contemporary history, a spirit of sincere impartiality. If you had taken the trouble to read that work, or had waited for its English translation, I think you would have dropped the reproach with which you begin and end your letter. Whenever I have honestly believed after careful scrutiny, that an officer had committed an error or fault, I have said so plainly, even when he bore the name of McClellan, Fitz John Porter, Hooker, or any other of my personal friends. And let me tell you, as you no doubt are not aware of it, that it is with that spirit of impartiality that I have warmly taken your defence on the occasion of the false despatch mentioning the capture of 10,000 prisoners in the spring of 1862, the responsibility of which General Halleck so unjustly threw upon your shoulders. I had expected, I confess, that, after a lapse of fourteen years, you would have judged events more calmly than when your heart was still full of that bitterness which ill success never fails to bring with it. I had expected that you would have frankly acknowledged facts which you disbelieved and tried to disprove at the time these questions were debated before a court-martial, but the reality of which has since been demonstrated beyond a doubt.

Nevertheless, I thank you for having put me under the obligation of examining again the whole matter, for it has afforded me the opportunity to correct my judgment upon some points of serious importance, and it is not my fault if the consequence is to lighten the blame, which in my account I had laid, I believe now, too heavily upon Fitz John Porter.

In order to give clearness to my answer, I must begin by stating what I think, after due consideration, can be regarded as an accurate account of the movement of Longstreet's forces on the 29th of August. This general, coming from Gainesville, reached with Lee the right of Jackson between 10 and 11 A.M. He brought with him the commands of Kemper (3 brigades), D. R. Jones (3 brigades), Wilcox (3 brigades), Hood (2 brigades), and Evans' brigade—Anderson, with 3 brigades, being too far behind to join him before night. At twelve, Longstreet's corps was deployed in two lines, each command holding a part of the front. Hood, who had the lead of the column, following the Warrenton pike, was in line before 11 A.M., having put Laws' brigade on the left and Wofford's on the right, while Wilcox's command coming into line, but remaining somewhat in reserve, connected on his left the first with the second corps of the Confederate army, near the hill where Lee had posted several batteries. On the right of Evans came Kemper's command—one brigade, Hunton's, being close to the latter, the two others stretching across a difficult country, and being rather loosely connected with that of D. R. Jones. The three brigades of the latter were posted on the extreme right of Longstreet's line, in very strong positions along the edges of some woods, resting on the Manassas Gap railroad, near the point where it is crossed by the road from Bristoe and Manassas Junction to Gainesville. Robertson's cavalry scouted further on the right.

Before the arrival of Longstreet the troops of Sigel somewhat outflanked Jackson's right, and even created an alarm behind his lines. Stuart's cavalry tried to stop that move which Sigel was not strong enough to develop, and by 11 o'clock the arrival of Hood gave full security to Jackson's flank. In the afternoon, very likely when Porter, just before the departure of King, made serious preparations for an attack, Robertson advised Longstreet of the appearance of a heavy force of the enemy menacing D. R. Jones' front on the Bristoe-Gainesville road. In order to check its expected attack, the commander of the First corps, whose twelve brigades had not yet fired a gun, withdrew Wilcox's command from his left to place his three brigades between Kemper and Jones, which place they reached about 5 P.M. During that time McDowell, having withdrawn King from the position he held next to Porter, was leading him by a circuitous move towards Groveton and the turnpike. Longstreet becoming aware of that new move, sent orders to Wilcox to retrace his steps and return to his first position; but this general did not leave the left *before sundown*, and when his command reached the ground where Hood and King had met late in the evening, the fight was already over. That fight was the only one in which the First corps was engaged that day. It began at sunset, viz., about 6:45 P.M. Jackson being severely pressed by Kearny, Longstreet, to relieve him, instructed Hood to advance along the turnpike, so as to flank the former. But just at that time, McDowell, arriving with King's division, had deployed the latter in order to accomplish the same move on Jackson's right, which he still believed to be uncovered. The result was a bloody encounter, in which neither party lost or gained much ground, between King on one side, Hood's command, Evans' and Hunton's brigades on the other. These five brigades alone took part in the fight on the Southern side, the second and third brigades of Kemper's command being too far on the right, and Wilcox's command, as aforesaid, arriving too late.

Believing that the accuracy of the above statement cannot be disputed, I shall now examine under its light the different allegations of your letter. But I must, in due justice, begin by acknowledging the mistake which I committed myself when I said that Longstreet had moved Hood from his right to his left, in order to support Jackson. As aforesaid, Hood did not move during the whole day from the ground on which he at last met King. Instead of Hood, it was Wilcox who was moved in that way, but he did not participate in the fight. The consequence is clear and important, and it is only just toward General Porter that I should avail myself of that opportunity to show how far it modifies the judgment which I had passed upon him. If, as it is now proved, not a single man of the troops forming the right of Longstreet took part in the fights engaged north of and about the turnpike, the consequence is that Porter's inaction had not the slightest influence on the results of those fights, as far as the direct attack of Kearny and afterwards of King is concerned. But it may be alleged that if Porter had attacked at once the forces which confronted him, he might have overcome their resistance soon enough to roll them back, and, accomplishing the task which you had prescribed to him and McDowell at a time when you were unaware of their presence, had fallen on the flank, not of Jackson, as you desired him to do, but of Hood and Evans. This hypothesis does not seem to me to bear a critical examination. For that examination I think the time during which Porter confronted the right wing of Longstreet should be divided into three periods: 1st. From the moment that McDowell and Porter, acting under your joint order, encountered that right wing, to the departure of the former with King's division toward Groveton; 2d. From that departure to the receipt by Porter of your order of 4:30 P.M.; 3d. After that receipt.

1st. During the first period it seems to me that there was a reasonable chance for the Federal forces massed near the Manassas Gap Railroad to overpower the Confederate troops opposed to them. These forces were composed of Porter's corps and King's division; in the whole three divisions; while the Confederates had only D. R. Jones' three brigades of infantry and Robertson's cavalry. But General McDowell interpreting, according to his judgment, your joint order, which left a great latitude to both corps commanders, and prescribed to them not to act so as to lose the facility of retreat that very night on the Bull Run, did not think it fit to make that attack. Seeing that the country on his right did not allow him to establish a direct connection with the forces posted on the turnpike, he left the ground with his command to join these forces by a circuitous and retrograde move. No one, sir, agrees better with you than I do in the eulogy which you pass upon General McDowell's military abilities. It is not because I am proud to consider myself a personal friend of this remarkable leader, not because I hope that nothing will impair that friendship which persisted through the painful difficulties which arose between him and my former chief, but only for truth's sake that I have exerted myself to exonerate him of the criticisms which were directed against him in many circumstances. Therefore I consider that what he did at the time was wisely done, and that the best support which he could give to the Federal army was to come and take part in the fight about Groveton. If something is to be regretted it is that he did not take with him the best of Porter's corps, leaving only a *rideau* before Longstreet's right wing, and I suspect that you share that opinion, if I understand correctly certain sentences of a late publication which you did me the honor to send me, and where, recognizing implicitly that Longstreet's presence impeded the direct march of Porter, you reproach him with not having sought another way to gain Groveton.

2d. The responsibility of Porter began, of course, only after the departure of McDowell. What could he, what should he have done during that second period? If he had attacked D. R. Jones immediately, or very soon after McDowell's departure, he would most likely have had still the advantage on the former, but he would soon have been met first by Kemper's command, and shortly afterwards by the reinforcements which Longstreet would have been able to oppose him, as shown by the movement prescribed to Wilcox at 4:30 P.M. Porter's two divisions would certainly have been no match for these eight or nine brigades, and, if not thoroughly defeated, would at all events not have been able to strike Jackson's flank or even to reach the turnpike. If he had attacked after 5:30 P.M., the presence of Wilcox in support of Jones would have rendered that attack still more fruitless. Whatever may have been Porter's energy, it is not likely that, having at least eight brigades (Jones 3, Wilcox 3, and Kemper 2, deducting that of Hunton) to oppose him, Longstreet would have removed a single man from the forces which met King on the turnpike. That Porter did a good show is proved by the fact that at 4:30 P.M. Longstreet took Wilcox away from his left to bring him on his right; in forcing that removal upon his adversary, Porter materially relieved the Federal troops which attacked the Confederate center, and it is likely that if Wilcox had remained next to Hood at the time of King's attack, the latter would have suffered much more than he did. It may be alleged that Porter's display of forces became after a time insufficient, as Wilcox's command was recalled from the right to the left late in the evening. But Longstreet himself states that this new change of position was prescribed to Wilcox because he saw McDowell's column moving towards Groveton. Therefore, examining the second question, viz: What Porter should have done, I say he was justified in not attempting, at a great risk, to crush the forces which were opposed to him. The situation in which he found himself was quite different from that supposed in the joint order; that order left a great latitude, both to him and McDowell; the latter availed himself of that latitude to move to the right, Porter to observe the troops which confronted him. He might have done more than he did to deceive the Confederates on the departure of King's division; without pressing an attack to the utmost, he might have made feints, or even engaged some partial fights, so as to draw as much as possible of the enemy's forces upon himself. But, if it can be regretted that he did not do so, if it can be alleged, as I did, that however insignificant the consequence would have been, it was a mistake, he can be charged only with an error of judgment. Under his first instructions, his duty would have been to attack the large and well-posted forces of the enemy, which he unexpectedly met near the railroad, only in two cases: 1st. If he had received from a superior a positive order to do so; 2d If he had been aware that a great battle was raging near enough for him to take a direct or indirect part in it. On the first head, whatever may be made out of the contradictory debate on McDowell's verbal orders to Porter, it seems clear that these were not such as to compel the latter to begin a fight by himself, far from any support at the very moment his superior was taking away the forces which would have assured the success of that attack. On the second head I strongly censured Porter because I believed that he remained positively inactive within hearing of the noise of the fight at Groveton. But, after a careful comparison of hours and testimonies, and, taking in consideration the nature of the country, I have come to the conclusion that in Porter's position nothing for a long time was heard of the fight engaged northwest of Groveton but some cannon shots, which sounded exactly like those artillery duels to whose noise neither officer nor soldier used to pay attention in Virginia. The first indication he had of a serious fight was given to him by the reports of the volleys of musketry fired by King shortly before dark, about the time he received your order dated 4:30 P.M., and, consequently, during the third period.

3. As for that period, the only question of importance is the precise hour at which it began, viz: the hour of the receipt by Porter of your order of 4:30. The state of affairs which that order supposed to exist was still so different from reality that indeed Porter may have pleaded the right to interpret it according to his judgment, for you informed him that his line of march brought him in the enemy's flank and prescribed him to take advantage of that position to engage his flank and rear, it being clear, both by the wording of the order and by your own reports and testimony, that by this enemy Jackson's corps was meant, while Porter, having made some prisoners of D. R. Jones' command, knew positively at that time that Longstreet's corps was interposed between him and Jackson. This move, as any move which he would have undertaken under your joint order, I called a turning movement (*un mouvement tournant*), not a flank move, and before the explanation which you gave me on the faith of a translation, I knew the difference between both. Examples to instruct me are not wanting in the very campaign we are discussing, such as Jackson's movement from Manassas Junction to the field of battle of the 29th, which was really a flank march, while in prescribing to Porter to fall on the flank and rear of the enemy you ordered a turning movement. But enough on that incident; I shall neither further discuss the latitude which his situation gave to Porter in the interpretation of your order, because in my opinion there is no ground for that. After a new examination, I maintain what I said that Porter received your order too late to make a serious attack upon Longstreet's right; in the absence of the written reply which Porter addressed to you, the weightiest testimony giving 6:30 as the precise hour of that receipt. So far from disobeying that order, Porter seems to have anticipated it, as he had made some preparations for an attack before it reached him. But only a part of Morell's division was deployed, the ground being most difficult and did not favor a night attack as did the clearings about the turnpike where King and Hood began their fight; the enemy was very strongly posted, and Porter's generals, considering the attack as extremely

hazardous, took most wisely some time in preparing it. Dark coming before it began, Porter could not act otherwise than he did. To have thrown his battalions at night through unknown woods and tangles was a folly which could be an inspiration of genius when it was accomplished by Jackson at Chancellorsville, because he had for chief a master in the art of war, but of which, after the experience of the preceding days, not one of the general officers of the Army of Virginia would have taken the responsibility.

Drawing now in a few words the conclusion of that long statement, I shall say, therefore: 1st, That Porter's inaction had not the slightest influence on the result of the battle of the 29th of August, 1862. 2d, That his dispositions during the time which elapsed between the departure of McDowell and the receipt of your order, in some respect are open to criticism, that therefore you could blame them, but, as he acted in a situation which left him full liberty of action, and as that action was attended with no serious consequences, that blame could not go further than the censures which you have passed in your report on several of your subordinates, such as Ricketts, Sigel, etc. 3d, That the charge of disobedience or failure to do his duty, which, even granting that the execution of your order would have led to no result at all, would not be the less serious, as a subordinate is bound to follow a clear and positive order, whatever may be the consequences, is entirely disproved by the facts.

After that, it is, no doubt, useless to discuss a point upon which you enter at great length. Taking exception against my opinion on the result of the fight of the 29th, you assert that it was no reverse but a success; adding that Porter's co-operation alone was wanting to turn it into a great victory, but that, even if it had been a reverse, his inaction if *criminal* in one case would have been just as much in the other. In that last opinion I agree with you; but I have shown that, whatever Porter might have done or tried to do, his action could have no serious influence on the issue of the fight engaged on the other part of the line, and therefore it does not matter for his case whether the result of that fight was favorable or not to your arms. You choose to consider that result as a success, and you use for that purpose the testimony of General McDowell. As I told you, I have the greatest respect for the latter's authority in military matters, but in this case, his whole argument rests on the assumption that Longstreet had not joined Jackson in the afternoon of the 29th, and as it is now proved that he was mistaken, it falls to the ground. I called the result of that fight a check, and alluded once to the general situation of the army that night as disastrous because you did not realize the object of the whole plan of battle as well as of the different attacks of Hooker, Kearny, and King, viz.: dislodging the Confederates from the positions which they held, and especially those on the Gainesville turnpike. However brave were the Federals in their attacks, however tenacious in the close fights engaged in different parts of the line, they never gained ground enough to imperil the position of their enemies, and it is clear therefore that the result of that day's fighting was against them.

It remains now for me, sir, to leave with you the domain of facts and to follow you on the more uncertain ground of opinions. You assail me first, for having said that the want of alacrity of Porter can be explained by the confusion which prevailed in the directions given since the beginning of the campaign to the different bodies of troops under your orders; and secondly, for my supposed sympathy for a political party to which you ascribe the most nefarious designs against the Government which its adherents in the army were at that time faithfully serving. It will be an easy task for me to show that in the first point my opinion is well founded, and in the second your attack groundless.

I regret to be called upon to explain in a letter addressed to yourself what I meant by the confusion which prevailed in the orders given to the several chiefs of your army. As I did so already in a note at the end of the volume, I think you might have spared me that painful task. I am fully aware of the difficulties of a command like that which you exercised in presence of adversaries such as Lee and Jackson. But if this can excuse, it does not disprove the alleged confusion in the orders given to your subordinates. This confusion appears nowhere more distinctly than in that very collection of orders to which you refer me as a refutation. Every single order, no doubt, is by itself perfectly clear, but their succession illustrates the constant changes of plan, the contradictory instructions, which from the opening of the campaign, puzzled the officers, tired and discouraged the soldiers by useless fatigues, scattered your divisions sent in every direction to *bag the whole crowd* of your enemies at a time when steadiness and concentration could alone have retrieved the fortunes of war, and finally offered to the Confederate leaders the grand opportunities which they turned to such good account for their cause. After ten days of those orders and counter-orders, marches and counter-marches, the corps and division commanders, seeing that their promptness had no other result than to tax so much more the strength of their soldiers, that instructions were given to them without due allowance for unavoidable delays or consideration for the soldiers' marching powers, and could often not be complied with, had a legitimate disposition not to go beyond the strict interpretation of these instructions, and it is natural that Porter should not have cared to assume by attacking Longstreet a responsibility, which, in his unforeseen situation, rested entirely upon him.

Now, sir, in a discussion which might have been conducted exclusively on military questions, I regret to see that you have tried to mix political ones. Your attempt is most unfortunate, for it shows that you have not even taken the trouble to inquire in what spirit my book has been written. It would be perhaps too bold to refer you to my chapters on Slavery and Emancipation. But for your information let me tell you that your criticisms fall upon one who joined the Federal Army because it fought for the cause of emancipation, who, with the due reserve imposed upon him by his double quality of a foreigner and a soldier, always professed the belief that the abolition of slavery would be the result of the victory of the North and the best guarantee of the Constitution; in a word upon one who had no better friend in the American political world than Charles Sumner.

I agree with you that *trop de zele* in political matters does not suit a military commander, to whatever opinion, I shall add, he may belong; but it was quite unnecessary to bring forward in this affair the name of the chief, who at Antietam retrieved the ill success of the Federal arms in Virginia, and to whom at least no one can reproach that he shrunk before fighting; still more to insinuate that you had been defeated less by Confederates than by a political party, for, in our time, the best way for an unsuccessful leader to be honored or even praised by his contemporaries is to assume openly the responsibility of the events in which he played a prominent part, instead of shaking it off upon others.

I am, respectfully, your obedient servant,

L. P. D'Orleans,
Comte de Paris

Headquarters, Department of the Missouri
Fort Leavenworth, Kansas, December 21, 1876

M. Le Comte de Paris
Sir:

Events of great consequences have for the past three months so absorbed the attention of everyone in this country that it has been almost impossible to think of anything else, and I trust that you will consider this as my excuse for not sooner acknowledging your letter of October 8, 1876.

That letter, I presume, is in some sense a reply to mine of May 29, 1876, though I may be permitted to say that it cannot be considered an answer to the objections I have felt constrained to make to certain portions of your history of our civil war. In it you discuss many points which I did not raise, and answer many questions which you yourself put, but it does not seem to me that you explain satisfactorily, if at all, the errors to which I called your attention. I pointed out to you several errors of very grave character in your history, and gave you my authority for the statements I made in contradiction to them, which I shall here briefly recapitulate:

1st. You state in your history that the Army under my command suffered a reverse on the evening of August 29, 1862 (the first day of the Second Battle of Bull Run). The answer to this statement I will leave General McDowell to make, merely premising his testimony by saying that he was second in command of that army, that he was personally with me hours before and after the time indicated, and was thoroughly acquainted with the condition of affairs in all respects. Your abrupt disposal of his testimony on the ground that he did not know of Longstreet's presence in front of Porter, is not at all justified by the facts, as it will be seen from McDowell's testimony quoted below that it covers the very point, that there might probably have been at the time in front of Porter a force large enough to have defeated him in open battle if he had attacked. Whether his opinion is weightier than your own on such a subject, especially in the view that his was sworn testimony before a Court, of what he knew, and yours an opinion formed at a distance, and without such solemn responsibility, I am quite willing to leave intelligent public opinion to decide.

Being a witness before a Court Martial, General McDowell, in reply to a question, said: "On the evening of that day (August 29, 1862), I thought the result was decidedly in our favor, as it was." In addition to this testimony of General McDowell, I may say that your statement of a reverse to our arms at that time or any other time during August 29, 1862 was the first intimation of such a thing I ever heard from any quarter, and certainly there was no man on that field who had such an idea at any time during that day if we except F. J. Porter, who was not on the field at all, but at a distance of four or five miles away, was finding excuses to fall back, and judged from sound and not from sight, which I may here remark is hardly consistent with your theory, which I will notice farther on, that Porter's Corps did not know that a severe action was going on with the rest of the army.

2d. Using your theory of this "reverse" as a basis, you proceed to say that whilst an attack by Porter would have probably prevented this "reverse," it could not have produced the results I expected from it.

If, however, as is the fact, there was no reverse but a success elsewhere, it will be necessary for you to reconsider your opinion of what the result of his attack would have been, and to assist you in doing so, I give again the testimony of General McDowell before the Court Martial on this very point. Being asked: "Please state the ground on which you formed the opinion that if the accused had attacked the right wing of the rebels as he was ordered, the battle would have been decisive in our favor?" he replied, "Because on the evening of that day, I thought the result was decidedly in our favor, as it was. But admitting that it was merely equally balanced, I think, and thought, that if the Corps of General Porter, reported one of the best, if not the best in the service, consisting of between twenty and thirty regiments and some eight batteries, had been added to the efforts made by the others, the result would have been in our favor very decidedly."

In reply to the question by the accused, "Will you state what in your opinion would have been the result of the battle of August 29 if the accused had attempted to execute the order of 4:30 P.M. to attack the enemy on his right flank and in the rear, if he, the accused, had been defeated?" General McDowell said: "To have defeated General Porter in that attack would have required a large force of the enemy, which would have relieved the attack in front, and I think would have still resulted in a success to our side; to our Army generally." The answer effectually disposes of your dismissal of McDowell's opinion because he did not consider the contingency of Longstreet's presence.

And again being asked: "What would probably have been the effect upon the fortunes of that battle, if between five and six o'clock in the afternoon General Porter, with his whole force, had thrown himself upon the right wing of the enemy as directed in this order of 4:30 P.M. of August 29, which has been read to you?" he replied: "I think it would have been decisive in our favor."

Again I say that I am perfectly willing to submit to an intelligent public opinion whether the testimony of General McDowell, based on his own full personal knowledge and observation of the facts, is, or is not, weightier than yours, based on an erroneous assumption and supported by mistaken theories.

3d. You make an excuse for Porter—and, of course, to the injury of the rest of the army and especially its commander—that although he did not go into battle at all (for which inaction you, yourself, say that he had no excuse), he nevertheless, by his mere presence, held Longstreet in check and thereby prevented him from falling upon the rest of the army.

Now, if the object of two armies, engaged in campaign, be only to keep each other in "check," war would be stripped of all its horrors and become an out-of-door exercise, very exciting and, no doubt, healthful. Unfortunately, however, the world generally does not hold this theory of the business of armies engaged in battle, and even if it did, Porter did not play his part in this exercise. I leave General Longstreet, himself, to say how he was held in "check," and I suppose his statement, like that of General McDowell, is entitled to at least equal weight with yours on that point.

In his official report, dated Winchester, Va., October 10, 1862, he says: "At a late hour in the day, Major General Stuart reported the approach of the enemy in heavy columns against my extreme right. I withdrew Wilcox with his three brigades from the left, and placed his command in position to support Jones in case of an attack on my right. After some few shots the enemy withdrew his forces, moving them round toward his front, and about four o'clock in the afternoon began to pass forward against General Jackson's position. Wilcox' brigades were moved back to their former position (that is Longstreet's left, which was probably opposite our left-center), and Hood's two brigades, supported by Evans, were quickly pressed forward to the attack, etc."

It is quite unnecessary to say that Porter's Corps was not the force which "pressed forward against General Jackson." How far Longstreet was held in "check"—admitting that to "check" each other is the business of armies engaged in battle—he, himself, tells in the foregoing extract from his report, and it is, I think, sufficient.

4th. I think your statement that the country between Bull Run and Gainesville was difficult and well nigh impracticable, will astonish if it does not amuse those who are familiar with that small district. It is rendered more absurd by the fact that the right wing of the enemy the very next day, and greatly to our cost, moved against our left over the very ground in front of Porter the day before, and certainly without any perceptible difficulty whatever. That this ground could be moved over by an army corps rapidly and effectively, the enemy completely demonstrated the very day after Porter found it so impracticable.

5th. You intimate, rather than absolutely state, that from the position Porter's Corps occupied, the sound of the battle, except perhaps the artillery, could not be heard, and inferentially, that Porter's command, himself included, could not know of the severe action going on. That a severe battle, the sounds of which were heard in the streets of Washington thirty miles away, could not be heard at four miles' distance by Porter's Corps, is certainly a singular idea, and one hard to substantiate by any witness in that corps.

I will, however, let Porter answer it himself, as he does in this extract from a letter written at the time and addressed to McDowell and King, in which he not only contradicts the assumption that he did not know of the battle, but actually judges from its sounds that the army to his right was falling back, being defeated, and the enemy advancing; and this opinion of the battle and its results he assigns as his reason for deserting the field.

The following extract from his letter covers the point in question:

Generals McDowell and King:
I found it impossible to communicate by crossing the roads to Groveton. The

enemy is in strong force on this road, and as they appear to have driven our forces back, the firing of the enemy having advanced and ours retired, I have determined to withdraw to Manassas etc., etc.

This extract may, I think, be considered conclusive proof of what Porter knew and believed, and it also, I think, pretty effectually disposes of the "checking operation."

In your letter you divide up the time occupied in these military operations into several periods, and undertake to treat them separately. As for instance, you include a period from early morning of the 29th of August, 1862, to about twelve o'clock in the day, when Porter, as you state, was with McDowell, his senior, and therefore under that senior's command, who thereby was responsible for what Porter did or did not do.

If this be so, your case is made even worse. In his testimony before the Court, General McDowell says that when he left Porter, with the enemy in sight of him, to move up the Sudley Springs Road to join the left of the army, he said to Porter: "You put your forces in here, and I will take mine up the Sudley Spring Road on the left of the troops engaged at that point with the enemy." "I left General Price with the belief and understanding that he would put his force in at that point."

If then, as you affirm, Porter were under McDowell's command at that time, he received precisely the orders from McDowell which I sent him four hours later, neither of which orders did he make any effort to obey.

You seem also to fancy that if you can establish the fact that there was a large force of the enemy in front of Porter, and that his attack might have been repulsed you have furnished him some justification for his offense. This seems to me a wholly untenable position either for a soldier or a man of ordinary fidelity or humanity.

A severe battle was going on in which all the forces of our army (except Porter's) were engaged; in which the most earnest efforts of every man were needed, both for the army and the country.

The greater the force of the enemy in our front, the greater the need there was of the help of Porter's corps, and the greater his obligation to render it, and if you could prove that the whole Southern Confederacy was in front of him on that day, you would only succeed in blackening his crime; the crime of deserting the field of battle and abandoning his comrades to the unequal odds he left behind him.

In his letter to McDowell and King above quoted, Porter states his purpose to withdraw to Manassas, three miles to the left and rear, because he thought the rest of the army was being defeated, and the reports both of Longstreet (above quoted) and of Stuart, who were in front of him, positively state that he did retire from their front, and that in consequence Longstreet did precisely what he was expected to do and ought to have done, viz: withdrew the forces sent to resist Porter's advance, and threw them on the rest of the army elsewhere engaged in battle.

It seems to me unnecessary to pursue this matter further in this way. A history of the campaign in Virginia in which I was concerned is being written by competent hands, and will, I trust, soon be published. In that history all of the controverted points will be treated, dispassionately, and without prejudices I know, and I hope with more complete knowledge of the facts than you seem to possess. Until then I am content to let the matter rest.

My only object in writing to you at all, I frankly told you, viz: "To caution the reading public in this country as far as I can do so by the publication of this letter" (my letter of May 29, 1876), "not to accept, without grave doubt, your account of any transactions related in your history, except such as fell under your own observation." It is rendered doubtful to me whether this exception was not a mistake; but however that may be, I am so certain that whatever my letter might lack to produce the effect I wished, has been supplied by yours, that I feel grateful to you for writing it, and shall take pains to give it all the circulation possible in connection with my own.

The moral precepts with which you so obligingly favor me, seem to me truly admirable; but they would have carried additional weight, had you illustrated them in the composition of your history of "The Civil War in America."
I am, sir,

Very respectfully,

Your obedient servant,

John Pope,

Brevet Major General, U.S.A., Commanding

Chateau D'Eu, Seine Inferieure, France
March 23, 1877

Major General Pope,
Fort Leavenworth, Kansas, U.S.A.
Sir:
Your letter of December 21, 1876, and its printed copy, posted on the same day, reached me some time ago while traveling abroad. Although I found in this no information which I had not previously examined and discussed, I thought it due to you to defer my answer till I could give again to the case my whole consideration with the help of the numerous documents which, of course, I had left at home. I did so and find no motive to alter the opinions expressed in my first letter. In fact it strikes me that the arguments which you bring again forward have already been answered by me, so that if, instead of printing my letter *between* your two, you had put it *after* both, I would feel perfectly satisfied that I need not add a line.

As such is not the case, although I do not expect that this present letter will find its place as a closing word at the end of a second edition of your pamphlet, I feel bound to answer briefly your argument.

1st. You remind me that in my history I stated that on the 29th of August, 1862, the army under your command suffered a reverse, and, knowing my high regard for General McDowell, you try to set up his testimony against me on that subject. But the fact is that my expressions are inaccurately quoted by you. I did not say that your command suffered a *reverse*, but suffered a check (*eprouva un echee*) at the *end* of the day. By this I mean that, notwithstanding the partial advantages gained by your right during the middle of the day, at a very heavy cost and through the great gallantry of the officers and men, the general result of that day's fighting was not satisfactory; you had not been able to crush Jackson while he was alone, the junction of the Confederate army had been accomplished during the battle, and, although hardly more than one half of this army had been engaged in the fight, you had not succeeded in dislodging it from its position. King, coming at the end of the day, and following the examples of Sigel's, Kearny's, and Hooker's soldiers, had attacked the center of the enemy's line and fought till dark without being able to break Hood's front or gain any ground upon him. These are facts which are no disparagement to the bravery of the Federal army; the assumption that Porter, following the direction you had given him, could have exerted any influence upon that fight, being based upon the supposition that Jackson's right was unsupported by any large portion of Longstreet's corps, falls to the ground before the opposite and now well established facts. As you have quoted the very report of Longstreet where this fact is proved, I would be tempted to call also your attention to a paragraph which follows immediately your own quotation and begins by these words: "The enemy seized that opportunity to claim a victory." But I refrain, such a testimony being unnecessary to sustain not what you make me say, but what I really said.

2d. Here again you draw from my words conclusions which are exactly the reverse of the meaning I intended to give them. If I have sinned against the English language, I beg to be excused as a foreigner. I wrote "I have shown that whatever Porter might have done or tried to do, his action could have no serious influence on the issue of the fight on the other part of the line, and therefore it does not matter for his case whether the result of the fight was favorable or not to your arms." Which opinion you translate in the following way for the benefit of your readers: "Using your theory of this reverse as a basis, you proceed to say, that whilst an attack by Porter would have probably prevented this reverse, it could not have produced the results I expected from it. If, however, as is the fact, there was no reverse but a success elsewhere, it will be necessary for you to reconsider your opinion of what the result of this attack would have been." In answer to this head, I take therefore the liberty merely to refer you to my first letter.

3d. I have shown in that letter that the position in which General Porter found himself after the departure of General McDowell was so different from the one supposed in your instructions—being ordered to fall on the flank of Jackson's corps and finding a large part of Longstreet's command in his front, while he was still bound not to engage himself in such a way which would have prevented him from retreating this very evening to the Bull Run—that it was necessary for him to judge how and how far those orders could be carried into effect. As for the fact that a Confederate force larger than that of Porter's was, by his appearance on Longstreet's right, kept off from the actual field of battle, it cannot be disposed of neither by a joke, nor by an incomplete quotation. Although, as you say, the duties of military leaders do not consist in merely keeping each other harmlessly in check, as on a chess-board, I dare say that if in those eventful days of August 1862, you had succeeded in keeping in check Lee's army, the authorities in Washington would not have found exception against the way in which you would have done so, with or without much bloodshed. As you quote Longstreet's report in order to prove that the troops opposed to Porter, having been withdrawn, took part in the fight on the Gainesville turnpike, I felt it my duty to verify the accuracy of your quotation, having already found, as stated in my work, that in another pamphlet on the same subject, you had been led in error by mistaking the dates in Jackson's report. It is true that Longstreet recalled late in the afternoon from his right Wilcox's brigades, but, if you refer to the latter's report, you shall see that he reached the battle-ground on the turnpike *after* the end of the fight between King and Hood. As for the latter as well as Evans, they never left the neighborhood of the turnpike; therefore, contrary to the impression which you intend to convey, the fact is that not a single soldier of those who were sent to meet Porter took part in the fight on the Confederate center and left.

4th. It so happens that the ground between the Manassas Gap Railroad and the turnpike is as familiar to me as to most of our readers—who, by the way, I do not expect to be much *amused* by this barren discussion—having spent several days at or in the neighborhood of Manassas Junction after its evacuation in March 1862. This ground offers excellent defensive positions, especially where Longstreet's right had established itself. Of course an army corps could easily cross it, if not at all or very weakly opposed, but the difficulty of reaching Jackson's flank, as prescribed by your order, either by walking over Longstreet's right, or by taking a straight line along its front toward Groveton, is conclusively shown by the fact that General McDowell, who was the best judge of the situation, did not make such an attempt, and chose a circuitous route to bring King's division on the turnpike.

5th. The question whether, from the place he occupied, Porter could hear more or less the noise of the fight, is of little weight as, unless one is very near, it is impossible to judge only by the noise of the importance of a fight engaged in a wood. I remember well that at the Battle of Williamsburg General Sumner, who never shrunk from a fight when he saw a chance for it, did not sustain Hooker's attack because, although near, the noise was so dampened by the woods that he remained for a long time unaware of its character. I said a word on that subject only because I thought that in my history I had taken against Porter a conclusion which another examination of the proceedings of his Court-Martial showed was not supported by facts, none of the witnesses who were with him having before evening heard any musketry fire. At all events, when the fight extended towards him by the attack of King against Hood, and therefore the noise of battle was more likely to reach him, he was, acting according to your order, preparing for an attack which darkness prevented him from carrying into effect and consequently was not retiring at the time when the other wing was fighting. From the way in which you quote the dispatch mentioning such an intention to retire one not conversant with the whole matter would be induced to assume that he really retired, while, as you well know, and knew a few hours afterwards, he never did so and remained on the ground he had occupied during the day. As for General McDowell's verbal order to Porter at the time he left him alone in the presence of Longstreet, I need add nothing to what I say in my former letter, having already fully treated that question.

Your last argument would be indeed all powerful, if, as you insinuate, the large forces unexpectedly brought by the enemy had been concentrated on the front of that part of your army which was actually engaged in battle and had themselves taken share in the fight, leaving Porter unopposed. But such is not the fact, as I have already proved that a force of the enemy larger than Porter's corps was in his front the greater part of the day, and was effectually prevented by his presence from taking any part whatever in the fight of the 29th.

With this I shall conclude, as I see, contrary to my expectations, that so many years elapsed have not soothed the bitter feelings which could find their excuse in recent disasters and that any further discussion would be useless. You may depend upon that nothing will induce me to take the pen to revive that debate. Allow me therefore to avail myself of this last opportunity I have in addressing you to express the hope that the long prepared history of your campaign in Virginia, which you announce as being nearly ready for publication, will prove as just towards those whom you had the honor to command as it shall certainly be instructive for the student of military events and of historical philosophy.

I am, sir, your obedient servant,

Louis Philippe D'Orleans,
Comte de Paris

Headquarters Department of the Missouri,
Fort Leavenworth, Kansas, April 19, 1877

M. Le Comte de Paris.
Sir:

I have just received your letter of the 23rd ult. as it is mainly a re-assertion of points already treated in my former letters, without any new facts to support them, it does not seem to me to require any answer other than the acknowledgment which courtesy demands.

If those who are interested in this correspondence (I suppose there are not many) will take the trouble to read your letters and the narrative of the same transactions as related in your History, they will not, I think, need from any other source the admonition "not to accept without grave doubts your account of any transactions related in your history, except such as fell under your own observation." As my object in beginning the correspondence was simply to convey this caution, I rest satisfied with the result.

Whilst the resolution you announce to write no more seems to me entirely wise, yet I confess that I am selfish enough to be glad that you did not adopt it sooner, as in that case I might have been deprived of your valuable assistance in accomplishing the purpose I had in view.

In terminating this correspondence, however, I beg to assure you that I entertain no ill-will whatever toward you, as I am well satisfied that your imperfect acquaintance with the facts and, what appear to me, your rather illogical deductions even from that, are faults altogether of the head; not at all of the heart.

Very respectfully,

Your obedient servant,

Jno. Pope,
Brevet Major General,
U.S. Army

Pope's Memoirs in the National Tribune

Listed below are the original *National Tribune* installments of Pope's memoirs, as they have been ordered in the chapters of this book.

CHAPTER 1

"War Reminiscences: Personal Recollections of Conspicuous People, Civil and Military: Gov. Dick Yates," December 11, 1890.

CHAPTER 2

"Missouri in 1861, I: Affairs in That State the First Year of the War," February 17, 1887.

CHAPTER 3

"Missouri in 1861, II: A Conscientious Effort to Restore Peace and Quiet," February 24, 1887.

"Missouri in 1861, III: Military Operations during the Early Winter," March 3, 1887.

"Missouri in 1861, IV: Gen. Frémont Superseded in Command by Gen. Hunter," March 10, 1887.

CHAPTER 4

"Island Number Ten, I: The First Success in Opening the Mississippi," May 5, 1887.

"Island Number Ten, II: The Patient Labors and Suffering of the Brave Soldiers," May 12, 1887.

CHAPTER 5

"Siege of Corinth, I: Halleck's Snail-like Approach to the Rebel Stronghold," May 17, 1888.

Notes

ABBREVIATIONS

JCR   *Reports of the Joint [Congressional] Committee on the Conduct of the War*, Washington, D.C., 1863–65

MOLLUS   *Military Essays and Recollections, Papers Read Before the Commandery of the State of Illinois*, Military Order of the Loyal Legion of the United States, Chicago, 1891

NT   *National Tribune*

OHS   Ohio Historical Society, Columbus

OR   U.S. War Department, *The War of the Rebellion: A Compilation of the Official Records of the Union and Confederate Armies*, 128 vols., Washington, D.C., 1880–1901. *OR* citations take the following form: volume number (part number, where applicable): page number. Unless otherwise indicated, all volumes cited throughout notes are from series 1.

ORN   U.S. War Department, *The War of the Rebellion: The Official Records of the Union and Confederate Navies*, 30 vols., Washington, D.C., 1894–1922

PMHSM   *Papers of the Military Historical Society of Massachusetts*, vol. 2, *The Virginia Campaign of 1862 under General Pope*, edited by Theodore F. Dwight, Boston, 1895

UOW   University of Washington, Spokane

INTRODUCTION

1. Pope, "War Reminiscences, X: Personal Recollections of Conspicuous People, Civil and Military: Edwin M. Stanton," *NT*, February 12, 1891.

2. Pope, "Army of Virginia, II: Campaign in Front of Washington in 1862: Virginia Fortitude," *NT*, August 9, 1888.

3. William T. Sherman, *Memoirs of General William T. Sherman* (New York, 1990), 903, 911; David S. Stanley, *Personal Memoirs of Major-General D. S. Stanley, U.S.A.* (Cambridge, Mass., 1917), 85. For examples of the high opinion western soldiers had of Pope, see Byron C. Bryner, *Bugle Echoes: The Story of the Illinois 47th* (Springfield, 1905), 35; Henry Eby, *Observations of an Illinois Boy in Battle, Camp, and Prison* (Mendota, Ill., 1910), 41; Oscar Jackson, *The Colonel's Diary* (Sharon, Pa., 1922), 60; Henry Clay McNeil to his sister, November 29, 1862, McNeil Papers, Iowa Public Museum, Sioux City; Lyman B. Pierce, *History of the Second Iowa Cavalry* (Burlington, 1865), 15; David T. Stathem to his family, n.d., Stathem Papers, and Joseph Strickling Reminiscences, 17, both in OHS; Marshall P. Thatcher, *A Hundred Battles in the West: St. Louis to Atlanta, 1861–1865* (Detroit, 1884), 43; C. W. Wills, *Army Life of an Illinois Soldier* (Washington,

D.C., 1908), 144; and William E. Smith and Ophia D. Smith, eds., *Colonel A. W. Gilbert: Citizen Soldier of Cincinnati* (Cincinnati, 1934), 89.

4. John Y. Simon, ed., *The Papers of Ulysses S. Grant*, 20 vols. (Carbondale, Ill., 1967–), 13:35–36, 78.

5. Manning F. Force, "John Pope, Major General U.S.A.: Some Personal Memoranda," in *Sketches of War History, 1861–1865: Papers Prepared for the Ohio Commandery of the Military Order of the Loyal Legion of the United States* (Cincinnati, 1888–1919), 4:355; Merlin G. Cox, "John Pope: Fighting General from Illinois" (Ph.D. diss., University of Florida, 1956), 294, 302; *OR* 48(2):568, 881–82.

6. Pope, "War Reminiscences," *NT*, February 18, 1890. Here Pope refers to *McClellan's Own Story* (New York, 1887), published posthumously and compiled by McClellan's literary executor, William C. Prime, who tampered freely with much of what McClellan had written. Contemporaneous reviews of *McClellan's Own Story* were almost universally hostile. See Stephen W. Sears, *General George B. McClellan: The Young Napoleon* (Boston, 1988), 403–4.

7. Pope, "Army of Virginia, III: Campaign in Front of Washington in 1862: Cedar Mountain," *NT*, August 16, 1888.

8. Pope, "War Reminiscences, XI," *NT*, February 19, 1891.

9. Pope to J. J. Abert, August 16, September 3, 1850, February 24, 1851; Abert to Joseph E. Johnston, November 27, 1850 and April 8, 1851, and Johnston to Abert, February 17, 1851, all in Letters Sent and Received, Topographical Bureau, Record Group 77, National Archives.

10. Pope, "War Reminiscences, III," *NT*, December 25, 1890.

11. Jacob D. Cox, *Military Reminiscences of the Civil War*, 2 vols. (New York, 1900), 1:246.

12. Pope repeatedly called for an end to the insidious Indian agent system, for strong measures against whites who encroached on Indian reservations, and for the benign assimilation of the Plains Indian into American society through education and self-help. His views are best expressed in House, *Report by Maj. Gen. John Pope, of the Condition and Necessities of the Department of the Missouri, February 25, 1866*, 39th Cong., 1st sess., H. Executive Doc. 76, serial 1263; in a letter to Judge J. Bright Smith, August 3, 1866, reprinted in *Missouri Democrat*, August 29, 1866; and in *The Indian Question: Address by General Pope, before the Social Science Association, at Cincinnati, Ohio, May 24, 1878* (Cincinnati, 1878).

13. Pope to Rutherford B. Hayes, January 2, 1872, Pope Letter Book, Hayes Presidential Library, Fremont, Ohio; Pope to Thomas C. H. Smith, March 17, 1874, October 23, 1875, Smith Papers, OHS; Pope to his sister, February 15, 1870, Abraham Lincoln Book Shop, Chicago; Pope to Manning F. Force, February 16, 1875, Force Papers, UOW.

14. Pope to G. W. Mindil, April 26, 1877, Abraham Lincoln Book Shop; Wallace J. Schutz, *Major General John Pope and the Army of Virginia* (N.p., 1986), 181; Pope to Manning F. Force, February 16, 1875, January 14, 1885, Force Papers, UOW.

15. Pope to Manning F. Force, February 16, 1875, Force Papers, UOW.

16. *Correspondence between General John Pope and the Comte de Paris, concerning the Second Battle of Bull Run* (N.p., 1876); "The Comte de Paris to General Pope," *U.S. Army and Navy Journal*, April 14, 1877; Pope to Thomas C. H. Smith, January 30, 1877, Smith Papers, OHS.

17. Pope to the Comte de Paris, April 19, 1877, printed copy in Thomas C. H. Smith Papers, OHS.

18. Stephen W. Sears, *The American Heritage Century Collection of Civil War Art* (New York, 1974), 12; Pope to Manning F. Force, July 22, 1885, Force Papers, UOW.

19. Pope, "The Second Battle of Bull Run," *Century* 31, no. 3 (January 1886): 441–66.

20. James Longstreet, "Our March against Pope," *Century* 31, no. 4 (February 1886): 601–14.

21. Jacob D. Cox, *The Second Battle of Bull Run, as Connected with the Fitz-John Porter Case* (Cincinnati, 1882).

22. Pope to Manning F. Force, February 25, 1886, Force Papers, UOW; Pope to Benjamin H. Grierson, December 16, 1887, Grierson Papers, Illinois State Historical Library, Springfield.

23. John Gibbon, "Pope at Bull Run," 4, 9, Fitz John Porter Papers, Library of Congress, Washington, D.C.

24. Pope to Manning F. Force, February 25, 1886, Force Papers, UOW.

25. Pope to Manning F. Force, February 25, 1886, January 14, 29, 1887, Force Papers, UOW.

26. Richard A. Sauers, *"To Care for Him Who Has Borne the Battle": Research Guide to Civil War Material in the National Tribune, Volume 1: 1877–1884* (Jackson, Ky., 1995), xi; Pope to Manning F. Force, January 29, 1887, Force Papers, UOW.

27. For the complete titles and dates of publication of Pope's articles in the *National Tribune*, see App. B.

28. J. F. Haynes to Manning F. Force, September 27, 1892, Appointment, Commission, and Personal Branch, Record Group 94, National Archives.

CHAPTER 1

1. Richard Yates (1815–73), Civil War governor of Illinois, was a staunch Republican and an ardent supporter of the Lincoln administration. Yates was one of the foremost of the "War Governors," a term applied to those Northern governors who supported an aggressive prosecution of the war. As governors were the constitutionally mandated commanders of volunteer forces raised within their states, the federal government depended on them for men, arms, and money. Patricia Faust, ed., *Historical Times Encyclopedia of the Civil War* (New York, 1986), 845–46; Mark Boatner, *Civil War Dictionary* (New York, 1959), 859, 951; William Hesseltine, *Lincoln and the War Governors* (New York, 1948), 5.

2. Yates was elected to the Senate from Illinois in 1865 and served a single term. He was a strong advocate of universal suffrage and an outspoken critic of President Andrew Johnson. His uncontrollable alcoholism made him an embarrassment to his party, ultimately costing him his bid for reelection. Richard Yates II and Catherine Yates Pickering, *Richard Yates: Civil War Governor* (Danville, Ill., 1966), 262–67.

3. George Brinton McClellan (1826–85) graduated second in the West Point class of 1846 and had a successful career as a military engineer before the Civil War. Governor William Dennison of Ohio appointed McClellan a major general of volunteers on April 23, 1861. He assumed command of the Department of the Ohio on May 13 but was relieved on July 25 to take command of the Department of Washington and the Department of Northeastern Virginia. Pope is correct in his assertion that McClellan acted from his headquarters in Cincinnati before taking the field with his troops in West Virginia. George B. McClellan, *McClellan's Own Story* (New York, 1887), 41; *OR* 2:762–63; Ezra J. Warner, *Generals in Blue* (Baton Rouge, 1964), 290.

4. William S. Harney (1800–89) of Tennessee began his long army career in 1818. He

served with distinction during the Seminole War and the Mexican War and against the Plains Indians. He was one of only four generals in the Regular Army until May 1861, commanding the Department of the West with headquarters in St. Louis. Harney's Southern sympathies caused his relief of command after he conditionally agreed to refrain from asserting Federal authority over the pro-Southern Missouri State Guard commanded by General Sterling Price. During the Mexican War Harney had run afoul of General Winfield Scott, who relieved him of command during the advance on Mexico City. Scott's low opinion of Harney probably also played a role in his dismissal from the Missouri command. Warner, *Generals in Blue*, 209; Dumas Malone, ed., *Dictionary of American Biography* (New York, 1928–44), 8:280–81.

5. Harney died in 1889, the year before Pope's article appeared, at the age of eighty-eight.

6. A Connecticut Yankee, Nathaniel Lyon (1818–61) graduated in the West Point class of 1841 and served with distinction in the Seminole and Mexican Wars (to which he was opposed). Lyon's unswerving Union sentiments made him a valuable, if volatile, asset in keeping Missouri in the Union. He worked aggressively to squelch secessionist power until he was killed in action during the Battle of Wilson's Creek on August 10, 1861.

7. Claiborne Fox Jackson (1806–62) was elected proslavery governor of Missouri in 1860 and worked tirelessly to bring Missouri into the Confederacy. When Lyon moved against him, he was forced to flee the state. Sterling Price (1809–67), a native Virginian, was a veteran of the Mexican War, a former congressman, and a former governor of Missouri. Although he was a conditional Unionist, he commanded the Missouri state militia in 1861. For more on Pope's opinion of Price, see Chapter 6.

8. Benjamin McCulloch (1811–62) was a Tennessee frontiersman who migrated to Texas and became one of the original Texas Rangers. He served brilliantly during the Mexican War and as a colonel of state troops in 1861; he accepted the surrender of Federal forces in Texas from General David Twiggs in February 1861. Three months later McCulloch was appointed a brigadier general in the provisional Confederate army and was given command in Arkansas. He fostered a healthy contempt for West Pointers and thus had some difficulty cooperating with other Confederate leaders. McCulloch fell in battle at the head of a mixed force of recruits, Indians, and Texas Rangers during the Battle of Pea Ridge on March 7, 1862, a disastrous Confederate defeat. For Pope's estimation of McCulloch and Twiggs, see Chapters 6 and 13. For a full biographical treatment of McCulloch, see Thomas W. Cutrer, *Ben McCulloch and the Frontier Military Tradition* (Chapel Hill, 1993).

9. Lyon fought the Battle of Wilson's Creek in an effort to stem the advance of the combined forces of Price and McCulloch. This decision was bolstered by other concerns. Supply shortages after active campaigning had reduced Lyon's force to half rations. He also faced losing much of his effective strength as his ninety-day volunteers neared the end of their service.

10. John Charles Frémont (1813–90) was appointed major general and took command of the Western Department on July 25, 1861, replacing Harney. The Western Department included Illinois and all states and territories west of the Mississippi and east of the Rocky Mountains, including New Mexico. *OR* 3:390, 406; Allan Nevins, *Frémont: Pathmaker of the West*, 2 vols. (New York, 1961), 2:473. Frémont had a noteworthy, if clouded, career. His fame and ambition, combined with his political clout, made him a potential threat to the Lincoln administration.

11. Colonel John J. Abert (1788–1863) of Virginia was an assistant professor of mathematics at West Point from 1808 to 1811. He was appointed major in the Topographical Engineers in 1814. In 1824 he was brevetted lieutenant colonel and in 1831 was named chief of the Topographical Bureau. He was Frémont's commanding officer when the young second lieutenant was appointed to the corps in 1838. Malone, *DAB*, vol. 21, supp. 1–3.

12. Pope was placed in command of the District of North Missouri, which comprised all forces north of St. Louis, under Frémont's Special Order No. 10 of July 29, 1861. *OR* 3:415.

13. The Brant mansion occupied a full city block on the south side of Chouteau Avenue between Eighth and St. Paul Streets. It was the most prominent building in the most affluent neighborhood of St. Louis. The stately house was rented by Frémont from Sarah Benton Brant, the widow of Joshua B. Brant. The widow Brant was the aunt of Frémont's wife, Jessie Benton Frémont. This raised eyebrows considering that government funds were used to rent the house at a cost of $6,000 per year. However, the practicality of having Frémont's staff "eat, and sleep, and do his work all under one roof" justified the expenditure, despite appearances. William Winter, *The Civil War in St. Louis* (St. Louis, 1994), 71. See also the testimony of Colonel Isaac C. Woods, *JCR* 3:69, 205.

14. Colonel Isaac C. Woods served as head of transportation on Frémont's staff. Before the war he gained notoriety when he fled to Australia after mismanaging the funds of Adams and Co., a financial institution in San Francisco that declared bankruptcy in 1855. William T. Sherman, who dealt with Woods in San Francisco, misidentifies him as Isaiah C. Woods in his memoirs. Dwight L. Clarke, *William Tecumseh Sherman: Gold Rush Banker* (San Francisco, 1969), 116; *JCR* 3:198; Sherman, *Memoirs of General William T. Sherman* (New York, 1875), 2:223.

15. After taking command in St. Louis, Frémont busied himself organizing a river ram fleet, planning an expedition to New Orleans, and building fortifications for the defense of St. Louis. He drew much criticism both for dealing with contractors of dubious reputation and for the great expense the fortifications entailed. He was absolved of wrongdoing after an investigation by the Joint Congressional Committee on the Conduct of the War. However, the twin defeats of Lexington and Wilson's Creek engendered criticism that he was neglecting military affairs. *JCR* 3:38–39.

16. Frémont's notorious isolation from visitors (official and private) was exploited by his political enemies, the most vocal of whom was Francis (Frank) P. Blair, brother of the Missouri political boss, Montgomery Blair, then serving in Lincoln's cabinet as postmaster general. Frémont himself denied any impropriety, testifying before the Joint Congressional Committee on the Conduct of the War that "all officers having reason to see me, having business with me, could readily find access to me, taking their turn." *JCR* 3:69. Frank Blair countered that lacking a special order of admission of the sort Frémont gave him, "it was almost impossible for any one to see him." Blair added that "governors of states, congressmen, colonels of regiments, men bearing information from the disturbed portions of the state, right from the hostile part of our state, would come with information to him, and could not get a glimpse of him." *JCR* 3:69, 179–80. William T. Sherman had to bully two sets of guards to gain an audience with Frémont. Sherman, *Memoirs*, 1:223–24. Not surprisingly, Isaac Woods said that Frémont was "not exclusive enough" in his dealings with callers, being too anxious to accommodate everyone. *JCR* 3:205.

17. Governor Hamilton Rowan Gamble (1798–1864) was the provisional (Union) governor of Missouri. He opposed Frémont's militant policies and instead urged conciliatory

measures. On September 14, 1861, at President Lincoln's request, Frémont and Gamble met to settle their differences. Frémont requested a second meeting but did not keep the appointment. Nevins, *Frémont*, 2:514–15.

18. As Pope correctly observed, Frémont's choice of Europeans for his personal staff offended many Americans. Know-Nothing (American-born) sentiment remained strong in the North despite that party's demise after the 1856 elections. Frémont's chief of staff was Alexander Asboth, an exiled Hungarian revolutionary. Other prominent staff officers included Major Charles Zagonyi (Hungarian), Captains Antonio Cattanco and Ajace Saccippi and Lieutenant Dominica Occidone (Italians). Frémont especially favored Germans, Prussians, and Frenchmen for service on his personal staff. Nevins, *Frémont*, 2:494.

19. Lincoln drafted the order relieving Frémont on October 24, 1861. David Hunter arrived to assume command on the evening of November 3. *OR* 3:533; Nevins, *Frémont*, 2:541.

20. Major General David Hunter (1802–86) was a graduate of the West Point class of 1822 and a personal friend of Pope. Hunter's acquaintance with Lincoln led to an invitation to accompany the president-elect on the inaugural train to Washington. Hunter was president of the court-martial that cashiered Major General Fitz John Porter after Second Bull Run.

21. General Winfield Scott retired as commander in chief on October 31, 1861. McClellan succeeded him despite Scott's recommendation that Halleck get the post. McClellan appeased the disappointed Halleck by giving him command of the Department of the Missouri. T. Harry Williams, *Lincoln and His Generals* (New York, 1952), 46–47; McClellan, *McClellan's Own Story*, 202.

22. Henry Wager Halleck (1815–72) graduated third in the West Point class of 1839. He gained the nickname "Old Brains" after authoring the widely read *Elements of Military Art and Science* and for his translations of the works of the Frenchman Henri Jomini. Halleck served in an administrative role in California and missed active service during the Mexican War. He resigned his commission to join California's foremost law firm in 1854.

23. Pope refers to Halleck's snail-like march upon Corinth after assuming field command in April 1862. Halleck's combined armies took twenty-seven days to march the twenty miles to Corinth.

24. There is a lot of circumstantial evidence to support Pope's speculation. In 1858 Stanton and Halleck were involved as adversaries in a legal dispute. Stanton was conducting an investigation into the California landholdings of the New Almaden Mine Co. Halleck testified on behalf of the company and was accused of perjury by Stanton because of his inconsistent and unsubstantiated answers to questions. Halleck's promotion to general in chief also threatened Stanton's influence in military decision making, a role to which he had grown accustomed. See Benjamin P. Thomas and Harold M. Hyman, *Stanton: The Life and Times of Lincoln's Secretary of War* (New York, 1962), 80–81, 217.

25. For a complete account of Pope's campaign against Island No. 10, see Chapter 4. Pope's plan of operations can be found in *OR* 8:655–56.

26. Halleck's reply is not found in the *OR*. Pope alleged that Halleck removed these official documents, which were damning to him and favorable to Pope, from the headquarters' file and took them with him when he went east. If this was in fact the case, his equivocal telegram to Pope before Island No. 10 may have been among them. Such a communication would have been characteristic of Halleck.

27. After the fall of Corinth, Halleck sent a dispatch to Washington claiming that Pope

had reported the capture of 10,000 prisoners; what, in fact, Pope reported was that 10,000 Confederates had straggled from the rebel army and might be expected to give themselves up. Halleck's distorted message caused Pope much public embarrassment and provoked ridicule from unfriendly generals and the Democratic press. After the war Pope tried unsuccessfully to convince Halleck to retract the damning message; Halleck simply ignored Pope's correspondence. For Pope's dispatch, see *OR* 10(2):249. For Halleck's telegram to Washington, see ibid. (1):669.

28. Pope is substantially correct in his assessment of Halleck's declining years. According to his biographer, Stephen E. Ambrose, Halleck succeeded in alienating most of his peers. This occurred partly as a result of his administration of the army and partly because he so often misrepresented himself or failed to communicate properly to his subordinates. Besides Pope, only Sherman was able to set aside his grievances and give Halleck some credit in his memoirs. Halleck died in 1872, lonely, misunderstood, and unappreciated. Stephen E. Ambrose, *Halleck: Lincoln's Chief of Staff* (Baton Rouge, 1962), 200–205.

CHAPTER 2

1. According to the 1860 census, there were 114,931 slaves in Missouri, about one-ninth of the total population. As the war progressed, thousands of slaves fled to Kansas, joined the army, or abandoned their masters and wandered at large over the countryside. Michael Fellman, *Inside War: The Guerrilla Conflict in Missouri during the American Civil War* (New York, 1989), 6–7, 66.

2. The disparity was greater than Pope suggests, although the secessionists made up for their lack of numbers in noisy vituperation. In a referendum on secession held on March 4, 1861, Union candidates outpolled secessionists 110,000 to 30,000. Fellman, *Inside War*, 5; William Winter, *The Civil War in St. Louis* (St. Louis, 1994), 30.

3. Elements of ethnicity and nativism were also at play here. Many Americans resented the large pro-Union population of immigrant Germans who had settled in northern Missouri. Most of Missouri's slave-holding population resided along the Missouri River, where hemp and tobacco flourished. Both of these crops were labor intensive and their success belies Pope's assertion that slavery was profitless. Fellman, *Inside War*, 6; *Encyclopedia of the Confederacy*, 3:1052–54.

4. Pope correctly described the near anarchy that reigned in Missouri. Raiders from Kansas, dubbed "jayhawkers," ravaged Missouri farms on the pretext of liberating slaves. Retaliation in kind by slaveholders replaced the rule of law, forcing hundreds of settlers to flee to Texas, Colorado, Idaho, California, and Oregon. Fellman, *Inside War*, 21, 74. In 1861 J. W. Brooks, a prominent Missourian, wrote Secretary of War Simon Cameron, "Union voters near the borders are being driven out, and large numbers of others with their families put in such extreme peril that self-preservation is rapidly joining them to the forces of the enemy." And General Frémont was informed that "many timid Union men . . . have left the state or are intending to leave it, while perhaps a large number think it of no use to struggle against it, and bow to the storm." *OR* 3:434, 458.

5. Pope refers to the numerous guerrilla attacks on trains on the Hannibal and St. Joseph Railroad that began in earnest in July 1861, interrupting the delivery of mail and army supplies. These raids destroyed several important bridges north of the Missouri River. *OR* 3:398. See also Pope's report to the Joint Congressional Committee on the Conduct of the War, *JCR*, supp. 2:5.

6. On June 12, 1861, the pro-secession governor of Missouri, Claiborne Fox Jackson, and the commander of the state militia, Sterling Price, met with ardent Unionist Congressman Francis P. Blair and Brigadier General Nathaniel Lyon in a halfhearted attempt to stem the violence. At this meeting Lyon declared a state of war between Missouri and the United States, and Jackson and his cabinet fled to southwestern Missouri. Price, who had been a conditional Unionist, now cast his lot with the Confederacy. Robert E. Shalhope, *Sterling Price: Portrait of a Southerner* (Columbia, 1971), 162–66.

7. Five railroads were operating in Missouri in 1861, only one of which traversed the state. In northern Missouri the Hannibal and St. Joseph line connected the Mississippi and Missouri Rivers. The Northern Missouri Railroad linked the Hannibal and St. Joseph Railroad to St. Louis. The Missouri Pacific paralleled the Missouri River to Jefferson City and beyond, whereas the Southern Railroad branched off at Franklin and ran to Rolla. Finally, the Iron Mountain Railroad connected St. Louis to Ironton. The swiftest means of delivering supplies, these railroads were prime targets of guerrilla attacks. George E. Turner, *Victory Rode the Rails* (Indianapolis, 1953), 96.

8. *OR* 3:403–4. The text of this notice as published in the *OR* is substantially the same as that presented here by Pope, which appears to be an unedited version of the order.

9. Pope said as much in his report to the Joint Congressional Committee on the Conduct of the War. *JCR*, supp. 2:7. However, sporadic incidents continued. See the letters of J. T. K. Hayward, in *OR* 3:460–61, which detail several attacks on trains on the Hannibal and St. Joseph Railroad after the promulgation of Pope's warning. John B. Wyman to Frémont (*OR* 3:466) reports an attempt to blow up a train near Rolla. In response to the attacks, Pope on July 31 instituted the policies outlined in General Order No. 3. On August 17 Pope reported that the citizens of Marion County, where most of the depredations occurred, were cooperating after he had Federal troops quartered in their homes at their expense for ten days. Pope wrote: "That order seems to have united all responsible persons who have anything to lose in efforts to preserve the peace, and they have organized for that purpose. If any skirmishing is done, it will be done by the people themselves, and who have a motive to do so which they had not before." *OR* 3:447.

10. Pope sent specific instructions to his subordinates regarding the selection of the Committees of Public Safety. See his directive to Colonel William H. Worthington of the Fifth Iowa, August 2, 1861, which reads in part: "In selecting members for the Committee of Public Safety you are directed to appoint, be sure to put upon it at least two, or, better still, three of the most worthy and prominent secessionists. It is the service of the secessionists I specially require, and I desire that you will give them plainly to understand that unless peace is preserved, their property will be immediately levied upon, and their contribution collected at once in any kind of property at hand." *OR* 3:422.

11. Pope's policy brought down a storm of protests and complaints from the citizenry. J. T. K. Hayward blamed the railroad attacks on outsiders and complained in a letter to Frémont that "it is the published purpose of General Pope to hold communities responsible for acts of violence committed among them. This might do in a foreign country, but I do not think it can be done here, without alienating friends and making the feeling still more bitter on the part of the enemies. . . . It is already creating great dissatisfaction. The principle of holding peaceable, quiet men responsible in a military contribution for damages done by lawless and violent men is one which can never meet with favor in the popular mind." *OR* 3:458–60. Pope justified his actions, including arrests and seizures of property, to Frémont in part as follows: "The policy of making the people along the lines of the railroad in North Missouri responsible for any damage done to the roads has per-

fectly secured them from destruction since it was established. . . . this policy alone, and the fear of the penalty to property prescribed in it, prevents the secessionists from driving out Union men and destroying their property. . . . Where outrages are so expensive, they will not be repeated." *OR* 3 : 456.

CHAPTER 3

1. According to the census of 1860, the population of Missouri was 1,182,012, of whom 114,931 were slaves. During the course of the war, Missouri sent 109,111 men to the Union armies and some 30,000 to the Confederate armies. Although the number of men who fought as irregulars or guerrillas was much greater, no reliable statistics can be had. Frederick Phisterer, *Statistical Record of the Armies of the United States* (New York, 1883), 10.

2. The full text of General Order No. 3 is in *OR* 3 : 417–18.

3. See also Chapter 2, n. 11. On August 24, 1861, twelve prominent Missourians sent a letter of protest to Frémont in response to the swift and severe action taken by Pope in retaliation for guerrilla attacks on passenger trains. *OR*, ser. 2, 1 : 214–15.

4. On August 5, 1861, Pope sent U. S. Grant, his subordinate, to Frémont to argue the necessity of General Order No. 3. Pope also explained his motives in a long letter to the president of the North Missouri Railroad, J. H. Sturgeon, and again to Frémont in a letter on August 23. *OR* 3 : 456–57 and ser. 2, 1 : 214–15, 199–200.

5. The attack occurred on August 7, 1861, near Palmyra, in Marion County. In response, Pope ordered Brigadier General Stephen A. Hurlbut to "shoot any who were concerned in the firing" and to compel the community to deliver up the guilty parties, warning him not to "fail in severity or in strict compliance with orders or upon yourself will rest a serious responsibility." Hurlbut acted with zeal and arrested several prominent Missourians, including John McAfee, the former speaker of the Missouri House of Representatives. *OR*, ser. 2, 1 : 202–3, 206–9.

6. Union forces occupied Marion County for ten days. On departing, their train was fired on as it passed through Palmyra and Hunnevell. Pope threatened a $10,000 levy on the county and one of $5,000 on the towns if the perpetrators were not surrendered within six days. The loud public outcry at this prompted Governor Gamble and Frank Blair to pressure Pope into retracting General Order No. 3. On August 30 Pope rescinded the order, explaining: "Neither the condition of the people nor the experience of the past month can fairly justify a departure from the policy which already has greatly reduced the extent and character of the disturbances in North Missouri, yet it is hoped that this cordial assent to the suggestions . . . of the executive and many of the most prominent citizens of the State will be received by the people in the spirit in which it is accorded and that the hopes of peace and quiet which these gentlemen base upon it will not be disappointed" (Special Order No. 13). *OR*, ser. 2, 1 : 212–13, 220–21.

7. On August 30, 1861, Frémont proclaimed martial law in Missouri. Among the provisions of his manifesto were death to anyone found bearing arms within Union lines and the emancipation of the slaves of any Missourian who took up arms against the United States. President Lincoln demanded that Frémont retract the edict of emancipation immediately. *OR* 3 : 466–67.

8. Governor Claiborne F. Jackson and the Missouri legislature fled from Jefferson City, to Booneville, at the approach of Lyon's army, ordering the railroad bridges burned behind them. On June 12 Jackson issued a proclamation calling for 50,000 volunteers of the state militia to repel the Federal invasion. This edict threw the state into war. James Peck-

ham, *Gen. Nathaniel Lyon and Missouri in 1861* (New York, 1866), 249–52. See also Chapter 2, n. 7.

9. To what work or competent authority Pope refers is unclear.

10. On July 22, 1861, a state convention met to replace the government of Missouri. After eight days of deliberation, the offices of governor and lieutenant governor were declared vacant. Hamilton R. Gamble was elected governor; Willard P. Hall, lieutenant governor; Mordecai Oliver, secretary of state; and George A. Bingham, treasurer. St. Louis was named the new seat of government. Peckham, *Lyon and Missouri*, 290–91.

11. For the text of this order, see *OR* 3:466–67.

12. Martin Green (1815–63) was a native Virginian who migrated to Missouri in 1836, settling in Lewis County, where he and his brothers operated a sawmill. When the Civil War began, he organized a cavalry command in the northeastern part of the state and was commissioned a general in the State Guard. Green fought with Price's army in the Battles of Lexington, Pea Ridge, and Corinth.

13. David Moore was a Mexican War veteran whose sons fought for the Confederacy. Steve Meyer, *Iowa Valor* (Garrison, Iowa, 1994), 19.

14. The incident occurred on the night of September 3, 1861; the bushwhackers believed the train to be loaded with Federal soldiers. Thirteen people were killed and seventy-five were injured. Thomas Goodrich, *Black Flag: Guerrilla Warfare on the Western Border, 1861–1865* (Bloomington, 1995), 8–10.

15. James A. Mulligan (1830–64) was born in Utica, New York. He moved to Chicago, where he was active in politics and worked as a lawyer and newspaperman. The dynamic, colorful Mulligan used his influence in the Irish community to raise a regiment and was named colonel of the Twenty-third Illinois Volunteer Infantry, the so-called Irish Brigade. Harold F. Smith, "Mulligan and the Irish Brigade," *Journal of the Illinois State Historical Society* 56, no. 2 (Summer 1963): 164–76.

16. The Battle of Lexington was fought during September 13–20, 1861. Price's army invested Mulligan's Irish Brigade in the town. After a sharp fight, Mulligan was forced to surrender before reinforcements could effect a junction with him. For Mulligan's account of this battle, see Robert Underwood Johnson and Clarence C. Buel, eds., *Battles and Leaders of the Civil War*, 4 vols. (New York, 1887), 1:307–13.

17. On September 16 Pope ordered the Sixteenth Illinois and the Third Iowa at Hudson, together with three pieces of artillery, to march to Lexington. Pope reported from Palmyra that these regiments, four guns, and 150 cavalrymen were expected to reach Lexington by the eighteenth. *OR* 3:176.

18. Pope was ordered to go to Booneville. *OR* 3:504.

19. Simon Cameron was Lincoln's secretary of war; Brigadier General Lorenzo Thomas was the adjutant general of the army.

20. Pope's contempt for Frémont was an open secret in the department, and he made sure that his views were known to Cameron and Thomas. He sent General David Hunter a frank letter expounding on his disgust with Frémont, which Hunter was to express freely with the secretary and the adjutant general. John Nicolay and John Hay, *Abraham Lincoln: A History* (New York, 1890), 4:431; *Philadelphia Inquirer*, July 4, 1862. For a sharply critical appraisal of Pope's behavior, see Allan Nevins, *Frémont: Pathmaker of the West*, 2 vols. (New York, 1961), 2:530–31, 534–35.

21. Most likely this was Francis A. Hoffman, the lieutenant governor of Illinois.

22. Pope queried Hunter, "What is to be accomplished, or rather what does any sane man suppose will be the result? The prospect before us is appalling . . . I think Frémont

crazy or worse." Pope and Hunter reached an accord not to move unless adequately supplied; i.e., they would disobey Frémont's orders. *OR* 3:727–28, 730–32; James Jay Monaghan, *Civil War on the Western Border, 1854–1865* (Boston, 1955), 200–203.

23. Franz Sigel (1824–1902), a native of Baden, Germany, emigrated to New York following the failed revolution of 1848. When the Civil War began, he was commissioned brigadier general of volunteers by virtue of his immense popularity among the immigrant German population and was assigned to duty in Missouri. Sigel and Pope detested one another. Manuscript notes on Federal generals, 1–2, Franz Sigel Papers, Western Reserve Historical Society, Cleveland.

24. Brigadier General Justus McKinstry (1814–97) led a division under Frémont.

25. Julian is identified only as "a well informed and reliable guide" in *OR* 3:559.

26. Pope was ordered to move forward "with the greatest alacrity to join the advanced corps at the place [Springfield]. . . . It is imperatively necessary that you should come here by forced marches." J. H. Eaton to Pope, ibid.

27. Eugene A. Carr (1830–1910) of New York was a graduate of the West Point class of 1850.

28. This meeting took place on the evening of November 3, 1861. Nevins, *Frémont*, 2:542.

29. Frémont maintained that he was about to give battle when he was improperly relieved by Hunter. For his account of the affair, see "In Command in Missouri," in Johnson and Buel, *Battles and Leaders*, 1:288.

30. On November 7, 1861, at the council of war, Hunter decided to fall back to Rolla and Sedalia. He withdrew despite information that Price was seventy-five miles away and over protests that a withdrawal would again surrender the region to the Confederates. Monaghan, *Civil War on the Western Border*, 206.

31. On October 24, 1861, Lincoln wrote to Hunter opining that if Price was retreating to Arkansas, Rolla and Sedalia should be occupied to secure the railroad. "An indefinite pursuit of Price . . . will be exhaustive beyond endurance," Lincoln advised. *OR* 3:553–54.

32. On November 9, 1861, General Order No. 97 created the Department of the Missouri and named Henry W. Halleck as commander. *OR* 3:567.

33. The District of Central Missouri was bounded by the area between the Osage River on the south and the Missouri River on the north. Pope assumed command on December 3, 1861. *OR* 8:403.

34. Price issued his "Proclamation to the People of Central and North Missouri," on November 26, 1861, calling for 50,000 volunteers to "drive the hireling bands of thieves and marauders from the State." *OR* 8:695–97; Albert Castel, *General Sterling Price and the Civil War in the West* (Baton Rouge, 1968), 61.

35. The response to his proclamation disappointed Price, who complained that only 5,000 men responded to his various calls for volunteers between June and November. *OR* 8:695–97. See also Castel, *Price*, 61–62.

36. Halleck ordered Pope to move against Price in the direction of Warrensburg. Pope predicted that the move would be too late and proposed Clinton, to the southwest, as his objective. *OR* 8:436.

37. Jefferson Columbus Davis (1828–79), of Indiana, a Mexican War veteran who commanded the Twenty-second Indiana Infantry, and Frederick Steele (1819–68).

38. Major William M. G. Torrence.

39. E. B. Brown, Seventh Missouri Cavalry.

40. Major J. M. Hubbard, First Missouri Cavalry, and Colonel Lewis Merrill, Second Missouri Cavalry.

41. This occurred on December 16, 1861. See Pope's report, *OR* 8:39.

42. Lieutenants Henry Gordon and Capley Amory, Fourth U.S. Cavalry.

43. For a full description of the action at Blackwater River, see Amory's report, *OR* 8:40–42.

44. Estimates of the number captured vary from 736 in Joanne C. Eakins's undocumented *Battle at Blackwater River* (Independence, Mo., 1995) to Pope's count of 1,300 in *OR* 8:40.

45. See Pope's report, *OR* 8:40.

46. December 22, 1861.

47. December 18, 1861.

48. Brigadier General Samuel R. Curtis (1805–61), commanding the Southwestern District of Missouri.

49. The Battle of Pea Ridge, or Elkhorn Tavern, was fought on March 7–8, 1862. The defeat was disastrous for the Confederate army under Earl Van Dorn.

50. Pope presumably was referring to Frémont's article on the Missouri campaign in Johnson and Buel, *Battles and Leaders*.

CHAPTER 4

1. This refers to Grant's failed effort to bypass the Vicksburg batteries by cutting a new channel for the Mississippi River. Grant describes his several failures in his *Personal Memoirs of U. S. Grant* (New York, 1885–86), 1:442–58. Grant does not mention Pope or Island No. 10 and states that he "never felt great confidence that any of the experiments resorted to would prove successful." The only book-length treatment of the campaign is Larry J. Daniel and Lynn N. Bock, *Island No. 10: Struggle for the Mississippi* (Tuscaloosa, 1995).

2. Pierre Gustave Toutant Beauregard (1818–93). For Pope's appraisal of Beauregard, see Chapter 14.

3. See Pope's report to the Joint Congressional Committee on the Conduct of the War, *JCR*, supp. 2:24, and *OR* 8:79–81. Brigadier General John P. McCown commanded the combined Confederate forces defending Island No. 10 and New Madrid. Daniel and Bock place the number of Confederate guns at 52 and the combined garrison at 7,432 at the opening of the campaign; *Island No. 10*, 30–34, 156.

4. Island No. 10 was so named because it was the tenth island on the Mississippi River south of the Ohio River from Cairo, Illinois. Estimates of its length vary from one mile to one and a half miles; its width has been calculated at 450 yards to half a mile. The island sank to the bottom of the Mississippi many years ago.

5. The distance is six miles by land but fifteen by the river, which twists and turns for great stretches here. See Manning Force, *From Fort Henry to Corinth* (New York, 1881), 67. See also Daniel and Bock, *Island No. 10*, 4–5.

6. The distance to Tiptonville is five miles overland but twenty-seven by river. Pope's estimates of distances here are surprisingly in error in view of the fact that he was formerly a topographical engineer. Force, *Fort Henry to Corinth*, 67.

7. Seven miles according to the map that accompanies Pope's report to the Joint Congressional Committee on the Conduct of the War. See Pope, *JCR*, supp. 2:56.

8. I.e., south of Tiptonville.

9. Pope again erred on distance; it is seven miles from Tiptonville to Island No. 10.

10. The regional topography was due in large part to the effects of the great earthquake of December 6, 1811, which transformed the once fertile region into dismal swampland. The region lay directly along a major fault line and the earthquake's epicenter was near New Madrid.

11. Cairo, Illinois, lay at the confluence of the Mississippi and Ohio Rivers. It was a strategically important staging base for troops and supplies going down the river throughout the war.

12. Brigadier General David S. Stanley, First Division; Brigadier General Schuyler Hamilton, Second Division; Brigadier General John M. Palmer, Third Division; and Colonel Gordon Granger, Cavalry Division. See OR 8:91–92.

13. Pope issued marching orders to Hamilton and Palmer on February 27. OR 8:571.

14. The command reached Hunter's Farm just before midnight on February 28, 1861. OR 8:102.

15. William P. Kellogg.

16. Meriwether "Jeff" Thompson (1826–76) was a former mayor and railroad executive from St. Joseph, Mo. An ardent secessionist, he was a brigadier general in the Missouri State Guard. His exploits leading troops in the swamps of southeastern Missouri and northeastern Arkansas earned him the moniker "Swamp Fox." See Bruce Allardice, *More Generals in Gray* (Baton Rouge, 1995), 219–20.

17. On March 1 Kellogg's Seventh Illinois Cavalry encountered Thompson's force near Sikeston and scattered it, capturing three guns. Thompson falsely claimed to have engaged Kellogg in a deliberate, seventeen-mile rearguard action toward New Madrid. OR 8:102, 173.

18. The lower redoubt, known as Fort Thompson, was armed with five 32-pounders, five 24-pounders, one 12-pounder, and three smaller guns. The upper fort, called Fort Bankhead, held a combination of seven 24- and 32-pounders. OR 8:163.

19. In addition to the twenty-one guns in the two forts, there were twenty-one guns in earthworks outside of New Madrid and six gunboats acting as floating batteries. When New Madrid fell, thirty-seven guns were captured. OR 8:163. David Dixon Porter claimed that seventy-five guns protected the area. See David D. Porter, *The Naval History of the Civil War* (New York, 1886), 161.

20. Pope's estimate was too high. The Confederate commander at New Madrid, Brigadier General A. P. Stewart, reported that fewer than 3,000 troops were on hand at New Madrid to face Pope, and brigade commander Edward W. Gantt placed the number at just under 3,500. OR 8:163, 167.

21. George N. Hollins (1799–1878) was a career naval officer dating to the War of 1812. He resigned in 1861 to offer his service to the Confederacy and was given command of the upper Mississippi naval forces. Hollins had six gunboats, not nine as credited by Pope, on duty near New Madrid. Charles W. Davis, "New Madrid and Island Number Ten," in MOLLUS 1:80.

22. Major General John Porter McCown (1815–79) commanded the Confederate forces at New Madrid before Pope's arrival. General Alexander Peter Stewart (1821–1908) graduated from West Point in 1842 but soon resigned to teach mathematics and philosophy at Cumberland University and other schools. He joined the Confederacy and, after several months of training new troops, saw action in the Battle of Belmont and was appointed brigadier general under Leonidas Polk. Acting Brigadier General Edward W. Gantt was a lawyer and politician who cast his lot with the Confederacy. He was colonel of the 12th

Arkansas Infantry but commanded a brigade at New Madrid. Ezra J. Warner, *Generals in Gray* (Baton Rouge, 1959), 199–200, 293–94; Allardice, *More Generals in Gray*, 95–96.

23. Josiah W. Bissell commanded the Engineer Regiment of the West, an organization consisting of twelve full companies of selected workmen, skilled mechanics, and officers. J. W. Bissell, "Sawing Out a Channel above Island Number Ten," in Robert Underwood Johnson and Clarence C. Buel, eds., *Battles and Leaders of the Civil War*, 4 vols. (New York, 1887), 1:460.

24. Bissell had gone to Cairo for four rifled 32-pounder guns but returned with three 24-pounders and one eight-inch howitzer. These were immediately shipped across the river to Bird's Point and sent on by rail to Sikeston, where they were mounted on carriages and moved to Pope over a road newly repaired by Bissell's engineers. The guns reached Pope on the evening of March 12, thirty-four hours after being delivered to Bissell. See Force, *Fort Henry to Corinth*, 74–75, and *OR* 8:82.

25. James D. Morgan commanded the First Brigade, consisting of the Tenth and Sixth Illinois Infantry regiments. *OR* 8:110.

26. Pope is incorrect. McCown reported on March 12 that Pope would be able to bring 24-pounders from Sikeston to use against New Madrid. *OR* 8:777.

27. Joseph A. Mower (1827–70) was a Mexican War veteran, later commissioned from the ranks to second lieutenant in the First U.S. Infantry. He commanded Pope's siege train during the Island No. 10 campaign. *OR* 8:96, 824.

28. March 14, 1862.

29. New Madrid lay to the northwest of Island No. 10 yet was downstream of it, thus "below," in river parlance. Pope's occupation of New Madrid and Point Pleasant, ten miles downriver, gave him command of that entire stretch of the river. This all but isolated the enemy forces at Island No. 10. *OR* 8:83.

30. Andrew Hull Foote (1806–63) began his naval career as a midshipman in 1822. During the Civil War he commanded the naval forces on the upper Mississippi River. His cooperation with Grant's army led to the fall of Forts Henry and Donelson in February 1862.

31. Pope voiced no objection to Halleck's order. *OR* 8:618–19.

32. Schuyler Hamilton (1822–1903), a grandson of Alexander Hamilton and brother-in-law of Henry Halleck, graduated from West Point in 1841 and served on the plains and as an instructor of tactics at West Point before the Mexican War. As a division commander under Pope, Hamilton suggested that a canal be cut that would allow Pope's transports to avoid the batteries at Island No. 10. The origin of the idea became a point of controversy between Hamilton and Bissell. See Johnson and Buel, *Battles and Leaders*, 1:462, and Daniel and Bock, *Island No. 10*, 104–18.

33. For Bissell's account of this operation, see Johnson and Buel, *Battles and Leaders*, 1:460–62. The only digging involved was to widen the pre-existing channel. See *OR* 8:87.

34. Bissell's canal was completed on April 6, and four steamers were immediately sent through. Bissell neither wrote an official report nor commented on the condition of his men in the *Century* article. See *ORN* 22:724, and Johnson and Buel, *Battles and Leaders*, 1:460–62.

35. On March 31 General Mackall reported that Pope was "endeavoring to cut a canal across the peninsula for the passage of transports," an attempt he thought would fail, leaving Island No. 10 safe until the river fell. *OR* 8:132.

36. For example, on March 26 Pope requested that Foote send him even the smallest gunboat in his flotilla, with or without guns. See *ORN* 22:701.

37. Pope to Halleck, March 27, 1862. *ORN* 22:703.

38. On April 2 Mackall reported that he had fifty guns mounted on floating and water batteries along twenty-five miles of riverbank, in addition to the defenses on the island itself. *OR* 8:132–33. See also the report of Captain A. B. Guy in ibid., 138–45.

39. Colonel Joseph B. Plummer occupied Point Pleasant on March 6–7.

40. Foote acceded to pressure from both Halleck and Assistant Secretary of War Thomas Scott. Walke's willingness to make the attempt also contributed. A career naval officer, Henry Walke (1808–96) was a commodore at the time of the Island No. 10 campaign. See Walke's account in Johnson and Buel, *Battles and Leaders*, 1:440–46.

41. Walke was promoted to captain in July 1862 and was favorably mentioned to Secretary of War Edwin Stanton by Assistant Secretary Thomas Scott, who was with Pope's army. Foote also commended Walke. *ORN* 22:712–13, 722.

42. Captain Charles Houghtaling, Battery C, First Regiment Illinois Light Artillery.

43. George A. Williams, First U.S. Infantry.

44. Pope to Paine, April 7, 1862. *OR* 8:670.

45. Foote reported the surrender of "seventeen officers, 368 privates, 100 of these sick, and also 100 men employed in transports," along with eleven earthworks with seventy heavy cannon. *ORN* 22:721.

46. General Mackall surrendered to Paine unconditionally at 2:00 A.M. on April 8, 1862, with what has been variously estimated as from 3,900 to 4,538 men. In the immediate aftermath of the surrender, Pope exuberantly reported 7,000 prisoners taken, a claim that caused him much embarrassment in the newspapers. See *OR* 8:110, and Daniel and Bock, *Island No. 10*, 157–59.

47. Colonel Napoleon B. Buford, Twenty-seventh Illinois Infantry.

48. In the *National Tribune* Pope repeated the numbers he had recited before the Joint Congressional Committee on the Conduct of the War. Daniel and Bock concluded that Pope had captured 109 guns of all calibers and 5,000 stands of small arms. Daniel and Bock, *Island No. 10*, 144–45; *OR* 8:90. General Stanley recalled that a lot of the equipment and tents was worn out. David S. Stanley, *Personal Memoirs of Major General D. S. Stanley, U.S.A.* (Cambridge, 1917), 91.

CHAPTER 5

1. April 14, 1862.

2. *OR* 10(2):107–8.

3. Graham N. Fitch, commander of the Second Brigade of Palmer's Third Division, remained with the Forty-third and Forty-sixth Indiana Infantry regiments. *OR* 8:92.

4. Pope means Brigadier General Eleazer A. Paine, not Payne as in the text.

5. Halleck was suffering from the effects of dysentery. See Jack Welsh, *Medical Histories of Union Generals* (Kent State University Press, Kent, 1996), 145.

6. Halleck left his headquarters in St. Louis and arrived at Pittsburg Landing on April 12, 1862. See *OR* 10(2):99, 104–5.

7. *OR* 10(2):116.

8. The roads were, in fact, in poor condition due to the effects of incessant rain. Ibid.

9. Grant was made second in command during the controversy that surrounded him

after the Battle of Shiloh. He was very aggrieved at this situation, of which he wrote, "For myself I was little more than an observer. . . . My position was so embarrassing in fact that I made several applications during the siege to be relieved." Grant, *Personal Memoirs of U. S. Grant* (New York, 1885–86), 1:248, 251.

10. Frustrated at his position, Grant requested to relocate his headquarters to Memphis. Sherman convinced him to stay with the army, lest he regret the move. According to David S. Stanley, Grant "commanded nothing and he looked like a man without employment." Grant, *Personal Memoirs*, 1:258; Stanley, *Personal Memoirs of Major General D. S. Stanley, U.S.A.* (Cambridge, 1917), pp. 102–3; for Sherman's account, see *Memoirs of W. T. Sherman*, 1:275–76.

11. Halleck's caution was due in part to his belief that the Union armies were overextended. He viewed Richmond and Corinth as the "great strategical points of war" and cautioned that "our success at these points should be insured at all hazards." *OR* 10(2):667.

12. Pope miscalculated. The distance is only seventeen miles.

13. Pope means Brigadier General Eleazer Paine, not Payne.

14. This action was a skirmish at Farmington on May 4, 1862. Four companies of the Third Michigan Cavalry engaged three hundred Confederates and drove them after a brisk hour-long fight. *OR* 10(1):728.

15. Halleck ordered Pope to "avoid any general engagement. I can get no reply from Buell, and he may not have received my orders to support you." Brevet Brigadier General Edward Bolton recalled that "it was the generally expressed opinion at the time, that had Pope been allowed to do so, he would have effected the capture or compelled the evacuation of Corinth in two days." *OR* 10(1):674 and (2):171, 177, 180–81; Edward Bolton, *Events of the Civil War* (Los Angeles, 1906), 38.

16. Pope was mistaken. Brigadier General Isaac Newton Palmer was serving on The Peninsula under McClellan at the time. Brigadier General John McCauley Palmer led the First Brigade, First Division, under Pope at Island No. 10 and Corinth.

17. Brigadier General Joseph Bennett Plummer (1816–62) commanded the Second Brigade, Second Division, of Pope's army.

18. On the night of May 9 Pope reported to Halleck on the success of the day's fighting and complained that he obeyed the order to avoid a general engagement "very reluctantly." Similarly, Colonel John Loomis of the Twenty-sixth Illinois wrote that his men could have held their advanced position if not ordered to retire. The Confederates withdrew into the Corinth entrenchments during the night. The following morning Assistant Secretary of War Scott tried unsuccessfully to convince Halleck to follow up Pope's action with a general advance. *OR* 10(1):804, 807.

19. Palmer's message is not in the *OR*.

20. Pope organized a cavalry division in his Army of the Mississippi under Colonel Gordon Granger, which was unprecedented at the time. According to the historian of the Second Iowa Cavalry, which participated in the raid, Pope "showed the world that he could make this branch of the service very effective. Instead of mixing them with infantry . . . he organized cavalry brigades and divisions, placing them under cavalry officers, and when thus organized he assigned them to their appropriate duty." Lyman B. Pierce, *History of the Second Iowa Cavalry* (Burlington, 1865). See also Stephen Z. Starr, *The Union Cavalry in the Civil War* (Baton Rouge, 1979–82), 3:57, 61; *OR* 8:93, 10(1):731.

21. Philip H. Sheridan (1831–88) graduated from West Point in 1853. During the early

part of the Civil War, he was chief quartermaster for the Army of Southwest Missouri before serving in the same capacity under Halleck at St. Louis. On May 25, 1862, he was appointed colonel of the Second Michigan Cavalry.

22. Edward Hatch (1832–87) of Maine managed a lumber company in Iowa prior to the Civil War. He was commissioned captain in the Second Iowa Cavalry and later became its colonel. He was assigned to Pope's army and led a brigade during the Island No. 10 and Corinth campaigns.

23. Washington (not William) L. Elliott (1825–88) ended the war a division commander in the Fourth Corps.

24. For the text of the order, see *OR* 10(1):217.

25. Colonel Elliott says that he left at midnight. *OR* 10(1):862.

26. Two A.M. is the time cited by Pope and Elliott in their reports. Ibid.

27. Pope and Elliott reported that one locomotive and twenty-six cars were destroyed. Ibid.

28. Pope reported that one brass and two iron fieldpieces were taken. Ibid.

29. These statistics were provided to Elliott by Brigadier General James B. McPherson, who was the engineer in charge of railcars at Corinth.

30. Stanley's report of this skirmish can be found in his *Personal Memoirs*, 99–100.

31. According to Stanley, a heated dispute erupted between Pope and General William B. Nelson over who was first. Stanley recalled: "As soon as day came the discovery was made that our foe was gone, and then commenced a foolish race between the different divisions of the army as to which should have the empty honor to enter first the miserable little town of Corinth. Our commander, Pope, at the head of one of his divisions, came face to face with General Nelson, commanding one of Buell's divisions, and, at the head of their troops, indulged in a general cursing match, to the horror and scandal of everybody. Pope threatened to arrest Nelson. The latter swore he would not respect the arrest. Finally they departed to become bitter enemies thereafter." Stanley, *Personal Memoirs*, 101. For a vivid account of the quarrel by a soldier in the ranks, see Joseph Strickling Diary, 16–17, OHS.

32. Confederate major general Earl Van Dorn.

33. The distance is twenty-two miles.

34. June 2, 1862.

35. Pope reported to Halleck that he had sufficient force to attack the enemy near Baldwin but, concerned with the enemy's strength and his own supplies, cautioned his own commanders not to pursue too much farther. *OR* 10(2):245–46, 250, 252–53.

36. Sherman wrote that the woods were full of deserters whom the army did not take prisoner but rather told to go home and stay there. Sheridan thought the disorganization on both sides was so great that it prevented the Union forces from destroying the Confederate army. Sherman, *Memoirs of General William Tecumseh Sherman* (New York, 1875), 1:281; Philip H. Sheridan, *Personal Memoirs of P. H. Sheridan*, 2 vols. (New York, 1887), 1:153.

37. *OR* 10(1):699.

38. Pope, in fact, rejoined his army on the evening of June 4. *OR* 10(2):249–55.

39. Pope sent numerous dispatches and updates to Halleck during the pursuit, but the official records do not reflect hourly communications from him. Ibid., 237–59.

40. Ohio brigadier general William Starke Rosecrans (1819–98), a graduate of the West Point class of 1842, was Pope's senior division commander during the pursuit from Corinth.

41. *OR* 10(2):249.

42. The correspondence eventually appeared in the official records. Ibid., 635–37. Pope also caused it to be published shortly after the war. See *Correspondence between Generals Pope and Halleck in Relation to Prisoners Captured at Corinth* (n.p, n.d.). Julia Dent Grant castigated Pope for his apparently fabricated prisoner count, but most senior officers on the scene seem to have accepted Pope's version of events. John Simon, ed., *Personal Memoirs of Julia Dent Grant* (New York, 1975), 101; William P. Carlin, "Military Memoirs," *NT*, February 19, 1885; Edward Bolton, *Events of the Civil War* (Los Angeles, 1906), 46–48.

43. Pope reported that the estimates came from Gordon Granger and that very few prisoners actually came in. See Pope's report, *JCR*, supp. 2:77.

CHAPTER 6

1. Pope, "War Reminiscences: Personal Recollections of Distinguished People, Civil and Military," *NT*, December 25, 1890.

2. Albert Sidney Johnston (1803–62) of Kentucky graduated from West Point in 1826. An excellent biography of Johnston is Charles P. Roland's *Albert Sidney Johnston: Soldier of Three Republics* (Austin, 1964).

3. Davis regarded Johnston as the "great pillar of the Confederacy; her outstanding general."

4. Johnston was fifty-eight years old in 1861.

5. James Pinckney Henderson (1808–58) was the first governor of Texas.

6. An unfair remark. Johnston distinguished himself at the Battle of Monterrey on September 21, 1846, when he rallied a demoralized Ohio regiment and repulsed a charge of Mexican lancers. This earned him the praise of (later Major General) Joseph Hooker, who wrote, "it was through (Johnston's) agency, mainly, that our division was saved from a cruel slaughter." Roland, *Albert Sidney Johnston*, 134–35, 138; Steven E. Woodworth, *Jefferson Davis and His Generals: The Failure of Confederate Command in the West* (Lawrence, 1995), 8–9.

7. Johnston's biographer confirms this. President Zachary Taylor appointed Johnston to the paymaster's post; Taylor was Jefferson Davis's father-in-law. Roland, *Albert Sidney Johnston*, 153–54.

8. Pope commanded the Division of the Pacific, with headquarters at the Presidio of San Francisco, from November 1883 to March 1886.

9. Braxton Bragg (1817–76) of North Carolina was a graduate of the West Point class of 1837.

10. Bragg's sour demeanor was legendary in the Old Army. Grant recalled: "Bragg was a remarkably intelligent and well-informed man, professionally and otherwise. He was also thoroughly upright. But he was possessed of an irascible temper, and was naturally disputatious." Sherman wrote that Bragg was a man of ability, discipline, and great organizational skill, but he was "exacting and severe, and not possessing the qualities to attract the love of his officers and men. Grant, *Personal Memoirs of U. S. Grant* (New York, 1885–86), 2:86–87; Sherman, *Memoirs of General William Tecumseh Sherman* (New York, 1875), 1:285.

11. Zachary Taylor, later president.

12. Thomas West Sherman (1813–79) graduated from West Point in 1836.

13. Sherman and one of his howitzers supported a fragmented line against a charge of Mexican lancers, earning him a brevet rank of major.

14. This is a lengthier version of the anecdote usually quoted from Grant's memoirs. See Grant, *Personal Memoirs*, 2:86–87.

15. William Joseph Hardee (1815–73) of Georgia was a graduate of the West Point class of 1838. A highly regarded officer, twice brevetted for gallantry during the Mexican War, Hardee was the author of *Rifle and Light Infantry Tactics*, which was adopted by the army for general use. For an excellent biography of Hardee, see Nathaniel C. Hughes, *General William J. Hardee: Old Reliable* (Baton Rouge, 1965).

16. Van Dorn (1820–63) brought with him an army that generally viewed him as an incompetent glory seeker. See Peter Cozzens, *The Darkest Days of the War: The Battles of Iuka and Corinth* (Chapel Hill, 1997), 9–11.

17. Van Dorn ranked fifty-second out of fifty-six in the class of 1842.

18. David Emanuel Twiggs (1790–1862) was cashiered after surrendering the soldiers and stores of the Department of Texas to authorities of the recently seceded state of Texas.

19. Pope dealt unfairly with Van Dorn, who was on leave of absence in Mississippi when Twiggs surrendered his command. The best biographical treatment of Van Dorn is Robert Hartje, *Van Dorn: The Life and Times of a Confederate General* (Nashville, 1967).

20. Van Dorn was murdered on May 7, 1863, in Spring Hill, Tennessee, by Dr. George B. Peters, the husband of Jesse Peters, with whom Van Dorn purportedly had been carrying on an indiscreet affair.

21. Major General Mansfield Lovell (1822–84) of Washington, D.C. After New Orleans, Lovell commanded a division at the Battle of Corinth and failed miserably. See Cozzens, *Darkest Days*, 271–73.

22. Admiral David Glasgow Farragut and Major General Benjamin Franklin Butler.

23. Pope is voicing his contempt for the man (McClellan) he believed responsible for his defeat at Second Bull Run and subsequent exile to Minnesota. For more on this, see Chapter 11.

24. Gustavus Woodson Smith (1821–96), a native Kentuckian who also graduated from West Point in 1842.

25. Pope, "War Reminiscences, III: Personal Recollections of Distinguished Leaders, Civil and Military," *NT*, December 25, 1890.

26. Gustavus Smith, *Confederate War Papers* (New York, 1884).

27. See Chapter 1, n. 7. Price was born in Virginia and moved to Missouri as a young man. The best biography of Price is Robert E. Shalhope, *Sterling Price: Portrait of a Southerner* (Columbia, 1971).

28. Francis Preston Blair Jr. was the son of the Republican party founder Francis P. Blair. He was an ardent Unionist who played a central role in keeping Missouri in the Union in 1861.

29. See Chapter 2, n. 7. For a less flattering appraisal of Price's motives, see Albert Castel, *Sterling Price and the Civil War in the West* (Baton Rouge, 1968).

30. Price favored neutrality for Missouri, but after the "Camp Jackson Massacre" on May 10, 1861, he accepted a commission as commander of the secessionist Missouri state militia.

31. Contrary to Pope's assertion, the Confederate government eagerly accepted Missouri troops and admitted the state and its exiled secessionist government into the Con-

federacy. Missouri was vital to Confederate interests because it controlled a large stretch of the Mississippi. There is truth, however, in Pope's conclusion that the Confederate cared little of Missouri for Missouri's sake. See Emory Thomas, *The Confederate Nation: 1861–1865* (New York, 1979), 94–95, and Clement Eaton, *A History of the Southern Confederacy* (New York, 1954), 155.

CHAPTER 7

1. For Pope's unflattering estimate of Halleck, see Chapter 1.

2. Grant makes no mention of such an encounter with Pope, instead crediting his appointment to Yates directly. Augustus Chetlain wrote that Grant had with him a letter of endorsement from Congressman Elihu B. Washburne. (Chetlain accompanied Grant to Springfield from Galena, having been elected captain of a company of volunteers, "the Jo Daviess Guards.") Chetlain said that Pope left Springfield abruptly when he lost the chance for a brigadier generalship to Benjamin Prentiss on May 3, 1861, thus inadvertently assisting Grant by leaving vacant the position of mustering officer at Camp Yates. Grant, *Personal Memoirs of U. S. Grant* (New York, 1885–86), 1:232–33; Augustus Chetlain, "Recollections of General U. S. Grant," in MOLLUS 1:13–15.

3. Grant's perspective on this was quite different. Though he acknowledged that Pope offered to intercede on his behalf, Grant divorced himself from the offer. Of his acquaintance with Pope in Springfield, he wrote: "On one occasion he said to me that I ought to go into the United States service. I told him I intended to do so if there was a war. He spoke of his acquaintance with the public men of the State, and said he could get them to recommend for me a position and that he would do all he could for me. I declined to receive endorsement for permission to fight for my country." Grant, *Personal Memoirs*, 1:239.

4. Pope misconstrued Grant's leaving. Grant took a leave from his clerical duties and visited Major General George B. McClellan in Cincinnati seeking a position on his staff. Rebuffed, Grant returned to Springfield. It was after this, on June 10, 1861, that Yates appointed Grant to the colonelcy of the Twenty-first Illinois Infantry. Ibid., 1:241, 242.

5. The controversy about rank was with Benjamin M. Prentiss, who was commissioned brigadier general on the same day as Grant, thus making Grant senior by virtue of his prior official army status. Grant described the affair but did not go into the detail provided here by Pope. Ibid., 1:262–63.

6. Brigadier General David S. Stanley recalled that Grant "occupied the ridiculous position of second in command, i.e., he commanded nothing and he looked like a man without employment. He rode about the camps everyday with a staff . . . stopped at the headquarters . . . where he knew officers, talked the military gossip of the day and rode away. He had no orders to give or suggestions to make." Stanley, *Personal Memoirs of Major General D. S. Stanley, U.S.A.* (Cambridge, 1917), 102–3.

7. Halleck ordered Grant to turn over his command to Charles F. Smith after the victories at Forts Henry and Donelson. Grant wrote: "General Halleck unquestionably deemed General C. F. Smith a much fitter officer for the command of all the forces in the military district than I was. . . . Indeed I was rather inclined to this opinion myself." Grant, *Personal Memoirs*, 1:326, 328.

8. According to Sherman, Grant was fed up with his anomalous position and was packing to leave for St. Louis. Sherman wrote: "I argued with him that, if he went away, events would go right along, and he would be left out; whereas, if he remained, some happy ac-

cident might restore him to favor and his true place." Sherman, *Memoirs of General William Tecumseh Sherman* (New York, 1875), 1:283.

9. On November 30, 1864, Pope was ordered to City Point, Virginia, for a conference with Grant, who gave Pope overall command of the Departments of the Northwest, Missouri, and Kansas in a new military division—the Military Division of the Missouri, headquartered in St. Louis. This ended what Pope called his exile in Minnesota. *OR* 41(4):716–17; Wallace J. Schutz and Walter Trennery, *Abandoned by Lincoln: A Military Biography of General John Pope* (Champaign, 1990), 179.

10. Major General William T. Sherman (1820–91) was born in Lancaster, Ohio, and graduated sixth in the West Point class of 1840.

11. Sherman was lionized by both veterans and the public at large after the war and spent his waning years much in demand as a public speaker. His biographer writes that Sherman's fame was "wider than North or South. It was international." He was a major public figure and was given "ready entree" everywhere he went. John Marszalek, *Sherman: A Soldier's Passion for Order* (New York, 1993), 362.

12. According to Sheridan, the difficulty stemmed from his attempt to thwart illegal profiteering by horse thieves who tried to sell animals to the army. Sheridan refused to obey Curtis's order to pay for the horses and was relieved from command at his own request. Philip H. Sheridan, *Personal Memoirs of P. H. Sheridan*, 2 vols. (New York, 1887), 1:133–35.

13. Austin Blair (1818–94).

14. For the details of this raid, see Chapter 5.

15. Pope could not possibly have been unaware of the case of Gouverner K. Warren, who was relieved from command by Sheridan at Five Forks, Va. (April 1, 1865). Sheridan's controversial action wrecked the career of this hero of Gettysburg fame. Warren was finally vindicated by a court of inquiry in November 1882, three months after his death. Of Sheridan, Major General George G. Meade wrote: "His determination to absorb the credit of everything done is so manifest as to have attracted the attention of the whole army." Sheridan himself treats the matter lightly in his memoirs, admitting no wrong, despite testifying at Warren's court of inquiry that "I do not know anything of what the commander of the Fifth Corps did during the operations of that day." Emerson G. Taylor, *Gouverner Kemble Warren* (Boston, 1932); 228–48; George G. Meade, *The Life and Letters of George Gordon Meade* (New York, 1913), 2:271; Sheridan, *Personal Memoirs*, 2:162–70.

16. Pope is referring to his own postwar service during the years Sheridan was commander of the Division of the Missouri and later commanding general of the army (1884–88).

17. Sheridan was often at odds with the War Department concerning the Indian policy in the West, especially in regard to reductions in manpower and restrictive orders governing military operations. Roy A. Morris, *The Life and Wars of Gen. Phil Sheridan* (New York, 1993), 332–66. See also Paul A. Hutton, *Phil Sheridan and His Army* (Lincoln, Nebr., 1985).

18. Major General George Henry Thomas (1816–70) was a native Virginian who graduated twelfth in the West Point class of 1840. Serving in the artillery for the next fifteen years, he saw combat in the Seminole War and the Mexican War and against the Indians in Texas. Thomas was one of several Southern generals who remained loyal to the Union. He was in Buell's Army of the Ohio at Shiloh and Corinth.

19. Port-fire is a composition of niter, sulfur, and melaf powder driven into a case

of strong paper. It was used to fire field guns prior to the invention of the friction primer.

20. Pope understated Thomas's ambition. Thomas keenly desired his own command, but he was unwilling to accept a command to the injury of a brother officer. Francis F. McKinney, *Education in Violence: The Life of George H. Thomas and the Army of the Cumberland* (Detroit, 1961), 139, 303–4, 468; Peter Cozzens, *No Better Place to Die: The Battle of Stones River* (Urbana, 1990), 21–22.

21. John McAllister Schofield (1831–1906) was commanding general of the U.S. Army from 1888 to 1895.

22. John M. Schofield to Henry M. Cist, September 15, 1880, printed copy in John P. Nicholson Collection, Henry Huntington Library, San Marino, Calif.

23. Thomas died of a stroke on March 28, 1870.

24. Major General James Birdseye McPherson (1828–64) of Ohio graduated first in the 1853 class of West Point and served with the Corps of Engineers on both east and west coast fortifications. During the Civil War he rose in rank from lieutenant of engineers to corps command.

25. *Coup d'oeilin* is the ability to rapidly and comprehensively assess a situation at a glance.

26. Grant described McPherson as one of the army's "ablest, purest and best generals." Grant, *Personal Memoirs*, 2:169.

27. John Alexander Logan (1826–86) was a native of southern Illinois. A career Democratic politician and supporter of Stephen A. Douglas, he came out strongly in favor of the Union at the start of the Civil War and joined the army as colonel of the Thirty-first Illinois Infantry. For an excellent biography of Logan, see James Pickett Jones, *Black Jack: John A. Logan and Southern Illinois in the Civil War Era* (Tallahassee, 1967).

28. Senator Stephen A. Douglas (1813–61).

29. Douglas was a member of the Senate's Committee of Thirteen, a group that tried to work a last-ditch compromise to the sectional conflict, a measure Congressman Logan loudly supported.

30. A probable reference to Senator (later Major General) John A. McClernand and Judge (later Brigadier General) Isham Haynie. Pope had declaimed on the inevitability of civil war in February 1861 in an intemperate speech before the Literary Society of Cincinnati that was reprinted in the *Cincinnati Gazette* and widely circulated in pamphlet form as *A Military View of the Southern Rebellion: Our National Fortifications and Defenses* (Cincinnati, 1861). Pope expressed similar views in a didactic seven-page letter to Lincoln dated January 27, 1861. Robert Todd Lincoln Papers, Library of Congress, Washington, D.C.

31. This refers to the peace conference that convened in January 1861 to reach a settlement that would forestall war, using the Crittenden Compromise as a starting point in negotiations. Arkansas and the states that had already seceded refused to participate. This conference was referred to as the "Old Gentlemen's Convention" because the majority of its participants were politicians already past their prime. Among the delegates was Pope's father-in-law, Congressman Valentine B. Horton of Ohio. Allan Nevins, *The Emergence of Lincoln* (New York, 1950), 1:411; James McPherson, *Battle Cry of Freedom* (Oxford, 1988), 256–57.

32. James Buchanan, fifteenth president of the United States.

33. In his Cincinnati speech, Pope castigated President Buchanan for his "lethargy" and ignorance of the "treasonable conspiracies of his associates and advisors." His words

nearly led to a court-martial, which only the intervention of Buchanan himself prevented.

34. This undoubtedly is a reference to Generals Henry Halleck and George B. McClellan, both of whom were highly touted for their "book smarts."

35. Oliver Otis Howard (1830–1909), a West Pointer assigned to army command by Sherman, wrote, "General Logan had taken command of the Army of the Tennessee by virtue of his seniority, and had done well; but I did not consider him equal to the command of three corps." There is evidence that Thomas, also a West Pointer, spoke out against Logan's appointment to army command. To his credit, Logan stayed with the army. See Sherman, *Memoirs*, 2:85, and Jones, *Black Jack*, 218–20. The often lavish praise that Pope bestowed on Logan throughout his memoirs was fundamentally an expression of personal gratitude. After the war, Senator Logan consistently and vehemently opposed congressional initiatives to rehabilitate Fitz John Porter.

36. Frustrated by Thomas's seeming refusal to attack John Bell Hood's Army of the Tennessee in December 1864, Grant sent Logan to Nashville to relieve Thomas of command of the Army of the Cumberland. On December 15 Logan reached Louisville, where he learned of Thomas's victory at Nashville. Logan's "magnaminity" is questioned by his own biographer, who writes, "It would have been impossible for Logan to have reached Nashville ahead of Thomas's attack." Grant, *Personal Memoirs*, 2:382; *OR* 45(2):171; Jones, *Black Jack*, 242–43.

37. Major General Don Carlos Buell (1818–98) of Ohio graduated from West Point in 1841 and served in the infantry during the Seminole and Mexican Wars.

38. Buell was relieved of command of the Army of the Ohio after the Battle of Perryville in October 1862, when he failed to pursue Bragg aggressively into East Tennessee. Buell's ouster was attributed in part to the hostility of some of the War Governors, especially Oliver Morton of Indiana and Andrew Johnson of Tennessee. For a detailed look at the circumstances surrounding Buell's removal, see James B. Fry, *Operations of the Army under Buell from June 10th to October 30th, 1862* (New York, 1884), 81–106. See also Henry Stone, "The Operations of General Buell in Kentucky and Tennessee in 1862," in *PMHSM* 7:255–92. Buell himself said that it "would be useless" to review the correspondence that led to his removal. See Don Carlos Buell, "East Tennessee and the Campaign of Perryville," in Robert Underwood Johnson and Clarence C. Buel, eds., *Battles and Leaders of the Civil War*, 4 vols. (New York, 1887), 3:31–51.

39. Sherman wrote that Buell "published a bitter, political letter, aimed at General Grant, reflecting on his general management of the war, and stated that both Generals Canby and Sherman had offered him a subordinate command, which he declined because he had once outranked us. This was not true as to me, or Canby either, I think, for both General Canby and I ranked him at West Point and in the old Army, and he (General Buell) was only superior to us in the date of his commission as major general, for a short period in 1862." Sherman, *Memoirs*, 2:7.

40. In April 1851 Pope was ordered to Fort Union, New Mexico Territory, as chief engineer of the Ninth Military District.

41. Major General William Nelson (1824–62) of Kentucky. Pope detested Nelson, having engaged in a violent quarrel with him over whose command had entered Corinth first. Said an Ohio soldier who witnessed the clash, which occurred on the steps of the Corinth courthouse: "Those of you who have served under Pope know what a universal knowledge he had of cuss words and with what artistic ease, grace, and vim he could use them. . . . He turned to Nelson and hurled such a torrent of abusive epithets at him that

it seemed he must soon exhaust the entire vocabulary. On this occasion he seemed to sur-
pass any former effort of his left, and he seemed to enjoy it too. I know the boys did. General Nelson sat on his horse as immovable as a statue and never replied. . . . When Pope
got tired of the fun he rode off. Our major resumed his place in the regiment and we took
up our line of march." Joseph Strickling Diary, 16–17, OHS.

42. On September 29, 1862, Jefferson C. Davis shot and killed Nelson after being
insulted by him during a quarrel. No charges were ever proffered against Davis for the
murder.

43. Gordon Granger (1822–76) of New York graduated from West Point in 1845. He and
Pope were well acquainted in the Old Army, and Granger served under Pope at New
Madrid and Island No. 10. For a critique of Granger's generalship and character flaws, see
Peter Cozzens, *This Terrible Sound*, 93–94, 438–62, and *The Shipwreck of Their Hopes:
The Battles for Chattanooga* (Urbana, 1994), 247–48, 349, 386, 393–94.

44. David S. Stanley, Schuyler Hamilton, John M. Palmer, Alexander McDowell Mc-
Cook, and Thomas J. Wood.

45. Pope again mentions the telegram sent by Halleck to Washington referring to
prisoners allegedly taken by Pope.

CHAPTER 8

1. Perhaps sardonically, Sherman called the campaign "a magnificent drill, as it served
for the instruction of our men in guard and picket duty, and in habituating them to out-
door life." Grant was less generous: "For myself, I am satisfied that Corinth could have
been captured in a two days' campaign commenced promptly on the arrival of reinforcements after the battle of Shiloh." Sherman, *Memoirs of General William Tecumseh Sherman* (New York, 1875), 1:282; Grant, *Personal Memoirs of U. S. Grant* (New York, 1885–
86), 1:381.

2. Pope was hardly alone in thinking Halleck ill-suited for field command. General
Stanley wrote: "Halleck was a mistake in the field. Large and corpulent, he could not ride
a horse out of a walk. General and staff rigged themselves out in soldier's blouses and
great stiff hats. . . . When this queer cavalcade came riding slowly, ponderously along our
lines, it was hard to suppress the boisterous laughter of the soldiers." Stanley, *Personal
Memoirs of Major General D. S. Stanley, U.S.A.* (Cambridge, 1917), 95. Here, however,
Pope is criticizing Halleck for the indecision he showed as general in chief during Pope's
tenure in command in Virginia. This is dealt with in greater detail in Chapter 11.

3. Thomas A. Scott (1823–81) had been vice president of the Pennsylvania Railroad
before the war. He organized the secret route Lincoln took into Washington before the
first inaugural and for his efforts was appointed assistant secretary of war. His duties included coordinating railroads for military use and inspecting armies in the field.

CHAPTER 9

1. Edwin McMasters Stanton (1814–69) of Ohio was a prominent lawyer and attorney
general during the Buchanan administration. Stanton was highly critical of Lincoln yet
accepted the post of secretary of war in his cabinet when Simon Cameron resigned in
1862.

2. Stanton's cryptic telegram of June 19 read in part, "If your orders will admit, and you

can be absent long enough from your command, I would be glad to see you at Washington." *OR* 17(2):17.

3. Pope wired Halleck requesting permission to leave on the twentieth: "The Secretary of War . . . desires to see me in Washington for a day or two . . . Shall I go?" Pope also wired Stanton that he would leave for Washington the following morning. Halleck responded to Pope: "the Secretary of War can order you to Washington, if he deems proper; but I cannot give you leave, as I think your service here of the greatest importance. Your command is directly in the face of Beauregard." Ibid., 17–18, 20.

4. Pope is possibly referring to Frémont and Sigel, with whom he had unpleasant dealings in Missouri. Or he may be referring to McClellan and Porter, anticipating events with the benefit of hindsight.

5. Pope reported to Stanton on June 25, 1862.

6. Stanton died from chronic asthma, exacerbated by overwork and worry.

7. July 7, 1865.

8. Methodist bishop Matthew Simpson, an old friend of Stanton, had been among President Lincoln's favorite preachers.

9. See Chapter 1, n. 24.

10. On June 23, 1862, Lincoln visited General Winfield Scott at West Point to seek his opinion of the military situation in Virginia. According to Lincoln biographer David Donald, the primary purpose of the trip was to decide whether it was better to reinforce McClellan on The Peninsula or to retain troops for the defense of Washington. On his return to Washington on June 25, Lincoln created a command for Pope. David H. Donald, *Lincoln* (New York, 1995), 357; Earl Schenck Miers, ed., *Lincoln Day by Day* (Washington, D.C., 1960), 2:122.

11. Major Generals Irwin McDowell (1818–85), Nathaniel P. Banks (1816–94), and Franz Sigel led independent armies against Confederate general Stonewall Jackson in the Shenandoah Valley campaign between March and June 1862. Jackson outmarched, outfought, and outgeneraled his opponents.

12. In April 1862 McClellan had taken the Army of the Potomac to The Peninsula between the York and James Rivers of Virginia in an unsuccessful effort to capture Richmond. McClellan's extreme caution, overestimation of Confederate strength, and incessant demands for reinforcements greatly annoyed Lincoln and his cabinet.

13. *McClellan's Own Story* (New York, 1887) was published after McClellan's death by William C. Prime, who compiled the memoir from the general's notes and papers. It is more his work than McClellan's. Stephen W. Sears, *General George B. McClellan: The Young Napoleon* (New York, 1988), 403–6.

14. McClellan's estimates of enemy strength were provided by his chief spy, Allan Pinkerton, who gleaned much of his information from interviews with slaves. However, McClellan himself was responsible for the exaggerated reports of Confederate strength. For a comprehensive discussion of this subject, see Edwin Fishel, *The Secret War for the Union* (Boston, 1996), 102–29.

15. In July 1864 as Ulysses S. Grant invested Lee's army at Petersburg, Jubal A. Early led a corps of Lee's army into the Shenandoah Valley and actually demonstrated against Washington, forcing Grant to detach the Sixth Corps to fend him off.

16. Pope was ordered to this position on June 26, 1862. His orders read: "The Army of Virginia shall operate in such manner as, while protecting Western Virginia and the national Capital from danger or insult, it shall in the speediest manner attack and overcome

the rebel forces under Jackson and Ewell, threaten the enemy in the direction of Charlottesville, and render the most effective aid to relieve General McClellan and capture Richmond." *OR* 12(3):435.

17. When he learned of the appointment of Pope, Frémont asked to be relieved. Banks and McDowell agreed to serve under Pope.

18. Pope visited Lincoln frequently, having been asked by the president to remain in Washington as his de facto military adviser until Halleck arrived to assume the post of general in chief.

19. The order appears in *OR* 12(3):435.

20. Between June 25 and July 1, McClellan and Lee fought a series of battles collectively known as The Seven Days. McClellan was beaten more mentally than tactically and withdrew his army from the gates of Richmond to Harrison's Landing.

21. Randolph B. Marcy (1812–87) was McClellan's father-in-law and served him as inspector general and chief of staff.

22. McClellan sent Marcy to Washington on July 4, 1862.

23. On July 14, 1862, Pope sent McClellan a letter offering cooperation and seeking McClellan's views: "Your position on the James River places the whole of the enemy's force around Richmond between yourself and Washington. Were I to move with my command direct on Richmond I must fight the whole force of the enemy before I could join you, and at so great a distance from you as to be beyond any assistance from your army. If my command be embarked and sent to you by James River the enemy would be in Washington before it had half accomplished the journey . . . I trust you will communicate your wishes to me . . . I need not repeat that I stand prepared to do all in my power for that purpose." On July 7 McClellan responded vaguely, applauding Pope's intention to concentrate his forces but offering no thoughts on what Pope should do with them: "As soon as Burnside arrives I will feel the force of the enemy and ascertain his exact position. If I learn that he has moved upon you I will move upon Richmond, do my best to take it, and endeavor to cut off his retreat. . . . To preserve the morale of my men I must maintain my present position as long as it is possible. Therefore I shall not fall back unless absolutely forced to do so." *OR* 11(3):295–97, 306.

24. On July 11, 1862, Lincoln appointed Halleck general in chief. Pope spoke out strongly on Halleck's behalf, but the decision was probably weighted more on the advice of Winfield Scott. Of Halleck, Gideon Welles wrote: "He is here, and came from the West, the friend of Pope, and is in some degree indebted to Pope for his position. Both were introduced here by an intrigue of the War and Treasury with the design of ultimately displacing McClellan." Kenneth P. Williams, *Lincoln Finds a General*, 5 vols. (New York, 1949–59), 1:135; Miers, *Lincoln Day by Day*, 127; Gideon Welles, *Diary of Gideon Welles: Lincoln's Secretary of the Navy*, 3 vols. (Boston, 1911), 1:119; Stephen E. Ambrose, *Halleck: Lincoln's Chief of Staff* (Baton Rouge, 1962), 60.

25. One of Halleck's first official acts as general in chief was to visit McClellan at Harrison's Landing. His mission was to ascertain whether McClellan would continue his operations without being heavily reinforced. Halleck left the meeting understanding that McClellan would be content with an additional 20,000 men; however, soon thereafter McClellan asked for 40,000 men, leading an exasperated Lincoln to order his withdrawal from The Peninsula. Ambrose, *Halleck*, 65–69; *OR* 11(1):80–81.

26. Secretary of the Navy Gideon Welles had a different recollection. Far from opposing Halleck's appointment, he said that Stanton had "wonderfully magnified" Halleck's abilities to President Lincoln. Welles, *Diary*, 1:108, 120.

1. Pope's article, "The Second Battle of Bull Run," was reprinted in Robert Underwood Johnson and Clarence C. Buel, eds., *Battles and Leaders of the Civil War* (New York, 1887), 2:449–94.

2. *McClellan's Own Story*, Charles L. Webster and Co. (New York, 1887), was compiled posthumously from McClellan's personal files by William C. Prime, McClellan's literary executor. Prime was a New York lawyer and journalist who befriended McClellan after he was relieved of command. For an in-depth analysis of McClellan's memoirs, see Stephen W. Sears, "The Curious Case of General McClellan's Memoirs," in *Civil War History* 34, no. 2 (June 1988): 101–14.

3. Pope refers to McClellan's private correspondence, some of which Prime chose to publish. For example, on July 17, 1862, McClellan wrote to his wife: "So you like my letter to the President? . . . You do not feel one bit more bitterly towards those people than I do. I do not say much about it, but I fear they have done all that cowardice and folly can do to ruin our poor country." *McClellan's Own Story*, 449.

4. McClellan's official treatment of and correspondence with Pope was neither improper nor judgmental. However, his private correspondence is quite revealing of his disdain for Pope. In an August 24, 1862, letter to his wife, McClellan wrote: "I fancy that Pope is in retreat though this is only a guess of mine, without anything to base it on. I don't see how I can remain in the service if placed under Pope; it will be too great a disgrace." Ibid., 528.

5. Frémont submitted his request on July 27, 1862. *OR* 12(3):435–36.

6. Major General Franz Sigel (1824–1902) was assigned to command Pope's First Corps on June 29, 1862.

7. Brigadier General Rufus King (1814–76) was an 1833 West Point graduate from New York. Brigadier General James B. Ricketts (1817–87) of New York graduated from West Point in 1839.

8. Sigel to Pope, July 5, 1862, *OR* 12(3):455.

9. Pope's report, *OR* 12(2):20–50.

10. A distance of seventy miles.

11. See King to Pope, July 4, 6, 1862; *OR* 12(3):452, 457.

12. *OR* 12(3):436–37.

13. On June 25–July 1, 1862, the series of battles known collectively as The Seven Days was fought.

14. McClellan was aware of this opportunity but failed to act upon it. On June 26 he wrote, "I believe we will surely win & that the enemy is falling into a trap." McClellan's biographer speculated that the general ultimately may have hesitated because he feared a second Austerlitz, the battle in which Napoleon lured his enemies into making a disastrous turning movement. Stephen W. Sears, ed., *The Civil War Papers of George B. McClellan* (New York, 1989), 315, and *General George B. McClellan: The Young Napoleon* (New York, 1988), 208.

15. Pope was then in Washington acting as Lincoln's de facto military adviser.

16. Fortress Monroe sat on Old Point Comfort at the tip of the Virginia Peninsula, where the James River entered Chesapeake Bay.

17. On July 4, 1862, Pope wrote to McClellan, "I beg you to understand that it is my earnest wish to cooperate in the heartiest and most energetic manner with you." *OR* 11(3):295–97.

18. McClellan replied on July 7. Ibid., 306.

19. Ibid., 338, 340.

20. The unabashedly partisan Joint Congressional Committee on the Conduct of the War was organized on December 20, 1861, by Radical Republican congressmen to investigate the management of military campaigns and affairs as well as contracts and expenditures.

21. Major General James Ewell Brown Stuart (1833–64), an 1854 graduate of West Point, joined the Confederacy as colonel of the First Virginia Cavalry and rapidly won distinction and promotion to head of the cavalry corps in the Army of Northern Virginia.

22. The Faquier Seminary, on Lee Street, founded in 1857 and headed by one Dr. Bacon. This was the only female school then in Warrenton.

23. For more on these raids, see *OR* 12(3):450, 454, 475–76, 478–79.

24. General Edward Hatch was ordered to Culpeper Court House on July 11, 1862.

25. Pope intended the cavalry movement to disrupt Lee's communications between Charlottesville and Lynchburg and to destroy the James River Canal. *OR* 12(3):475, 481, 484.

26. Hatch reported encountering Major General Richard S. Ewell's infantry division at Gordonsville on July 16. Ibid., 481.

27. Brigadier General John Buford (1826–63), whom Pope selected to command his reserve cavalry brigade in the Army of Virginia after Hatch's missteps.

28. More commonly known as Robertson's River.

29. Brigadier General George D. Bayard (1835–62), an 1856 graduate of West Point and a veteran of the Shenandoah Valley campaign. Pope chose him to command the cavalry of the Third Corps, Army of Virginia.

30. Pope and Sigel heartily disliked one another. For a better understanding of the relations between these generals, see Stephen D. Engle, *The Yankee Dutchman: The Life of Franz Sigel* (Fayetteville, Ariz., 1993), 128–32.

31. Brigadier General Samuel Wylie Crawford (1829–92) of Pennsylvania.

32. Pope was furious. His aide, Lieutenant Colonel T. C. H. Smith, informed Sigel: "The general commanding orders . . . you are to march direct to Culpeper Court House by the turnpike. He's surprised that you make this inquiry after his definite instructions of this morning." Lieutenant Colonel Charles P. Heston said of Sigel, "being unable to decide between the merits of two parallel roads, and equally attached in either direction, remained like the ass between two bundles of hay." *OR* 12(2):54; Charles Heston, "The Campaign of General Pope in Virginia: Its Object and Purpose," *PMHSM* 2:46.

33. Pope vented his rage openly, telling Halleck, "Sigel, as you know, is perfectly unreliable, and I suggest that some officer of superior rank be sent to command his army corps." *OR* 12(2):12.

34. Pope's instructions became a cause célèbre with Banks. In his official report, Pope said he intended that Banks take up a strong position beside Crawford to "check the advance of the enemy, and to determine his forces and the character of his movements as far as practicable." Before the Joint Congressional Committee on the Conduct of the War, Pope grew more specific: "I directed [Banks] when he went forward from Culpeper Court House, if the enemy advanced to attack him on the strong position which I had instructed him to take up, that he should push his skirmishers well to the front and notify me immediately." Pope dispatched Colonel Marshall to convey his orders orally to General Banks. Pope may have wished Banks to act as he later alleged, but, if so, he failed to com-

municate his intentions clearly to Marshall. Banks and his adjutant general, Lieutenant Colonel Louis H. Pelouze, who claimed that he wrote down Marshall's precise words on the spot, said Marshall told them:

Culpeper, 9:45 A.M., August 9, 1862

General Banks to move to the front immediately, assume command of all the forces in the front, deploy his skirmishers if the enemy approaches, and attack him immediately as soon as he approaches, and be reinforced from here.

Marshall later challenged Banks and Pelouze's claim. In a letter to the Joint Congressional Committee on the Conduct of the War, Marshall insisted that the exact language he used to Banks was as follows:

GENERAL: The general commanding directs that you move to the front and take up a strong position near the position held by General Crawford's brigade; that you will not attack the enemy unless it becomes evident the enemy will attack you; then, in order to hold the advantage of being the attacking party, you will attack with your skirmishers well to the front.

Marshall understood that Pope wished Banks to hold the enemy in check without bringing on a general engagement until the remainder of the army came up, and to attack with his skirmishers only. Years later Brigadier General George H. Gordon concluded, "there can be no doubt that [Pope] did not authorize or expect [Banks's corps] to attack, single-handed, the whole of Jackson's army." And did Pope communicate his intentions clearly to Banks? Without question he did, according to Gordon. "Miscellaneous Papers: Battle of Cedar Mountain," *JCR*, 2d ser., 3:45, 55; Gordon, *History of the Second Massachusetts Regiment of Infantry: Third Paper* (Boston, 1875), 214–20.

35. Benjamin Stone Roberts (1810–75), a graduate of the West Point class of 1835, was a loyal subordinate of Pope, whom he served as inspector general and chief of cavalry.

36. On August 6, 1862, Pope issued General Order No. 18, a directive enjoining constant marching readiness and deploring straggling. In addition to two days' rations, soldiers were also ordered to carry one hundred rounds of ammunition. *OR* 12(2):52–53.

37. Banks sent two dispatches to Pope, at 2:25 and 4:50 P.M. He reported sighting enemy cavalry and one infantry regiment with artillery support. Ibid., 55.

38. Pope praised Banks's conduct during the battle, if not his actions prior. See ibid., 28.

39. Pope's redundancy here is a result of the serial form of the original in the *National Tribune*.

40. But Roberts himself may have goaded Banks to attack with the disdainful remark, "there must be no backing out this day." Fred H. Harrington, *Fighting Politician: Major General N. P. Banks* (Westport, Conn., 1970), 81–82.

41. Jackson had defeated Banks several times in the Shenandoah Valley in the spring of 1862. He raided Banks's supply trains so successfully that Jackson's men christened the Yankee general "Commissary."

42. Union losses at Cedar Mountain were 2,353 of 8,030 engaged. Confederate losses were 1,338 of 16,686 engaged. *OR* 12(2):139.

43. Lieutenant Colonel David H. Strother, of Pope's staff, wrote that Banks was thrown while trying to mount and was hit on the hip by another horse. Pope "stuck his head down and, striking spur, led off at full speed." It was a narrow escape for the entire party.

Strother, *A Virginia Yankee in the Civil War* (Chapel Hill, 1961), 77; Harrington, *Fighting Politician*, 85; George H. Gordon, *Brook Farm to Cedar Mountain in the War of the Great Rebellion, 1861–62* (Boston, 1883), 320–22.

44. Pope had between 23,000 and 25,000 troops in all, consisting of Rickett's Division, Sigel's Corps, and Banks's men. John C. Ropes, *The Army under Pope* (New York, 1881), 31.

45. Pope told Halleck on August 6 that he wanted King to advance to Culpeper and on the eighth ordered King to march when he was ready. King sent two brigades forward on August 9 and two more on the tenth. *OR* 12(3):539, 548–49, 553; Ropes, *The Army under Pope*, 29.

46. Jackson retreated on August 11, believing that Pope had been largely reinforced and hoping to draw him into pursuit. *OR* 12(2):184–85.

47. Brigadier General General John W. Geary commanded the Second Brigade of Christopher C. Augur's Second Division of Bank's Corps. Brigadier General Samuel S. Carroll led a brigade under Ricketts.

48. Major General Jesse L. Reno (1823–62), a graduate of the West Point class of 1846, brought with him twelve infantry regiments, four artillery batteries, and two companies of cavalry.

49. On August 16 Pope's cavalry captured a dispatch from Lee to Stuart detailing Lee's advance. Halleck informed Pope on the eighteenth that Jackson was being heavily reinforced from Richmond. *OR* 12(2):29, (3):590–91.

50. Lieutenant General Daniel Harvey Hill (1821–89) of South Carolina.

51. The captured staff officer was Norman R. Fitzhugh.

52. John Codman Ropes thought that Pope acted "with promptitude and decision . . . without any loss in men or material." Ropes, *The Army under Pope*, 33.

CHAPTER 11

1. George Henry Gordon (1823–86) of Massachusetts graduated from West Point in 1846. He was wounded twice during the Mexican War and was promoted for gallantry at the Battle of Cerro Gordo. Gordon resigned from the army to study law at Harvard. He started the Civil War as colonel of the Second Massachusetts Infantry and served under Banks in the Shenandoah Valley; he led a brigade under Banks at Cedar Mountain, where his men were in the heaviest part of the fighting, sustaining 466 casualties out of fewer than 1,500 engaged. Gordon later wrote prolifically of his war service. His account of the Second Bull Run campaign, published in 1880, entitled *History of the Campaign of the Army of Virginia* (Boston, 1889), was highly critical of Pope's generalship.

2. Pope exaggerated the importance of the information in Gordon's report, but not the impropriety. Gordon defended his actions but conceded that Pope was justified in placing him under arrest. For Gordon's report, see *OR* 12(2):807–8; for Gordon's own account of this incident, see his *Campaign of the Army of Virginia*, 39.

3. The arresting officer is identified by Gordon only as "an officer from Pope's staff." Gordon, *Campaign of the Army of Virginia*, 39.

4. Undercurrents of contempt run through Gordon's books. Here are but two examples: "Pope is a thick set man, of an unpleasant expression, of about fifty years of age" (Pope was forty); "He was a vain man, rather proud of his power of using words." See George H. Gordon, *Brook Farm to Cedar Mountain in the War of the Great Rebellion, 1861–62* (Boston, 1883), 274–75, and *Campaign of the Army of Virginia*, 80.

5. Gordon died at Framingham, Massachusetts, on August 30, 1886.

6. As Jackson advanced toward Sulphur Springs, Lee probed northward, seeking a point where he could force a crossing of the Rappahannock. Lee hoped to concentrate his army against Pope before the Federals could be reinforced. *OR* 12(2):552.

7. Lee planned to have his cavalry destroy the railroad bridge over the Rappahannock in Pope's rear while Longstreet and Jackson crossed the Rapidan to attack his left flank. Pope's rapid retreat prevented this.

8. Lee was aware of reinforcements from the Army of the Potomac coming to Pope. On August 11 he learned that Burnside was forwarding men to Pope from Fredericksburg, and by the sixteenth he knew that McClellan was leaving The Peninsula. Pope does himself a disservice here, as his forces effectively blocked all of Lee's attempts to force a passage of the river.

9. McClellan was first ordered to leave The Peninsula on August 3, 1862. The last of his army embarked on August 16.

10. Major General Ambrose E. Burnside (1824–81) was commander of the Ninth Corps of the Army of the Potomac.

11. *OR* 12(2):56–57.

12. Pope expected Sigel to reach Waterloo Bridge by sunset. Ibid., 61.

13. Brigadier General John F. Reynolds (1820–63) of Pennsylvania graduated from West Point in 1841. He led a brigade under McClellan on The Peninsula and was assigned to McDowell's Third Corps during the Second Bull Run campaign.

14. Major General George Gordon Meade (1815–72), a graduate of the West Point class of 1835, led a brigade under Reynolds.

15. Pope understates the importance of the captured correspondence, which revealed to Lee both Pope's strength and his orders to hold the Rappahannock line until reinforcements arrived via Fredericksburg. Pope's hat, plume, and dress uniform were captured and the incident was highly publicized. After the war Pope's adjutant, Thomas C. H. Smith, claimed that the papers had been overlooked in a valise and burned; however, Lee reported the content of Pope's captured correspondence to Richmond. For more on this, see T. C. H. Smith, *Memoir and Review of Pope's Campaign*, Smith Papers, OHS. See also John Hennessy, *Return to Bull Run: The Campaign and Battle of Second Manassas* (New York, 1992), 76–79; *OR* 12(3):630–31, 941–42; and Edwin Fishel, *The Secret War for the Union* (Boston, 1996), 196.

16. The wagons were guarded by 130 members of the Forty-second Pennsylvania (Bucktails). Only fifteen men were assigned to picket duty on this rainy night, oblivious to the presence of Stuart's force.

17. Pope ordered Sigel to cross the Rappahannock at Waterloo Bridge and directed McDowell to Warrenton.

18. "The Second Battle of Bull Run," *Century* 31, no. 3 (January 1886): 441–66, reprinted in Robert Underwood Johnson and Clarence C. Buel, eds., *Battles and Leaders of the Civil War* (New York, 1887), 2:449–94.

19. Pope is referring to Porter's alleged failure to promptly obey his marching orders. Porter obeyed but was several hours late due to troop fatigue, darkness, and obstructions in the road. Franklin was ordered to move to Warrenton on August 26.

20. Pope blamed his failure in part on the sluggishness of Porter and Franklin. He also criticized McClellan and Halleck for not hastening reinforcements from the Army of the Potomac to him.

21. On July 29 Pope reported his strength to be 28,500. *OR* 12(2):24.

22. The last corps of the Army of the Potomac left Harrison's Landing on August 16 to meet transports awaiting them at Yorktown and Newport News.

23. *OR* 11(1):85.

24. On August 11 Pope complained to Halleck that "the supineness of the Army of the Potomac renders it easy for the enemy to reinforce Jackson." On the twelfth McClellan told Halleck, "it is not possible for anyone to place the army where you wish it . . . in less than a month." *OR* 11(1):88, 12(3):561.

25. *OR* 11(1):89, 91.

26. Ibid., 86, 92.

27. Major General William B. Franklin (1823–1903) graduated first in the West Point Class of 1843. He commanded the Sixth Corps, Army of the Potomac, which was 10,000 strong.

28. Major General Samuel Porter Heintzelman (1805–80), from the West Point class of 1826, commanded the Third Corps, Army of the Potomac.

29. Major General Fitz John Porter (1822–1901) was a graduate of the West Point class of 1845. Porter led the Fifth Corps, Army of the Potomac, and was devoted to McClellan. Pope recalled Porter as having "a high reputation in the army and for services since the outbreak of the war . . . I was . . . exceedingly glad that he had joined the army under my command . . . he appeared to me . . . of a soldierly and striking appearance." Porter's open contempt for Pope and subsequent events would greatly change Pope's opinion. See Pope, "The Second Battle of Bull Run," in *Battles and Leaders*, 2:462–63.

30. U.S. Senate, Executive Documents, *Letter of the Secretary of War Transmitting the Report of the Organization of the Army of the Potomac and of Its Campaigns in Virginia and Maryland under the Command of Major General George B. McClellan*, 38th Cong., 1st sess. (Washington, D.C., 1864), 185.

31. Major General Darius Couch (1822–97) commanded a division in the Fourth Corps of the Army of the Potomac.

32. *OR* 11(1):95.

33. Colonel Herman Haupt (1817–1905) was chief of construction and transportation on U.S. military railroads.

34. Major General Henry Warner Slocum (1827–94) led a division in Franklin's Sixth Corps.

35. *OR* 11(1):96.

36. Major General Edwin V. Sumner (1797–1863) commanded the Second Corps, Army of the Potomac.

37. *OR* 11(1):96.

38. *OR* 12(3):707.

39. Brigadier General Amiel Weeks Whipple (1816–63) reported Confederates moving in force at Vienna and Fairfax Court House. Ibid.

40. Brigadier General John G. Barnard (1815–82) commanded Washington's defenses.

41. Forts Ethan Allen and Marcy were part of the extensive Washington defenses.

42. Colonel Samuel B. Holabird (1826–1907) was chief quartermaster of the Second Corps, Army of Virginia.

43. *OR* 12(3):708.

44. Ibid., 709.

45. Site of Fort Ramsey, part of Washington's defenses.

46. *OR* 11(1):97.

47. Brigadier Generals Erastus B. Tyler (1822–91) and Jacob D. Cox (1828–1900).

48. *OR* 12(3):709.

49. Ibid., 710.

50. Colonel Gustav Waagner.

51. *OR* 12(3):710.

52. Brigadier General Daniel P. Woodbury (1812–64) commanded the Engineer Brigade, Army of the Potomac.

53. Brigadier General Thomas Francis Meagher (1823–67).

54. *OR* 11(1):97–98.

55. *OR* 12(3):722.

56. Ibid., 722.

57. Ibid.

58. Ibid., 723.

59. *OR* 11(1):99–100.

60. Brigadier General David Bell Birney (1825–64).

61. *OR* 12(3):723–24.

62. *OR* 11(1):99–100, 12(2):17. See also Herman Haupt, *Reminiscences of General Herman Haupt* (New York, 1901), 113–14.

63. *OR* 11(1):101.

64. *OR* 12(3):746–47.

65. Ibid., 747.

66. *OR* 11(1):101.

67. Ibid., 98.

68. Lincoln was distressed by this dispatch, believing that McClellan wanted Pope to be defeated. Among other disparaging remarks about Pope, McClellan wrote to his wife Marcy that "two of my corps will either save that fool Pope or be sacrificed for the country." John Hay, *Lincoln and the Civil War in the Diaries and Letters of John Hay* (New York, 1939), 45; Stephen W. Sears, ed., *The Civil War Papers of George B. McClellan* (New York, 1989), 417.

69. *OR* 12(3):744.

70. For a discussion of available transportation, see Haupt, *Reminiscences*, chap. 2.

71. *OR* 11(1):100–101.

72. For Porter's explanation of why he wrote what he did, see *Gen. Fitz John Porter's Statement of the Services of the Fifth Army Corps, in 1862, in Northern Virginia* (New York, 1878), 19–20.

73. This is a reference to Confederate raids on the railroad in the vicinity of Manassas. See *OR* 12(3):693–96.

74. Ibid., 699–700.

75. Major General George W. Morell (1815–83) led the First Division of Porter's Fifth Corps.

76. *OR* 12(3):699.

77. Ibid., 732–33.

78. Pope learned of Sigel's fight at Groveton late on the evening of August 28.

79. *OR* 12(3):733.

80. On August 27 Porter was at Warrenton Junction, where Pope had ordered him to remain until relieved by Banks. On the twenty-ninth he was at Bristoe Station, from whence he was ordered to Centreville. Porter claimed that Pope never informed him of the details of the plan of campaign. Porter confessed ulterior motives in his dispatches to Burnside; they were meant to prompt the government to act "through General McClel-

lan, the only officer in whom . . . both armies had confidence." *OR* 12(2):40; Porter, *Porter's Statement*, 17, 72–73.

81. *OR* 12(2):18.

82. Like Porter, Franklin was an ardent partisan of McClellan.

83. Pope reported to Washington that "not much could be expected" from the troops of the Army of the Potomac, because they were "listless and dejected." *OR* 12(2):19.

84. For a discussion of McClellan's return to command, see Hennessy, *Return to Bull Run*, 451–55.

CHAPTER 12

1. Mason Lock Weems (1759–1825) penned the idolatrous, fictionalized *Life and Memorable Actions of George Washington* (ca. 1800) in which the hatchet and cherry tree story first appeared.

2. For an interesting parallel to Pope's thesis, see "George the Made Over," in *The Collected Works of Ambrose Bierce* (New York, 1966), 9:48–52. Bierce discusses the effects of deifying historical figures.

3. This meeting probably occurred in July 1850. Pope was on leave recovering from illness contracted while on a surveying expedition in Minnesota. Lincoln was in Chicago trying cases before the U.S. District Court.

4. Lincoln's inaugural train stopped in Indianapolis on February 11, 1861. Captain John Pope boarded the train and joined Colonel Edwin Sumner, Major David Hunter, and Colonel Elmer Ellsworth as the president-elect's military escort. The party also included Ward Hill Lamon, Captain George W. Hazzard, John Nicolay, John Hay, William S. Wallace, David Davis, Norman B. Judd, Ozias Hatch, Jesse duBois, Richard Yates, and Orville Browning.

5. Virginia did not secede until after the firing on Fort Sumter in April, when Lincoln called for 75,000 volunteers to put down the rebellion. Georgia seceded on January 19 by a majority of 208–89. Among the other Southern states, Tennessee, North Carolina, Arkansas, and Missouri initially rejected secession.

6. For example, on February 11, 1861, at Indianapolis, Lincoln stated: "I will only say that to the salvation of this Union there needs but one single thing—the hearts of a people like yours. . . . It is your business to rise up and preserve the Union and liberty, for yourselves, and not for me. I desire they shall be Constitutionally preserved." On February 13, at Columbus, he said: "We entertain different views upon political questions, but nobody is suffering anything. This is a most consoling circumstance, and from it we may conclude that all we want is time, patience and a reliance on that God who has never forsaken this people." Don E. Fehrenbacher, *Abraham Lincoln* (Stanford, 1964), 199–201.

7. February 21, 1861.

8. For transcripts of Lincoln's speeches along this journey, see Ray P. Basler, ed., *The Collected Works of Abraham Lincoln*, vol. 4 (Rutgers, N.J., 1953).

9. Fernando Wood (1812–81), a Tammany Hall politician, was mayor of New York from 1861 to 1862 and an outspoken critic of Lincoln.

10. For Lincoln's remarks, see Basler, *Collected Works of Lincoln*, 4:232–33.

11. The detective Allan Pinkerton had learned of an assassination plot while investigating the security of bridges along the Pennsylvania, Wilmington, and Baltimore Railroad. He urged Lincoln to alter his schedule and pass through Baltimore at night.

12. Pinkerton informed Lincoln that a group of conspirators, including some police-men, would attack the president as he exited the train at Baltimore's Culvert Street Station and crossed town to the Camden Street Station.

13. William Henry Seward (1801–72) of New York was Lincoln's chief rival for the presidential nomination and also his choice for secretary of state.

14. Republican governor Andrew Curtin (1817–94) of Pennsylvania.

15. Ward Hill Lamon (1828–93) was a former law partner of Lincoln.

16. The surreptitious trip took place on the evening of February 22, 1861.

17. John S. Gittings of the Baltimore and Ohio Railroad.

18. This is a reference to the riot that occurred on April 19, 1861, as Union troops (Sixth Massachusetts Infantry) crossed town to entrain for Washington. The soldiers were pelted with bricks and fired upon; they returned fire, killing twelve rioters.

19. John G. Nicolay and John Hay's ten-volume biography of Lincoln was first serialized in *Century Magazine*. Ward Hill Lamon left an account of the journey in his *Life of Abraham Lincoln* (New York, 1885).

20. Salmon P. Chase (1808–73) of Ohio was a powerful Republican boss and a fervent abolitionist. He was appointed to Lincoln's cabinet as secretary of the Treasury. Chase was an intimate friend of Pope's father-in-law, Congressman Valentin B. Horton of Ohio.

21. Francis P. Blair (1821–75), an influential Missouri Republican, was a major general serving in Sherman's army at the time Lincoln appointed him.

CHAPTER 13

1. Joseph Holt (1807–94) was a professional lawyer and Democrat from Kentucky. As judge advocate general of the Union army, he was the government's chief prosecutor in the Fitz John Porter court-martial.

2. Pope addressed the society on February 13, 1861.

3. John B. Floyd (1806–63).

4. Pope told the literary society that war was inevitable. Secession, he said, was a "revolutionary measure" that demanded the "inevitable penalty of revolution." He castigated President James Buchanan for his inaction in defending coastal forts and military installations. Only Major Robert Anderson, the defender of Fort Sumter, had shown backbone in dealing with secessionists, said Pope: "His prompt and soldierly conduct was the first exhibition of patriotism, the first evidence of any honorable sense of duty on the part of the executive department."

5. Stanton and Holt voiced the only opposition to the conciliatory policies of the Buchanan administration prior to the inauguration of Lincoln.

6. Mary Surratt, one of the convicted Lincoln conspirators, was the first woman executed for a capital offense in the United States.

7. Stanton was incensed at what he felt was Holt's bungling of the assassination trial, thus his reticence. Holt came under fire for not presenting to President Johnson the petition for clemency for Mrs. Mary Surratt that was signed by five of the nine members of the commission. Johnson steadfastly denied having seen the petition, which was a source of controversy then and has been ever since. See William Hanchett, *The Lincoln Murder Conspiracies* (Urbana, 1983), 86–88.

8. Major General John Ellis Wool (1784–1869), of New York, a Regular Army veteran of the War of 1812, served as Zachary Taylor's principal lieutenant during the Mex-

ican War. Immediately prior to the Civil War, he commanded the Department of the Pacific.

9. Wool was generally disliked by his subordinates because of his preoccupation with military form and ceremony.

10. Zachary Taylor (1785–1853), the thirteenth president of the United States, commanded the Army of the Rio Grande in the Mexican War.

11. The First Illinois Infantry Regiment under Colonel John J. Hardin and the Second Illinois Infantry Regiment under Colonel William Bissell. The battery was commanded by Captain J. M. Washington.

12. The Battle of Buena Vista was fought on February 23, 1847. Taylor's army had occupied an advanced position despite orders to remain on the defensive.

13. Taylor's army numbered 4,757; the Mexicans, led by Santa Anna, numbered 14,000. For a fine account of the battle by a distinguished American participant, see William B. Franklin, "The Battle of Buena Vista," in *Papers of the Military Historical Society of Massachusetts*, 13:545–57.

14. Pope was then a lieutenant of topographical engineers, temporarily assigned to duty on Taylor's staff.

15. Saltillo lay six miles north of Buena Vista.

16. Arkansas troops also strongly disliked Wool and were openly insubordinate to him.

17. The battery commanders were Braxton Bragg and Thomas West Sherman (1813–79), who rose to a division command in the Union army.

18. James Pinkney Henderson, first governor of Texas.

19. Agua Nueva lay twenty miles south of Saltillo. McCulloch and a company of Texas Rangers joined Taylor's army and did advance scouting duty for him. During one of these reconnaissances, McCulloch learned that Santa Anna was at Encornaleon with 20,000 men.

20. The Texas Rangers were organized in 1823 as the law enforcement agency of Texas. In time their numbers swelled to 250. They also served as the first line of defense against hostile Indian raiding parties.

21. Major General David E. Twiggs (1790–1862) of Georgia.

22. Twiggs, who at age seventy was the oldest officer to take up arms for the Confederacy, was commissioned major general in the provisional army of the Confederacy and was assigned to the District of Louisiana. He soon retired, being too old for field service.

23. Major General Joseph King Fenno Mansfield (1803–62) graduated second in the West Point class of 1822 and was assigned to the construction of coastal fortifications in the southeast. During the Mexican War he was chief engineer for Zachary Taylor and won three brevets for gallantry in combat. He spent the immediate pre–Civil War years in the Inspector General's office and helped design the Washington defenses in 1861.

24. The bold, ornate signature of Captain Drake DeKay on passes issued by General Mansfield made him something of a celebrity in Washington. Drake presumably signed his name in such a manner that it might not be easily imitated. At the outbreak of the war, DeKay closed his shipping and commissions office in New York abruptly, with no further notice beyond a note pinned to the door which read: "Gone to Washington. Back at close of war." DeKay served on Pope's staff at Second Bull Run.

25. The Battle of Monterrey was fought during September 21–25, 1846.

26. Captain L. B. Webster, First U.S. Artillery.

27. Samuel Cooper (1798–1876) graduated from West Point in 1815 and served continuously in the army until 1861. In 1852 he was named adjutant general. He resigned

from the Regular Army to become the ranking general in the Confederacy, serving throughout the war as inspector and adjutant general.

28. Brigadier General Lorenzo Thomas (1804-75). Secretary of War Stanton had no use for Thomas and in 1863 banished him from Washington to the Trans-Mississippi, where he organized black regiments.

29. Simon Cameron, secretary of war during 1861-62.

30. Edward Davis Townsend (1817-93) graduated from West Point in 1837 and after brief service in the Seminole War was assigned to the Adjutant General's Office, where he remained until the Civil War. He filled this position throughout the war as acting head of the department, with a brevet rank of brigadier general.

31. Charles Pomeroy Stone (1824-87) of Massachusetts was a graduate of the West Point class of 1845. He won two brevets in the Mexican War. As inspector general of the District of Columbia in 1861, Stone was responsible for the safety of the capital and the president. He fought as a regimental commander in the First Battle of Bull Run and was afterward promoted to brigadier general. Stone's command was routed at Ball's Bluff, Va., on October 21, 1861, an engagement in which one of Lincoln's closest associates, the former U.S. senator Edward Baker of California, perished.

32. On February 9, 1862, Stone was arrested and imprisoned at Fort Layfayette for 189 days. For a full account of this affair, see Edward G. Longacre, "Charles P. Stone and the 'Crime of Unlucky Generals,'" *Civil War Times Illustrated*, November 1974.

33. This is a reference to McClellan, who withdrew support from Stone and ordered his arrest when pressure was brought to bear. The men behind the charges were Governor John Andrew of Massachusetts and Senators Charles Sumner and Benjamin Wade. Stanton drew up the arrest order, which McClellan enacted. No charges were preferred against Stone, then or afterward.

CHAPTER 14

1. Winfield Scott (1786-1866) of Virginia was a career soldier who first won fame on the Canadian frontier during the War of 1812. He rose to become general in chief of the army in 1841 and remained in that capacity until his retirement in 1861.

2. Joseph Eggleston Johnston (1807-91), of Virginia, a member of the West Point class of 1829, was a veteran of both the Seminole War and the Mexican War. He joined the Confederacy in 1861 as its fourth ranking general.

3. Pope's kind recollections of Johnston are surprising, as the two had a falling out while Pope was assigned to Johnston's command in Florida. The cause of the rift is unclear, but it was serious enough to cause Johnston to refuse to accept then Brevet-Captain Pope as a subordinate in his command following the Mexican War. For his part, Pope wanted nothing to do with Johnston. "My relations with Colonel Johnston are and have been such for some years that it would be exceedingly unpleasant to serve with him," Pope told the chief of the topographical engineers. The assignment was broken. Joseph Johnston to J. J. Abert, February 17, 1851, and Pope to Abert, February 24, 1851, Letters Received, Topographical Bureau, RG 77, NA.

4. Riflemen.

5. Johnston was U.S. commissioner of railroads under President Grover Cleveland. He died on March 21, 1891.

6. Smith was brevetted three times for gallantry during the Mexican War.

7. G. W. Smith, *Confederate War Papers* (New York, 1884).

1. Edward Willitt, *The Life of Ulysses Sidney Grant, General, U.S. Army* (New York, 1865).

2. Major General Irvin McDowell.

3. Robert Patterson (1792–1881), an Irish immigrant, served in the U.S. Army from the War of 1812 as a colonel of Pennsylvania militia. During the Mexican War, he was a major general of volunteers. His friendship with Scott won him appointment to command the Department of Pennsylvania in the early stages of the Civil War.

4. Patterson was ordered to hold Joseph Johnston's force of 11,000 in the Shenandoah Valley to prevent his joining with Beauregard at Manassas. Patterson's timidity allowed Johnston to get away undetected.

5. For McDowell's report, see *OR* 2:316–25.

to be relieved from command in Virginia, 127

Front Royal, Va., 129

Gainesville, Va., 148, 150, 159, 166, 168
Galena, Ill., 89
Galt House, 101
Gamble, Hamilton R., 11
Gantt, Edward W., 50
Geary, John W., 140
Georgetown, Mo., 31
Georgia, 109, 178, 209
Gibbon, John, xxiv
Gilder, Richard W., xxiv
Gittings, John S., 181
Gordon, George H., 143, 144
Gordonsville, Va., 123, 130, 131, 132, 133, 140, 141, 150
Grand Army of the Republic, xxvi
Granger, Gordon, 47, 57, 71, 92, 102–3
Grant, Ulysses S., xviii, xix, xx, xxvii, 43, 46, 64, 65, 75, 88, 89–91, 92, 93, 95, 100, 108, 109, 190, 191, 210; Pope's acquaintance with, 89–91; as second in command at Corinth, 90–91
Great Mingo Swamp, 46, 47
Great Run, 147
Green, Martin, 28, 30
Greenwich, Va., 169
Grierson, Benjamin H., xxiv
Groveton, Va., Battle of, 165, 166
Guerrilla warfare, 25, 28
Gunboats, 51, 53, 54, 55; *Carondelet*, 55; *Pittsburg*, 55

Halleck, Henry W., xviii, 13, 14, 36, 46, 47, 51, 53, 62, 63, 64, 67, 70, 71, 74, 75, 83, 88, 89, 91, 92, 95, 103, 104, 106, 107, 108, 114, 117, 124, 131, 142, 145, 150–64 passim, 169; character of, 14, 108; correspondence with Pope, 70–74; as general-in-chief, 124
Hamburg, Tenn., 64, 65
Hamilton, Schulyer, 47, 48, 50, 51, 56, 103
Hannibal, Mo., 18
Hanover Courthouse, Va., 130, 167
Hardee, William J., 81, 89
Harney, William S., 6, 7, 197; description of, 7
Harrisburg, Pa., 180, 182
Harrison's Landing, Va., 122, 129, 130, 131, 132, 149, 150, 191

Hatch, Edward, 67
Haupt, Herman, 152, 159, 162
Hay, John, 181
Hayes, Rutherford B., xxiv
Hazel River, 134, 135
Health, of troops, 61
Heintzelman, Samuel P., 151, 152, 159, 168
Henderson, James P., 77, 196
Hill, Ambrose P., 160, 166
Hill, Daniel H., 141, 150
Hilton Head, S.C., 80
Holabird, Samuel B., 154
Hollins, George N., 50
Holt, Joseph, 188–91
Hooker, Joseph, 169
Houghtaling, Charles, 55
Howard, Oliver O., xxvi, 99
Huger, Benjamin, 166
Humansville, Mo., 33, 36
Hunter, David, 12, 13, 34, 35, 36, 86, 176
Hunter's Lane, 156

Illinois, xxvii, 4, 5, 15, 98, 175, 183, 193, 205, 206
Illinois troops: 7th Cavalry, 48; 10th Infantry, 50; 16th Infantry, 50; 51st Infantry, Houghtaling's Battery, 55
Indianapolis, Ind., 176
Indians, xx, xxii, 6, 7, 12, 35, 206
Iowa, 16
Iowa troops: 1st Cavalry, 37; 2nd Cavalry, 56, 57, 67
Island No. 10, xxvi, xxvii, 14, 39, 43, 44, 45, 46, 49, 51, 55, 56, 61, 62, 105, 109; canal dug at, 52
Iuka, Miss., 68

Jackson, Claiborne F., 8, 85
Jackson, Thomas J. "Stonewall," xviii, xx, 118, 130, 132, 133, 137, 140, 141, 148, 159, 165, 166
James River, 122, 129, 130, 132, 149, 186
Jefferson City, Mo., 11, 26, 31, 36, 39, 46, 85
Johnson, Andrew, 103, 191
Johnston, Albert S., 77, 78, 79, 196
Johnston, Joseph E., xxi, 92, 206–7, 215
Johnstown, Mo., 37
Joint Congressional Committee on the Conduct of the War, xx, xxvi, 132, 206

Kansas, xix, 15

Kearny, Philip, 169
Kellogg, William P., 48
Kelly's Ford, 142, 144, 146, 152, 167, 168
Kentucky, 25, 106, 107, 208
King, Rufus, 129, 132, 133, 140, 149
Knob Noster, Mo., 39

Lamon, Ward H., 180
Lee, John F., 190
Lee, Robert E., xviii, 130, 131, 132, 134, 141, 144, 145, 148, 150, 156, 165, 166, 167, 209
Lexington, Mo., 11, 30, 31, 32, 37, 38, 86
Liberty Mills, Va., 141
Lincoln, Abraham, xvii, xviii, xxvii, 20, 96, 97, 120–29 passim, 163, 166, 173–87 passim, 216; journey to Washington, 176–82
Logan, John A., 75, 88, 96, 98–99
Longstreet, James, xxiv, xxv, 130, 166, 168
Louisa Courthouse, Va., 141
Louisville, Ky., 6, 101
Lovell, Mansfield, 83, 84
Luray Gap, 129
Lynchburg, Va., 131
Lyon, Nathaniel, 6, 7, 8, 29, 36, 85, 86; Pope's impressions of, 8

McClellan, George B., xix, xx, xxii, xxiii, 6, 83, 84, 119, 120, 121, 122, 123, 126, 127, 129, 130, 131, 141, 145–65 passim, 169, 170, 186, 191, 192, 212
McCook, Alexander McD., 103
McCown, John P., 50
McCulloch, Benjamin, 8, 83, 86, 196, 197
McDowell, Irvin, 118, 119, 120, 127, 129, 132, 136, 138, 146, 147, 148, 152, 166, 168, 213–16
McElroy, John, xxvi
McKinstry, Justus, 33
McPherson, James B., 75, 88, 95–96, 99
Madison Courthouse, Va., 123, 133, 134, 136, 137, 141
Manassas Junction, Va., xxvii, 128, 148, 151, 153, 158, 167, 168, 169, 209
Mansfield, Joseph K. F., 198–200
Marcy, Randolph B., 122, 123
Martial law, 20, 22, 27
Massachusetts, 16
Meade, George G., 146
Meagher, Thomas F., 157
Memphis, Tenn., 75, 108
Merrill, Lewis, 37

Mexican War, xxvii, 77, 78, 84, 89, 175, 191, 192, 196, 197, 198, 208, 213
Mexico, Mo., 20, 90
Mexico City, 198
Michigan troops: 2nd Cavalry, 67, 92, 102
Middleton, Va., 118, 128
Milford, Mo., 38
Military Division of the Missouri, xix
Military Division of the Pacific, xxiv
Minnesota, xix, xx, xxi
Mississippi, xix, 82, 89
Mississippi River, xix, 14, 43, 44, 47, 57, 62, 86, 106, 109
Missouri, xix, xxvi, 6, 8, 9, 10, 11, 12, 15, 17, 20, 25, 26, 27, 28, 29, 33, 39, 46, 84, 85, 86, 87, 90, 106
Missouri River, 11, 17, 18, 30, 36, 37, 86
Missouri troops: 2nd Cavalry, 37
Monocacy River, 167
Monterrey, 80, 191; Battle of, xxvii, 94, 193, 196, 199
Moore, David, 28
Moore, Frank, xxvi
Morgan, James D., 50
Mormons, 78
Mower, Joseph A., 50, 57
Mulligan, James A., 30

Nashville, Tenn., 75, 99, 100, 108; Battle of, 95
National Tribune, xxvi, xxvii
Nelson, William, 101–2
Nevada, xix
New Jersey, 178
New Madrid, Mo., xxvii, 39, 44–57 passim, 109; desciption of defenses, 49; capture of, 49–50
New Orleans, La., 83
Newport, Ky., 189
Newspapers: Macon Telegraph, xix; The Nation, xxv; Chicago Tribune, 90; New York Tribune, 128
New York, 118
New York, N.Y., 179, 180, 200, 201, 203, 208
New York troops: 2nd Artillery, 156; 1st Cavalry, 168; 6th Cavalry, 168
Nicolay, John, 181

Occoquan Creek, 167
Ohio, xxii, xxvii, 6
Ohio River, 46, 62

Okolona, Miss., 70
Orange Courthouse, Va., 134, 140, 167
Orleans, Louis Philippe Albert d', Comte de
    Paris, xxiii; correspondence with Pope,
    217–37
Osage River, 33, 36, 37, 38, 86
Osceola, Mo., 33, 36, 37, 39
Otterville, Mo., 36, 39

Paducah, Ky., 62
Paine, Eleazor A., 55, 56, 62, 63, 66
Palmer, Isaac N., 66
Palmer, John M., 47, 57, 66, 67, 103
Pamunkey River, 130, 149
Parkersburg, Va., 145
Patterson, Robert, 215
"Peace Convention," 182
Pea Ridge, Ark., Battle of, 82, 83, 86, 89
Peninsula, 122, 124, 141, 144, 145, 149, 150,
    151, 192
Pennsylvania troops: Reserves, 146; 12th
    Cavalry, 157
Perryville, Ky., Battle of, 100
Philadelphia, Pa., 180, 215
Pittsburgh, Pa., 6
Pittsburg Landing, Tenn., 62, 63, 113
Platte River, 28, 30
Plummer, Joseph B., 67
Point Pleasant, 54
Poolsville, Md., 157
Pope, Clara, xxiv, xxvi, xxvii; death of, xxi
Pope, Major General John, xvii–xxviii pas-
    sim, 145, 150, 155, 159, 160, 161, 162, 163,
    164, 165, 166, 167, 170; death of child,
    xvii; as foil to Lee, xviii; Indian policy of,
    xx; correspondence with Comte de Paris,
    xxiii, 217–37; as mustering officer, 4; at
    Frémont's headquarters, 9; impressions of
    Frémont, 12; on Missouri politics, 16; as-
    sumes command in Missouri, 17; issues
    warning to people, 19; appeals to citizens,
    22; ordered to take Island No. 10, 46–47;
    and canal at Island No. 10, 51–52; arrival
    at Pittsburg Landing, 64; reflections on
    Grant, 64–65, 89–91; pursuit by after
    Corinth, 70; correspondence with Halleck,
    70–74; assessment of A. S. Johnston, 77–
    80; description of Bragg, 79–81; on Van
    Dorn, 81–83; on Lovell, 83; on Price, 84–
    87; on Sherman, 91–92; on Sheridan, 92–
    94; on Thomas, 94–95; on McPherson,

95–96; on Logan, 98–99; on Buell, 99–
    101; on Nelson, 101–2; on Granger, 102–3;
    on Thomas Scott, 109–10; description
    of Pittsburg Landing, 113–14; on Stanton,
    114–25; offered command in Virginia,
    120–23; arrival in Washington, 127; de-
    scription of Blue Ridge, 132–33; orders
    to Banks, 135–36; during Battle of Cedar
    Mountain, 137–39; orders Gordon's ar-
    rest, 144; correspondence with Porter,
    168–70; on George Washington, 173–75;
    on Abraham Lincoln, 175–76; inaugural
    train ride, 176–82; on Holt, 188–90;
    address to Cincinnati Literary Society,
    188–89; on Wool, 191–96; on McCulloch,
    196–97; on Mansfield, 198–200; on
    Stone, 203–4; on Joseph E. Johnston,
    206–7; on Beauregard, 207–8; opinion
    of West Point, 210–13
Porter, Fitz John, xxii, xxiii, xxiv, 151, 152,
    159, 166, 167, 168, 169, 170, 190, 215
Potomac River, 132, 150, 156, 198, 213
Price, Sterling, 8, 10, 28, 29, 30, 31, 32, 33,
    34, 35, 36, 37, 83, 84–87, 89; popularity
    of, 36; personality of, 84–87
Provost marshals, 17, 25, 27

Raccoon Ford, 134, 141, 142
Railroads, 18, 19, 20, 26, 66, 85, 106, 158,
    176, 177; North Missouri, 18, 19, 31;
    Hannibal & St. Joseph, 18, 30, 31; attacks
    on, 19, 26, 28, 29; Memphis & Charleston,
    66, 68; Mobile & Ohio, 68, 69; Missouri
    Pacific, 86; Orange & Alexandria, 131,
    134, 142, 146, 147; Virginia Central, 133;
    Baltimore & Ohio, 181; Northern Pennsyl-
    vania, 181
Rapidan River, 130, 132, 134, 140, 141, 142,
    145, 150
Rapidan Station, Va., 135, 136, 137, 138
Rappahannock River, 129, 130, 131, 141, 144,
    145, 146, 147, 148, 149, 165, 167, 192
Rappahannock Station, Va., 142, 144, 145,
    146, 148, 152
Rebellion Record, xxvi
Rectortown, Va., 148
Reelfoot Lake, 45, 46, 56, 57
Regular Army, xxii, 4, 6, 12, 37, 57, 67, 197,
    203
Reno, Jesse L., 141, 142, 145, 146, 147, 152,
    168, 169